Ibn Qayyim al-Jawziyya on Knowledge

OTHER TITLES BY IBN QAYYIM AL-JAWZIYYA
AVAILABLE FROM THE ISLAMIC TEXTS SOCIETY

Medicine of the Prophet

Ibn Qayyim al-Jawziyya on the Invocation of God

Ibn Qayyim al-Jawziyya
ON KNOWLEDGE

from Key to the Blissful Abode

Miftāḥ Dār al-Saʿāda

Translated by

TALLAL M. ZENI

THE ISLAMIC TEXTS SOCIETY

This first edition published 2016 by
THE ISLAMIC TEXTS SOCIETY
MILLER'S HOUSE
KINGS MILL LANE
GREAT SHELFORD
CAMBRIDGE CB22 5EN
UNITED KINGDOM
www.its.org.uk

British Library Cataloguing-in-Publication Data.
A catalogue record for this book is available from the British Library.

ISBN: 978 1903682 968 cloth
ISBN: 978 1903682 975 paper

Printed and bound in the UK by TJ Books, Padstow, PL28 8RW.

CONTENTS

Acknowledgements vii

Translator's Introduction ix

PROLOGUE 1

CHAPTER ONE: Attesting to God's Oneness is One of the Greatest Benefits of Being Knowledgeable 6

CHAPTER TWO: The Importance of Having Knowledge of the Qur'ān, the Sunna and Wisdom, and then Teaching them 14

CHAPTER THREE: The Superiority of the Scholar over the Worshipper and that the Former are the True Heirs of the Prophets 42

CHAPTER FOUR: The Most Eminent Types of Knowledge are Those which Concern God, His Names and His Attributes 71

CHAPTER FIVE: An Exposition on the Question: Does Knowledge Inevitably Lead to Guidance or is Ignorance the Only Reason that Many Do not Become Believers? 94

CHAPTER SIX: Knowledge Leads to Spiritual Bliss and Elevates One's Rank 123

CHAPTER SEVEN: Knowledge Allows One to Protect Oneself from Doubts, Temptations and Evil 136

CHAPTER EIGHT: The Superiority of Knowledge over Waging Battle for His Sake and over Supererogatory Deeds 153

CHAPTER NINE: An Exposition of a Tradition by ʿAlī Discussing the Characteristics of the True Scholars and Students of Knowledge 167

CHAPTER TEN: Knowledge is Essential to Attaining Certainty and to Calling to God 221

CHAPTER ELEVEN: God Commended Muḥammad, Abraham, the Messiah and many other Prophets due to their Knowledge 239

CHAPTER TWELVE: The Importance of Contemplation and Reflection 269

Bibliography 283

Index 289

ACKNOWLEDGEMENTS

I would like to thank Andrew Booso for his meticulous and excellent editing as well as his exceptional advice. He has made many significant contributions, which improved the fluency and readability of the text. I am also grateful for the advice and efforts of Zahra Azad. I must express my deep appreciation to Fatima Azzam, the Director of the Islamic Texts Society, for her endless support of this project, invaluable advice and enduring patience; without her efforts this book would not have been otherwise possible. Any errors within it are, of course, due to my inadequacies and faults.

May God reward them as well as my parents and family for all the good they have done. All praise and gratitude is due to God. I ask God to accept this work and make it a source of goodness for others. In the Name of God, Most Beneficent, Most Merciful, we begin.

TRANSLATOR'S INTRODUCTION

Ibn al-Qayyim was one of the most important scholars of the late-Ḥanbalī school, along with figures like Ibn al-Jawzī and Ibn Taymiyya. Although Ibn al-Qayyim closely adhered to the stances of his teacher Ibn Taymiyya, he wrote on original topics and explored some common subjects in greater depth. In fact, his scholarly output was so vast that he composed works on nearly all the major areas of the religious disciplines. Ibn al-Qayyim's foremost goal was to explain and establish the primacy of the Qur'ān and the Sunna, as well as the congruousness of reason and revelation. In addition, he was committed to refuting what he considered to be extremes in Sufi mysticism, such as monism (*waḥdat al-wujūd*) and antinomianism (*suqūṭ al-taklīf*), and repudiating groups that he felt stripped God of His Attributes or denied His wisdom and causality.

A Brief Biography

Abū ʿAbd Allāh Shams al-Dīn Muḥammad b. Abī Bakr b. Ayyūb b. Saʿd al-Zurʿī al-Dimashqī, better known as Ibn Qayyim al-Jawziyya, was born outside of Damascus, Syria, in 691/1292. Some brief biographical descriptions about Ibn al-Qayyim have been provided by his most well-known students, including Ismāʿīl ʿImād al-Dīn b. ʿUmar b. Kathīr (in *al-Bidāya wa'l-nihāya* and his famous *Tafsīr*), ʿAbd al-Raḥmān Zayn al-Dīn b. Rajab (in *Jāmiʿ al-ʿulūm wa'l-ḥikam*) and Muḥammad b. Aḥmad al-Dhahabī (in *Siyar aʿlām al-nubalā'*).[1] Ibn Kathīr reported that '[Ibn al-Qayyim] was very loving, and he never envied others or caused harm to them. He never pointed out

1 Bakr Abū Zayd, *Ibn Qayyim al-Jawziyya: ḥayātuh āthāruh mawāriduh* (Riyadh: Dār al-ʿĀṣimah, 1995), pp. 179–181.

the inadequacies of others nor harboured envy of them. I was one of his best friends and most beloved to him. I do not know of anyone living in our time who is a greater worshipper than him. His custom in prayer was to prolong it greatly, including the bowing and prostrating. Many of his colleagues would occasionally criticize him for that, but he would not respond to them nor would he abandon [his practice]. May God (Exalted is He) have mercy on him.'[1]

Furthermore, Ibn Rajab stated:

> Ibn al-Qayyim (may God have mercy on him) performed great acts of worship and would spend the night in prayer. He would greatly prolong his prayer. He would engage in the remembrance [of God] with great devotion and fervent love. He constantly repented and sought forgiveness [from God], and acknowledged his dependence upon God with humility to Him. I have not seen anyone act like him in this regard, nor have I seen anyone possess a greater amount of knowledge than him. I have not seen anyone with a greater understanding of the true meanings of the Qur'ān, the Sunna and faith than him. He is not infallible, but I just have not seen anyone like him ever ... He performed the pilgrimage many times and resided in the holy vicinity of Mecca. The people of Mecca considered his intense worship and multiple circumambulations of the Kaʿba to be astonishing. I remained with him for more than a year before his death; and I learned his lengthy [poem] *al-Qaṣīda al-nūniyya* [or *al-Kāfiyya al-shāfiyya*] during that year, as well other books of his.[2]

As is evident in the aforementioned testaments to him, Ibn al-Qayyim was a devout worshipper of God. He states in *Madārij al-sālikīn*: 'Once the door to experiencing the sweetness of worship

1 Ibn Kathīr, *al-Bidāya wa'l-nihāya* (Damascus: Dār al-Fikr, 1986), vol. xiv, pp. 234–235.

2 Ibn Rajab al-Ḥanbali, *Dhayl ṭabaqāt al-Ḥanābila* (Riyadh: Maktabat al-ʿUbaykān, 2005), vol. v, pp. 171–173.

is opened, one can almost never become satiated. One will find pleasure and comfort therein many times over what one would find in the pleasure of fun and games or the attainment of one's desires. It will reach such a level that once one enters into prayer, one will not want to exit it.'[1]

Ibn al-Qayyim's Relationship with Ibn Taymiyya

Ibn al-Qayyim's name is inevitably attached to that of his famous teacher Taqī al-Dīn b. ʿAbd al-Ḥalīm Ibn Taymiyya (1263–1328 CE). Although Ibn al-Qayyim had other teachers—such as Ṣafī al-Dīn al-Hindī and ʿImād al-Dīn Abū al-ʿAbbās Aḥmad b. Ibrāhīm al-Wāṣiṭī—he dedicated himself almost exclusively to Ibn Taymiyya, after meeting him at the age of twenty-one, until the latter's death. Ibn al-Qayyim's devotion for Ibn Taymiyya was great indeed. In *al-Qaṣīda al-nūniyya* and other writings, Ibn al-Qayyim acknowledges his indebtedness to Ibn Taymiyya for 'saving' him from the Ashʿarī doctrine. In fact, it has been argued that Ibn al-Qayyim's *al-Ṣawāʿiq al-mursala ʿala'l-Jahmiyya wa'l-muʿaṭṭila* 'represents one of the most sophisticated critiques of Ashʿarī doctrines ever written'.[2]

Moreover, Ibn al-Qayyim often writes of his spiritual debt to Ibn Taymiyya; for instance: 'When we were seized with fear and our thoughts [about God's decree] turned negative, and the earth grew narrow for us, we would go to [Ibn Taymiyya]. No sooner did we look at him and hear his words than all these [feelings] would leave us, to be replaced by relief, strength, certainty and tranquillity.'[3]

1 Ibn Qayyim al-Jawziyya, *Madārij al-sālikīn* (Beirut: Dār al-Kitāb al-ʿArabī, 1996), vol. III, p. 352.

2 Yasir Qadhi, 'The "*Unleashed Thunderbolts*" of Ibn Qayyim al-Ğawziyyah: An Introductory Essay'. In Caterina Bori and Livnat Holtzman (eds.), *A Scholar in the Shadow: Essays in the Legal and Theological Thought of Ibn al-Qayyim al-Ğawziyyah* (Oriente Moderno XC, no. 1. Rome: Istituto per l'Oriente C. A. Nallino, 2010), p. 148.

3 Michael Abdurrahman Fitzgerald and Moulay Youssef Slitine (trans.), *Ibn Qayyim al-Jawziyya: The Invocation of God* (Cambridge: The Islamic Texts Society, 2000), p. 58.

In the *Madārij al-sālikīn*, he recounts some examples of the amazing vision (*firāsa*) of Ibn Taymiyya, such as his prediction that the Syrians would be victorious over the Mongols, who had previously destroyed Baghdad. He then adds that a complete documentation of such occurrences would require a voluminous book.[1]

On Ibn Taymiyya's magnanimity, he writes: 'I never saw [Ibn Taymiyya] supplicate against [those who opposed him]; instead he would pray for them. One day I approached him and gave him the glad tidings of the death of a person who showed him great enmity and inflicted much harm upon him. At that [Ibn Taymiyya] chided and rebuked me. He immediately got up and went to the home of this person's family to pay his respects. He told them: "If only it had been me instead of him! If you desire any assistance, I am ready to help"—or something like that. They were very happy to hear that and prayed for him. They appreciated that gesture from him very much. May God have mercy upon [Ibn Taymiyya] and be pleased with him.'[2]

Ibn al-Qayyim was imprisoned with Ibn Taymiyya in Damascus in 1326 CE for two years, as a result of their verdict that journeying with the intention of only visiting the tomb of Abraham, the friend of God (*khalīl Allāh*), was impermissible.[3] He was released by the authorities only after Ibn Taymiyya's death. It was at that point that Ibn al-Qayyim earnestly began writing his books, in addition to ensuring that the works of Ibn Taymiyya were edited and promulgated.

Even after Ibn Taymiyya's death, it seems that Ibn al-Qayyim would always evaluate his own thoughts through the lens of his teacher. For example, Ibn al-Qayyim writes: 'The fruit of contentment (*riḍā'*) is experiencing happiness and joy with the Lord (Most Blessed and Exalted is He). I saw the Shaykh of Islam Ibn Taymiyya

1 Ibn al-Qayyim, *Madārij*, vol. II, pp. 458–459.

2 Ibid., vol. II, p. 329.

3 Ibn Rajab, *Dhayl*, vol. V, p. 172.

(may God sanctify his spirit) in a dream. I mentioned to him some actions of the heart, which I deemed to be great and beneficial—I cannot remember them exactly now. But he responded: "As for me, my way is experiencing happiness and joy with the Lord"—or something like that. Indeed this was [Ibn Taymiyya's] state during his life and it was outwardly apparent.'[1]

Ibn al-Qayyim's Writings

Bakr Abū Zayd calculates Ibn al-Qayyim's works to be ninety-eight, of which thirty are extant.[2] He is best known for his magnum opus *Madārij al-sālikīn*, which was written after *Miftāḥ dār al-saʿāda*. Bakr Abū Zayd writes: 'Both the proponents and critics of Ibn al-Qayyim agree that his books (may God, Exalted is He, have mercy on him) are characterized by beautiful expressions and genuine clarity. He also simplifies arguments, with an agreeable manner that eschews tediousness or unnecessary complexity. This allows readers to be commonly attracted to his books and read them.'[3]

Ibn al-Qayyim's writings spanned over more than twenty years. Holtzmann divides his works into early, middle and late periods.[4] His earliest works include *Kitāb al-rūḥ* and *al-Wābil al-ṣayyib min al-kalim al-ṭayyib*. A segment of the latter book, which mentions one hundred benefits of the remembrance of God, has been translated into English by Michael Abdurrahman Fitzgerald and Moulay Youssef Slitine under the title *The Invocation of God*.

Ibn al-Qayyim's works on jurisprudence also tended to be from the early period. Abdul-Rahman Mustafa, who translated a section of Ibn al-Qayyim's *Iʿlām al-muwaqqiʿīn ʿan-Rabb al-ʿālamīn*, states: 'His works in the fields of legal and political theory (*Iʿlām al-muwaqqiʿīn*

1 Ibn al-Qayyim, *Madārij*, vol. II, p. 174.

2 Abū Zayd, *Ibn Qayyim al-Jawziyya*, pp. 200–309.

3 Ibid., p. 115.

4 See Livnat Holtzmann, 'Ibn Qayyim al-Jawziyyah'. In Joseph E. Lowery and Devin Stewart (eds.), *Essays in Arabic Literary Biography II: 1350–1850* (Wiesbaden: Harrassowitz Verlag, 2009), pp. 202–203.

and *al-Ṭuruq al-ḥukmiyya*), Sufism (*Madārij al-sālikīn*) and Prophetic biography (*Zād al-maʿād*) are ground-breaking, as each marks a new way of thinking and writing in its respective genre.'[1]

Ibn al-Qayyim's writings on theology, complex doctrinal issues and Sufism were written later. As mentioned previously, one of Ibn al-Qayyim's teachers was the Ḥanbalī Sufi ʿImād al-Dīn Abū al-ʿAbbās Aḥmad b. Ibrāhīm al-Wāṣiṭī. Wāṣiṭī began, but did not finish, a commentary on ʿAbd Allāh al-Harawī al-Anṣārī's (d. 481/1089) *Manāzil al-sā'irīn* [The Stations of the Journeyers]. Later, in his own life, Ibn al-Qayyim was to complete the commentary of *Manāzil al-sā'irīn*, with his *Madārij al-salikīn bayn manāzil iyyāka naʿbudu wa-iyyāka nastaʿīn* [Stations of the Travellers between [the Verse] *Thee Alone We Worship and Thee Alone We Ask for Help*]. Joseph Bell states: 'Throughout *Ṭarīq al-hijratayn* and *Madārij al-sālikīn*, works totalling more than fifteen hundred pages in the printed editions, [Ibn al-Qayyim] has skilfully reproduced model mystical treatises and has manipulated the technical vocabulary of Sufism with the virtuosity of a true master.'[2]

Ibn al-Qayyim expounds on the one hundred stations mentioned in *Manāzil al-sā'irīn* in light of the servitude and reliance that one must manifest towards God as per the verse *Thee alone we worship and Thee alone we ask for help*.[3] He affirms that such obedience allows the believer to enter all of these spiritual stages simultaneously, rather than it being a case of the spiritual aspirant attaining each level one after the other.[4] Another objective of Ibn al-Qayyim in this work was to refute the contention of some that Harawī was a monist, so

1 Abdul-Rahman Mustafa. *On Taqlīd: Ibn al-Qayyim's Critique of Authority in Islamic Law* (New York: Oxford University Press, 2013), p. 2.

2 Joseph N. Bell, *Love Theory in Later Ḥanbalite Islam* (Albany: State University of New York Press, 1979), p. 180.

3 Q. 1.5.

4 See Ovamir Anjum, 'Sufism without Mysticism? Ibn Qayyim al-Ǧawziyyah's Objectives in *Madāriǧ al-Sālikīn*'. In Bori and Holtzman (eds.), *A Scholar in the Shadow*, pp. 161–188.

he endeavours to reconcile the text of *Manāzil al-sā'irīn* with those of Harawī's other writings. Furthermore, Ibn al-Qayyim negates a contention of some Sufis that the highest spiritual station is achieved by 'annihilating oneself' (*fanā'*) in order to achieve 'spiritual union' with God. Rather, he repetitively affirms that the highest goal is to make one's will subservient to God's religious will and His commandments. By confirming this, Ibn al-Qayyim also repudiates the antinomianism of some Sufis.

Moreover, Ibn al-Qayyim sought to refute mysticism, which Anjum defines as 'a mode of cognition which does not merely experience ecstasy or divine illumination (*kashf* or *mukāshafa*) of scriptural knowledge, but also turns that experience into discursive knowledge independent of scriptural knowledge'.[1] Anjum adds that the purpose of the *Madārij* is 'presented in its opening discourse, namely that the truth is not known by the greatness of saints, but by a patient, loving, and reasoned encounter with the Scripture available to all believers...Mystical knowledge, therefore, cannot be presented as superior or equal to the Scripture.'[2] Upon reading the *Madārij*, the reader is struck by Ibn al-Qayyim's profound love for God, His Prophet and Islam.

In comparing Ibn al-Qayyim and Ibn Taymiyya, one is able to identify a significant difference between them. While Ibn Taymiyya seems overly concerned with correcting the Arab philosophers and speculative theologians, Ibn al-Qayyim's focus in his later writings was to bring the Sufi mystics and their likes back into the fold of orthodox Islam. This is seen in particular in his *Madārij* and *Ṭarīq al-hijratayn*, which are tracts of love and spirituality, rather than works of philosophical or speculative enquiry. Although one can posit that Ibn al-Qayyim saw the importance of Ibn Taymiyya's repudiation of the philosophers and speculative theologians, as Ibn

1 Ibid., p. 166. Of note, Dr Anjum is currently working on a complete translation of *Madārij al-sālikīn*.

2 Ibid., p. 172.

al-Qayyim refers to Ibn Taymiyya's philosophical writings *al-Radd ʿala'l-manṭiqiyyīn* and *Naqd al-manṭiq* in *Miftāḥ dār al-saʿāda*, Ibn al-Qayyim in fact distanced himself from such pursuits.

A further significant work from Ibn al-Qayyim's late oeuvre is *Shifāʾ al-ʿalīl fi-masāʾil al-qaḍāʾ wa'l-qadar wa'l-ḥikma wa'l-taʿlīl* [The Cure for those Ailed by Questions of Predetermination, Divine Will, Wisdom and Causality], which addresses the complex issues stated in the title. Ibn al-Qayyim sets out in *Shifāʾ al-ʿalīl*, as well as in his other books including *Miftāḥ dār al-saʿāda*, to affirm that God has wise purposes for His actions. Hoover states: 'The notion of wise purpose in both God's creation and God's command appears in other works [besides *Miftāḥ dār al-saʿāda* and *Shifāʾ al-ʿalīl*] as well, and Ibn Qayyim al-Jawziyyah may well be the most prolific optimist in the Islamic tradition.'[1]

One of Ibn al-Qayyim's last works was *Zād al-maʿād*, which he actually wrote while travelling. It is a five-volume book on the life of the Prophet Muḥammad, with practical guidance on how one may emulate him (may God bless him and grant him peace). An abridged translation has been rendered into English.[2] It should also be noted that Ibn al-Qayyim was a physician. On the subject, he wrote *al-Ṭibb al-nabawī*, which is actually a portion of *Zād al-maʿād,* and has been translated into English by Penelope Johnstone as *Medicine of the Prophet*.[3]

Miftāḥ dār al-saʿāda wa-manshūr wilāyat al-ʿilm wa'l-irāda

Miftāḥ dār al-saʿāda is mentioned by Ibn al-Qayyim in *Madārij al-sālikīn*: 'This principle [of denying God's wisdom and causality] leads to many false requisites and conclusions. We have mentioned

1 Jon Hoover, 'God's Wise Purposes in Creating Iblīs: Ibn Qayyim al-Ǧawziyyah's Theodicy of God's Names and Attributes'. In Bori and Holtzman (eds.), *A Scholar in the Shadow*, p. 116.

2 See *Provisions for the Hereafter* (*Mukhtaṣar Zād al-Maʿād*) (Riyadh: Darussalam, 2003).

3 Penelope Johnstone (trans.), *Medicine of the Prophet* (Cambridge: Islamic Texts Society, 1998).

close to sixty of them in our great book named *Miftāḥ dār al-saᶜāda wa-maṭlab ahl al-ᶜilm wa'l-irāda*.[1] That book's contents are wonderful indeed.'[2]

Ibn al-Qayyim's writing of the *Miftāḥ* was a turning point in his career. The fact that he refers to it in many of his later books illustrates the importance he ascribed to it. Joseph Bell states: 'With the writing of *Miftāḥ Dār Al-Saᶜāda* Ibn al-Qayyim moved into a new period with respect to style and method alike.' He notes that earlier works of Ibn al-Qayyim only had 'glimpses of the polished and sophisticated expression which is the hallmark of *Miftāḥ Dār Al-Saᶜāda* and the works which follow it.'[3] Salāhud-Din ᶜAbd al-Mawjūd comments on the originality of many of the issues investigated within *Miftāḥ dār al-saᶜāda*, as well as Ibn al-Qayyim's other writings such as *Zād al-maᶜād*, *Hādī al-arwāḥ* and *Badā'iᶜ al-fawā'id*, and how they cannot be found in the writings of Ibn Taymiyya.[4]

Ibn al-Qayyim wrote the *Miftāḥ* while he was travelling and worshipping at the Kaᶜba. He mentions in the beginning of Chapter One: 'These are some of the inspirations (*nuzl*) and gems that God disclosed to me when I was at His House [the Kaᶜba], withdrawn [from all others] except for Him alone. I had cast myself at His door in submission and humility, and had exposed myself to His bountiful gifts and immense power throughout the day and night. The one who depends on God for his needs, attaches his hopes to Him, resides permanently at His gate for His assistance, and seeks refuge under His protection will never be disappointed.'[5]

1 Note the subtle change in sub-title by Ibn al-Qayyim. In this quote from the *Madārij*, it is rendered as *maṭlab ahl* rather than *manshūr wilāyat*. Ibn al-Qayyim will occasionally refer to his book titles with slight variations. Another example involves *Ṭarīq al-hijratayn wa-bāb al-saᶜādatayn*, which he refers to in the *Madārij* (vol. 1, p. 112) as *Safar al-hijratayn wa-ṭarīq al-saᶜādatayn*.

2 Ibn al-Qayyim, *Madārij*, vol. 1, p. 112.

3 Bell, *Love Theory*, p. 101.

4 Abdul-Rāfi Adewale Imām (trans.), *The Biography of Imām Ibn al-Qayyim* (Riyadh: Darussalam, 2006), p. 85.

5 See below, p. 3.

As the title suggests, Ibn al-Qayyim's main objectives were to expound on the power of knowledge and willpower, through which one may attain Paradise. In the *Madārij* Ibn al-Qayyim proclaims that remembrance (along with knowledge and willpower) is also powerful and an evidence of one's loyal support (*manshūr al-wilāya*) to God: 'Remembrance (*dhikr*) is a proclamation of sovereignty. One who is given it becomes [spiritually] proximate [to God], whereas those who are denied it are cut off. It is the sustenance of seekers, and if one abandons it then the body [dies spiritually and] becomes like a grave.'[1] Ibn Taymiyya and Ibn al-Qayyim always maintained that 'leadership in religious affairs is granted through patience and certainty'.[2] So certainty can only result from extensive knowledge and persistent remembrance of God, while patience is due to and results in a strong willpower.

Ibn al-Qayyim begins the *Miftāḥ* by explaining the wisdom of creating humanity and making them reside on earth. A discussion follows about whether Adam was placed in Paradise, or whether the Garden was in the heavens or on earth, and the wisdom associated with it. This was discussed in a more summarized fashion by Ibn al-Qayyim in an earlier book entitled *Hādī al-arwāḥ ila-bilād al-afrāḥ*. The discussion in the *Miftāḥ* is quite lengthy and repetitive as Ibn al-Qayyim brings forth the arguments of each viewpoint, and then presents their respective rebuttals. Ultimately, Ibn al-Qayyim's objective in mentioning the different viewpoints about the location of the Garden 'is to recount some of the wisdoms and benefits that occur as a result of Adam's exit from the Garden and being settled onto this earth, which is the abode of tribulation and testing. The objective is to refute those who say that God's wisdom is inconsistent with allowing Adam to commit a sin that results in his exit from the Garden or that there is no benefit in that. It is also to refute those who negate [God's] wisdom and [claim humanity's exit from the

1 Ibn al-Qayyim, *Madārij,* vol. II, p. 395.

2 See below, p. 80.

Garden] occurred solely because God had willed it.'[1] Ibn al-Qayyim then maintains that humanity was substituted with something better than the Garden: God's covenant and knowledge. It is only through them that one can attain bliss in this world and the Hereafter.

He then discusses the importance of knowledge, its benefits, wisdom, the necessity of pursuing it, and finally applying it. This section represents nearly one-half of Volume I and it is what forms *Ibn al-Qayyim on Knowledge*. Ibn al-Qayyim mentions 153 points and adds another forty proofs within Point 129 regarding the superiority of knowledge over wealth. In addition, he mentions many proofs within other points, such that they reach approximately 200.[2]

He starts Chapter One with Q. III.18 in order to show the connection between knowledge and bearing witness that there is no deity worthy of worship except for Him. Ibn al-Qayyim discusses the superiority of knowledge, in particular that which pertains to God and His Attributes, and that it is the greatest matter as it allows one to achieve spiritual bliss and the status of being truly faithful. He emphasizes the importance of knowing the Qur'ān, the Sunna and wisdom, and then teaching them. Thus only the true scholars and students of knowledge are capable of such an undertaking, and so their status is higher than that of one who is only a worshipper.

The author expounds at length on a saying of ʿAlī b. Abī Ṭālib that includes a description of the true scholars and students, those who are appropriate for Islamic knowledge, and the benefits of knowledge over wealth and other worldly matters. He states that the perfection of the offspring of Adam is achieved in this life through sincere repentance, while in the Hereafter it is by being protected from Hellfire and entered into Paradise.

Ibn al-Qayyim affirms, however, that knowledge is not enough to attain guidance. He lists in Chapter Five ten reasons why one may

1 Ibn al-Qayyim, *Miftāḥ dār al-saʿāda wa-manshūr wilāyat al-ʿilm wa'l-irāda* (Cairo: Dār al-Ḥadīth, 1994), p. 24.

2 Ṣaliḥ Aḥmad al-Shāmī, *Faḍl al-ʿilm wa'l-ʿulamā'* (Beirut: al-Maktab al-Islāmī, 2001), p. 6.

not be guided despite having knowledge. In the end, he emphasizes that being guided requires knowledge with submission to God and following His Prophet. *Ibn al-Qayyim on Knowledge* concludes with the importance of contemplation and reflection in order to attain further knowledge and guidance.

A portion of Volume I is dedicated to a discussion of God's creation of natural and scientific wonders, including those of the heavens, earth and humanity, and how they lead to belief in the fact that God is omnipotent and omniscient. Segments of this have been previously translated.[1]

Ibn al-Qayyim ends Volume I of the *Miftāḥ* with a discussion of the wise purposes and secrets associated with allowing people to sin (which should be viewed within the context of knowledge). He also posits that God is more apt to forgive the sins of those who are knowledgeable and sincere because of the preponderance of their good deeds. Finally, Ibn al-Qayyim emphasizes that the higher levels of Paradise can only be reached by 'traversing a bridge of hardships and tribulations'.[2] If one contemplates that reality, then one recognizes that this can only be achieved with extensive Islamic knowledge and a strong willpower.

He later states in Volume II: 'As for the Divine Law (*sharīʿa*), it is established to notify us which of our freely-chosen actions are pleasing to God and which displease Him.'[3] Ibn al-Qayyim maintains that God commands that which He has disposed us to innately recognize as good, and prohibited us from that which our innate disposition and reason recognize to be repugnant. Abdullah Sliti has asserted that 'Ibn al-Qayyim argues that God has established two kinds of legal conveyance (*ḥujja*) upon man: rational moral values and a messenger—the former which is firmly embedded in man's intellect

1 See Anas Abdul-Hameed al-Qoz, *Men and the Universe: Reflections of Ibn al-Qayyem* (Riyadh: Darussalam, 2004).

2 Ibn al-Qayyim, *Miftāḥ*, p. 339.

3 Ibid., p. 353.

so that he may differentiate between good and evil'.[1] On the other hand, the Ashᶜarīs consider that what God commands is good by virtue of His command alone, and what God forbids is repugnant as a result of His prohibition alone, without reason being able to identify whether something is good or bad in the absence of revelation. In this regard, Ibn al-Qayyim presents the deterministic position of Fakhr al-Dīn al-Rāzī (d. 606/1209): 'since our actions are not freely-chosen, they cannot be [intrinsically] deemed good or repugnant'.[2] In other words, the Ashᶜarī position can be understood as asserting, in the words of Sliti, that '[i]f man is not the agent of his actions then none of man's actions are detestable since God is the sole agent; therefore morality is only determined by God, and not reason'.[3] Ibn al-Qayyim then proceeds to negate Rāzī's position in twelve points. Of note, Ibn al-Qayyim had previously studied Rāzī's *Muḥaṣṣal* and *ᶜArbaᶜīn* with Ṣafī al-Dīn al-Hindī, but later viewed these tracts in a different light after reading and analysing them with Ibn Taymiyya.

He then maintains: 'Reason can establish whether something is good or repugnant, but punishment [in this world] only occurs after a messenger is sent [and people disbelieve]...The absence of punishment before the sending [of a messenger] is not due to the non-existence of its causes and requisites, but rather due to the absence of the condition [i.e. the absence of the messenger who can give them glad tidings or warn them] that would otherwise lead to it.'[4] The Muᶜtazila affirmed that reason could differentiate between good and evil, but also believed that punishment in this world could occur prior to the sending of a messenger.

Ibn al-Qayyim also discusses the beauty of the pillars of Islam

1 Abdullah Sliti, 'A Lost Legacy of Critical Engagement: Ibn al-Qayyim on Divine Determination (*qadar*)' (PhD thesis, Durham University, 2015), p. 125.

2 Ibn al-Qayyim, *Miftāḥ*, p. 376. For more on Rāzī's determinism and ethics, see Ayman Shihadeh, *The Teleological Ethics of Fakhr al-Dīn al-Rāzī* (Leiden: Brill, 2006), pp. 30–33, 37–9, 45–6, 56–7, 63–4.

3 Sliti, 'Ibn al-Qayyim on Divine Determination', p. 127.

4 Ibn al-Qayyim, *Miftāḥ*, p. 391.

and the Divine Laws: 'The Divine Laws are based upon attaining what is purely good or preponderantly advantageous, while prohibiting the impure and preponderantly evil. But if there are competing evils [within a preponderant good], then the [evils] that may cause the greatest harm are annulled, while the lesser ones are allowed. It is upon these principles that the Most Wise has established His Divine Laws. These all testify to His omniscience, perfect wisdom, providence and benevolence to His servants.'[1] He does briefly mention that the Qur'ān and the Sunna refer to causality in more than a thousand instances; but he reserves an expanded and lengthy discussion of this, as well as of God's wisdom, for *Shifā' al-ʿalīl*.

Nevertheless, in relation to the issue of God legislating good and prohibiting evil, Ibn al-Qayyim in the *Miftāḥ* discusses many examples of abrogation (*naskh*), like the changing of the qibla from Jerusalem to Mecca. He maintains that God never 'commands something and then totally invalidates or nullifies it; rather, He maintains some aspect of it [even after abrogation].' He goes on to explain that this is concordant with God's wisdom at the time of the initial commandment and then at the time of the abrogation.[2] A further noteworthy example is also given in this regard: 'The benefit in commanding His friend Abraham to sacrifice his son was not so that the sacrifice would occur, but rather so that both the father and the son would submit firmly and completely to His commandment. Once that benefit occurred, the [actual carrying out of the] killing became harmful for them both. Therefore God abrogated it [and commanded Abraham to sacrifice a lamb instead]. This is the true and curative answer in this matter.'[3]

Ibn al-Qayyim then discusses the Muʿtazilī claim that God is obligated to act in a manner that is beneficial and advantageous

1 Ibid., p. 373.

2 Ibid., pp. 381–384. Ibn al-Qayyim discusses here Q. II.106–144, and the wisdom in changing the qibla.

3 Ibn al-Qayyim, *Miftāḥ*, p. 392.

(*al-ṣalāḥ wa'l-aṣlaḥ*). Ibn al-Qayyim enumerates eighteen necessary concomitants of that claim and shows how they are inconsistent with the Qur'ān, the Sunna, reason and reality.[1] Ibn al-Qayyim ultimately maintains that God's actions are consistent with His wisdom, mercy, benevolence and justice. He then expounds upon sixty-three points establishing that both reason and revelation are congruous when assessing whether something is good or evil.[2] Yet a discussion of the aforementioned arguments is beyond the scope of this introduction.

He subsequently continues with a lengthy repudiation of astrology and belief in omens (*taṭayyur*), as they may either lead to a weakening of one's willpower or a deviation thereof. In this regard, Livingston writes on Ibn al-Qayyim's efforts to nullify those astrologers who claimed that 'periodicity of the fixed and moving stars were the key to divine secrets which by the expert interpretation of the initiated could be known to man. But for Ibn al-Qayyim, the heavens offered divine proofs of the perfection of God's cosmic creation, the product of a wisdom so great that it would be the height of folly for one to claim knowledge of even the smallest scrap of it.'[3]

Ibn al-Qayyim concludes Volume II with a discussion of the ramifications of the *ḥadīth* regarding the 70,000 who shall enter Paradise without being held to any accounting. The Prophet (may God bless him and grant him peace) stated: 'They are those who do not undergo cauterization, do not believe in spells, nor partake in omens—they only rely upon their Lord.'[4] Hence Ibn al-Qayyim ends the work by emphasizing the need to avoid astrology and belief in omens because they lead to disbelief (in the worst case) or a weakening of one's knowledge and willpower (in the case of minimum harm). Thus they

1 Ibid., pp. 403–407.

2 Ibid., pp. 414–458.

3 John W. Livingston, 'Ibn Qayyim al-Jawziyyah: A Fourteenth Century Defense against Astrological Divination and Alchemical Transmutation', *JAOS* 91 (1971), no. 1, p. 97.

4 Bukhārī 5707; Muslim 372; Tirmidhī 2446; Aḥmad 3806.

have the same effect as doubts and temptations, which also undermine one's knowledge and willpower. In conclusion, Ibn al-Qayyim addresses not only how to strengthen one's knowledge and willpower, but also how to avoid what may weaken them.

Ibn al-Qayyim and Ghazālī

Ibn al-Qayyim's discussion on knowledge is worthy of comparison with Ghazālī's *Book of Knowledge*[1] in his magisterial and greatly revered *Iḥyā' ʿulūm al-dīn*.[2] Now Ghazālī and Ibn al-Qayyim mention and discuss many of the same points; however, Ibn al-Qayyim tends to comment on the verses of the Qur'ān and *ḥadīth*s more extensively. For example, they both begin discussing Q. III.18, but Ibn al-Qayyim explains it in greater detail. Ghazālī also briefly mentions in two places a tradition by ʿAlī that is mentioned by Ibn al-Qayyim in Point 129; however, Ibn al-Qayyim goes on to expound on it for seventy-four pages.[3]

Ibn al-Qayyim actually refers in the *Miftāḥ* to Ghazālī's denouncement of philosophy and speculative theology from the beginning of the *Iḥyā'*: 'Know that all the beneficial proofs found in speculative theology are encompassed within the Qur'ān and the Traditions of the Prophet.'[4] Such sentiments are truly in keeping with Ibn al-Qayyim's own position.

1 For a recent translation, see Kenneth Honerkamp, *The Book of Knowledge: Book 1 of The Revival of the Religious Sciences* (Louisville: Fons Vitae, 2016).

2 The efforts of Ghazālī in writing the *Iḥyāʿ* and other works would lead to a 'Sunni revival'. See Abdul Rahman Azzam, *Saladin: The Triumph of the Sunni Revival* (Cambridge: Islamic Texts Society, 2014), pp. 8 and 12.

3 See below, Chapter Nine.

4 See below, p. 205-6; Abū Ḥāmid Muḥammad b. Muḥammad al-Ghazālī, *Iḥyā' ʿulūm al-dīn* (Beirut: Dār al-Maʿrifa, 2004), vol. 1, p. 22. Ghazālī further states: 'Knowledge of God (Exalted is He), His Attributes and actions (which is all included in that which unveils the realities (*ʿilm al-mukāshafa*)) is completely absent in speculative theology. Moreover, speculative theology is a barrier and obstacle to attaining this knowledge.' See Ghazālī, *Ihyā'*, vol. 1, p. 23.

About the Truly Faithful or Saints (Ṣiddiqūn)

At this point, it seems appropriate to discuss one issue that stands out in the *Miftāḥ*: Ibn al-Qayyim's repetition of the Prophet's *ḥadīth*: 'This knowledge [inherited from the Prophet] will be conveyed by the successors [of this Community] who are upright and trustworthy (*ʿudūl*). They will repudiate the distortions of the extremists (*taḥrīf al-ghālīn*), those who attempt to break-up [the religion] by negating [its precepts] (*intiḥāl al-mubṭilīn*), and the misinterpretations of those who are ignorant (*ta'wīl al-jāhilīn*).'[1] Ibn al-Qayyim includes it within the first ten points, which discuss the greatness of Q. III.18. He then repeats it in Point 136 and discusses it in greater detail.[2]

It seems that Ibn al-Qayyim repeats this *ḥadīth* because he wants to first illustrate that scholars possessed of strong willpower must work to repudiate falsehood. But more importantly, and God knows best, he is attempting to allude to one characteristic, or maybe even the most important characteristic possessed by those who are truly faithful (*ṣiddīqūn*). He states in the *Madārij*: 'Whoever worships God by striving against His enemy has attained a great share of [the characteristic of] being truly faithful. The greater the servant's love and loyal support for his Lord, as well as his enmity towards His enemy, the greater his participation in striving...This form of servitude [to God] is only realized by a few. Whoever has tasted its sweetness will lament the time he spent beforehand [in heedlessness of it].'[3] Ibn

1 Bayhaqī (*Sunan*) 20,911; Ibn ʿAdī, vol. I, p. 211; Haythamī 601; al-Khaṭīb al-Baghdādī (*Sharaf*), pp. 47–52; Tammām 899; al-Muttaqī al-Hindī 28,918; *Bidāya*, vol. x, p. 337. It is 'authentic' according to Albānī (*Mishkāt* 248). Ibn al-Qayyim also mentions this *ḥadīth* in other books of his, like *al-Ṣawāʿiq al-mursala* (Riyadh: Dār al-ʿĀṣima, 1987), vol. III, p. 927. It should also be mentioned that Imam Aḥmad b. Ḥanbal utilized it in his *al-Radd ʿala'l-zanādiqa wa'l-Jahmiyya* (Kuwait City: Ghirās, 2005), p. 170.

2 The Prophet (may God bless him and grant him peace) also said: 'You must be truthful. The truth guides one to righteousness, and righteousness guides one to Paradise. A person will persist in being truthful and credible until God writes him as being truly faithful (*ṣiddīq*).' Muslim 2607; Tirmidhī 1971; Aḥmad 3638.

3 Ibn al-Qayyim, *Madārij*, vol. I, p. 241.

al-Qayyim also states in Point 64: 'Furthermore, his followers are knowledgeable and carry out [the Prophet's message] by [spreading] knowledge, [performing good] actions, guiding and advising people, being patient, and striving [for His sake]. These are the truly faithful ones (*ṣiddīqūn*)—they are the best of the Prophet's followers; and their leader and imam is Abū Bakr al-Ṣiddīq (may God be pleased with him).'[1]

Although no one can reach the faith of Abū Bakr al-Ṣiddīq, Ibn al-Qayyim maintains in Point 66 that scholars can attain the level of the truly faithful: 'Thus if the scholar's writings reach the level of true faith then his ink becomes better than the blood of a martyr, as long as the latter is not considered to be one of the truly faithful.' Then in Point 70, based on Q. xxxii.24, he states that 'leadership in religious affairs is granted through patience and certainty. It is one of the highest levels of the truly faithful ones.'

Incidentally, Ghazālī also mentions in the *Iḥyā'* that the rank of the truly faithful is occupied by those 'whose existence [in this world is devoted] to their Lord, not to themselves...Their firm resolve in carrying out righteous actions is characterized by strength without any deviation, weakness or hesitation.'[2] He further argues: 'Some of the knowers (*ʿārifūn*) state that there are ranks for those who are patient. The first rank is to avoid desires; and this represents those who are repentant. The second is contentment with what has been decreed; and this rank describes the ascetics. The third is to love what the Lord uses him for; and this is rank of the truly faithful.'[3]

The Methodology of this Translation

The initial Arabic text that was utilized was edited by Sayyid b. Ibrahīm b. Ṣādiq ʿImrān and ʿAlī Muḥammad and published by Dār al-Ḥadīth in 1994. Subsequently a critical edition edited by ʿAbd

1 See below, p. 73.
2 Ghazālī, *Iḥyā'*, vol. iv, p. 389.
3 Ibid., vol. iv, p. 69.

al-Raḥmān b. Qā'id and published by Dār ʿAlām al-Fawā'id in 2015 was utilized. This translation, *Ibn al-Qayyim on Knowledge*, represents a significant portion of Volume 1 of *Miftāḥ dār al-saʿāda*.

The English translations of the Qur'ānic verses were derived from Pickthall in the vast majority of cases, with his older English style often retained, although his use of 'lo!' was largely omitted. The translations of Yusuf Ali and Muhammad Asad were utilized on occasions when they more accurately portrayed the meaning put forward by Ibn al-Qayyim in his text. Of note, as per Islamic Texts Society usage, *God* is used in place of *Allah*.

The English translations of the six canonical books of *ḥadīth*—Bukhārī, Muslim, Tirmidhī, Ibn Māja, Nasā'ī and Abū Dāwūd—published by Darussalam have also been utilized, adapted and referenced. *Ḥadīth*s were also found in the following collections: *Muwaṭṭa' al-Imām Mālik, Musnad al-Imām Aḥmad, Sunan al-Dārimī*, Bayhaqī's *Sunan* and *Shuʿab al-īmān*, Ḥākim's *al-Mustadrak ʿala'l-Ṣaḥīḥayn*, *Ṣaḥīḥ Ibn Ḥibbān*, Abu Nuʿaym's *Ḥilya*, Mundhirī's *al-Targhīb wa'l-tarhīb*, Haythamī's *Majmaʿ al-zawā'id*, Ibn ʿAbd al-Barr's *Jāmiʿ bayān al-ʿilm wa-faḍlih*, Ibn ʿAdī's *al-Kāmil fī-ḍuʿafā' al-rijāl*, Ibn Kathīr's *al-Bidāya wa'l-nihāya*, Tabrīzī's *Mishkāt al-maṣābīḥ*, al-Khaṭīb al-Baghdādī's *al-Faqīh wa'l-mutafaqqih* and *Tārīkh Baghdād*, al-Muttaqī al-Hindī's *Kanz al-ʿummāl*, Tammām's *Fawā'id*, and Zabīdī's *Itḥāf al-sāda al-muttaqīn*. When quoted, the *ḥadīth* numbers are referenced to editions of these books which are included on the website shamela.ws or its application, and mentioned in the Bibliography. In addition, any chains of narrators have been shortened to only include the immediate Companion of the Prophet who narrates it. Furthermore, in order to prevent the referencing of *ḥadīth* from being over-bearing for the reader, if a tradition was found in either *Ṣaḥīḥ al-Bukhārī* or *Ṣaḥīḥ Muslim* then references were limited to the 'Six Books' and *Musnad al-Imām Aḥmad*. If not present in the two *Ṣaḥiḥ*s, then the aforementioned collections were also cited. Also, in the footnote references, there is usually only the mention of the collector's name and the number of the tradition; however, in other instances, in regards to some lesser-known collections, the author, page number and volume is given (with the Bibliography considered sufficient for clarifying publication details in both instances). Finally, all *ḥadīth*s other than those present in *Ṣaḥīḥ al-Bukhārī* and *Ṣaḥīḥ Muslim* were categorized as 'authentic' (*ṣaḥīḥ*), 'sound' (*ḥasan*), 'weak' (*ḍaʿīf*) or 'fabricated' (*mawḍūʿ*) according to the opinion of the prominent *Ḥadīth* scholar Nāṣir al-Dīn al-Albānī wherever possible.

In an effort to assist the reader, the overarching theme of each point or group of points that Ibn al-Qayyim discusses is summarized between brackets before the point(s). The book is also divided into twelve chapters along with a Prologue, rather than the mere three chapters in the Arabic edition. As Ibn al-Qayyim was in Mecca away from his library when he authored the work, his order is not always logically sequential, so he tended to return later in the book to points raised earlier. Therefore the chapters may include other themes within them besides those mentioned within their titles.

Ibn al-Qayyim's writing style has been correctly explained by Ibn Ḥajar in the following terms: 'His writings can be long-winded and prolix in an attempt to clarify issues.'[1] Therefore in the *Miftāḥ* there are many instances of repetition, which Ibn al-Qayyim himself acknowledges, as he accepts his own tendency to sometimes digress. Some repetition is, however, retained in order to clarify or reinforce some points. Nonetheless, in order to shorten this book and make it more readable, repetition and digression not immediately relevant to a theme being discussed has been abridged. In addition, numerous grammatical discussions and many instances of poetry were also omitted. Yet none of the 153 points listed by Ibn al-Qayyim (even if repeated) were removed, so as to not disturb his numbering. The outcome is that approximately 20% of the text—derived from pages 59–222 of 343 in Volume I—has been abridged in this presentation.

1 Ibn Ḥajar, *al-Durar al-kāminah fī-aʿyān al-mā'ata al-thāminah* (Hyderabad: Maṭbaʿat Majlis Dā'irat al-Maʿārif al-ʿUthmāniyyah, 1972), vol. v, p. 139.

From KEY TO THE BLISSFUL ABODE
Miftāḥ Dār al-Saʿāda

[PROLOGUE]

In the Name of God, Most Compassionate and Merciful

When God's wisdom and mercy dictated that Adam and his offspring descend from the Garden, He substituted for them something better: His covenant. He made it a means of attaining unto Him, and it is a clear and obvious path. Whoever holds on [to His covenant] is successful and guided; and those who shun it are wretched transgressors.

This noble covenant—[which is] the straight path and the great tiding—cannot be fulfilled except through the door of willpower and knowledge. In this manner, willpower is the door; and knowledge is the key without which the former cannot be opened. A person's perfection can only be achieved by fulfilling two requirements: firm resolve to elevate his [rank] and knowledge to enlighten and guide him.

If one of these [two latter requirements] is absent, the ranks of bliss and success will elude a servant. In that case, he either does not have knowledge, and so he does not know how to pursue those [high ranks]; or he lacks a firm resolve, and so he cannot rise up to them. In those cases, he remains motionless in a lowly state while his heart is barred and impeded from the perfection he was created for. If both are absent, then he becomes a degenerate, allowing himself to graze untended along with livestock,[1] finding pleasure in the abyss of relaxation and inactivity, and comfort in the bed of incapacity and laziness.

1 Ibn al-Qayyim gives a detailed explanation of this analogy in Chapter Nine.

This [aforementioned person] is not like someone for whom knowledge is esteemed and so he embarks towards it. The latter is blessed in his unrivalled pursuit. He adheres firmly to the path and is upright upon it. His overwhelming and fervent longing for God refuses everything but the emigration to God and His Messenger. He disdains to have any companions except those who accompany him on this path.

Since the perfection of willpower is related to what one intends and the eminence of knowledge is associated with that which it concerns, the servant achieves his ultimate bliss by making his will subservient to that of the Desired One, Who never wanes or eludes. One cannot attain any bliss or [spiritual] life except by having a firm resolve to act in accordance [with the religious commands] of the Ever-Living One Who never dies.

There is no way for one to reach this high goal and good fortune except with knowledge inherited from His servant [Muḥammad]—His Messenger, friend and beloved one—who He has sent for such a purpose and established as a guide on this path. He made the Messenger an intermediary between Him and the people, whereby he invites them by His will to the peaceful abode [of Paradise].

The Sublime refused to grant success or open [the gates to Paradise] for anyone except through the Prophet. God will not accept anyone's efforts unless they begin with the Prophet and end by being devoted to Him. All of the paths are now blocked except the way of the Prophet Muḥammad (may God bless him and grant him peace). All hearts are barred and obstructed except for those of the followers of the Prophet.

It is thus obligatory upon someone who seeks bliss for himself, and whose heart is alive and aware, to make these two principles [i.e. knowledge and willpower] the bases for all his sayings and actions. One should hold them dear like a hidden treasure, and rely on them to pave the way during any of life's frightening situations.

This book's intent is to reveal the eminence of these two principles. I named it *Key to the Blissful Abode: Proclamation of the Sovereignty of Knowledge and Willpower* as these are some of the inspirations and gems that God disclosed to me when I was at His House [the Kaᶜba], withdrawn [from all others] except for Him alone. I had cast myself at His door in submission and humility, and had exposed myself to His bountiful gifts and immense power throughout the day and night. The person who depends on God for his needs, attaches his hopes to Him, resides permanently at His gate for His assistance, and seeks refuge under His protection, will never be disappointed.

Since knowledge comes before willpower, takes precedence over it, qualifies it and guides it, we will discuss the importance of knowledge first. Upon the completion [of these two] we will follow this, God willing, with [another] book about love.[1] We will include here the sections, wisdoms, benefits, fruits and causes, as well as what strengthens, weakens or hinders [knowledge or willpower]. We will seek evidence for it through all means, whether transmitted [from the Qur'ān and the Sunna] or through reason, or the innate disposition, or analogy, or through taste and experience [of the truth] (*al-dhawq wa'l-wajd*).[2] Our [will and love should only] be attached to the True God—there is no god but Him—and it is wholly inap-

1 Since love of God leads to a stronger willpower, Ibn al-Qayyim discusses it at length in his other books. Whether Ibn al-Qayyim had initially intended to discuss love in *Miftāḥ dār al-saᶜāda* or not is debatable. His earlier book *Rawḍat al-muḥibbīn wa-nuzhat al-mushtaqīn* discusses love, and is extant; but his *al-Mawrid al-ṣāfī*, which he wrote afterwards on the topic of love, is now lost.

2 *Dhawq* and *wajd* are popular Sufi terms. Ibn al-Qayyim derives them from two *ḥadīths*. Firstly, 'He who is content with God as his Lord, Islam as his religion, and Muḥammad as his Prophet has tasted (*dhāq*) the sweetness of faith' (Muslim 54; Tirmidhī 2623; Aḥmad 1778). Secondly, 'If one possesses these three [characteristics], then he has experienced (*wajada*) the sweetness of faith: [1] he who finds nothing more beloved to him [than following] God and His Messenger; [2] he who only loves another person for the sake of God; and [3] he who hates to return back to disbelief—after God has saved him from that—just as he would hate to be thrown in Hellfire' (Bukhārī 6941; Muslim 67; Tirmidhī 2624; Ibn Māja 4032; Nasā'ī 4988; Aḥmad 12,002). See Ibn al-Qayyim, *Madārij*, vol. II, p. 67.

propriate to act to the contrary. We will also respond to those who deny this and show their errors.

These [aforementioned matters] are included in this gem, and the best of its meanings will now be shining before you. It is like an astonishingly beautiful bride, with her dress trailing as she proceeds in the wedding ceremony towards you. Be one who accepts this shining bliss, and do not be like one who is blind and paralysed. You can choose for yourself either [knowledge or ignorance] and have either [a strong or weak will].

Inevitably, each blessing has those who are envious of it; and each truth has its deniers and those who stubbornly reject it. The author will be exposed to the attacks of the envious and unjust, who fire arrows at him and [attempt to] defame him. But you, the reader, will find here the quintessential arguments and fruits that the author has taken upon himself to plant. I ask God to excuse my errors and mistakes, and those of His believing servants.

I seek God's protection from those who lack knowledge and have sold their religion. They are insolent in their ignorance and use all their capabilities to harm Your servants. Due to their ignorance, such people consider benevolence to be evil, the Sunna [of the Prophet] to be blameworthy innovation in religion, and good tradition to be strange. Due to their injustice, they recompense a good deed with evil and one evil with ten. They also disregard the rights of others and despise people, so that they may attain their false desires and pleasures. They do not acknowledge what is good except that which accords with their wishes, nor do they renounce what is abominable unless their desires oppose it. They act arrogantly with the loyal supporters (*awliyā'*) of the Messenger and they quicken to sit amongst those who are astray and ignorant. They may think that [in knowledge] they are the foremost, but God, His Messenger and the believers consider them to be cut off from the Prophet's inheritance.

Now, when journeying on this path, one should only accompany those who are [spiritually] alive, rather than dead. A poet said it best:

> There is a [spiritual] death before the [physical] one for
> those who are ignorant.
> And for their bodies, there are [spiritual] graves before
> the [physical] ones.
> Their spirits are estranged from their bodies.
> There will be no resurrection for them until the Day of
> Resurrection.

O God, You are deserving of praise and we seek Your assistance and help regarding our grievances. We rely on You, and there is no power nor any strength save in You. You are sufficient as our Guardian and the best Trustee. We will now commence with our objective, by the power of God and His strength.

CHAPTER ONE

Attesting to God's Oneness is One of the Greatest Benefits of Being Knowledgeable

[POINTS 1–10: THE IMPORTANCE OF KNOWLEDGE ACCORDING TO THE VERSE: THERE IS NO GOD BUT HE: THAT IS THE WITNESS OF GOD, HIS ANGELS AND THOSE ENDUED WITH KNOWLEDGE.]

God (Exalted is He) said: *There is no god but He: That is the witness of God, His angels and those endued with knowledge, standing firm on justice. There is no god but He, the Exalted in Power, the Wise.*[1] The Sublime has cited (*istashhada*)[2] that the knowledgeable are the ones who bear witness to His Oneness—the noblest testimony—by saying: *There is no god but He: That is the witness of God, His angels and those endued with knowledge.* This proves the excellence of knowledge and the knowledgeable in numerous ways:

1. Citing only the testimony of those with knowledge from amongst all of humanity.
2. Linking their testimony to His.
3. Linking their testimony to that of His angels.
4. Implying their righteousness and just nature. Indeed, God would

1 Q. III.18 (Yusuf Ali translation).

2 The meaning of 'cite' (*istashhada*) is not that God (Glory be to Him) is in need of His angels or scholars to bear witness to His Oneness: *God sufficeth as a Witness* (Q. XLVIII.28). Rather, God cites the knowledgeable for many reasons, as Ibn al-Qayyim mentions in Points 8, 15, 20 and 81. Similarly, God cites the believers' words on the Day of Judgment: *Lo! there was a party of My slaves who said: Our Lord! We believe, therefore forgive us and have mercy on us for Thou art Best of all who show mercy* (Q. XXIII.109).

not cite their testimony unless they were upright. It has been related in a known tradition that the Prophet (may God bless him and grant him peace) said: 'This knowledge [inherited from the Prophet] will be conveyed by the successors [of this Community], who are upright and trustworthy (*ʿudūl*). They will repudiate the distortions of the extremists (*taḥrīf al-ghālīn*), those who attempt to break up [the religion] by negating [its precepts] (*intiḥāl al-mubṭilīn*), and the misinterpretations of those who are ignorant (*ta'wīl al-jāhilīn*).'[1] A discussion will follow, God willing, about this *ḥadīth* in its appropriate place.[2]

5. He described them as being knowledgeable, and this signifies that they are specialized in [knowledge], devoted to it, and are permanently associated with it, rather than being only temporarily so.

6. The Sublime bore witness to it Himself, and He is the Most Glorious witness. Then He linked the best of His creation to it: His angels and the knowledgeable from amongst His servants. It is a sufficient distinction for them that they receive this grace and honour.

7. He cited their testimony of the noblest, greatest and highest thing to be witnessed: that there is no deity worthy of worship except God. Clearly, the Exalted and Greatest will only mention the greatest and most elevated of His creation in this regard.

8. The Sublime rendered their testimony as evidence against the deniers. Therefore, He gave them the status of being considered as one of His proofs, signs and evidences that indicate His Oneness.

9. The Sublime used only a single verb to encompass His testimony as well as that of His angels and the knowledgeable. This is indicative of the powerful connection of their testimony to His. It is as if He (Glory be to Him) testified to His Oneness through their speech and made them utter His testimony. Thus He is the One Who bore witness to His Oneness by certifying, speaking and teaching it to

1 Bayhaqī (*Sunan*) 20,911; Ibn ʿAdī, vol. 1, p. 211; Haythamī 601; al-Khaṭīb al-Baghdādī (*Sharaf*), pp. 47-52; Tammām 899; al-Muttaqī al-Hindī 28, 918; *Bidāya*, vol. x, p. 337. It is 'authentic' according to Albānī (*Mishkāt* 248).

2 Ibn al-Qayyim discusses it further in Chapter Ten, Point 136.

others, while the knowledgeable bear witness by affirming, knowing, believing and attesting to it.

10. The Sublime allowed them, by virtue of their testimony, to fulfill His rights upon humanity. It is incumbent upon the creation to affirm [His Oneness]—this alone will bring them the highest degree of happiness in this life and the Hereafter. In addition, the [knowledgeable] will receive the same reward of those who become guided and affirm [His Oneness] as a result of their testimony. The extent of this great blessing is not appreciated by anyone except God. The above are ten aspects relevant to this verse.[1]

[Point 11: God negated any equivalence between the knowledgeable and the ignorant.]

The Sublime negated equivalence between the knowledgeable and others, just like He negated equivalence between the inhabitants of Paradise and the denizens of Hellfire. The Exalted said: *Say (unto them, O Muḥammad): Are those who know equal with those who know not?*[2] The Exalted also said: *Not equal are the owners of the Fire and the owners of the Garden.*[3] This indicates their excellence and eminence.

[Point 12: Those who are ignorant are described in the Qur'ān as being blind.]

The Sublime made those who are ignorant similar in status to those who are blind: *Is he who knoweth that what is revealed unto thee from thy Lord is the truth like him who is blind?*[4] Thus one is either knowledgeable

1 Ibn al-Qayyim has discussed Q. III.18 elsewhere: 'This verse and this testimony includes proof for: [1] His Oneness, which negates polytheism; [2] His justice, which negates injustice; [3] His Almightiness, which negates incapability; and [4] His wisdom, which nullifies ignorance or inadequacy. Therefore, it testifies to His Oneness, His justice, and His omnipotence, knowledge and wisdom. For these reasons it is the greatest testimony.' See Ibn al-Qayyim, *Madārij*, vol. III, pp. 418–432.

2 Q. XXXIX.9.

3 Q. LIX.20.

4 Q. XIII.19.

or blind. The Sublime has described those who are ignorant as deaf, dumb and blind in other instances in His Book.

[POINT 13: GOD COMMENDED THOSE WHO ARE KNOWLEDGEABLE.]

The Sublime commended the scholars because they acknowledge the truth of the Lord's revelations. The Exalted said: *Those who have been given knowledge see that what is revealed unto thee from thy Lord is the truth.*[1]

[POINT 14: GOD COMMANDS US TO REFER BACK TO THE SCHOLARS.]

The Sublime commanded us to ask the scholars and refer back to their statements. He said: *And We sent not (as Our messengers) before thee other than men whom We inspired. Ask the followers of the Remembrance if ye know not!*[2] The *followers of the Remembrance* is a reference to the scholars, since they are knowledgeable regarding that which was revealed unto the prophets.

[POINT 15: GOD ATTESTED TO THE GREATNESS OF THOSE WHO ARE KNOWLEDGEABLE.]

The Sublime cited the knowledgeable due to their testimony that what God revealed to His Messenger is the truth. The Exalted said: *Shall I seek other than God for judge, when He it is Who hath revealed unto you (this) Book, fully explained? Those unto whom We gave the Book (aforetime) know that it is revealed from thy Lord in truth. So be not thou (O Muḥammad) of the waverers.*[3]

[POINT 16: GOD CONSOLED THE PROPHET BY REMINDING HIM OF THE FAITH OF THOSE WHO ARE KNOWLEDGEABLE.]

The Sublime consoled His Prophet by reminding him of the faith of the knowledgeable. He also commanded him to avoid concerning himself with the ignorant. The Exalted said: *And (it is) a Qur'ān*

1 Q. XXXIV.6.
2 Q. XVI.43.
3 Q. VI.114.

that We have divided, that thou mayst recite it unto mankind at intervals, and We have revealed it by (successive) revelation. Say: Believe therein or believe not; those who were given knowledge before it, when it is read unto them, fall down prostrate on their faces, adoring, saying: Glory to our Lord! Verily the promise of our Lord must be fulfilled.[1] This represents a great honour for the knowledgeable. Implied within this is the fact that those who are knowledgeable recognize, believe and affirm [the truth of the Qur'ān], regardless of whether others have believed or not.

[Point 17: God selected those who are knowledgeable by placing His Book in their hearts.]

The Sublime honoured the scholars by placing [and preserving] the verses of the Qur'ān in their hearts. This allows them to prove the veracity of the Qur'ān itself.

This is a special characteristic and virtue of theirs, which is not present in others. The Exalted said: *In like manner We have revealed unto thee the Book, and those unto whom We gave the Book aforetime will believe therein; and of these (also) there are some who believe therein. And none deny Our revelations save the disbelievers. And thou (O Muḥammad) wast not a reader of any (Divine) book before it, nor didst thou write it with thy right hand, for then might those have doubted, who follow falsehood. But it is clear revelations in the hearts of those who have been given knowledge, and none deny Our revelations save wrongdoers.*[2]

One interpretation is that the scholars have memorized the verses of the Qur'ān so that they have become preserved in their hearts. Moreover, these verses indicate the veracity of [the Qur'ān] itself. Alternatively, it can be interpreted to mean that the verses of the Qur'ān are clear signs preserved in their hearts and well known to them. Both viewpoints are necessary concomitants. In either case, they are praised and commended. This is a testament to them, so deeply reflect on that.

1 Q. XVII.106–108.

2 Q. XXIX.47–49.

[Point 18: God commanded His Prophet to ask for more knowledge.]

The Exalted said: *Then exalted be God, the True King! And hasten not (O Muḥammad) with the Qur'ān ere its revelation hath been perfected unto thee, and say: My Lord! Increase me in knowledge.*[1] It is a sufficient distinction for knowledge that God (Glory be to Him) commanded His Prophet to ask for more of it.

[Point 19: The knowledgeable occupy an elite status exclusive to them.]

The Sublime revealed the elite status exclusive to those characterized by knowledge and faith when He (Exalted is He) said: *O ye who believe! When it is said unto you, Make room! in assemblies, then make room; God will make way for you (hereafter). And when it is said, Come up higher! Go up higher, God will exalt those who believe among you, and those who have knowledge, to high ranks. God is Informed of what ye do.*[2] The Sublime notified us in His Book of four instances in which one's rank is elevated—the first is mentioned here.

The second is His statement: *They only are the (true) believers whose hearts feel fear when God is mentioned, and when His revelations are recited unto them they increase their faith, and who trust in their Lord; who establish worship and spend of that We have bestowed on them. Those are they who are in truth believers. For them are grades (of honour) with their Lord, and pardon, and a bountiful provision.*[3]

The third is the statement of the Exalted: *But whoso cometh unto Him a believer, having done good works, for such are the high stations.*[4]

The fourth instance is the statement of the Exalted: *God hath bestowed on those who strive a great reward above the sedentary; degrees of rank from Him, and forgiveness and mercy.*[5]

1 Q. xx.114.
2 Q. lviii.11.
3 Q. viii.2–4.
4 Q. xx.75.
5 Q. iv.95–96.

Those who are faithful are bestowed three of the four elevated ranks. These groups are characterized as having beneficial knowledge and doing pious deeds. The fourth group is elevated because they battle [in His path]. Therefore, an elevated status is due to either knowledge or waging battle [for His sake]. It is upon these two that the religion is established.

[Point 20: God cites the knowledgeable on the Day of Resurrection.]

The Sublime cited the statement of those having knowledge and faith on the Day of Resurrection to show the falsity of the disbelievers' statements. The Exalted stated: *And on the day when the Hour riseth the guilty will vow that they did tarry but an hour—thus were they ever deceived. But those to whom knowledge and faith are given will say: The truth is, ye have tarried, by God's decree, until the Day of Resurrection. This is the Day of Resurrection, but ye used not to know.*[1]

[Point 21: God informs us that only the knowledgeable are fearful of Him.]

The Sublime revealed that they are the ones who are truly fearful of Him. Furthermore, it is He Who selected them exclusively [to have that attribute] from amongst all people. The Exalted said: *The erudite among His servants fear God alone. God is Mighty, Forgiving.*[2] This verse specifies that [the characteristic of] fearing Him is exclusive to those who have knowledge. The Exalted also said: *Their reward is with their Lord: Gardens of Eden underneath which rivers flow, wherein they dwell for ever. God hath pleasure in them and they have pleasure. This is (in store) for him who feareth his Lord.*[3]

If the above two verses are considered together, the reward mentioned [in the latter verse] is proven to be for the knowledgeable.

1 Q. xxx.55–56.

2 Q. xxxv.28.

3 Q. xxviii.8.

Ibn Masʿūd[1] (may God be pleased with him) said: 'It is sufficient that knowledge results in fear of God, and it is sufficient that ignorance leads to becoming deluded away from Him.'[2]

[Point 22: God informs us that only the knowledgeable benefit from His similitudes.]

The Sublime informed us that the similitudes that He has revealed to His servants prove the veracity of [the Qur'ān], and only those who are knowledgeable derive benefit from them or have knowledge of their meanings. The Exalted said: *As for these similitudes, We coin them for mankind, but none will grasp their meaning save the wise.*[3]

There are around forty similitudes in the Qur'ān. If a Predecessor read one of them but could not understand it, he would weep and say 'I am not one of the knowledgeable.'

1 ʿAbd Allāh b. Masʿūd (d. 29/650) was a prominent Companion and is reported to have been the sixth man to accept Islam. He was one of the foremost reciters of the Qur'ān. He also narrated 848 *ḥadīths*.

2 Ibn ʿAbd al-Barr 1514.

3 Q. xxix.43.

CHAPTER TWO

The Importance of Having Knowledge of the Qur'ān, the Sunna and Wisdom and then Teaching Them

[POINT 23: ABRAHAM PREVAILED OVER HIS FATHER AND HIS PEOPLE BY USING EVIDENCE.]

The Sublime recounted the debate between Abraham, his father and his people, and how Abraham prevailed over them by using evidence. He also mentioned how He blessed him and elevated his rank due to this knowledge. The Exalted said after mentioning Abraham's debate with his father and his people in *Sūrat al-Anʿām*: *That is Our argument. We gave it unto Abraham against his folk. We raise unto degrees of wisdom whom We will. Thy Lord is Wise, Aware.*[1] Zayd b. Aslam[2] (may God be pleased with him) said: 'His raising of whom He wills to higher ranks is according to their knowledge and use of evidence.'

[POINT 24: WISDOM CAN BE SEEN IN GOD'S CREATION BECAUSE IT SHOWS THAT HE IS OMNISCIENT.]

The Sublime revealed that He originated the creation, established His Holy House [Kaʿba] and the holy month, and established marked and unmarked sacrificial animals[3] so that His servants would come to know that He is Omniscient and Omnipotent. The Exalted said: *God it is Who hath created seven heavens, and of the earth the like thereof. The commandment cometh down among them slowly, that ye may know that*

1 Q. VI.83.

2 Abū Usāma Zayd b. Aslam (d. 136/754) was a Successor.

3 This is mentioned in Q. V.97.

God is Able to do all things, and that God surroundeth all things in knowledge.[1] This proves that the servants' knowledge of the Lord and His Attributes, as well as their worshipping Him alone, is the desired objective of His creating and His commandments.

[Points 25–26: God informs us that knowledge is better than any wealth, and that it is the best bounty.]

25. God (Glory be to Him) commanded the knowledgeable to rejoice with what He has bestowed upon them. He informed us that knowledge is better than what people may accumulate [of wealth in this world]. The Exalted said: *Say: In the bounty of God and in His mercy: therein let them rejoice. It is better than what they hoard.*[2] *The bounty of God* has been interpreted to mean 'faith', while *His mercy* is interpreted as the Qur'ān itself. Faith and the Qur'ān represent beneficial knowledge, righteous deeds, guidance and the true religion; and these denote the most superior types of knowledge and deeds.

26. The Sublime has borne witness that whosoever has been given knowledge, has been given a great bounty. The Exalted said: *He giveth wisdom unto whom He will, and he unto whom wisdom is given, he truly hath received abundant good. But none remember except men of understanding.*[3] Ibn Qutayba[4] and others defined *wisdom* (*ḥikma*) here as 'possessing the truth and acting upon it'. Thus it indicates beneficial knowledge and righteous deeds.

[Point 27: God's greatest blessings upon the Prophet are the Book, wisdom and knowledge.]

The Sublime has recounted His blessings and grace upon His Messenger, with the most distinguished being that He bestowed upon him the Book and wisdom, and taught him that which he did

1 Q. LXV.12.

2 Q. X.58.

3 Q. II.269.

4 ʿAbd Allāh b. Muslim b. Qutayba al-Dinawārī (d. 276/889) was a scholar and judge during the Abbasid Caliphate.

not previously know. The Exalted said: *God revealeth unto thee the Book and wisdom, and teacheth thee that which thou knewest not. The grace of God towards thee hath been infinite.*[1]

[POINT 28: GOD REMINDS THE BELIEVERS OF HIS BLESSINGS IN SENDING THE MESSENGER MUḤAMMAD TO THEM.]

The Sublime reminded His pious servants of these [above-mentioned] blessings and commanded them to thank Him and remember Him for what He has conferred upon them. The Exalted said: *Even as We have sent unto you a messenger from among you, who reciteth unto you Our revelations and causeth you to grow, and teacheth you the Book and wisdom, and teacheth you that which ye knew not. Therefor remember Me, I will remember you. Give thanks to Me, and reject not Me.*[2]

[POINT 29: GOD'S FAVOUR UPON ADAM BY ENDOWING HIM WITH KNOWLEDGE.]

When the Sublime informed the angels that He would place a viceroy on the earth, they asked Him: *Wilt thou place therein one who will do harm therein and will shed blood, while we hymn Thy praise and sanctify Thee? He said: Surely I know that which ye know not. And He taught Adam all the names, then showed them to the angels, saying: Inform Me of the names of these, if ye are truthful. They said: Be glorified! We have no knowledge saving that which Thou hast taught us. Thou, only Thou, art the Knower, the Wise.*[3] Then His commandment was given to the angels to prostrate before Adam, but Iblīs[4] refused. Thus God damned the Devil and expelled him from the heavens.

There are numerous points in this story that show the excellence of knowledge. Firstly, the Sublime responded to the angels—when they inquired why He would place humans on the earth, since they

1 Q. IV.113.

2 Q. II.151–152.

3 Q. II.30–32.

4 Iblīs is one of the names of the Devil or Satan (*Shayṭān*). It is derived from the word *ablasa*, which means 'to despair of any hope or goodness'.

felt that they were more obedient to Him—by stating: *Surely I know that which ye know not.*[1] Thus He responded that He knows hidden matters and their realities, that these [issues] are unknown to them, and that He is the Most Knowledgeable and Most Wise. It thereafter became apparent that some of the best of His creation arose from this viceroy: His messengers and prophets, the pious servants, martyrs, truly faithful ones (*ṣiddīqūn*), scholars, and other ranks of knowledgeable and faithful people who are better than the angels.

It also became evident that the most evil of creation arose from the Devil. Thus He (Glory be to Him) brought forth both types of [creatures]. The angels had no prior knowledge of this, nor could they have anticipated the dazzling wisdoms ensuing from the creation of Adam and the settling [of his progeny] on earth.

Secondly, when the Sublime wanted to manifest Adam's superiority and excellence over [the angels], He favoured him with knowledge. God taught him all of the names and then presented them to the angels saying: *Inform Me of the names of these, if ye are truthful.*[2] It has been narrated in some exegeses that the angels thought that their Lord would not create anyone more honourable than them, and that they would be better than the viceroy that God established for the earth. Once they were tested with knowledge that He had only taught this viceroy, they acknowledged their incapacity and ignorance, and said: *Be glorified! We have no knowledge saving that which Thou hast taught us. Thou, only Thou, art the Knower, the Wise.*[3] Thus when He said *O Adam! Inform them of their names, and when he had informed them of their names,*[4] they acknowledged his superiority.

Thirdly, once the Sublime manifested the excellence of Adam, He said to them: *Did I not tell you that I know the secret of the heavens and the earth? And I know that which ye disclose and which ye hide.*[5] Thus the

1 Q. II.30.
2 Q. II.31.
3 Q. II.32.
4 Q. II.33.
5 Q. II.33.

Sublime made Himself known to them by manifesting His Attribute of being the Most Knowledgeable. His knowledge has encompassed what is apparent and what is hidden about them, in addition to the Unseen in the heavens and earth. This is sufficient to show the eminence of knowledge.

Fourthly, the Sublime created Adam with more characteristics of perfection than any other creature. Furthermore, He (Glory be to Him) wanted to show the angels Adam's excellence and honourable nature, so He manifested to them his greatest characteristic: his knowledge. This indicates that knowledge is the most eminent thing a person can possess, and that one's superiority and excellence is due to it.

[Point 30: The beauty of knowledge is greater than physical beauty, as illustrated in the story of Joseph.]

A similar situation occurred when He willed to manifest Joseph's (peace be upon him) superiority and eminence over all the people of his time. Joseph's knowledge was manifested to the King and people of Egypt when he interpreted [the King's] dreams—something that the [Egyptian] masters of interpreting [dreams] failed to do. Recall that the King had previously imprisoned him, even though Joseph's appearance was the most handsome and beautiful. But once the excellence and beauty of his knowledge became apparent to the King, he released Joseph from prison, gave him authority and handed over the treasury of the land to him.

This is proof that the projection of knowledge—when it comes to the progeny of Adam—is more magnificent and superior than a person's physical image, even if the latter is the most beautiful.

[Point 31: God has in many verses rebuked those who are ignorant.]

The Sublime has in many verses in His Book rebuked those who are ignorant. The Exalted said: *Howbeit, most of them are ignorant;*[1] *But most of them know not.*[2] The Exalted also said: *Or deemest thou that most of them hear or understand? They are but as the cattle—nay, but they are farther astray?*[3] He (Glory be to Him) did not deem it sufficient to equate those who are ignorant with animals, but instead went further by declaring them more astray than animals.

He also said: *The worst of beasts in God's sight are the deaf, the dumb, who have no sense.*[4] Here, He informed us that some of those who are ignorant are the worst of beasts. There is nothing more harmful to the religion of the messengers than those who are ignorant.

The Exalted protected His Prophet [from foolishness] while advising him: *So be not thou among the foolish ones.*[5] And Moses—the one whom God spoke to—said: *God forbid that I should be among the foolish!*[6] And He said to His first messenger Noah (peace be upon him): *I admonish thee lest thou be among the ignorant.*[7]

God (Glory be to Him) has also informed us that He punished His enemies by preventing them from having knowledge of the Book, His [Attributes] and His Laws. The Exalted said: *And when thou recitest the Qur'ān We place between thee and those who believe not in the Hereafter a hidden barrier; and We place upon their hearts veils lest they should understand it, and in their ears a deafness.*[8] He also commanded His Prophet to avoid them: *Turn away from the ignorant.*[9]

God also commended His servants who avoid and abandon the [ignorant], by saying: *And when they hear vanity they withdraw from it and say: Unto us our works and unto you your works. Peace be unto you! We*

1 Q. VI.111.
2 Q. VI.37.
3 Q. XXV.44.
4 Q. VIII.22.
5 Q. VI.35.
6 Q. II.67.
7 Q. XI.46.
8 Q. XVII.45–46.
9 Q. VII.199.

desire not the ignorant.[1] The Exalted also said: *And when the foolish ones address them answer: Peace.*[2]

All of the above illustrates the repulsive nature of ignorance in God's sight and His hatred of the ignorant. Likewise, [the innate disposition leads] people to [hate ignorance], so they will deny being [ignorant] even if they are in fact so.

[Point 32: The Qur'ān and faith are two spiritual lights that God has placed in the hearts of the believers.]

The [pursuit of] knowledge is a life [of its own] and it lights [the way], while ignorance leads to [spiritual] darkness and death. All evilness is due to the privation of [spiritual] life and light, while all virtue is due to the presence of that [spiritual] light and life. Light elucidates the reality of things and reveals their levels. Being [spiritually] alive allows a person to perfect his character, statements and deeds.

Traits that emanate from [a spiritual] life are all good. One example is modesty, which is due to one's heart being perfectly alive [in spiritual terms]. This allows it to then recognize the reality and repugnant nature of a sin. The opposite of it is insolence and indecency, which are due to the [spiritual] death of the heart and its failure to flee from that which is repugnant.

The Exalted also said: *Is he who was dead and We have raised him unto life, and set for him a light wherein he walketh among men, as him whose similitude is in utter darkness whence he cannot emerge?*[3] Previously this person was [spiritually] dead because of his ignorance, but God brought him back to life by gracing him with knowledge and a [spiritual] light. The Exalted also said: *O ye who believe! Be mindful of your duty to God and put faith in His Messenger. He will give you twofold of His mercy and will appoint for you a light wherein ye shall walk, and will forgive you. God is Forgiving, Merciful; that the People of the Book may know that*

1 Q. xxviii.55.
2 Q. xxv.63.
3 Q. vi.122.

they control naught of the bounty of God, but that the bounty is in God's hand to give to whom He will. And God is of Infinite Bounty.[1]

The Exalted also said: *God is the Protecting Guardian of those who believe. He bringeth them out of darkness into light. As for those who disbelieve, their patrons are false deities. They bring them out of light into darkness. Such are rightful owners of the Fire. They will abide therein;*[2] *And thus have We inspired in thee (Muḥammad) a Spirit of Our command. Thou knewest not the Book, nor what is faith. But We have made it a light whereby We guide whom We will of Our servants. And lo! thou verily dost guide unto a right path.*[3] Therefore God revealed to us that the Qur'ān brings about a [spiritual] life, and that it is a [spiritual] light by which one can elucidate [the straight path]. Thus He combined [in this verse] between the two principles of [spiritual] life and light.

The Exalted says: *Now hath come unto you light from God and a plain Book, whereby God guideth him who seeketh His good pleasure unto paths of peace. He bringeth them out of darkness unto light by His decree, and guideth them unto a straight path.*[4] *So believe in God and His Messenger and the light which We have revealed. And God is Informed of what ye do.*[5] *O mankind! Now hath a proof from your Lord come unto you, and We have sent down unto you a clear light.*[6] *Now God hath sent down unto you a reminder, a messenger reciting unto you the revelations of God made plain, that He may bring forth those who believe and do good works from darkness unto light.*[7]

The Exalted also said: *God is the Light of the heavens and the earth. The similitude of His light is as a niche wherein is a lamp. The lamp is in a glass. The glass is as it were a shining star. (This lamp is) kindled from*

1 Q. LVII.28–29.
2 Q. II.257.
3 Q. XLII.52.
4 Q. V.15–16.
5 Q. LXIV.8.
6 Q. IV.174.
7 Q. LXV.10–11.

a blessed tree, an olive neither of the East nor of the West, whose oil would almost glow forth (of itself) though no fire touched it. Light upon light. God guideth unto His light whom He will. And God speaketh to mankind in similtudes, for God is Knower of all things.[1] Ubayy b. Kaᶜb[2] (may God be pleased with him) narrated that this is a similitude that God drew for the [spiritual] light that He has placed in the heart of a believer. At the end of the verse *light upon light* represents the [spiritual] light of faith superimposed upon the light of the Qur'ān. Some of the Predecessors have said that the believer is almost able to express the truth despite having not heard the revealed [Book]. Once he has heard it though, it becomes described as *light upon light*.

God (Glory be to Him) has mentioned these two lights—the Book and faith— together in another verse in His Book: *Thou knewest not the Book, nor what is faith. But We have made it a light whereby We guide whom We will of Our servants.*[3]

In a *ḥadīth* narrated by al-Nawwās b. Samᶜān (may God be pleased with him), the Prophet said: 'Indeed God has drawn a similitude of the straight path: at the sides of the path there are two walls with open doors, each door having a curtain. There is a caller at the head of the path and a caller above it, and they are both announcing: *And God invites to the abode of peace and guides whomever He wills to the straight path.*[4] The doors, which are on the sides of the path, are the legal limitations of God; but once one breaches the legal limitations of God, that curtain is lifted. The one calling from above it is an advisor of the Lord.'[5] This is the

1 Q. XXIV.35.

2 Abū Mundhir Ubayy b. Kaᶜb (d. 29/649) was a prominent Companion who witnessed the Battle of Badr. The Prophet (may God bless him and grant him peace) mentioned him as one of the four that his contemporaries should learn the Qur'ān from.

3 Q. XLII.52.

4 Q. XVI.25.

5 Tirmidhī 2859; Aḥmad 17634; Ḥākim 245; Bayhaqī (*Shuᶜab*) 6821. It is 'authentic' according to Albānī (*Ṣaḥīḥ al-Jāmiᶜ al-ṣaghīr* 3887).

wording narrated in Tirmidhī.[1] Imam Aḥmad's[2] wording [for the last part] is: 'The caller at the head of the path is the Book of God and the caller above the path is the advisor of God present in every believer's heart.'

Therefore the Prophet mentioned two principles: the calling of the Qur'ān and that of faith.[3] Ḥudhayfa[4] narrated that, 'The Messenger of God (may God bless him and grant him peace) said to us: "The trust (*amāna*) was preserved within the base of the hearts of men, and then the Qur'ān was revealed. Thus they learned faith and then they learned the Qur'ān."'[5]

The Prophet said in another *ḥadīth* narrated by Abū Mūsā al-Ashʿarī:[6] 'The similitude of [a believer] who recites the Qur'ān is like that of a citron, which tastes good and smells good. And [a believer] who does not recite the Qur'ān is like a date, which tastes good but has no smell. The similitude of a hypocrite who

1 Abū ʿĪsā Muḥammad b. ʿĪsā al-Sulamī al-Tirmidhī (d. 279/892) was a student of Imam Bukhārī and Imam Muslim. His major collection *Jāmiʿ* or *Sunan al-Tirmidhī* includes 3956 *ḥadīths*.

2 Abū ʿAbd Allāh Aḥmad b. Muḥammad b. Ḥanbal (d. 241/855) was the eponymous founder of the Ḥanbalī school of jurisprudence. He studied under Shāfiʿī and collected the massive collection of *ḥadīth* named *Musnad al-Imām Aḥmad*. He became particularly famous after rejecting the Muʿtazilī doctrine that the Qur'ān was created. He was imprisoned during the Inquisition (*Miḥna*), first by the Abbasid Caliph Ma'mūn and later by his successors Muʿtaṣim and Wāthiq only to be finally released by Mutawakkil. Ibn al-Qayyim often refers to Imam Aḥmad in his works.

3 Ibn al-Qayyim is here drawing the conclusion—based on the wording of the *ḥadīth* in *Musnad al-Imām Aḥmad*—that the faith in the heart of a believer is one of God's advisors to him.

4 Hudhayfa b. al-Yamān (d. 35/656) was a Companion who participated in all the battles after Uhud. He was known as the 'Keeper of the Secret of the Messenger of God', as the Prophet revealed to him the identities of the Hypocrites.

5 Bukhārī 6497; Muslim 367; Tirmidhī 2179; Ibn Māja 4053; Aḥmad 23,255.

6 Abū Mūsā ʿAbd Allāh b. Qays al-Ashʿarī (d. 42-52/662-672) was a prominent Companion, who accepted Islam before the migration to Medina. He became governor of Yemen during the Prophet's time and later assumed the same position in Basra and Kufa during the Caliphates of ʿUmar and ʿUthmān. He narrated 360 *ḥadīths*.

recites the Qur'ān is like sweet basil, which smells good but tastes bitter. And the similitude of a hypocrite who does not recite the Qur'ān is like a bitter apple, which tastes bitter and has no smell.'[1]

Thus the Prophet divided people into four groups. Those who are faithful and adhere to Qur'ān are the best. Those who are faithful but do not recite the Qur'ān are below the first group, but are still blessed. The wretched hypocrites are divided into two groups: the first are those who recite the Qur'ān; and the second are neither faithful nor do they read the Qur'ān.

The point is that the Qur'ān and faith are the [spiritual] lights that God has placed in the hearts of those whom He wills of His servants. These two are the bases of every good in this life and the Hereafter. Knowledge of them both is the noblest and most virtuous type. There is no knowledge that is truly beneficial for a person except of them both: *God guideth whom He will unto a straight path.*[2]

[Point 33: A trained dog's prey is permissible because of the former's knowledge.]

God (Glory be to Him) forbade eating the killed prey of an ignorant wild dog but allowed eating that of a trained dog. This is also due to the eminence of knowledge. God (Exalted is He) said: *They ask thee (O Muḥammad) what is made lawful for them. Say: (All) good things are made lawful for you. And those beasts and birds of prey which ye have trained as hounds are trained, ye teach them that which God taught you; so eat of that which they catch for you and mention God's name upon it, and observe your duty to God. Lo! God is swift to take account.*[3] Had it not been for the distinction of knowledge as well as the excellence of teaching it, then the [ruling regarding the] killed prey of a trained and an ignorant dog would have been the same.

1 Bukhārī 5427; Muslim 1860; Tirmidhī 2865; Abū Dāwūd 4829; Ibn Māja 214; Nasā'ī 5041; Aḥmad 19,664.

2 Q. II.213.

3 Q. V.4.

[Point 34: Moses travelled to be with Khiḍr for the sole purpose of increasing his knowledge.]

God (Glory be to Him) informed us how [Moses]—His selected one whom He spoke to and wrote the Torah for with His Hand—travelled to learn from the learned man [Khiḍr], and endeavoured to further his knowledge. He said: *And when Moses said unto his servant: I will not give up until I reach the point where the two rivers meet, though I march on for ages.*[1]

Moses was keen to meet this learned man and acquire [wisdom] from him. Upon meeting him, he adopted the mannerism of a student with his teacher: *Moses said unto him: May I follow thee, to the end that thou mayst teach me right conduct of that which thou hast been taught?*[2] Therefore, after greeting him, he asked permission to follow him. Moses could not have followed him otherwise. He did not approach [Khiḍr] to test or inconvenience him, but instead to learn and further his knowledge. The excellence and eminence of knowledge is sufficiently illustrated in the three matters [that occurred between them both].[3] Their story contains many lessons, signs and wisdoms; however, they are beyond the scope of this book.

[Point 35: Acquiring knowledge and thereafter teaching it is equivalent to waging battle for His sake.]

The Exalted said: *Nor should the believers all go forth together: if a contingent from every expedition remained behind, they could devote themselves to studies in religion, and admonish the people when they return to them, that thus they (may learn) to guard themselves (against evil).*[4]

Hence the Exalted ordered the believers to acquire religious knowledge. This includes learning it, and then admonishing and apprising their people when they return to them. There is a differ-

1 Q. xviii.60.

2 Q. xviii.66.

3 See Q. xviii.65–82.

4 Q. ix.122 (Yusuf Ali translation).

ence of opinion about this verse. Some have said the meaning implies that not all believers must travel to acquire an understanding [of the religion] and study; rather, only some of them should go out, and after their return, they should teach those who stayed behind. In this sense, [the verse solely] concerns the pursuit of knowledge.

Others have said the meaning is that not all believers should battle [for His sake], but rather only some should do so, while others stay behind pursuing religious knowledge. Then, when the group that went out [to wage war] returns, those who stayed behind will teach the former what has been revealed of the religion, in terms of the permitted and forbidden. This is the opinion held by the majority, who maintain that the word *nafīr* technically means 'going out to battle'; and when it is used, it should be understood to indicate waging battle [for His sake]. For example, God (Exalted is He) said: *Go forth, light-armed and heavy-armed, and strive with your wealth and your lives in the way of God! That is best for you if ye but knew.*[1] The Prophet (may God bless him and grant him peace) said: 'There is no migration (*hijra*) [from Mecca to Medina] after the Conquest [of Mecca], but waging battle and good intention remain. Should you be called to go to battle [by the Muslim ruler], immediately go forth.'[2]

Nevertheless, both opinions encourage one to pursue religious knowledge, and thereafter to teach it. It is comparable to waging battle [for His sake] and perhaps superior to it. This will be discussed in Point 108,[3] God willing.

[Point 36: The excellence of knowledge and good deeds is evidenced in Sūrat al-ʿAsr.]

The Exalted said: *By the declining day, man is a state of loss, save those who believe and do good works, and exhort one another to truth and exhort*

1 Q. ix.41.

2 Bukhārī 2783; Muslim 4831; Tirmidhī 1590; Abū Dāwūd 2480; Nasā'ī 4174; Aḥmad 2396.

3 Also discussed in Point 66.

one another to endurance.[1] Shāfiʿī[2] (may God be pleased with him) said: 'If all people would simply think about this *sūra*, it would suffice them.'

There are four levels [in this matter]; and completion of them leads one to ultimate perfection. The Exalted (Glory be to Him) mentioned them in this *sūra* and swore by time (*wa'l-ʿaṣr*) that all are in loss except those who believe and do good deeds. Thus they include those who learn and know the truth, and that is [the first] level. Those who do good deeds are those who act according to what they have learned of the truth; this is the second level. The third level is to exhort [to the truth] by teaching and guiding one another. Finally, the fourth level is to be patient upon the truth and exhort one another to be patient and perseverant.

This [last level] represents the utmost perfection, since it entails being perfect and then working to perfect others. Such perfection represents the improvement and strengthening of one's knowledge and deeds; the former occurs through faith while the latter is through further good deeds. [Helping to] perfect others is by teaching them while being perseverant, and then exhorting them to be patient in learning that knowledge and carrying out those actions.

This *sūra*, although short, is one of the most comprehensive *sūras* of the Qur'ān—it encompasses all good. All praise is due to God Who made His Book sufficient above all else, a cure for every spiritual disease and the guide to every good.

1 Q. CIII.1–3.

2 Abū ʿAbd Allāh Muḥammad b. Idrīs al-Shāfiʿī (d.204/820) was the eponymous founder of the Shāfiʿī school of jurisprudence. Shāfiʿī was a descendant of the Banū Muṭṭalib tribe of Quraysh. He was born in Gaza in 150/767 and at the age of 2 his mother took him to Mecca. He later moved to Medina to study under Mālik b. Anas (see footnote 3 on page 45 for further details). He is famous for writing the book *al-Risāla*, which is the earliest surviving documentation of Islamic jurisprudence that is relatively elaborate.

[Point 37: God reminds us of His grace in bestowing knowledge upon His prophets Muḥammad, Joseph, Moses, Jesus son of Mary, David and Solomon.]

The Sublime reminded us of His grace and favour in bestowing knowledge upon His prophets, messengers, loyal supporters (*awliyāʾ*) and believing servants. He recounts His blessings upon [Muḥammad], the seal of His prophets and messengers, by saying: *God revealeth unto thee the Book and wisdom, and teacheth thee that which thou knewest not. The grace of God towards thee hath been infinite.*[1]

He said regarding Joseph: *And when he reached his prime We gave him wisdom and knowledge. Thus We reward the good.*[2] And He said regarding Moses, whom He spoke directly to: *And when he reached his full strength and was ripe, We gave him wisdom and knowledge. Thus do We reward the good.*[3] Due to the fact that Moses was chosen to endure a great ordeal—and only the mighty of firm resolve could remain steadfast [in such circumstances]—God prepared Moses only after he had reached full and complete strength.

He said regarding the Messiah: *O Jesus, son of Mary! Remember My favour unto thee and unto thy mother; how I strengthened thee with the holy Spirit, so that thou spakest unto mankind in the cradle as in maturity; and how I taught thee the Book and wisdom and the Torah and the Gospel.*[4] God made his teaching of the Book, wisdom, the Torah and the Gospel a bearer of glad tidings for his mother and a delight for her eyes.

He said regarding David: *We made his kingdom strong and gave him wisdom and decisive speech.*[5] He said regarding Khiḍr, the companion of Moses: *Then found they one of Our servants, unto whom We had given mercy from Us, and had taught him knowledge from Our presence.*[6] Thus

1 Q. IV.113.
2 Q. XII.22.
3 Q. XXVIII.14.
4 Q. V.110.
5 Q. XXXVIII.20.
6 Q. XVIII.65.

God mentioned His blessings, which included His teachings and bestowal of mercy upon [Khiḍr].

The Exalted has also recounted His blessing upon David and Solomon: *And David and Solomon, when they gave judgment concerning the field, when people's sheep had strayed and browsed therein by night; and We were witnesses to their judgment. And We made Solomon to understand (the case); and unto each of them We gave judgment and knowledge.*[1] He mentioned these two noble prophets, praising them both for their wisdom and knowledge, but selecting only one of them to [perfectly] understand the matter.

The legal judgments of David and Solomon [and their merits] have been debated. Some of the scholars preferred the former's verdict while others preferred the latter's. Nonetheless, Solomon's legal judgment is superior in many aspects, including its concordance with analogical reasoning and the foundational principles of the Divine Law, [as discussed] in the book *al-Ijtihād wa'l-taqlīd*.[2]

The Exalted said: *Say (unto the Jews who speak thus): Who revealed the Book which Moses brought, a light and guidance for mankind, which ye have put on parchments which ye show, but ye hide much (thereof), and (by which) ye were taught that which ye knew not yourselves nor (did) your fathers (know it)? Say: God.*[3] This indicates that the [Book] that the Sublime revealed and taught them also proves the veracity of [Muḥammad's] prophethood and message, since it is not possible to acquire that knowledge except through the messengers. Therefore how can [the disbelievers] contend that God has not revealed anything [through Muḥammad] to humanity? This [evidence for the veracity of Muḥammad's prophethood] is all due to the excellence and eminence

1 Q. XXI.78–79.

2 Ibn al-Qayyim may be referring to his book more commonly known as *Iʿlām al-muwaqqiʿīn ʿan-Rabb al-ʿālamīn*, as this discussion—which has not been fully translated into English—is on p. 244 of the Dār al-Kitāb al-ʿArabī edition that was published in Beirut. However, Abū Zayd maintains that *al-Ijtihād wa'l-taqlīd* is a distinct but not extant book. See Abū Zayd, *Ibn Qayyim al-Jawziyya*, p. 200.

3 Q. VI.91.

of knowledge itself. God alone grants success to achieve guidance.

The Exalted said: *God verily hath shown grace to the believers by sending unto them a messenger of their own who reciteth unto them His revelations, and causeth them to grow, and teacheth them the Book and wisdom; although before (he came to them) they were in flagrant error.*[1] The Exalted also said: *He it is Who hath sent among the unlettered ones a messenger of their own, to recite unto them His revelations and to make them grow, and to teach them the Book and wisdom, though heretofore they were indeed in error manifest, along with others of them who have not yet joined them. He is the Mighty, the Wise. That is the bounty of God; which He giveth unto whom He will. God is of Infinite Bounty.*[2]

There is a difference of opinion regarding the connotation of *yalḥaq* ('to join'). For instance, it is said that [*others of them who have not yet joined them*] is a matter of timing [because they will be born in the future]. The other [opinion] is that [it refers to] those who are trying to catch up with the [former's] excellence and precedence. In either case, the Sublime blessed them in that He taught them after they were ignorant and guided them after they were astray. This is such a great, lofty and priceless grace [from God] that we cannot fully appreciate it.

[Point 38: God has graced humanity by teaching them what they did not previously know.]

The first *sūra* that God revealed in the Qur'ān was *Sūrat al-ʿAlaq*. He mentioned how He has blessed humanity by teaching them that which they did not previously know. God also mentions how He chose them due to what He has taught them. This illustrates the great importance of teaching after knowing something. The Exalted said: *Read, in the name of thy Sustainer, Who has created man out of a germ-cell. Read—for thy Sustainer is the Most Bountiful One, Who has taught* [*man*]

1 Q. III.164.
2 Q. LXII.2–4.

the use of the pen—taught man what he did not know![1] Thus He began this *sūra* with the command to read as a requirement for knowledge, and then He mentioned His creation, both specifically and in general, by saying: *Who has created man out of a germ-cell. Read—for thy Sustainer is the Most Bountiful One.*[2]

He selected humans from amongst all of His creation because of what He has conferred upon them. This bestowal includes all of His marvels and signs, which indicate His sovereignty, power, knowledge, wisdom, perfect mercy and prove that there is no deity worthy of worship or any lord besides God. He informed us that His creation of humanity began with a germ cell, which is the first stage of many that a sperm passes through.

God then repeats the command to read. He reminds us that He is the Most Generous (*al-Akram*). This is the superlative form of *karam* ('generous') and it indicates [His] great generosity. There is nobody worthier of this attribute than the Sublime as all good is in His hands, all goodness comes from Him, all blessings are planned by Him, and all perfection and glory are His. God truly is the Most Generous.

He then mentioned His teaching both generally and specifically: *Who has taught [man] the use of the pen.*[3] This encompasses His teaching of both the angels and humans [in general]. Then He mentions teaching humans specifically by saying: *Taught man what he did not know.*[4] These verses indicate that He has originated all things in existence.

There are four grades of existence. One of them is the exterior being, as evidenced by His statement: *Created.* The second is the intellectual: *Taught man what he did not know.*[5] The third and fourth are the spoken and written words. The written is explicitly men-

1 Q. xcvi.1–5 (Muhammad Asad translation).
2 Q. xcvi.1–3.
3 Q. xcvi.4.
4 Q. xcvi.5.
5 Q. xcvi.5.

tioned in His statement: *Who teacheth by the pen.*[1] The spoken word is a necessary prerequisite for instruction using the pen. Writing is a branch of speech and speech is a branch of conception.

Again, these verses include all of the grades of existence, and that He (Glory be to Him) brought them about by creating and then instructing them. God is the Creator and Instructor. Every entity exists because it was created by Him, every knowledge in the intellect exists because He taught it, and every utterance by the tongue, or script written by the finger, exists due to His determination, creation and instruction. These are some of the signs of His power and wisdom. There is no god but Him, the Beneficent, the Merciful.

The point is that the Sublime made Himself known to His creation through the script, [its] expression or meanings that He has instructed them in accordance with His wisdom. Thus knowledge is one of the methods used to prove Him [i.e. His existence, Names and Attributes]. In fact, it is one of the greatest and clearest means. This is sufficient to illustrate the importance of knowledge.

[Point 39: The power of knowledge is great because God has specified that it signifies authoritative evidence.]

The Sublime specifies that all knowledge-based evidence has *sulṭān* [lit. powerful authority]. Ibn ʿAbbās[2] (may God be pleased with him) said that every *sulṭān* in the Qur'ān signifies authoritative evidence. The Exalted said: *They say: God hath taken (unto Himself) a son—Glorified be He! He hath no needs! His is all that is in the heavens and all that is in the earth. Ye have no warrant for this. Tell ye concerning God that which ye know not?*[3] This indicates that the disbelievers have no evidence, regardless of what they may contend; in fact, theirs are only ignorant claims about God.

1 Q. xcvi.4.

2 ʿAbd Allāh b. al-ʿAbbās (d. 68/687) was a Companion and cousin of the Prophet. He was known as the expert interpreter (*tarjumān*) of the Qur'ān. He also narrated 1660 *ḥadīths*.

3 Q. x.68.

The Exalted also said: *They are but names which ye have named, ye and your fathers, for which God hath revealed no warrant. They follow but a guess and that which [they] themselves desire. And now the guidance from their Lord hath come unto them.*[1] This indicates that He did not reveal any evidence or proof for it, but rather it is [only a contention of] theirs and their fathers. The Exalted also said: *Or have ye a clear warrant? Then produce your writ, if ye are truthful;*[2] that is, bring forth clear evidence if you are indeed truthful in your contention.

There is, however, one instance [where *sulṭān* may indicate a different meaning] according to the opinion of some: *My wealth hath not availed me, my power (sulṭān) hath gone from me.*[3] Some have said that it indicates that a disbeliever will lose all of his power in the Hereafter. Others have said that it still indicates the aforementioned explanation, i.e. 'my evidence [or argument] will be invalidated and rendered null'.

Actually, the point is that the Sublime specified that knowledge of evidence is a powerful authority (*sulṭān*) because it allows one to have dominance and power over those who are ignorant. Moreover, the power of knowledge is stronger than the might of force as people are more willing to follow evidence than force. In reality, hearts follow evidence while only the body surrenders to force.

Evidence captivates the heart and guides it. Even if someone is apparently stubborn and arrogant, his heart must surrender to its power and be overcome by it. Moreover, the power of rulers, if not accompanied by knowledge to administer it, is like the power of predatory beasts, lions and the like, i.e. force without knowledge or mercy. Yet the power of authoritative evidence is [best exhibited] when it is accompanied by knowledge, mercy and wisdom.

Finally, if someone is not empowered by knowledge it is either because his evidence is weak or because the force used against him is

1 Q. LIII.23.

2 Q. XXXVII.156–157.

3 Q. LXIX.28–29.

overwhelming. Otherwise, evidence itself is necessarily victorious over falsehood.

[Point 40: God described the denizens of Hellfire as being ignorant, and drew many analogies regarding them that show the repugnant nature of ignorance.]

God (Exalted is He) described the denizens of Hellfire as being ignorant and informed us that He closed off the paths of knowledge for them. The Exalted conveyed what they will say [on the Day of Judgment]: *Had we been wont to listen or have sense, we would not have been among the dwellers in the flames. So they acknowledge their sins; but far removed [from mercy] are the dwellers in the flames.*[1] Thus the disbelievers admit that they could not hear or comprehend; and hearing and comprehension are the bases and means by which knowledge is acquired.

The Exalted also said: *Already have We urged unto Hell many of the jinn and humankind, having hearts wherewith they understand not, and having eyes wherewith they see not, and having ears wherewith they hear not. These are as the cattle—nay, but they are worse! These are the neglectful.*[2] Thus He notifies us that the disbelievers failed to attain knowledge by using any one of the three means: the intellect, hearing or vision. Similarly, in another verse, He states: *Deaf, dumb, blind, therefor they have no sense.*[3]

The Exalted also said: *Have they not travelled in the land, and have they hearts wherewith to feel and ears wherewith to hear? For indeed it is not the eyes that grow blind, but it is the hearts, which are within the bosoms, that grow blind.*[4] The Exalted said: *And verily We had empowered them with that wherewith We have not empowered you, and had assigned them ears and eyes and hearts; but their ears and eyes and hearts availed them naught since they denied the revelations of God; and what they used to mock befell them.*[5]

1 Q. LXVII.10–11.
2 Q. VII.179.
3 Q. II.171.
4 Q. XXII.46.
5 Q. XLVI.26.

Thus God makes clear that the fate of the wretched is due to their lack of knowledge. He portrayed them in various instances: as being similar to grazing animals or even more astray than them; as similar to donkeys that carry books; as the worst and most evil of beasts; as being [spiritually] dead, rather than alive; as being astray; and residing in the darkness of ignorance. He also depicted their hearts and eyes as being covered, and their ears as completely hollow.

The aforementioned analogies all denote the condemnation of those who are ignorant and indicate the repugnant nature of ignorance, as well as His hatred of them. As indicated previously, though, God loves the knowledgeable, and He commends and praises them. We depend on God alone.

[Point 41: Knowledge accompanied by good deeds is a sign that God wants good for that believer.]

It is related in the *Ṣaḥīḥs* [of Bukhārī[1] and Muslim[2]] that Muʿāwiya[3] (may God be pleased with him) narrated that he heard the Messenger of God (may God bless him and grant him peace) say: 'If God wants good for someone, He grants him *fiqh*[4] of the religion.'[5]

Fiqh connotes a deep understanding of necessary religious knowledge, which inevitably results in [one doing good] deeds. This

1 Abū ʿAbd Allāh Muḥammad b. Ismāʿīl b. Ibrāhīm b. al-Mughīra al-Bukhārī (d. 256/870) was born in the city of Bukhara. Imam Bukhārī went on to collect the most authentic collection of *ḥadīths*, *Ṣaḥīḥ al-Bukhārī*. It is comprised of 7275 *ḥadīths* with repetition, or 2230 without repetition.

2 Abū al-Ḥusayn Muslim b. al-Ḥajjāj b. Muslim b. Ward al-Naysābūrī (d. 261/875) was a student of Imam Bukhārī and Imam Aḥmad. He is the compiler of the second most authentic collection of *ḥadīths*, *Ṣaḥīḥ Muslim*. It is comprised of 7563 *ḥadīths* with repetition, or 3033 without repetition.

3 Muʿāwiya b. Abī Sufyān (d. 60/680) was a Companion. He was first appointed as the governor of Syria by ʿUmar b. al-Khaṭṭāb. He later became the first Umayyad Caliph. He narrated 163 *ḥadīths*.

4 Since the actual connotation of *fiqh* is multifaceted, the transliterated form of the Arabic word will be used throughout the text.

5 Bukhārī 71; Muslim 2389; Tirmidhī 2645; Ibn Māja 221; Aḥmad 16,837.

indicates that if God does not give someone *fiqh* of the religion, then He does not will goodness for that person. Moreover, if one only possesses knowledge [unaccompanied by good deeds], then it is not proof that He has willed goodness for such a person. And God knows best.

[Point 42: The analogy between knowledge and guidance and abundant rain and water.]

The Messenger of God (may God bless him and grant him peace) said: 'The similitude of the guidance and knowledge which God has sent me with is like abundant rain falling on the earth. In some places there was fertile soil that absorbed the rainwater and brought forth vegetation and grass in abundance. In others it was hard and held the rainwater, whereby God allowed people to benefit and drink from it and [allowed it to] be used to irrigate the land for cultivation. However, a portion of it was barren, such that it could neither hold water nor bring forth vegetation. The first is the similitude of the person to whom God has given *fiqh* of the religion and who has benefitted from that which God revealed through me. He understands and then teaches others. The last is a metaphor for a person who does not care for it and does not accept God's guidance, which He has revealed through me.'[1]

Thus the Prophet (may God bless him and grant him peace) taught us by [first] drawing an analogy between knowledge and abundant rain: both knowledge and rain bring about life, benefit, sustenance, cures and other goods for people. Next, he drew an analogy between [people's] hearts and the earth: many beneficial plants grow in areas where the rain falls; similarly, the hearts holding of knowledge results in the growth of fruits and blessings.

The Prophet then divided people into three groups. The first group includes those who have memorized and preserved [the religion], and have understood and comprehended its meanings. They

1 Bukhārī 79; Muslim 5953; Aḥmad 19,573.

are then also able to derive [the relevant] rulings, wisdoms and morals from it. So they are like the earth that holds water, thereby allowing pastures and grass to grow forth. These people have preserved [this religion] and have a deep understanding of it. Indeed they are the transmitters and guardians of this religion.

The second group has been graced with the blessing of memorizing, conveying and recording knowledge, but they have not been blessed with deeper comprehension of its meanings nor the ability to derive the legal rulings, wisdoms or morals from it. ʿAli b. Abī Ṭālib[1] (may God be pleased with him) said: 'God bestows upon His servants an understanding of His Book, but people are greatly varied in their ability to understand [what has been revealed by] God and His Messenger. Perhaps one individual may understand from a passage one or two wisdoms while another will understand one hundred or two hundred.'

Ultimately, these first two groups are the blissful ones; but the first attain a loftier level and higher reward: *That is the bounty of God, which He giveth unto whom He will. God is of Infinite Bounty.*[2]

The third group is composed of those who have no share in it, because they cannot memorize, understand, transmit or instruct on religious matters. Instead, they are like barren lowland that does not bring forth vegetation and cannot retain water. They did not accept God's guidance, and therefore they are worse than grazing animals. These people are wretched, and they are the fuel for Hellfire.

Again, this great *ḥadīth* draws our attention to the eminence of knowledge and teaching it. It also divides the children of Adam into [those who are either] blissful or wretched. The blissful are divided into those who surpass others and are given proximity (*sābiq muqarrab*), and those who strive on the right path (*yamīn muqtaṣid*). It also

1 ʿAlī b. Abī Ṭālib (d. 40/660) was a Companion and a cousin of the Prophet, and the first youth to accept Islam. He later married the Prophet's daughter Fāṭima, and became the fourth Rightly-Guided Caliph. He was one of the ten promised Paradise. He narrated 537 *ḥadīths*.

2 Q. LXII.4.

proves that people require knowledge in the same way as or even more than they need water.

The Exalted also said: *He sendeth down water from the sky, so that valleys flow according to their measure, and the flood beareth (on its surface) swelling foam—from that which they smelt in the fire in order to make ornaments and tools riseth a foam like unto it—thus God coineth (the similitude of) the true and the false. Then, as for the foam, it passeth away as scum upon the banks, while, as for that which is of use to mankind, it remaineth in the earth. Thus God coineth the similitudes.*[1] Here the Sublime likened the knowledge that He revealed upon His Messenger to the water that He made fall from the sky: each one of them results in life, and benefits people in this world and when they return [in the Hereafter].

Then God likened hearts to valleys: a big heart can contain much knowledge just like a large valley can hold a large quantity of water, whereas a smaller heart holds less knowledge just like a smaller valley holds less water. He said: *So that valleys flow according to their measure, and the flood beareth (on its surface) swelling foam.*[2] God (Exalted is He) drew an analogy to how knowledge removes invalid doubts once they enter the heart. These [doubts] emerge and appear on the surface of the heart to then be thrown out. This is like floodwater as it removes the scum from a valley, which then floats on the surface of the water [to be taken away]. Therefore what remains established in one's heart is what benefits its owner: the true religion and being guided to it, just like pure water remains in a valley. Ultimately, no one can comprehend the similitudes of God except the knowledgeable sages.

Then the Sublime drew another analogy by saying: *from that which they smelt in the fire in order to make ornaments and tools riseth a foam like unto it.*[3] Thus when the progeny of Adam kindle gold, silver, copper and iron, they remove their impurities, which are expelled because

1 Q. XIII.17.
2 Q. XIII.17.
3 Q. XIII.17.

of [the fire], thereby leaving only the pure metal. The Sublime drew the analogy with water because it contains life, coolness and benefit, whereas the analogy with fire was drawn because it has light, heat and burning.

Now the verses of the Qur'ān enliven the heart just as water revives the earth. The Qur'ān also expels evilness, doubts and darkness, just as fire burns away what is thrown into it. [The Qur'ān] separates and differentiates what is pure from the impure, just like fire separates out the impurities from gold, silver, copper and the like. These are some of the lessons and knowledge contained in this great analogy. God (Exalted is He) said: *As for these similitudes, We coin them for mankind, but none will grasp their meaning save the wise.*[1]

[Points 43–45: The excellence of the person teaching and guiding others, and that the teacher receives the same reward as those whom he has taught.]

43. Sahl b. Saᶜd[2] (may God be pleased with him) narrated that the Messenger of God (may God bless him and grant him peace) told ᶜAlī (may God be pleased with him): 'By God, if one person is guided to the right path[3] through you, it would be better for you than [a tremendous number of] red camels (*ḥumr al-naᶜam*).'[4]

This again shows the excellence of knowledge and instruction, and the eminence of those who hold that status. This *ḥadīth* [addresses] the guidance of only one person, so can you imagine how great [the reward and rank of the Prophet is] as it is through his efforts that a multitude of people is guided at each moment?

1 Q. xxix.43.

2 Abū al-ᶜAbbās Sahl b. Saᶜd b. Mālik (d. 95/713) was a Companion. He was one of the Anṣār. He lived to be 101 years old by some estimates and was the last Companion to die in Medina. He narrated 188 *ḥadīths*.

3 'The right path' in this context is guiding a non-Muslim to Islam.

4 Bukhārī 3009; Muslim 6223; Aḥmad 22,821.

44. Abū Hurayra[1] (may God be pleased with him) narrated that the Messenger of God (may God bless him and grant him peace) said: 'Whoever calls to guidance shall receive a reward similar to the one who follows him, without diminishing anything from the latter's reward. And whoever calls to misguidance shall receive a sin similar to the one who followed him, without that diminishing anything from the latter's sin.'[2]

Thus the Prophet informed us that the one who guided another will have the same reward as the person who was guided through him. Similarly, one who led another person astray will have the same recompense of the person whom he led astray. The former strove with all his might to guide people while the latter strove with all his might to lead them astray, thus each of them is accorded the full recompense of those influenced by them. This is a fundamental rule of the Divine Law (which will be discussed later).

The Exalted said: *That they may bear their burdens undiminished on the Day of Resurrection, with somewhat of the burdens of those whom they mislead without knowledge. Ah! evil is that which they bear!*[3] And the Exalted said: *But they verily will bear their own loads and other loads beside their own.*[4] This proves that the one who calls this Community to other than the Sunna of the Messenger of God is a true enemy, since he prevented the Prophet from receiving the reward of those who would have otherwise been guided through his Sunna. This represents one of the greatest forms of enmity towards [the Prophet]. We ask for God's protection from being forsaken.

45. Ibn Masʿūd (may God be pleased with him) narrated that the Messenger of God (may God bless him and grant him peace) said: 'Do not wish to be like anyone except in two cases: one to

1 This refers to ʿAbd al-Raḥmān b. Ṣakhr al-Azdī, who was better known as Abū Hurayra (d. 61/681). He was a prominent Companion, who narrated 5374 *ḥadīths* with repetition (or about 1500 without repetition).

2 Muslim 6804; Tirmidhī 2674; Abū Dāwūd 4609; Ibn Māja 206; Aḥmad 9160.

3 Q. XVI.25.

4 Q. XXIX.13.

whom God has given wealth and he spends it righteously; or one to whom God has given wisdom, so he acts according to it and teaches it to others.'[1]

Thus the Prophet (may God bless him and grant him peace) [first] informed us that one should not envy anyone else [as a general rule]. Yet he did allow one to wish to be like two others: those who use either knowledge or wealth as charity. But this can only occur on the condition that one does not desire that such a blessing is lost by the other person in order to attain it for oneself.

1 Bukhārī 73; Muslim 1896.

CHAPTER THREE

The Superiority of the Scholar over the Worshipper and that the Former are the True Heirs of the Prophets

[Point 46: On the scholar being superior to the worshipper, and the prayers of the angels and the rest of creation for the scholar.]

Abū Umāma al-Bāhilī[1] narrated that two men—one of them a scholar and the other a worshipper—were mentioned to the Messenger of God (may God bless him and grant him peace), whereupon he said: 'The superiority of the scholar over the worshipper is like my superiority over the least of you. Indeed God, His angels, the inhabitants of the heavens and the earths—even the ant in its hole and the fish in the sea—say prayers [and blessings] for the one who teaches people to do good.'[2]

Al-Fuḍayl b. ʿIyāḍ[3] said: 'A scholar who is active [in doing good deeds] and instructing others is named a "great one" (*kabīr*) by those in the heavens.' Similar statements exist from the Companions. Ibn ʿAbbās said: 'The scholars of this Community are of two types: one whom God has bestowed knowledge and he expends it for the people without desiring to secure [some favours] or requesting reimbursement from them. For them is the praise of the birds, whales,

1 Abū Umāma Sudayy b. ʿAjlān al-Bāhilī (d. 81/700) was a Companion. He narrated 250 *ḥadīths* and was the last of the Companions to die in Syria.

2 Tirmidhī 2685. It is 'authentic' according to Albānī (*Ṣaḥīḥ al-Jāmiʿ al-ṣaghīr* 4213).

3 Abū ʿAlī al-Fuḍayl b. ʿIyāḍ (d.187/803) studied under Abū Ḥanīfa after repenting from a life of being a robber and other sins. He later became well known for his asceticism.

everything living on this earth and the noble angels who record our deeds. In contrast is one who, although God gave him knowledge, withheld it from His servants, attempted to secure favours and desired monetary gain. These will come on the Day of Resurrection and will be bridled with fire.' Ibn ʿAbd al-Barr[1] attributed this statement to the Prophet,[2] but that is disputable.

The Prophet's statement 'God, His angels, the inhabitants of the heavens and the earths... say prayers for the one who teaches people to do good' is because the [scholar's] instruction causes people's salvation, bliss and purification. The [scholar] also teaches people what is good, makes evident the religion of the Lord and His rulings, and explains His Names and Attributes to them. Therefore God recompenses the [scholar] in accordance with his deeds and bestows upon him His blessings as well as the blessings of His angels and people on this earth. These represent a tribute and honour for the scholar, and they are causes that result in his salvation, bliss and success.

[Point 47: On the superiority of the scholars, who are the heirs of the prophets.]

Abū al-Dardā'[3] (may God be pleased with him) narrated that the Messenger of God (may God bless him and grant him peace) said: 'Whoever takes a path in search of knowledge, God makes the path to Paradise easy for him. The angels lower their wings in approval of the one seeking knowledge. Forgiveness is sought for the scholar by whoever is in the heavens and the earth, even the fish in the sea. The superiority of the scholar over the worshipper is like the superiority of the moon over the rest of the celestial bodies. Indeed the scholars are the heirs of the prophets. The prophets did not leave behind a

1 Yūsuf b. ʿAbd Allāh b. Muḥammad b. ʿAbd al-Barr (d. 463/1071) was a great Mālikī scholar who lived in Muslim Spain.

2 Ibn ʿAbd al-Barr 182.

3 Abū al-Dardā' ʿUwaymir b. Ziyād (d. 32/652) was a Companion. He was well known for his ascetic lifestyle. He was later appointed as a deputy governor in Syria.

dinar or dirham. Instead, their only legacy is knowledge, so whoever acquires it has gained the most abundant share.'[1]

Abū al-Dardā' also narrated that the Messenger of God (may God bless him and grant him peace) said: 'Whoever goes out seeking knowledge, God will pave the path to Paradise for him. The angels will spread out their wings and the angels of the heavens will bless him along with the fish of the sea. The superiority of the scholar over the worshipper is like the superiority of the moon on the night of Badr over the rest of the celestial bodies. The scholars are the inheritors of the prophets. The prophets did not bequeath a dinar or dirham but instead bequeathed knowledge. Whoever acquires it has attained the most abundant share. The death of a scholar is a calamity that cannot be remedied and a void that cannot be filled. It is like a star that has been annihilated. Even the death of a whole tribe is less significant than the death of a scholar.'[2]

The scholar's traversing of the path of knowledge is so pleasing to the Lord that he is compensated with the path to Paradise. The angels' spreading of their wings is a sign of humility, reverence and honour for what [the scholars] carry of the Prophet's inheritance. It is also a sign of the angels' love and exaltation [for the scholars] since they help people attain [spiritual] life and salvation.

There are many similarities between the angels [and the scholars]. [In the first instance,] the angels are the best advisors of God's creation and the most beneficial for the children of Adam, and all bliss, knowledge and guidance occurs as a result of their actions. For example, the angels ask [God] to forgive those who commit sins and commend the believers; and to assist them against their enemies and devils. Furthermore, they are many times more intent on striving

1 Tirmidhī 2682; Abū Dāwūd 3641; Ibn Māja 223. It is 'authentic' according to Albānī (*Ṣaḥīḥ al-Jāmiʿ al-ṣaghīr* 6297).

2 Bayhaqī (*Shuʿab*) 1576; Ibn ʿAbd al-Barr 179. It is 'very weak' according to Albānī (*Ḍaʿīf al-Targhīb* 73). Albānī stated that the portion of the tradition beginning from 'The death of the scholar is a calamity…' is 'very weak' (*Silsilat al-aḥādīth al-ḍaʿīfa* 4838).

on behalf a person than the person himself, and they wish goodness for him in this life and the Hereafter more than he would desire or could ever imagine. Some of the Successors said: 'We have found that the angels are the sincerest well-wishers of God's creation for His servants, and we have found the devils to be the most deceptive.'

The Exalted said: *Those who bear the Throne, and all who are round about it, hymn the praises of their Lord and believe in Him and ask forgiveness for those who believe (saying): Our Lord! Thou comprehendest all things in mercy and knowledge, therefor forgive those who repent and follow Thy way. Ward off from them the punishment of Hell. Our Lord! And make them enter the Gardens of Eden which thou hast promised them, with such of their fathers and their wives and their descendants as do right. Thou, only Thou, art the Mighty, the Wise. And ward off from them ill-deeds; and he from whom Thou wardest off ill-deeds that day, him verily hast Thou taken into mercy. That is the supreme triumph.*[1] Is there any better appeal than this except for that of the prophets?

If a servant seeks knowledge, then he has undertaken the greatest endeavour. Therefore the angels love that servant, extol him, and spread out their wings in approval, love and exaltation.

Abū Ḥātim al-Rāzī[2] related that Ibn Abī Uways said that he heard Mālik b. Anas[3] mention that 'the reason "the angels lower their wings" is so that they can spread them out and supplicate for the student of knowledge'. Aḥmad b. Marwān al-Mālikī[4] wrote in his book *al-Majālisa* that Zakariyya b. ʿAbd al-Raḥmān al-Baṣrī

1 Q. XL.7–9

2 Abū Ḥātim Muḥammad b. Idrīs al-Rāzī (d. 277/890) was a great *Ḥadīth* scholar and traditionist.

3 Mālik b. Anas b. Mālik b. Abī ʿĀmir al-Aṣbaḥī (d. 179/795) was the eponymous founder of the Mālikī school of jurisprudence. He lived in Medina and was one of the Successors to the Successors. He studied under Imam Abū Ḥanīfa and he also taught Shāfiʿī. He compiled *al-Muwaṭṭa'*, which includes mostly *ḥadīths* but also some juristic statements of the Companions, and he would go on to revise it many times over the span of his life.

4 Abū Bakr Aḥmad b. Marwān b. Muḥammad al-Dinawārī al-Mālikī (d. 333/945) was a scholar who wrote *al-Majālisa wa-jawāhir al-ʿilm*.

related that he heard Aḥmad b. Shuᶜayb say: 'We were sitting amongst the scholars of *Ḥadīth* in Basra when one of them related the *ḥadīth* of the Prophet (may God bless him and grant him peace) that "The angels lower their wings out of approval for the one seeking knowledge." At that point, a Muᶜtazilī in the gathering began mocking that *ḥadīth* and said: "By God, I am going to hammer some nails into my shoes tomorrow so that I can use them to step on the wings of the angels." He actually did that. Then once he began walking with those shoes, both of his legs became useless and subsequently became gangrenous.'

Ṣafwān b. ᶜAssāl [went to the Messenger of God and] said: 'I have come to seek knowledge.' The Prophet said: 'Welcome, seeker of knowledge! The angels surround the student of knowledge and shade him with their wings, one on top of the other until they reach the lowest heaven. That is out of their love for what he seeks.'[1] In this *ḥadīth* the angels enclosed him with their wings, whereas in the previous *ḥadīth* they spread out their wings. The spreading out of wings is out of humility, respect and deference, while the enclosure with wings is to protect, defend and preserve them. Thus the two *ḥadīth*s mention the angels' exaltation of [the student of knowledge] and their love, enclosure and protection of him. Had the student of knowledge not received any other good fortune besides this, it would have been sufficient.

The meaning of the Prophet's statement (may God bless him and grant him peace) 'Forgiveness is sought for the scholar by whoever is in the heavens and the earth, even the fish in the sea'[2] is that since the scholar's sole aim is to be instrumental in spreading knowledge, which leads to people's salvation from a variety of destructive perils, he is recompensed in accordance with his deeds. Therefore all of those in the heavens and the earth supplicate for

1 Ibn Māja, 226; Aḥmad 18,089; Haythamī 550. It is 'authentic' according to Albānī (*Ṣaḥīḥ al-Jāmiᶜ al-ṣaghīr* 5702).

2 Tirmidhī 2682; Abū Dāwūd 3641; Ibn Māja 223. It is 'authentic' according to Albānī (*Ṣaḥīḥ al-Jāmiᶜ al-ṣaghīr* 6297).

his protection from all types of disasters and for his forgiveness. Furthermore, if the angels supplicate for the forgiveness of the believers, they are more likely to do so for the purest and most elite of them [i.e. the scholars].

It has been said that those asking forgiveness for the scholar include all those in the heavens and the earth, whether it be animals endowed with intelligible speech or not, birds or otherwise. This is supported by the Prophet's statement 'even the ant in its hole and the fish in the sea'.[1] It has been said that the reason for this is because the scholar teaches people how to care for these animals, instructs them in what is allowed, what is forbidden, and how to consume, ride, benefit from or slaughter them in the best and most merciful way. Thus the scholar is the most merciful person to animals and is the most able to expound on how to treat them. In general, only through knowledge is the merciful and benevolent purpose for which animals have been created recognized. Since the scholar is the one who best explains that, it is most appropriate that animals should ask forgiveness for him in particular. And God knows best.

The Prophet's statement 'The superiority of the scholar over the worshipper is like the superiority of the moon over the rest of the celestial bodies'[2] is an analogy that resembles the state of the moon and the celestial bodies at night-time. The moon lights up even the remotest parts wherein people live, and this is similar to the scholar. In the case of a celestial body, however, its light does not extend beyond itself or to that which is nearby; this is similar to the worshipper as his [spiritual] light is limited to himself and does not extend to others. If it did extend to others, it would only be to those who are proximate to him.

A narrated tradition states: 'On the Day of Resurrection, God will say to the worshipper: "Enter Paradise even though your benefit

1 Tirmidhī 2685. It is 'authentic' according to Albānī (*Ṣaḥīḥ al-Jāmiʿ al-ṣaghīr* 4213).

2 Tirmidhī 2682; Abū Dāwūd 3641; Ibn Māja 223. It is 'authentic' according to Albānī (*Ṣaḥīḥ al-Jāmiʿ al-ṣaghīr* 6297).

was limited to yourself." Yet He will say to the scholar: "Intercede and you will be allowed intercession since your benefit extended to the others."'[1] Ibn Jurayj[2] mentioned that ʿAṭā'[3] related from Ibn ʿAbbās (may God be pleased with him and his father) that on the Day of Resurrection it will be said to the worshipper: 'Enter Paradise!' Yet it will be said to the scholar: 'Intercede, for you will be allowed intercession!'

In addition, the religion is established, adorned and illumined by its scholars and worshippers, just like the night sky is lit and adorned by the moon and the celestial bodies. Therefore, if all of the scholars and worshippers die, then the religion also ceases to exist. Furthermore, once the moon is eclipsed and the celestial bodies are scattered, the arrival of that which is promised [i.e. the Day of Judgment] will occur.

If it is asked, 'Why are scholars likened to the moon and not the sun as the latter possesses a far greater degree of light?', we would reply that there are two reasons. Firstly, since the light of the moon is derived from [the sun], and the scholar's [spiritual] light is derived from that of the Messenger, it is more appropriate to compare the [scholars] to the moon rather than the sun. Secondly, the light of the sun is such that it is never absent, nor does it vary [significantly] in its intensity. On the other hand, the moon's light may wane or wax. Likewise, scholars are of varying levels, whereby some are preferred over others based on the extent of their knowledge and the degree to which they spread it. Some scholars are perfect, just like the full moon on the night of Badr, while others are less so, like the moon as it wanes on subsequent nights.

1 Ghazālī, *Iḥyā'*, vol. 1, p. 26; al-Khaṭīb al-Baghdādī (*Faqīh*), vol. 1, p. 111. A similar *ḥadīth* has been declared to be 'weak' by Albānī (*Ḍaʿīf al-Jāmiʿ al-ṣaghīr* 291).

2 ʿAbd al-Malik b. ʿAbd al-ʿAzīz b. Jurayj (d. 150/767) was a Successor to the Successors. He studied under ʿAṭā' b. Abī Rabāḥ.

3 ʿAṭā' b. Abī Rabāḥ (d. 115/733) was a prominent Successor and student of the Companions Ibn ʿAbbās and Ibn ʿUmar.

The following question could be raised: 'There is a well-known tradition of the Prophet (may God bless him and grant him peace) wherein he said: "My Companions are like the stars,"[1] so why are they likened [in the previous *ḥadīth*] to the moon?' The reply is that this analogy shows that just as the stars provide guidance in the dark, whether on land or at sea, so too do the scholars. Also just like the stars are ornaments in the sky, the scholars are ornaments for this earth. There are also shooting stars against the devils to prevent them from eavesdropping and thereafter confounding [people when they hear] God's revelation after it is transmitted to the messengers by His angel [Gabriel]. Similarly, the scholars shoot down the vain and deceptive ideas that the devils, whether human or jinn, suggest to others. God empowered the scholars to be the defenders and protectors of this religion against His and His Messenger's enemies. For these reasons they were compared to the stars.

As for [the *ḥadīth*] that compares the scholars to the moon, it shows their superiority over those who are only worshippers. Thus both analogies are appropriate in their respective context; and praise be to God.

His statement 'Indeed the scholars are the heirs of the prophets'[2] illustrates one of the greatest virtues of the scholars. Since the prophets are the best of God's creation, those who inherit from them are the best of His creation after them. Everyone passes their inheritance to their heirs and the heirs take their place afterwards, but there is no one who can take the place of the messengers and fulfill what they have been sent with except for the scholars. Thus the scholars are the most suitable people to inherit from [the Prophet]. It is also proof that the scholars are the closest people to the messengers, since only the closest people inherit. God selects those whom He wills for His mercy.

1 Ibn ʿAbd al-Barr 1684; Zabīdī, vol. II, p. 223. It is 'fabricated' according to Albānī (*Silsilat al-aḥādīth al-ḍaʿīfa* 58).

2 Tirmidhī 2682; Abū Dāwūd 3641; Ibn Māja 223. It is 'authentic' according to Albānī (*Ṣaḥīḥ al-Jāmiʿ al-ṣaghīr* 6297).

Within this [latter *ḥadīth*] is also an advice and a command to the Community to obey, respect, support and honour the scholars since they are the heirs of the Prophet; yet these are simply *some* of this Community's obligations towards them. Loving the scholars is also part of the religion itself. On the other hand, hating or fighting against them is contradictory to it and is like opposing and fighting against God. ʿAlī (may God ennoble his face and may He be pleased with him) said: 'Loving the scholars is part of the religion.' The Prophet (may God bless him and grant him peace) said [in the *ḥadīth qudsī*] that God (Great and Glorious is He) said: 'I will declare war against those who show hostility to a pious servant of Mine.'[1] The heirs of the prophets [i.e. the scholars] are the elite of those who are considered to be loyal supporters (*awliyā'*) maintained by God.

Within the aforementioned there is also an advice to the scholars that they must follow the guidance of the prophets and their methodology in conveying the message, such as having patience, forbearance, countering the evilness of people with righteousness, being gentle with them, bringing them closer to God by the best of means, and advising them as much as possible. It is in this fashion that the scholars will attain their share of this very great and distinguished inheritance.

Furthermore, it instructs the scholars to raise and educate the Community, just like a parent would raise his or her child. In other words, it should be in a gradual and orderly fashion, starting with the basics and then moving on to more advanced knowledge. One should only teach them what they can bear and should not burden them. The spiritual [state] of people compared to the prophets is like a child compared to his or her parents or even much less so. Every spirit that has not been raised or educated by the messengers [or their heirs] cannot be successful or achieve righteousness.

The Prophet's statement 'The prophets did not bequeath a dinar

1 Bukhārī 6502; Ibn Māja 3989.

or dirham but instead bequeathed knowledge'[1] reveals the perfect character of the prophets and the great manner by which they counseled their nations. It is from the complete nature of God's blessings upon the prophets and their nations that He protected them and put an end to any speculations or doubts that may lead some people to think that the prophets desired this world or wanted to be like kings.

People often desire this world to the point that that they will strenuously strive for it and even deny themselves so as to pass it on to their children. But God also prevented people from claiming that the prophets desired this world for their children. The Prophet (may God bless him and grant him peace) said: 'Our [the Prophet's] property will not be inherited. Whatever we leave is charity (*ṣadaqa*).'[2]

As for the Exalted's statement: *And Solomon was David's heir,*[3] the consensus of the exegetes is that this concerns the inheritance of knowledge and prophethood, and nothing else. Since David (peace be upon him) had many children besides Solomon, if the inheritance alluded to in this verse had been only that of money, then Solomon would not have been singled out. In addition, the Words of God are too exalted to mention something like that; it would have been like saying 'so-and-so died and his son inherited from him'. It is well known that everyone's son inherits from him, and there is no benefit in mentioning something obvious like that.

In addition, what preceded the verse and what came after it also reveals that the meaning of this inheritance was knowledge and prophethood, not wealth. The Exalted said: *And We verily gave knowledge unto David and Solomon, and they said: Praise be to God, Who hath preferred us above many of His believing servants! And Solomon was David's heir.*[4] The purpose here was to show Solomon's virtue and how God

1 Tirmidhī 2682; Abū Dāwūd 3641; Ibn Māja 223. It is 'authentic' according to Albānī (*Ṣaḥīḥ al-Jāmiʿ al-ṣaghīr* 6297).

2 Bukhārī 3094; Muslim 4579, 4580, 4582 and 4585; Tirmidhī 1610; Abū Dāwūd 2963; Nasā'ī 4152; Aḥmad 9.

3 Q. xxvii.16.

4 Q. xxvii.15–16.

had selected him and his father for prophethood and [bestowed upon them] knowledge: *This surely is evident favour.*[1]

Similarly, Zachariah (peace and blessings be upon him) said: *I fear my kinsfolk after me, since my wife is barren. Oh, give me from Thy presence a successor who shall inherit of me and inherit (also) of the house of Jacob. And make him, my Lord, acceptable (unto Thee).*[2] This refers to the inheritance of knowledge, prophethood and calling to God. It should not be thought that a noble prophet would be fearful that someone else of his relatives would inherit his wealth and thus ask God (Exalted is He) to grant him a son. God has purified His prophets and messengers from such concerns. Those who alter the Book of God, repudiate the traditions of His Messenger, or attribute to the prophets what they are blameless of and infallible from are deserving of banishment. Praise be to God for His guidance and success!

It is mentioned that Abū Hurayra (may God be pleased with him) was walking in the market and upon seeing [the Companions] trading and selling he said: 'You are all here doing that while the inheritance of the Messenger of God (may God bless him and grant him peace) is being distributed in his mosque.' Thereafter they hastened to the mosque only to find a gathering discussing knowledge of the Qur'ān and remembrance of God. They asked: 'Where is what you mentioned, O Abū Hurayra?' He replied: 'This is the inheritance of Muḥammad being distributed amongst his heirs. It is not like the worldly type you bequeath.'

The Prophet's statement, 'So whoever acquires it has gained the most abundant share'[3] represents the greatest, most beneficial and lasting fortune a servant can attain. Even if other fortunes cease to exist, this share of religious knowledge will benefit him con-

1 Q. XXVII.16.

2 Q. XIX.5–6.

3 Tirmidhī 2682; Abū Dāwūd 3641; Ibn Māja 223. It is 'authentic' according to Albānī (*Ṣaḥīḥ al-Jāmiʿ al-ṣaghīr* 6297).

tinuously and forever. Since it is connected to God, the Everlasting who never dies, it will never cease or escape one. All other fortunes will become non-existent once the entities they are connected to become null.

The Exalted also said: *And We shall turn unto the work they did and make it scattered motes.*[1] Since their ultimate [vain] objectives vanished, their works followed suit. This occurs [on the Day of Judgment] when the doer is most in need of his [good] deeds. There is no way to treat or [reverse] this; and we seek refuge in God. We ask for His assistance as we are in dire need of Him. We rely on Him and there is no might or power save in God.

The Prophet's statement, 'The death of a scholar is a calamity which cannot be remedied, and a void that cannot be filled. It is like a star that has been annihilated. Even the death of a whole tribe is less significant than the death of a scholar'[2] is due to the virtuous nature of the scholar. If it had not been for them, people would have been like animals or even worse. Thus the death of a scholar is a calamity that can only be ameliorated by another one succeeding him. In addition, scholars direct the conduct of people, states and kingdoms; thus their death results in the corruption of this worldly system. Therefore, God has allowed the scholars to succeed the Predecessors so as to protect His religion and Book, and ensure [the well-being of] His servants.

Now, imagine if there existed a person with a vast wealth who most generously satisfied all of the needs of the people. What would happen when he dies and his wealth is cut off from them? Yet the death of a scholar is a greater calamity than the death of a person like that, even if an entire nation, which is dependent upon that person, dies off as a result. It has been said:

1 Q. xxv.23.

2 Bayhaqī (*Shuʿab*) 1576; Mundhirī 149; Ibn ʿAbd al-Barr 179. Albānī stated that this additional portion of the tradition is 'very weak' (*Silsilat al-aḥādīth al-ḍaʿīfa* 4838).

Do you know what a calamity is? It is not to lose money
Or the death of a sheep or a camel.
Instead a calamity is the loss of a noble person
Whose death leads to the death of a great many people.

[Point 48: 'A jurist is more formidable against the Devil than a thousand worshippers', as well as some anecdotes about the potential for ignorance amongst the latter.]

It has been narrated that the Messenger of God (may God bless him and grant him peace) said: 'A jurist (*faqīh*) is more formidable against the Devil than a thousand worshippers.'[1]

Abū Hurayra (may God be pleased with him) narrated that the Messenger of God (may God bless him and grant him peace) said: 'God is not worshipped through anything better than *fiqh* of the religion.'[2] Abū Hurayra then added: 'It is more beloved to me to spend one hour gaining a deep understanding of knowledge that I can apply than to spend an entire night in prayer. The jurist is more formidable against the Devil than a thousand worshippers. Everything has its pillars and the pillars of this religion consist of *fiqh* [that is practised].'[3]

Muzanī[4] related that Ibn ᶜAbbās said:

> The demons asked Satan: 'Our leader! Why do we see that you are happier with the death of a scholar more than the death of a worshipper, since we cannot deceive a scholar whereas we can deceive a worshipper?' He said: 'Let's go.'

1 Tirmidhī 2681; Ibn Māja 222; Bayhaqī (*Shuᶜab*) 1586; Ibn ᶜAbd al-Barr 121. It is 'fabricated' according to Albānī (*Ḍaᶜīf al-Jāmiᶜ al-ṣaghīr* 3987).

2 This tradition has been narrated by Ibn ᶜUmar; see Bayhaqī (*Shuᶜab*) 1583. It is 'weak' according to Albānī (*Silsilat al-aḥādīth al-ḍaᶜīfa* 6912).

3 Haythamī 487; Mundhirī 137; Dāraquṭnī 3085. It is 'fabricated' according to Albānī (*Silsilat al-aḥādīth al-ḍaᶜīfa* 5159).

4 Abū Ibrāhīm Ismāᶜīl b. Yaḥyā b. Ismāᶜīl al-Maṣrī al-Muzanī (d. 264/877) was a student of Shāfiᶜī and author of *Mukhtaṣar al-Muzanī fī-furūᶜ al-Shāfiᶜiyya*.

> So they went to a worshipper and found him worshipping. They said: 'We want to question you, so stop [your prayers].' Iblīs then said: 'Can your Lord put this universe inside an egg?' The worshipper replied: 'I do not know.' Then Satan said to them: 'See how he just disbelieved.' Then they went to a scholar, who was lecturing and entertaining his students in his gathering circle. They said to him: 'We want to ask you a question. Can your Lord put this universe inside an egg?' He said yes. They asked him: 'How?' The scholar said: 'He [the Lord] will say: *Be! and it is*.'[1] Then Satan said to the demons: 'Do you see how the worshipper's [disbelief] was limited to himself, yet if the scholar had been the same then many others would have also become corrupted?'[2]

This story has also been narrated in another fashion. They asked the worshipper: 'Can your Lord create a being like Himself?' He replied: 'I do not know.' So they said: 'Do you see how his worship does not benefit him and he remains ignorant?' When they asked a scholar the same he replied: 'That is an absurd question! If a being was like Him, it could not have been created. Therefore it is impossible to create a being like Him. If it was created, it could only be one of His servants or one of His creation.' Thus the Devil said to the demons: 'Do you not see how a scholar can demolish [with his correct knowledge] what it took me years to build.'

It has been narrated that ʿAbd Allāh b. ʿUmar[3] said: 'A scholar is superior to a worshipper by seventy levels [in Paradise]—between each level is the distance that a horse travels in seventy years.' That is because if the Devil tries to spread a blameworthy innovation in religion, the scholar will recognize it as such and forbid others from

1 Q. XVI.40.

2 Ibn ʿAbd al-Barr 127.

3 Abū ʿAbd al-Raḥmān ʿAbd Allāh b. ʿUmar (d. 74/693) was a prominent Companion and son of ʿUmar b. al-Khaṭṭāb. He narrated more than 2600 *ḥadīths*.

it. On the other hand, a worshipper—although he is worshipping his Lord—will not sense or realize it for what it is. The scholar will prevent whatever evil Satan has tried to perpetrate and will demolish whatever he has invented. Thus there is nothing more desirable to the Devil than the death of a scholar, so that he can then corrupt the religion and tempt the Community. The only objective of a worshipper is to struggle against the Devil in order to protect himself alone; but sometimes he cannot even achieve that.

[Point 49: On everything in life being worthless except knowledge and the remembrance of God.]

Abū Hurayra (may God be pleased with him) narrated that he heard the Messenger of God (may God bless him and grant him peace) say: 'Indeed the world is cursed; everything in it is cursed except for the remembrance of God and what is conducive to it, the scholar and the student.'[1]

Since this world is worthless in the sight of God—not even worth the wing of a mosquito—and everything in it is far removed from Him [except piety], it is in reality cursed. The Sublime only created it as a bridge to the Hereafter so that His [believing] servants could equip themselves [with good deeds]. They could not have become proximate to Him except by establishing His remembrance and doing what He loves, which includes attaining knowledge. Such actions allow one to know God and worship, remember, praise and glorify Him. It is only for these reasons that He created it and its inhabitants.

The Exalted says: *I created the jinn and humankind only that they might worship Me.*[2] He also said: *God it is who hath created seven heavens, and of the earth the like thereof. The commandment cometh down among them slowly, that ye may know that God is Able to do all things, and that God sur-*

1 Tirmidhī 2322; Ibn Māja 4112; Bayhaqī (*Shuʿab*) 1580. It is 'sound' according to Albānī (*Silsilat al-aḥādīth al-ṣaḥīḥa* 2797).

2 Q. LI.56.

roundeth all things in knowledge.[1] Thus the two verses imply that the Sublime only created the heavens and the earth so that He may be known through His Names and Attributes. In this manner we can better worship Him alone, for that is our obligation. God (Glory be to Him) loves that His servants remember, worship, know and love Him. [He also loves] whatever leads to these [actions]or is a necessary concomitant of them. On the other hand, everything else is hated and blameworthy in His sight and is, therefore, deserving of censure.

[Point 50: Seeking knowledge is part of striving in God's cause, and it can only be done by the elite.]

Al-Rabīᶜ b. Anas narrated that the Messenger of God (may God bless him and grant him peace) said: 'Whoever goes out seeking knowledge, he is striving in God's cause until he returns.'[2] Seeking knowledge is part of striving in God's cause because it establishes the foundations of Islam in the same way that they are established by waging battle [for His sake].

For this reason striving is of two kinds: one is by fighting with force and weapons [for His sake], which is done by many, while the second is by confronting others with evidence and clear proofs. The latter represents the striving of the elite [scholars] and leading imams, for they are the successors of the messengers. It is superior to the first because it leads to great benefits, the stress of its burden (*shiddat mu'natih*) is greater, and because of the large number of His enemies [that they must refute].

The Exalted said in *Sūrat al-Furqān*, which was revealed in Mecca: *If We willed, We could raise up a warner in every village. So obey not the disbelievers, but strive against them herewith with a great endeavour.*[3] The striving against them is by using [the evidence of] the Qur'ān.

1 Q. LXV.12.
2 Tirmidhī 2647. It is 'weak' according to Albānī (*Silsilat al-aḥādīth al-ḍaᶜīfa* 2037).
3 Q. XXV.51–52.

The [second] is also the type of striving undertaken against the hypocrites. The hypocrites did not [openly] wage war against the believers, but instead appeared to be with them—even fighting on the same side of the believers against the latter's enemies. Despite this, the Exalted said: *O Prophet! Strive against the disbelievers and the Hypocrites.*[1] It is well known that striving against the hypocrites is through evidence and the Qur'ān. The point is that following the path of God includes striving, seeking knowledge and calling people to God.

Muʿādh[2] (may God be pleased with him) said: 'You must pursue knowledge as learning it for God's sake represents fear [of God], studying it is [a form of] worship, instructing it represents glorification [of God], and seeking it out is [a form of] striving.'

The Sublime juxtaposed the revealed Book with iron [weaponry] as both lead to victory. The Exalted said: *We verily sent Our messengers with clear proofs, and revealed with them the Book and the Balance, that mankind may observe right measure; and He revealed iron, wherein is mighty power and (many) uses for mankind, and that God may know him who helpeth Him and His messengers, though unseen. God is Strong, Almighty.*[3] Therefore the foundations of the religion are established upon the Book and waging battle.

God (Great and Glorious is He) stated: *O ye who believe! Obey God, and obey the Messenger and those of you who are in authority.*[4] The Companions (may God be pleased with them) interpreted His statement *those of you who are in authority* as the rulers and scholars. These latter two groups both strive in the path of God: the first group does so by force and the latter by speech.

1 Q. LXVI.9.

2 Muʿādh b. Jabal (d. 18/639) was a prominent Companion. The Prophet sent him to Yemen to call the people to Islam. He later moved to Syria and taught there.

3 Q. LVII.25.

4 Q. IV.59.

Kaᶜb al-Aḥbār[1] said: 'The student of knowledge is always going back and forth in the path of God (Great and Glorious is He).' According to some of the Companions (may God be pleased with them), a student who dies whilst he is pursuing religious knowledge dies a martyr. Sufyān b. ᶜUyayna said: 'Whoever pursues knowledge has pledged allegiance to God (Great and Glorious is He).'

[Point 51: God will ease the path to Paradise for those who seek knowledge.]

Abū Hurayra narrated that the Messenger of God (may God bless him and grant him peace) said: 'Whoever embarks on a path seeking knowledge, God eases the path to Paradise for him.'[2] In addition, Ibn ᶜAdī[3] related a tradition narrated by ᶜĀ'isha[4] traceable to the Prophet: 'God inspired to me that He will facilitate a path to Paradise for whoever pursues a path seeking knowledge.'[5] These two *ḥadīth*s contain a principle which is substantiated by the Divine Law and His predestination: recompense is in accordance with the deed. Since the [seeker of knowledge] pursued a way to enliven his heart and save himself from destruction, God will facilitate a path for him to achieve that.

[Points 52–53: The importance of understanding, memorizing and conveying the Prophet's message.]

52. The Prophet (may God bless him and grant him peace) supplicated for the person who hears his traditions, understands and conveys them with a face characterized by *naḍra*, which means 'delightful,

1 Abū Isḥāq Kaᶜb b. Matīᶜ al-Himyarī al-Aḥbār (d. 32/653) was one of the Successors, who converted from Judaism to Islam during the time of ᶜUmar and narrated many Israelite traditions.

2 Muslim 6853; Tirmidhī 2682; Abū Dāwūd 3641; Ibn Māja 223; Aḥmad 8316.

3 Abū Aḥmad ᶜAbd Allāh b. ᶜAdī al-Jurjānī (d. 365/975) was a traditionist and author of the book *al-Kāmil fī'l-jarḥ wa'l-taᶜdīl*.

4 ᶜĀ'isha bint Abī Bakr al-Ṣiddīq (d. 58/678) was a wife of the Prophet and a Mother of the Believers. She narrated 2210 *ḥadīth*s.

5 Ibn ᶜAdī, vol. vii, p. 353. It is 'authentic', with a slightly different wording, according to Albānī (*Ṣaḥīḥ al-Jāmiᶜ al-Ṣaghīr* 6298).

brilliant and gleaming'. Ibn Masᶜūd narrated that the Prophet (may God bless him and grant him peace) said: 'May God make brilliant the face of a man who hears a tradition of mine, understands, remembers, and conveys it. Perhaps he spreads its precepts to another who has a deeper understanding than him. There are three things which, if done, will prevent the heart of a Muslim from harbouring rancour: sincerity to God, giving advice to the leaders of the Muslims, and sticking to the Community. Indeed this call envelops and protects all.'[1]

Even if no other *ḥadīth* existed to show the eminence of knowledge, this would suffice. All levels of knowledge are described here. The first and second are that one must hear and then understand or retain (*ᶜaqala*) [the Prophet's tradition] in his mind. It then settles in the heart just like when something remains enclosed within its container and cannot exit it. Similarly, *ᶜaqalahu* is used when one confines a camel or an animal in order to prevent them from straying or leaving. And comprehending something entails more than just knowing it.

The third level involves committing [the *ḥadīth*] to memory so that one will not forget it or allow it to become lost. Then the fourth level is conveying and spreading it amongst the Community, which is the ultimate objective. If that does not occur, then it will be like an unused hidden treasure. In addition, knowledge that is not spread is at risk of being lost [and forgotten]. Yet if it is utilized and spread, it will lead to the growth and progress [of the Community].

Whoever performs these four is included in the supplication of the Prophet; and this will result in both external and internal beauty. In addition, having faith leads one's heart to attain delight (*bahja*), happiness, joy (*surūr*) and pleasure (*iltidhādh*). This then manifests itself in the brilliance and beauty that appears upon the face. It is for this reason that the Sublime (Exalted is He) linked delight, joy and brilliance together in His statement: *Therefor God hath warded off*

1 Tirmidhī 2658; Ibn Māja 230; Aḥmad 21,590; Dārimī 234; Ḥaythamī 583. It is 'authentic' according to Albānī (*Silsilat al-aḥādīth al-ṣaḥīḥa* 404).

from them the evil of that day, and hath made them find brightness and joy.[1] Thus brilliance appears on their faces, while joy is present in their hearts. The Exalted also said: *Thou wilt know in their faces the radiance of delight.*[2] The point is that this brilliance is manifested upon the face of one who has heard the traditions of the Messenger of God (may God bless him and grant him peace), then understood, memorized and conveyed them; and this is a sign of the sweetness, delight and joy present in his heart and soul.

The Prophet's statement (may God bless him and grant him peace) 'Perhaps he spreads its precepts to another who has a deeper understanding than him' is a notification of the benefit in conveying [a Prophetic tradition]. It may be that the one to whom it is conveyed achieves a deeper level of understanding than the conveyor. Alternatively, the meaning may be that the one to whom it is conveyed applies it better than the conveyor. Thus, once he hears the *ḥadīth*, he interprets it to best derive the correct laws from it, and has more insight into the intent of it.

And the Prophet's statement 'There are three things which, if done, will prevent the heart of a Muslim from harbouring rancour…' indicates that these three [actions] will obliterate rancour and deceptive behaviour. Otherwise these would lead to wickedness and ill will from the heart. The sincerity of those who are devoted to God prevents rancour from overtaking their hearts. Yet if [rancour] is present beforehand, then [devotion] will remove and obliterate it altogether. By ignoring the desires of their hearts, and instead pursuing what pleases their Lord, no place remains for rancour or wickedness.

The Exalted also said: *Thus it was, that We might ward off from him evil and lewdness. He was of Our chosen slaves.*[3] Once Joseph devoted himself sincerely to his Lord, He protected him from anything that would have otherwise provoked him to evil or fornication. Since Iblīs knows

1 Q. LXXVI.11.

2 Q. LXXXIII.24.

3 Q. XII.24.

that there is no way to deceive or destroy those who are sincere, he excluded them from his stipulation: *Then, by Thy might, I surely will beguile them every one, save Thy single-minded (mukhlaṣīn) servants among them.*[1] The Exalted said: *As for My servants, thou hast no power over any of them save such of the froward as follow thee.*[2] Thus sincerity is the path to salvation, Islam is its vehicle, and faith seals one's safety.

As for the Prophet's statement 'giving advice to the leaders of the Muslims', this also eradicates rancour and deceptive behaviour since giving [sincere] advice is the opposite of harbouring malice.

Finally, the Prophet's statement 'sticking to their Community' indicates that this also purifies the heart from rancour and ill will. Due to a person's attachment to his Community, he will love for others what he loves for himself, hate for them what he hates for himself, become sad if they are saddened, and become joyous if they are joyous. This is in contrast to those who are disposed against them and work to attack, defame and criticize [the Community], such as the Rāfiḍa,[3] Khawārij,[4] and Muʿtazila,[5] amongst other groups. They

1 Q. xxxviii.82–83.

2 Q. xv.42.

3 Rāfiḍa is derived from the Arabic word *rafaḍa*, meaning 'to reject'. It refers to those who rejected the Caliphate of Abū Bakr, ʿUmar and ʿUthman. They claimed that ʿAlī b. Abī Ṭālib should have instead succeeded the Prophet. The earliest use of this term may have emanated from the Shiites of Kufa, Iraq, who rejected Zayd b. ʿAlī after he gave legitimacy to the Caliphates of Abū Bakr and ʿUmar.

4 Khawārij is derived from the Arabic word *kharaja*, meaning 'to abandon or revolt against'. The Prophet foretold of their coming. This sect initially supported ʿAlī, but later revolted against him. They assassinated ʿAlī after he agreed to arbitration with Muʿāwiya b. Abī Sufyān. One of their well-known tenets was that they considered a Muslim who perpetrated any major sin to be a disbeliever.

5 The Muʿtazila began after Wāṣil b. ʿAṭā' (d. 131/748) withdrew (*iʿtazala*) from the scholarly circle of al-Ḥasan al-Baṣrī due to Wāṣil's belief that a Muslim who commits a major sin and does not repent is neither a Muslim nor a disbeliever, but rather occupies an intermediary position (one of the five tenets of the Muʿtazila). Prominent Muʿtazila include Abū Hudhayl al-ʿAllāf (d. 235/849) and both Abū ʿAlī (d. 303/915) and Abū Hāshim al-Jubbā'ī (d. 321/933). Ibn al-Qayyim has named such individuals and repudiates many of the Muʿtazila beliefs in the second volume of *Miftāḥ dār al-saʿāda*.

have hearts that are filled with rancour and they act with deception.

The Prophet's statement 'This call envelops and protects all' is an eloquent and concise phrase, which has a magnificent meaning. He likened the call of the Muslims to a shield guarding them and preventing the enemy from approaching them. He also informed us that whoever is connected to them and within their fold will be likewise protected. This call unifies the Community, reunites them and guards them.

53. The Prophet (may God bless him and grant him peace) commanded us to convey his message. ʿAbd Allāh b. ʿAmr[1] narrated that the Messenger of God said: 'Convey my teachings even if only a single verse. And tell others the stories of the Children of Israel for it is not sinful to do so. But whoever fabricates a lie about me intentionally, he will surely take his place in Hellfire.'[2] The Prophet also said: 'It is incumbent upon those who are present to inform those who are absent.'[3]

Thus he (may God bless him and grant him peace) commanded that we convey his teachings, since it may result in guidance. The more his message is conveyed, the greater the reward of the Prophet. He will receive the reward of every person who conveys the message and of every person who is guided by it, since he was the [initial] caller to it. This is above and beyond the reward [the Prophet] will receive for his direct actions. If there was no benefit in conveying the Prophet's knowledge except that he (may God bless him and grant him peace) loves it, it would be sufficient.

A sign of true love is that one pursues what one's beloved loves and exerts his utmost ability to attain it. It is well known that noth-

1 ʿAbd Allāh b. ʿAmr b. al-ʿĀṣ (d. 65/684) was a Companion. His devotion to worship and fasting was so great that the Prophet advised him to limit his fasting to every other day and his reading of the entire Qur'ān to every third day. He narrated 700 *ḥadīths*.

2 Bukhārī 3461; Tirmidhī 2669; Abū Dāwūd 3662; Aḥmad 6486.

3 Bukhārī 67; Muslim 3304; Tirmidhī 809; Ibn Māja 233; Abū Dāwūd 1278; Nasā'ī 2876; Aḥmad 20,419.

ing is more beloved to the Messenger of God (may God bless him and grant him peace) than conveying the guidance to all of the Community.[1] Hence a person who conveys the message strives to achieve what is beloved to the Prophet. In the process, such a person becomes one of the closest and most beloved people to the Prophet. In fact, he is also considered to be a viceroy of the Prophet in his Community. This alone is sufficient to show the excellence and eminence of knowledge and the scholars.

[POINT 54: THE PROPHET GAVE PREFERENCE TO THOSE WITH SUPERIOR LEVELS OF KNOWLEDGE WHEN IT CAME TO RELIGIOUS APPOINTMENTS.]

The Prophet (may God bless him and grant him peace) gave preference to those with superior levels of knowledge when it came to [making] the highest religious appointments. Abū Masᶜūd al-Badrī narrated that the Prophet (may God bless him and grant him peace) said: 'The one who is able to recite the most of the Book of God should lead the people [in prayers]. If they are equal in recitation, then the most knowledgeable in the Sunna among them should. If they are equal regarding the Sunna, then the earliest of them to emigrate should. If they are equal in their emigration, then it should be the eldest amongst them.'[2]

Thus the Prophet gave preference to knowledge over when they first became Muslim or when they emigrated. Since knowledge of the Qur'ān is superior to knowledge of the Sunna, he gave preference to the former. Then he gave preference to knowledge of the Sunna over an earlier emigration, even though the latter may entail having done more righteous deeds. The Prophet took care to give preference to knowledge over deeds and to give preference to the most superior types of knowledge over others. This indicates the

1 This can be extended to the whole of humanity.

2 Muslim 1532; Tirmidhī 235; Abū Dāwūd 582; Nasā'ī 781; Ibn Māja 980; Aḥmad 17,097.

eminence of knowledge and its excellence. It also indicates that scholars should be given preference when it comes to the highest religious appointments.

[Point 55: The best of the Community of Muḥammad are those who have learned the Qur'ān and taught it to others.]

ʿUthmān b. ʿAffān[1] (may God be pleased with him) narrated that the Prophet (may God bless him and grant him peace) said: 'The best amongst you are those who learn the Qur'ān and teach it [to others].'[2] Learning the Qur'ān includes learning its words and meanings. The latter is the more eminent of the two types. Then one must teach them both. The meanings are the ultimate objective while the pronunciation is only the means to it. The difference between the two is like that between the ends and their means.

[Points 56–57: The believer must never be satisfied with his level of knowledge or wisdom and must strive to attain more.]

56. Abū Saʿīd[3] narrated that the Prophet (may God bless him and grant him peace) said: 'A believer will never be satisfied with the good [knowledge that] he hears until he enters Paradise.'[4]

Thus the Prophet (may God bless him and grant him peace)

1 ʿUthmān b. ʿAffān (d. 36/656) was a prominent Companion. He converted to Islam soon after Abū Bakr, and was one of the ten promised Paradise. He married two of the Prophet's daughters: Ruqayya and, later, Umm Kulthūm after the former died. He was well known for his generosity, particularly in the Battle of Tabuk. He was the third of the Rightly-Guided Caliphs, and during that time standardized the Qur'ān in accordance with the dialect of Quraysh. He narrated 146 *ḥadīths*.

2 Bukhārī 5027; Tirmidhī 2907; Abū Dāwūd 1452; Ibn Māja 211; Aḥmad 412.

3 Saʿīd b. Mālik Sinān al-Khazrajī al-Khudrī, known as Abū Saʿīd (d. 74/693), was a Companion. He was too young to fight in the Battle of Uḥud, but fought in later expeditions. He narrated 1170 *ḥadīths*.

4 Tirmidhī 2686; Tabrīzī 222. It is 'weak' according to Albānī (*Ḍaʿīf al-Jāmiʿ al-ṣaghīr* 4783).

made having a voracious appetite for knowledge and never becoming satiated with it a necessary concomitant of faith and an attribute of the believers. He also informed us that the believers will persevere tirelessly to attain it until they enter Paradise. Therefore when the scholars of Islam such as ʿAbd Allāh b. Mubārak[1] and Aḥmad b. Ḥanbal were asked 'Until when will you pursue knowledge?', they would reply 'Until death.'

ʿAbd Allāh b. Bishr al-Ṭāliqānī said: 'I hope that the command [of death] will not come upon me except that I have a pen in my hand. I hope that I will always be seeking and writing down knowledge.' [2] Ḥamīd b. Muḥammad b. Yazīd al-Baṣrī said: 'Al-Ḥāfiẓ b. Busṭām came to ask me about a *ḥadīth*, so I said to him: "You are so avid in your pursuit of *ḥadīths*." He said: "I do not want to be at the tail end of the followers of the Messenger (may God bless him and grant him peace)."' It was said to some of the scholars: 'How long is it appropriate for a person to learn?' They would say: 'As long as he is alive.' Ḥasan[3] was asked about an eighty year old: 'Is it appropriate for him to seek knowledge?' He said: 'He should, if he is alive.'

57. Abū Hurayra (may God be pleased with him) narrated that the Messenger of God (may God bless him and grant him peace) said:

1 Abū ʿAbd al-Raḥmān ʿAbd Allāh b. Mubārak (d. 181/797) was a prominent Successor to the Sucessors and traditionist. He studied under Mālik b. Anas and Awzāʿī.

2 In a subsequent section, Ibn al-Qayyim discusses further the importance of recording *ḥadīths* stating: 'A man said to al-Muʿāfā b. ʿImrān: "Is it more beloved to you that I would pray all night or that I record *ḥadīths*?" He said: "I would love more that you record the *ḥadīths* than pray from the beginning of the night to the end." He also said: "To [acquire] one *ḥadīth* is more beloved to me than praying the night."' Ibn ʿAbd al-Barr 111. See Ibn al-Qayyim, *Miftāḥ*, p. 212. Al-Muʿāfā b. ʿImrān al-Mawṣilī (d. 185/801) was a traditionist and scholar. He authored *Kitāb ṭabaqāt al-muḥaddithīn*. He was also known for his asceticism and wrote *Kitāb al-zuhd*.

3 Abū Saʿīd al-Ḥasan b. Abī al-Ḥasan Yasār al-Baṣrī (d. 110/728) was a prominent Successor. He was born in Medina. He later moved to Basra, Iraq. He was a devoted ascetic and scholar attracting large numbers to his teaching circle. Ibn al-Qayyim mentions many of his sayings.

'Wisdom [or a wise saying] is the lost property of a believer—he is the most deserving of it wherever he finds it.'[1]

This is one of the best metaphors. Wisdom is a part of knowledge; and if a believer is deprived of it, he is akin to someone who has lost a cherished gem. Only when the latter finds [that jewel] will his heart become content and happy. The believer feels the same about anything pertaining to his heart or spirit. The heart of a believer should always be seeking knowledge [and wisdom] wherever it can be found. That is a greater pursuit than seeking a lost material item.

[Point 58: Fiqh and good manners will not be coupled together in a hypocrite.]

Abū Hurayra (may God be pleased with him) narrated that the Prophet (may God bless him and grant him peace) said: 'Two characteristics—good manners and having *fiqh* of the religion—will never be coupled together in a hypocrite.'[2]

This is a testament to the fact that if good manners and *fiqh* of the religion are present in a person, then he is a believer. Good manners and *fiqh* of the religion are the most specific markers of belief. God will not allow them to be present together in a hypocrite as hypocrisy is contrary to them and vice versa.

[Point 59: The importance of reviving the Sunna of the Prophet.]

Anas b. Mālik[3] (may God be pleased with him) narrated that the Messenger of God (may God bless him and grant him peace) said: 'O my son, if you are capable of [waking up in] the morning and [reaching] the evening without allowing your heart to debase others,

1 Tirmidhī 2687; Ibn Māja 4169. It is 'very weak' according to Albānī (*Ḍaʿīf al-Jāmiʿ al-ṣaghīr* 4302).

2 Tirmidhī 2684; Tabrīzī 219. It is 'authentic' according to Albānī (*Silsilat al-aḥādīth al-ṣaḥīḥa* 278).

3 Anas b. Mālik b. Naḍar al-Khazrajī al-Anṣārī (d. 93/711) was a Companion who served the Prophet. He narrated 2286 *ḥadīths*.

then do so. O my son, that is from my Sunna. Whoever revives my Sunna has truly loved me. And whoever loves me shall be with me in Paradise.'[1] This is part of a long *ḥadīth*.

Kathīr b. ʿAbd Allāh b. ʿAmr b. ʿAwf al-Muzanī narrated that the Prophet (may God bless him and grant him peace) said to Bilāl b. al-Ḥārith: 'Know, O Bilāl!' He said: 'What should I know, O Messenger of God?' The Prophet said: 'Whoever revives a sunna of mine that has died out after me will receive a share of the same reward as the one who carries it out, without that diminishing anything from the latter's reward. And whoever introduces a false innovation which displeases God and His Messenger will receive the sin of the one who perpetrates it, and that will not diminish anything from the latter's sin.'[2]

The principle outlined in this *ḥadīth* is corroborated by other *ḥadīths*, such as: 'Whoever calls to guidance will receive a reward similar to that of whosoever follows him, without that diminishing anything from latter's reward.'[3] Another *ḥadīth* states: 'Whoever guides to good will receive the same reward as the one who acts upon it.'[4]

[Point 60: The Prophet encouraged and entrusted the Muslims to treat the students of knowledge well.]

The Prophet (may God bless him and grant him peace) entrusted people to treat the students of knowledge well, because of the excellence of that which they pursue. Tirmidhī related that Abū Hārūn said: 'We went to Abū Saʿīd [al-Khudrī] and he said: "Welcome, for the Messenger of God (may God bless him and grant him peace) counseled us saying: 'Surely the people will fol-

1 Tirmidhī 2678; Tabrīzī 175. It is 'weak' according to Albānī (*Ḍaʿīf al-Jāmiʿ al-ṣaghīr* 6389).

2 Tirmidhī 2677; Ibn Māja 210. It is 'weak' according to Albānī (*Ḍaʿīf al-Jāmiʿ al-ṣaghīr* 5359).

3 Muslim 6804; Tirmidhī 2674; Abū Dāwūd 4609; Ibn Māja 206; Aḥmad 9160.

4 Muslim 4899; Tirmidhī 2671; Abū Dāwūd 5129; Aḥmad 17,084.

low you. They will come to you from distant regions of the earth to gain an understanding in the religion. So when they come, take care to advise them well.'"'[1]

[POINT 61: SEEKING KNOWLEDGE ATONES FOR ONE'S PAST SINS.]

Sanḥabra narrated that the Prophet (may God bless him and grant him peace) said: 'Seeking knowledge atones for one's past [sins].'[2] This principle is only found in this *ḥadīth*; however, the [chain of narration] is not sound. Nonetheless, it was previously mentioned that those in the heavens and earth ask that the scholar be forgiven.[3]

In addition, there are many reports from the Companions that have a similar meaning. Ibn ᶜAbbās said: 'A student seeking knowledge is accompanied by an angel [during his travels]. When he returns home, [all of his sins] are forgiven.' ᶜAlī said: 'The sins of a student of knowledge are forgiven from the moment he gets dressed, puts on his shoes/leather slippers, and leaves his home seeking knowledge.' Ibn ᶜAdī attributed this [latter statement] to the Prophet.[4] ᶜĀ'isha said: 'Whoever puts on their shoes to pursue good knowledge is forgiven before they step out.'[5] Now these sayings may not be considered as evidence; but since seeking knowledge is one of the best pious deeds, and good deeds annul sins,[6] it is more appropriate that seeking knowledge for God's sake expiates one's past sins.

It is reported that ᶜUmar b. al-Khaṭṭāb (may God be pleased with him) said: 'A man will leave his house having sins like the mountain

1 Tirmidhī 2650 and 2651; Ibn Māja 247 and 249. It is 'weak' according to Albānī (*Ḍaᶜīf al-Jāmiᶜ al-ṣaghīr* 1797).

2 Tirmidhī 2648. It is 'fabricated' according to Albānī (*Ḍaᶜīf al-Jāmiᶜ al-ṣaghīr* 5686).

3 Tirmidhī 2682; Abū Dāwūd 3641; Ibn Māja 223. It is 'authentic' according to Albānī (*Ṣaḥīḥ al-Jāmiᶜ al-ṣaghīr* 6297).

4 Ibn ᶜAdī, vol. 1, p. 499; Haythamī 557. It is 'fabricated' according to Albānī (*Silsilat al-aḥādīth al-ḍaᶜīfa* 2676).

5 Al-Muttaqī al-Hindī 28,816. It is 'fabricated' according to Albānī (*Ḍaᶜīf al-Jāmiᶜ al-ṣaghīr* 5489).

6 This refers to Q. XI.114: *Lo! good deeds annul ill-deeds.*

of Tihamah but, once he [joins and] hears knowledge [in a circle of learning], he will become fearful and repent, and thus will seek forgiveness. For those [reasons he is forgiven] and therefore returns home sinless. Do not abandon the gatherings of the scholars.'

[Point 62: The teaching of fiqh is better than supplication alone.]

Ibn Māja[1] relates in his *Sunan* that ʿAbd Allāh b. ʿAmr b. al-ʿĀṣ (may God be pleased with him) narrated that 'The Messenger of God (may God bless him and grant him peace) went out and found two groups in the mosque. One was learning knowledge and the other supplicating God (Exalted is He). The Prophet said: "Both groups are good: one supplicates God and the other pursues learning and teaching *fiqh* to those who do not know. However, the latter are better since they seek the knowledge that I have been sent with." Then he sat with them.'[2]

1 Abū ʿAbd Allāh Muḥammad b. Yazīd b. Māja al-Qazwīnī (d. 273/887) was the compiler of *Sunan Ibn Māja*, which is one of the six canonical collections of *Ḥadīth*. It includes 4341 *ḥadīths*.

2 Ibn Māja 229. It is 'weak' according to Albānī (*Ḍaʿīf al-Jāmiʿ al-ṣaghīr* 4242).

CHAPTER FOUR

The Most Eminent Types of Knowledge are Those which Concern God, His Names and His Attributes

[Point 63: On how God mentioned to His angels the magnificence of those who sit in circles remembering Him and His Attributes.]

God (Most Blessed and Exalted is He) mentions to His angels the magnificence of those who remind each other with knowledge, and remember and praise God for what He has bestowed upon them. Tirmidhī related that Muᶜāwiya narrated that God's Messenger (may God bless him and grant him peace) went out to a gathering of his Companions and said: 'What makes you sit here?' They said: 'We are sitting here in order to remember God, praise Him for guiding us to the path of Islam, and for conferring His favours upon us through you.' Thereupon the Prophet said: 'I adjure you by God, is it only for that purpose that you all sit here?' They said: 'By God, we are only sitting here for that very purpose.' The Messenger then said: 'I am not asking you to take an oath due to any suspicion, but instead because Gabriel came to me and informed me that God (Exalted is He) mentioned your magnificence to the angels.'[1]

Only those who are firmly rooted (*rāsikhūn*) in knowledge would sit to perform the above. It encompasses knowing God, His Attributes and actions, His religion and His Messenger. Furthermore, it involves love of all of that, glorifying Him, and being content. So it is most befitting that God would mention the magnificence of those who possess that knowledge to His angels.

1 Muslim 6857; Tirmidhī 3379; Nasā'ī 5428; Aḥmad 16,835.

Indeed the Prophet (may God bless him and grant him peace) gave glad tidings to a man who loved *Sūrat al-Ikhlāṣ*. The latter said: 'I love it because it contains the description of the Most Beneficent (Great and Glorious is He).' The Prophet then said: 'Your love for it has allowed you to enter Paradise.' In another wording, he was informed that God loves him.[1] This proves that God loves those who love His Attributes, and will enter them into Paradise as a consequence.

The Jahmiyya[2] are the most averse and most likely to deter others from learning about His Attributes of perfection. They criticize those who mention [His attributes], learn about or take care to compile them. For these reasons [the Jahmiyya] are hated and criticized by the Community and the scholars of Islam. Indeed God (Exalted is He) hates and detests them to an even greater degree; and they will have a recompense that is commensurate with that.

[Point 64: The highest level in the sight of God is that of the messengers and the prophets followed by the truly faithful ones.]

The highest level in the sight of God is that of the messengers and prophets. God has selected messengers from amongst both the angels and mankind. How can they not be the most superior creation in the sight of God, since they are intermediaries between Him and His servants in conveying His message? They also elucidate His Names, Attributes and actions as well as His Laws, what He loves and what He dislikes, His reward, and His punishment to His servants. He

1 Bukhārī 774; Tirmidhī 2901; Aḥmad 12,432. Q. lxii: *Say: He is God, the One! God, the eternally Besought of all! He begetteth not nor was begotten. And there is none comparable unto Him.*

2 The Jahmiyya doctrine, founded by Jahm b. Safwān (d. 128/746) and al-Jaʿd b. Dirham (d. 118/736), denied and negated the majority of the Attributes of God (*taʿṭīl*), including His ability to speak. They only affirmed His ability to create and His power. They also claimed that humans do not have free choice, but rather are subject to divine compulsion (*jabr*). This doctrine was also the first to maintain that the Qur'ān was created, which was later adopted by the Muʿtazila.

selected them for His revelation, distinguished them with His grace, and made them the purest of mankind. In addition, the prophets have the noblest character, the greatest extent of knowledge, the most excellent deeds, the finest physical appearance, and are the most beloved to the hearts of people. God also absolved them of any inadequacy, faults or contemptible manners.

He made the next most honourable level after them that of their successors and heirs. This is because they follow their methodology and tradition in giving people advice, correcting those who are astray, teaching those who are ignorant, supporting victims, guiding those who are oppressors [to change their ways], enjoining good and doing it, and forbidding evil and forsaking it. They call those who respond to [the religion of] God through wisdom, and use good advice [to address] those who reject it out of ignorance, and debate amicably with those who stubbornly shun [the message].

The Exalted said: *Say: This is my way: I call on God with sure knowledge. I and whosoever followeth me.*[1] The meaning may be: 'I [the Prophet Muḥammad] and those who follow me have sure knowledge, and I call to God.' Alternatively it may be interpreted as: 'I call to God with sure knowledge.' Both meanings are concordant by necessity. In fact, a person is not a true follower unless he calls to God with sure knowledge and insight. Furthermore, his followers are knowledgeable and carry out [the Prophet's message] by [spreading] knowledge, [performing good] actions, guiding and advising people, being patient, and striving [for His sake]. These are the truly faithful ones (*ṣiddīqūn*)—they are the best of the Prophet's followers; and their leader and imam is Abū Bakr al-Ṣiddīq (may God be pleased with him).

God (Exalted is He) said: *Whoso obeyeth God and the Messenger, they are with those unto whom God hath shown favour, of the prophets and the truly faithful ones and the martyrs and the righteous. The best of company are they! That is a bounty from God, and God sufficeth as Knower.*[2] Thus God

1 Q. XII.108.
2 Q. IV.69–70.

has informed us of four levels of those who are blissful. He started with the highest level and then mentioned those who follow them in rank. These four groups are all in Paradise. May God, by His grace and generosity, make us from amongst them!

[Point 65: Humans are distinguished from animals by their knowledge and oral rhetoric.]

Humans are distinguished from other living creatures by virtue of their knowledge and rhetoric. Otherwise, many beasts and predatory animals eat more than them, are stronger, have intercourse more often, have more children, and live longer. Thus if a human becomes devoid of knowledge, there is nothing left to differentiate him from other beasts. God (Exalted is He) said regarding this type of people: *The worst of beasts in God's sight are the deaf, the dumb, who have no sense.*[1]

He also said: *Had God known of any good in them He would have made them hear.*[2] This indicates that these ignorant people do not have any means by which they can accept goodness. Were they to have any goodness, then *He would have made them hear*, meaning that He would have given them understanding. 'Hearing' here indicates that which is associated with understanding. Otherwise, the perception of sound has already occurred for them—through it the evidence of God has been established against them. The Exalted said: *Be not as those who say: We hear, and they hear not.*[3]

The Exalted also said: *The similitude of those who disbelieve (in relation to the Messenger) is as the similitude of one who calleth unto that which heareth naught except a shout and cry. Deaf, dumb, blind, therefor they have no sense.*[4] The meaning of this analogy may be that although the caller may exclaim [the message] to the disbelievers, they are simply beasts that only perceive sound. Alternatively, the interpretation may be

1 Q. VIII.22.
2 Q. VIII.23.
3 Q. VIII.21.
4 Q. II.171.

that the disbelievers, after hearing the message, are like beasts that croak out, as they can only perceive the sound of the summons. Both meanings are concordant by necessity. The second interpretation, though, is closer to the wording and more eloquent in meaning. Nonetheless, in both interpretations they did not benefit at all from the message except for the sound that even a grazing animal would hear. Thus the characteristics of humanity, which allow people to be distinguished from animals, are absent in them.

'Hearing' (*samʿ*) can connote perception of sound, or understanding of the meaning, or accepting and complying [with the message]. All three meanings are in the Qur'ān. An example of the first is His statement: *God hath heard the saying of her that disputeth with thee (Muḥammad) concerning her husband, and complaineth unto God. And God heareth your colloquy. God is Hearer, Knower.*[1] This is the clearest [verse] that establishes His Attribute of hearing. In it God mentioned the past, present and active participle: heard (*samaʿa*), heareth (*yasmaʿu*), and Hearer (*samīʿ*). ʿĀ'isha (may God be pleased with her) said: 'Praise be to God Whose hearing encompasses all voices. The woman who complained to the Prophet about her husband came while I was sitting in a corner of the room, yet I did not hear some of what she said. Then God revealed: *God hath heard the saying of her that disputeth with thee (Muḥammad) concerning her husband.*'[2]

Next is hearing associated with understanding, [as mentioned] in His statement: *Had God known of any good in them He would have made them hear, but had He made them hear they would have turned away, averse.*[3] Their [aversion] is due to the arrogance and obstinacy of their hearts. Therefore they committed two sins: first, they did not understand the truth because of their ignorance; and [second], even if they were to understand it, they would have turned away and shunned it due to their arrogance.

1 Q. LVIII.1.
2 Ibn Māja 188; Aḥmad 24195. It is 'authentic' according to Albānī (*Ṣaḥīḥ Ibn Māja* 188).
3 Q. VIII.23.

The third meaning is hearing associated with acceptance and compliance [to the message], as in the Exalted's statement: *Had they gone forth among you they had added to you naught save trouble and had hurried to and fro among you, seeking to cause sedition among you; and among you there are some who would have listened to them.*[1] Here *listened* means [that the believers would have] accepted and complied with [the suggestions of the Hypocrites]. Another example is His statement: *Listeners for the sake of falsehood!*[2] This means that the disbelievers accepted and complied with the falsehood of those espousing it.

The Prophet also said (may God bless him and grant him peace): 'When the imam says "God hears those who praise Him" (*samiʿa Allāh liman ḥamida*) you should say "Our Lord! All praise is due to You" (*Rabbanā wa-laka'l-ḥamd*). God will then hear you.'[3] This means that God will respond to those who praise Him. Similarly, God responds to those who supplicate to Him.

The point is that if a person does not have knowledge of what benefits him in this life and the Hereafter, then livestock animals are better than him. At least they will not be punished in the Hereafter whereas the ignorant person will be.

[Point 66: Knowledge is the judge of whether something is good or not.]

Knowledge is the judge of everything and nothing can supersede it. Therefore knowledge settles disagreements about whether something is existent or not, right or corrupted, beneficial or harmful, and it [discerns] its degree of goodness. Once knowledge passes a verdict, disagreement should cease and, following that, judgement becomes incumbent.

It also passes judgments in regards to the affairs of kings, politi-

1 Q. IX.47.

2 Q. V.42.

3 Bukhārī 796; Muslim 913; Tirmidhī 267; Abū Dāwūd 848; Ibn Māja 875; Nasā'ī 1064.

cians, finances and writings. A king who does not utilize knowledge is not upright, a sword without knowledge is used for unjust or foolish ends, and a pen without knowledge is a vain movement.

There is disagreement regarding whether the ink of scholars or the blood of the martyrs is better. There are proofs for each opinion, but the sole presence of this controversy is proof for the excellence of knowledge. Since the judge in this issue is knowledge itself, it must be the better of the two.

If it is asked, 'How can [knowledge] accept a judgment on its behalf?', we would reply that this is another evidence of its excellence, superior status and eminent nature. A [court] judge would not be justified to preside over [a matter involving] himself because of the suspicion of bias; however, no accusations can be made against knowledge when it does so. If [knowledge] is the judge, it decides the matter in an [unbiased fashion] with reason and reflective insight.

Ultimately, this debate is decided by returning to a point of agreement; that is, the types and ranks of perfection. There are four levels of perfection: prophethood, true faith (*ṣiddīqiyya*), martyrdom and loyal support (*wilāya*). Indeed God (Glory be to Him) mentioned them in His statement: *Whoso obeyeth God and the Messenger, they are with those unto whom God hath shown favour, of the prophets and the truly faithful ones and the martyrs and the righteous. The best of company are they! That is bounty from God, and God sufficeth as Knower.*[1]

The Exalted also mentioned these four in *Sūrat al-Ḥadīd*: *Lo! those who give alms, both men and women, and lend unto God a goodly loan, it will be doubled for them, and theirs will be a rich reward. And those who believe in God and His messengers, they are the loyal, and the martyrs are with their Lord; they have their reward and their light; while as for those who disbelieve and deny Our revelations, they are owners of Hellfire.*[2] He mentioned the hypocrites beforehand and, thus, these verses encompass all of the divisions of humanity—both wretched and blissful.

1 Q. IV.69–70.
2 Q. LVII.18–19.

Hence the highest level is that of a prophet and messenger. This is followed by sincere truthfulness, so the truly faithful ones lead those who follow the messengers. Their rank is the highest after prophethood. Thus if the scholar's writings reach the level of true faith, then his ink becomes better than the blood of a martyr, as long as the latter is not considered to be one of the truly faithful. But if the blood of the martyr flows with true faith, then it is better than the ink of the scholar. And God knows best.

True faith represents the perfection of the faith that the Messenger conveyed. It is fulfilled through knowledge and attesting [to the truth] completely. The essence of it is based on knowledge. True faith is like a tree: the trunk of it is knowledge, its branches are attesting [to the truth], and its fruits are [pious] deeds. This represents a summarized discussion regarding who is superior, the scholar or the martyr.

[Point 67: The best of deeds is faith in God, which requires knowledge.]

There is a mass of narrations (*tawātur*) that relate Prophetic texts stating that the best of deeds is faith in God, with deeds following thereafter. Faith has two pillars: first is knowledge and recognition (*maʿrifa*) of what the Messenger has conveyed. Second is to attest to it in word and deed. Attesting without knowledge and recognition is impossible.

The relationship of knowledge to faith is like that of the spirit to the body: the tree of faith cannot stand up except upon the trunk of knowledge and recognition. Therefore knowledge is the most honourable pursuit and most brilliant gift.

[Point 68: Knowledge is essential for willpower.]

Having a perfect character is based on the extent of one's knowledge and ability. Willpower is a branch of knowledge because it is dependent upon knowing what the desired objectives are. Capability is not manifested unless it is directed by willpower, but knowledge is not dependent upon anything else. This proves the excellence and eminent status [of knowledge].

[Point 69: Being Most Knowledgeable is the most expansive and generalized attribute of God.]

Knowledge is the most generalized attribute. It encompasses what is considered to be obligatory, possible, impossible, allowable, as well as what exists and what is non-existent. The Lord's Being, Attributes and Names (Glory be to Him) are only known to Him alone. The servants only know what He, the Most Knowledgeable and All-Cognizant, has taught them.

As for His power and will, they are specific to what they are connected to. His power only pertains to what is possible—not to what is impossible or even to what is [deemed by some to be] obligatory. Thus His power is more specific than His knowledge, but more general than His will. His will only pertains to some of the possibilities, i.e. only what He has willed to exist. Hence knowledge is essentially more expansive and generalized.

[Point 70: God appoints those who are the most knowledgeable to be leaders.]

God (Glory be to Him) notified us that He has appointed those who are knowledgeable to be leaders. They lead and guide others by His commandments; and they continue to lead even after they have passed on. The Exalted said: *And when they became steadfast and believed firmly in Our revelations, We appointed from among them leaders who guided by Our command.*[1]

In another verse, He said: *And who say: Our Lord! Vouchsafe us comfort of our wives and of our offspring, and make us patterns for (all) those who ward off (evil).*[2] This implies that they will become leaders who are emulated

1 Q. xxxii.24.
2 Q. xxv.74.

even after they have died. Thus the Sublime informed us that leadership in religious affairs is granted through patience and certainty. It is one of the highest levels of the truly faithful ones. Certainty indicates perfect knowledge, and it is the ultimate goal. Therefore, by achieving perfect knowledge, religious leadership is attained.

[Point 71: People's need for religious knowledge is greater than their need for food.]

A person's need for knowledge is greater than his body's need for food. Moreover, a person's need for knowledge [is vast like the] number of his breaths. A person needs faith and wisdom to accompany each breath. If he is bereft of faith or wisdom for even a moment, then he will be ruined and his wretchedness becomes imminent. One cannot attain faith or wisdom except through knowledge.

Thus the need for knowledge is higher than any other need. Imam Aḥmad alluded to this when he stated: 'People are more in need of knowledge than food or drink. Food and drink are only needed once or twice daily, while one needs knowledge all of the time.'

[Point 72: The knowledgeable person who teaches receives a greater reward than others even if he exerts himself less physically.]

The knowledgeable exert themselves less and do less, yet they are compensated with a greater reward. Take, for example, a labourer or an employee who have very strenuous jobs versus an instructor who sits while he teaches: the latter is compensated [with a salary] that is many times more than the former.

The Prophet (may God bless him and grant him peace) intimated the [aforementioned meaning] when he said: 'The best of deeds are faith in God followed by waging battle in the path of God.'[1] Waging battle requires one to sacrifice himself, and it is the most extreme

1 Aḥmad 7641; Abū Nuʿaym, vol. III, p. 156; al-Mutaqqī al-Hindī 241. It is 'authentic' according to Albānī (*Ṣaḥīḥ al-Jāmiʿ al-ṣaghīr* 1092).

hardship. Faith represents knowledge within the heart, followed by one acting and demonstrating [the truth of that faith]. Faith is the best of deeds even though the hardships associated with waging battle surpass its difficulties many times over.

Through knowledge one can know the merit of an action relative to another and which is better; and then one will only choose the best of actions to carry out. Yet those who act without knowledge may believe that the greater the hardship, the greater the virtue, and so they endure them. But it may be that something less virtuous is associated with greater hardship.

In this regard, we should remind ourselves of [Abū Bakr] al-Ṣiddīq, as he is the best of this Community. It is well known that amongst [the Companions] there were some who carried out more good deeds, did more pilgrimages, fasted more days, prayed more, and recited the Qur'ān more than him. Abū Bakr b. ʿAyyāsh[1] said: 'Abū Bakr did not surpass them by fasting or praying more, but rather due to the [faith] that settled (*waqara*) in his heart.' That is the theme of the following well-known analogy:

> Who is like you when you guide me on a journey?
> You may walk leisurely but you still arrive first.

[Points 73–74: Actions done without knowledge may not be accepted.]

73. Knowledge is the leader and commander of action. Every action that is not guided by knowledge is not beneficial to the doer, and can even be harmful to him. Some of the Predecessors have said: 'Whoever worships God without adequate knowledge may cause more harm then benefit.' Furthermore, [worship] may be accepted or rejected depending on whether it accords with knowledge or is inconsistent with it. Consequently, knowledge is the balance scale and the litmus test.

1 Abū Bakr b. ʿAyyāsh (d. 193/809) was one of the two transmitters of ʿĀṣim's Qur'ānic reading (the other being Ḥafṣ). He was also a renowned narrator of *ḥadīth*.

The Exalted said: *Who hath created life and death that He may try you which of you is best in conduct; and He is the Mighty, the Forgiving.*[1] Al-Fuḍayl b. ʿIyāḍ said: 'This [conduct] refers to the sincerest and most correct of deeds.' Some asked him: 'O Abū ʿAli, which are the sincerest and most correct?' He replied: 'If the action is sincere but not correct, it will not be accepted. Likewise, if it is correct but not done with sincerity, it will not be accepted. It has to be done with sincerity and correctness. Sincerity means doing it for God's sake, while correctness is doing it according to the [Qur'ān] and the Sunna.'

The Exalted said: *And whoever hopeth for the meeting with his Lord, let him do righteous work, and make none sharer of the worship due unto his Lord.*[2] God will not accept deeds otherwise. They need to be in accordance with the traditions of the Messenger of God (may God bless him and grant him peace) and seeking the Countenance of God. It is only through knowledge that one can fulfill these two requirements. Knowledge is therefore evidence of one's sincere devotion and of being a follower [of the Prophet].

God (Exalted is He) said: *God accepteth only from those who ward off (evil).*[3] The best interpretation of this verse is that God accepts only those deeds done by the pious. Piety indicates that one seeks His Countenance and acts in accordance with His commandments—this can only occur with knowledge. If this is the status of knowledge, then it becomes known that it is the most eminent thing. And God knows best.

74. A scholar without knowledge is like a traveller without a guide. It is well known that the [traveller] may very likely be injured [during his journeys], and his remaining safe is by accident and unlikely

1 Q. LXVII.2.
2 Q. XVIII.110.
3 Q. V.27.

[without a guide]. Ibn Taymiyya,[1] the Shaykh of Islam, used to say: 'Whoever abandons evidence has strayed from the path, and there is no evidence except that which the Messenger conveyed.'

Ḥasan [al-Baṣrī] said: 'Seek knowledge and do not harm it by worshipping [with blameworthy innovations in religion]. Worship and do not ruin it by your [lack of] knowledge. A group of people worshipped whilst abandoning knowledge[2] to the extent that they fought with their swords against the Community of Muḥammad (may God bless him and grant him peace). Had they been knowledgeable, they would have found no evidence for their actions.'

The difference [between point 73 and point 74] is that in the former point knowledge is obeyed, followed and emulated. In the latter point it is a guide, which leads to the desired objectives.

[Point 75: A discussion of the four types of guidance, and that the believer perpetually needs guidance from God.]

The Prophet (may God bless him and grant him peace) used to say: 'O God, Lord of Gabriel, Michael and Isrāfīl, the Originator of the heavens and the earth, Who knows the Unseen and the seen. You judge the differences amongst Your servants. By Your permission, guide me to the truth concerning what people have differed on. It is

1 Taqī al-Dīn Aḥmad b. ʿAbd al-Ḥalīm b. Taymiyya (d. 728/1328) was born in Ḥarrān (in present-day Turkey). His father—a scholar himself—moved his family to Damascus, Syria, due to the Mongol invasion. Ibn Taymiyya is often referred to by Ibn al-Qayyim as 'the Shaykh of Islam' or 'my Shaykh'. He wrote many books to refute the philosophers and speculative theologians. His major books include *Dar' taʿāruḍ al-ʿaql wa'l-naql*, *Minhāj al-Sunna al-nabawiyya*, *al-Radd ʿalā'l-manṭiqiyyīn*, *Majmūʿat fatāwā Ibn Taymiyya*. Ibn al-Qayyim was, of course, his most prominent student.

2 This is referring to the Khawārij. The Prophet said about them: 'A group will emerge from amongst you. You will deem insignificant your prayer in comparison to their prayer; your fasting relative to their fasting; and your deeds in comparison to their acts. They will recite the Qur'ān, but it will not go beyond their throats.' Bukhārī 5058; Aḥmad 11,579.

only You Who guides those whom You will to the straight path.'[1] It was narrated in some of the traditions that the Prophet would start the night prayer by exclaiming 'God is Most Great' and then supplicate with it.[2]

Being guided means that one knows the truth, and then pursues, desires and prefers it over everything else. It is the greatest blessing that God bestows upon a servant of His. For this reason, the Sublime has commanded us to ask Him to guide us to the straight path in our five daily prayers.

The servant first needs to know the truth, and then what is pleasing to God. Thereafter, he is in need of One to inspire him to pursue it, instill in his heart the will to carry it out, and enable him to do so. It is well known that what the servant is ignorant of is many times greater than what he knows. Furthermore, his body will often not follow his [heart's] will, even if it knows it to be correct. And sometimes, even if he wants to do something, he is incapable of [achieving] much of it.

Therefore the servant needs guidance in every moment, with regards to all matters, past, present or future. As regards the past, he must hold himself accountable for it: if he performed good, then he should thank God and ask for its continuation. But if it is otherwise, then he should repent to God (Exalted is He) and ask for His forgiveness; and he should also resolve to not do it again. Regarding guidance in the present, he needs to know the legal rulings concerning actions, especially if he is uncertain as to their correctness or wrongness. Regarding the future, his need of guidance is clearly obvious: it is so that he remains on the [straight] path.

The corrupt question that some people pose is: 'If we are already guided, then why would we need to ask God to guide us any more?' Such an enquiry is sufficient evidence that these people have not

1 Muslim 1811; Tirmidhī 3420; Abū Dāwūd 767; Ibn Māja 1357; Nasā'ī 1626; Aḥmad 25,225.

2 Abū Dāwūd 767 and 768; Aḥmad 25,225. It is 'authentic' according to Albānī (*Ṣaḥīḥ Abī Dāwūd* 767–768).

attained the essence of guidance, nor have they understood its reality due to their [lack of] knowledge. They claimed that [asking for guidance] only serves to ensure that God makes it permanent.

One who has completely understood the reality of guidance, and the need for it, knows that what one has not attained of it is many times greater that what one has realized, and that one needs guidance to be renewed in every moment. Moreover, since God (Exalted is He) is the Creator of the heart's and body's actions, one needs God to create a specific guidance for his every movement. Furthermore, if God does not turn away the barriers and diversions which prevent the induction of guidance, then one will not benefit from guidance nor will its reality be achieved.

As a rule, it is not sufficient for only prerequisites to exist, but the barriers or what would negate [the effect] from occurring must also be absent. It is well known that the misgivings, doubts and seductive temptations present in a person's heart may prevent the realization of guidance for him. Therefore, if God does not turn all of these away from him, he will not be guided completely.

This is why the Prophet (may God bless him and grant him peace) mentioned the Attributes of God and His sovereignty in this great and valuable supplication [at the beginning of this point], which are concordant with that which is being requested. Saying 'Originator of the heavens and the earth' uses this Attribute to entreat God as it entails guiding us back to the innate disposition (*fiṭra*) that He originated the creation upon.

Since learning and being guided to the truth is being requested [in the supplication], the Prophet mentioned that the Sublime has knowledge of the Unseen and the seen. It is most befitting that the servant should only ask the One Who is Omniscient to teach, lead and guide him. This is similar to beseeching the Self-Sufficient to bestow His [favours] upon the servant, or the Most Forgiving to forgive, or the Most Merciful to have mercy on him and pardon him.

The Prophet then recounted the Exalted's lordship over Gabriel,

Michael and Isrāfīl. This is due to—and God knows best—the fact that the request is for guidance to enliven the heart, and these are the three angels who have been enabled by God (Exalted is He) to be instruments for the well-being of people. Gabriel is the angel who transmits the revelation of God to the prophets; and this is the source of [spiritual] life in this world and the Hereafter. Michael is entrusted with water,[1] and this is the [source of] life for all creatures. Isrāfīl is the angel who blows the horn at the time when God will resurrect the dead.

Guidance is divided into four categories, which are recounted in the Qur'ān. The first is a general type of guidance, which includes all of creation, whether animals or human beings, so that they can carry out those matters beneficial to them. The Exalted said: *Praise the name of thy Lord the Most High, Who createth, then disposeth; Who measureth, then guideth.*[2] Here God describes four issues: creation, arrangement, measure and guidance. He arranged and perfected His creation with precision. Then He willed in due measure and guided them to the means to achieve their well-being and livelihood. Nevertheless, guidance also needs to be taught, so He mentioned that He is the One Who created and taught. This is akin to what He mentioned in the first *sūra* [Q. LXLVI] revealed to His Messenger. It is also what Moses said to God's enemy, Pharaoh: *Our Lord is He Who gave unto everything its nature, then guided it aright.*[3]

The second category of guidance involves the clear proofs that God has established as evidence for His servants. This does not necessarily result in complete guidance [which is the third type]. The Exalted said: *And as for Thamūd, We gave them guidance, but they preferred blindness to the guidance.*[4] This indicates that He made [the

1 Elsewhere Ibn al-Qayyim discusses this and mentions that the angel Michael 'is entrusted with water and plantation ... sustenance and mercy'. See Ibn al-Qayyim, *Miftāḥ*, pp. 545–6.

2 Q. LXXXVII.1–3.

3 Q. XX.49–50.

4 Q. XLI.17.

evidence] clear and known to them, but they preferred to remain astray and [spiritually] blind. The Exalted also said: *And (the tribes of) ʿĀd and Thamūd! (Their fate) is manifest unto you from their (ruined and deserted) dwellings. Satan made their deeds seem fair unto them and so debarred them from the way, though they were keen observers (mustabṣirīn) [aware of the guidance].*[1] The second category is more specific than the first, but more generalized than the third.

The [third category of guidance] involves granting them success and inspiration. God (Exalted is He) said: *And God summoneth to the abode of peace, and leadeth whom He will to a straight path.*[2] Therefore the summons is generalized to all of His creation, but He selected only those whom He willed to be guided. The Exalted also said: *Thou (O Muḥammad) guidest not whom thou lovest, but God guideth whom He will;*[3] *And thou verily dost guide unto a right path.*[4] Thus God has affirmed [that the Prophet] may guide people by summoning them [to Islam] and making it clear to them. But He withheld [from the Prophet the ability to ensure] that they are successfully guided. The Prophet (may God bless him and grant him peace) said [in recognition of this]: 'Whomever God guides cannot be led astray; and whomever He allows to go astray, no one can guide.'[5] The Exalted also said: *Even if thou (O Muḥammad) desirest their right guidance, still God assuredly will not guide him who misleadeth. Such have no helpers.*[6]

The third type of guidance necessarily and inevitably leads to guidance; yet the second [type of guidance] is conditional, so it does not necessarily do so. It is not impossible that guidance would fail to result from [the second], whereas with the third it is impossible.

The fourth category occurs in the Hereafter, and this is guidance

1 Q. XXIX.38.

2 Q. X.25.

3 Q. XXVIII.56.

4 Q. XLII.52.

5 Muslim 2007; Tirmidhī 1105; Abū Dāwūd 2118; Ibn Māja 1892; Nasāʾī 1405; Aḥmad 2749.

6 Q. XVI.37.

to the path of either Paradise or Hellfire. The Exalted said: (*And it is said unto the angels*): *Assemble those who did wrong, together with their wives and what they used to worship instead of God, and lead them to the path to Hell.*[1] With regards to the statement of the inhabitants of Paradise, *And they say: Praise be to God, Who hath guided us to this. We could not truly have been led aright if God had not guided us,*[2] it is possible that they mean guidance to the path of Paradise [in the Hereafter]; or it could just indicate the guidance that had occurred in this world, which made it possible for them to reach the blessed abode. If it is said that they are praising God for both, then the latter is the best interpretation.

God (Exalted is He) has also drawn a similitude regarding those who did not attain knowledge or follow the truth. The Exalted said: *Say: Shall we turn back after God hath guided us, like one bewildered whom the devils have infatuated in the earth, who hath companions who invite him to the guidance (saying): Come unto us? Say: The guidance of God is the Guidance, and we are ordered to surrender to the Lord of the Worlds.*[3]

[Point 76: On the merit and eminence of knowledge.]

The merit and eminence of something sometimes manifests itself as a result of its widespread benefit; sometimes due to the great need for it and the inability to suffice without it; sometimes because of some fault or evil that results if it is absent; sometimes because it results in great pleasure, joy and delight; and sometimes because it results in effects, end objectives (*al-ʿilla al-ghāʾiya*) and pursuits that are perfect and noble. All of these facets and others like them occur and manifest themselves due to their attachments (*mutaʿalliqāt*). If [the cause] is perfect and eminent, and its attachments are too, then all aspects of eminence and excellence are gathered together.

It is well known that all of the aforementioned apply to knowledge since its benefits are the most comprehensive, most numerous

1 Q. xxxvii.22–23.
2 Q. vii.43.
3 Q. vi.71.

and permanent. Indeed the need for it is greater than the need for food and even greater than the need to breathe. The worst case in the absence of [food or air] is only that the body will expire, whereas if one is devoid of knowledge, it leads to the heart and spirit being deprived of [spiritual] life. And the servant cannot dispense with the latter for even the twinkling of an eye.

As for [knowledge] resulting in pleasure and delight, it is because it is perfect, in and of itself, and is rightly suited to the soul. On the other hand, ignorance is a disease and it represents a deficiency; it is the greatest source of pain and harm to the soul. If people do not sense the rightness [of knowledge] and the inappropriateness [of ignorance], it is only because they have lost their senses and soul, like a dead person who does not feel any pain upon being wounded. The soul seeks knowledge because it recognizes the greatness of its beloved and it feels connected to it; and this is the ultimate pleasure and happiness. Of course, such [privileged states] depend on the [type of] knowledge itself. People's knowledge of their Creator and Originator, love of Him and desire to become closer to Him is not like knowledge of nature and its states. This is clarified next.

[Points 77–78: The greatest and most eminent types of knowledge are those which concern the Names and Attributes of God and Islam.]

77. The eminence of knowledge is in accordance with what it concerns. The soul's [delight] occurs when it knows the proofs and evidences for His existence [and His Attributes]; and it derives many great benefits from that. There is no deity but Him. He is the Lord of the universe, the Sustainer of the heavens and the earth, and the True Clear King. His Attributes are perfect, sublime and infallible above any fault, or imperfection, or any similitude or anthropomorphism. There is no doubt that knowledge of Him and His Names, Attributes and actions are the most noble and best types of knowledge.

Knowledge of God is the basis of all knowledge, just as He (Glory be to Him) is the Originator, Lord and Owner of everything. There is no doubt that if one wants to attain a complete understanding of an effect and why it has occurred, one must first apprehend the causative factor. Knowledge of the complete cause (*ʿilla*) results in understanding the effect (*maʿlūl*). Now everything other than God is dependent upon its Creator to exist. Thus knowledge of the Sublime's Essence, Attributes and actions necessarily results in knowledge of others. He is in His Essence the Lord and Owner of everything. Thus whoever knows God understands others, and whoever is ignorant about His Lord is more uninformed about others.

The Exalted said: *And be not ye as those who forgot God, therefor He caused them to forget their souls.*[1] Reflect on this verse and you will find a great and eminent meaning: God will cause whosoever disregards his Lord to neglect his soul. Thus he will not know his reality nor what is beneficial for him in this life and the Hereafter. He will become idle and negligent, like stray grazing animals. It may even be that grazing animals are more aware of what is beneficial for them as a result [of the first category of] guidance that the Creator has endowed them with. On the other hand, this [disbeliever] has even strayed from the innate disposition that he was created upon.

God (Exalted is He) also said: *Obey not him whose heart We have made heedless of Our remembrance, who followeth his own lust and whose case hath been abandoned.*[2]Since [the disbeliever] became heedless of the remembrance of God, his affairs were lost and his heart became scattered and forsaken.

78. There is nothing sweeter or more pleasurable to the servant, nor more beneficial or blessed for his heart and his life, than love of his Creator and Originator, remembrance of Him continuously,

1 Q. LXIX.19.

2 Q. XVIII.28.

and pursuit of His pleasure. Indeed without the aforementioned a servant cannot attain perfection. God originated the creation, inspired His revelation, sent His messengers, fashioned the heavens and the earth, created Paradise and Hellfire, prescribed the Divine Laws, [commanded] that the Holy Mosque [the Kaᶜba] be erected, and made pilgrimage obligatory—all so that the servants may love Him and be content with Him.

It is also for these reasons that He commanded us to battle [in His cause] against those who have stubbornly refused [to worship and obey] Him and instead have preferred others. He has made [Hellfire in] the Hereafter an everlasting and eternal abode of humiliation for those disbelievers. It is for these great reasons that the religious Community was founded and the direction of the Kaᶜba was established—they both revolve around it. In fact, knowledge is the only way to participate in all of the aforementioned.

Love of something results when one recognizes it. Therefore those who have the most knowledge about God love Him the most. In truth, everyone who knows God loves Him. Likewise, whoever actually knows this world and its inhabitants, refrains from them. Thus knowledge opens up the path [to loving Him], which is the secret of His creating and commanding. This will be clarified subsequently, God (Exalted is He) willing.

[Point 79: The love one feels towards God is concordant with the strength of one's knowledge.]

The pleasure that one experiences towards the beloved decreases and increases according to the relative weakness or strength of one's love. For this reason, the enjoyment of a person drinking cold water is greater if he is thirsty; and the same is the case for a person who is hungry. Hence love proceeds from knowledge and recognition of the external and internal beauty of the beloved.

The pleasure of seeing God after meeting Him [in Paradise] is concordant with the strength of one's love and hope [to be proximate to Him]. This, in turn is dependent upon one's knowledge of Him and His perfect Attributes. Thus knowledge is the closest path to this great pleasure.

[POINT 80: KNOWLEDGE IS ALSO AN ACTIVE CHARACTERISTIC.]

Existence is twofold: existence of His creating and that of His commandments. They both derive and emanate from the Lord's knowledge and wisdom. It is only through His knowledge that the heavens and the earth were originated, the messengers were sent and the Books were revealed. Moreover, it is only through knowledge that God alone is worshipped, praised and glorified. And it is only through knowledge that what is permissible can be distinguished from what is forbidden and the superiority of Islam over other [religions] is appreciated.

There is a disagreement on whether knowledge is an active (*fiʿliyya*) characteristic or whether it is an influential one (*infiʿāliyya*). One group opined that it is of a character whereby one uses it to act, because it is a condition or a cause for the existence of an effect. So a freely chosen action requires an actor who is alive, knowledgeable, capable, and who has a will; and one's existence cannot be envisioned without these characteristics.

Another group states that [knowledge] influences one since it is associated with that which is known and is connected to it. For example, the scholar is aware of what is known, and since his awareness follows [knowledge], [they ask] how can [knowledge] be said to precede [awareness]?

The correct view is that knowledge includes both types, and the first is acted upon. Here it represents the knowledge possessed by an actor who can freely choose what he wills to do. It is dependent upon his will, which in turn is dependent on his conception and knowledge of his intent. This knowledge precedes an action and influences it.

The other type of knowledge is one that follows what is known already and has no effect in bringing it about. It is like our knowledge of the existence of the prophets, the prior nations, kings and all other existents. This type of knowledge does not have an effect on what is known nor is it a condition that leads to an [action].

Each of the two groups considered only part of the issue, yet rendered an opinion that they deemed to be definitive. This is an area where many people make mistakes. Both types of knowledge are perfect characteristics and if either is absent, then one is considered to be grossly inadequate. This is expanded further next.

CHAPTER FIVE

An Exposition on the Question: Does Knowledge Inevitably Lead to Guidance or is Ignorance the Only Reason that Many Do Not Become Believers?

[Point 81: An exposition on the question: Does knowledge inevitably lead to guidance or is ignorance the only reason that many do not become believers?]

The virtue and beauty of something is known by comparing it to its opposite. There is no doubt that ignorance is the basis of every evil and harm that afflicts the servant both in this world and in the Hereafter. For example, if one has full knowledge that some food is poisoned and that whoever eats it will suffer from an intestinal perforation at a set time, no one would eat it. If it was destined that he did, due to being overcome with hunger or wanting to die, it is only because his intent is concordant with his knowledge, and it is more preferable to him [to eat] than to suffer from hunger.

Here there is a difference of opinion on a major question: Does guidance only fail to occur due to the absence or deficiency of knowledge? The speculative theologians, Sufis, as well as others have argued about this.

One group opined that it is impossible for those who have deep knowledge of the truth—to the extent that they no longer have any uncertainties—to not become guided. [It is argued that] if they are in fact astray, it is only because their knowledge is inadequate. Such people use the following verses as proof. The Exalted said: *But those of them who are firm in knowledge and the believers believe in that which is revealed unto thee, and that which was revealed before thee.*[1] Thus the Exalted testified that every person who is deeply rooted in knowledge is a believer. The Exalted also said: *The erudite among His servants fear God alone;*[2] *Those who have been given knowledge see that what is revealed unto thee from thy Lord is the truth;*[3] *There is no god but He: That is the witness of God, His angels and those endued with knowledge, standing firm on justice;*[4] *Is he who knoweth that what is revealed unto thee from thy Lord is the truth like him who is blind?*[5]

Thus [they contend that] people have been divided into two groups: the first are those who know that what has been revealed by their Lord is the truth. The second are those who are blind. Consequently, there is no middle ground in this matter. [They also refer to] the statements of the Exalted which characterize the disbelievers: *Deaf, dumb, blind, therefor they have no sense;*[6] *God hath sealed their hearts so that they know not;*[7] *God hath sealed their hearing and their hearts, and on their eyes there is a covering.*[8] Accordingly, all three means to gain knowledge have become impaired.

There is also the statement of the Exalted: *Hast thou seen him who maketh his desire his god, and God sendeth him astray purposely, and sealeth up his hearing and his heart, and setteth on his sight a covering? Then who will lead him after God (hath condemned him)? Will ye not then heed?*[9] Saʿīd b. Jubayr[10] interpreted *God sendeth him astray purposely* as being due to

1 Q. IV.162.
2 Q. XXXV.28.
3 Q. XXXIV.6
4 Q. III.18 (Yusuf Ali translation).
5 Q. XIII.19.
6 Q. II.171.
7 Q. IX.93.
8 Q. II.7.
9 Q. XLV.23.
10 Abū Muḥammad Saʿīd b. Jubayr (d. 95/714) was one of the prominent Successors and transmitters of *ḥadīth*.

the Exalted's prior knowledge regarding [that disbeliever]. Zajjāj[1] interpreted it as being due to the Exalted's knowing, before he was created, that he will be astray. *Sealeth up his hearing* indicates that [the disbeliever] cannot hear [with understanding]. Inclusion of *his heart* means that he cannot comprehend the guidance. Finally, *setteth on his sight a covering* means that he is not enlightened as to the causes that otherwise would have led to guidance.

The Exalted has also said: *Among them are some who give ear unto thee (Muḥammad) till, when they go forth from thy presence, they say unto those who have been given knowledge: What was that he said just now? Those are they whose hearts God hath sealed.*[2] Had they known what the Messenger said, they would not have asked the scholars nor would their hearts be sealed. The Exalted also said: *Say: Believe therein or believe not, those who were given knowledge before it, when it is read unto them, fall down prostrate on their faces, adoring, saying: Glory to our Lord! Verily the promise of our Lord must be fulfilled.*[3] This represents a testimony from God (Exalted is He) that those who have knowledge believe in Him and His words.

On the other hand, the Exalted has said regarding the denizens of Hellfire: *And they say: Had we been wont to listen or have sense, we had not been among the dwellers in the flames.*[4] This proves that those who are astray do not listen in order to try to understand. The Exalted also said: *As for these similitudes, We coin them for mankind, but none will grasp their meaning save the wise.*[5] Therefore the Exalted informed us that only the wise understand His similitudes. Conversely, the disbelievers are not included amongst the wise since they do not understand them.

The Exalted said: *Nay, but those who do wrong follow their own*

1 Abū Isḥāq Ibrāhīm b. Sahl b. al-Sārī al-Zajjāj (d. 311/923) was a prominent linguist, grammarian and exegete.

2 Q. XLVII.16.

3 Q. XVII.107–108.

4 Q. LXVII.10.

5 Q. XXIX.43.

lusts without knowledge. Who is able to guide him whom God hath sent astray?[1] *And those who have no knowledge say: Why doth not God speak unto us, or some sign come unto us?*[2] The Qur'ān is replete with examples wherein knowledge and recognition are absent in the disbelievers. In some instances, He describes them as not having knowledge, sometimes as not having understanding or comprehension, and sometimes that they do not have sense, hear or see. As a result, all of these prove that disbelief and ignorance are necessary concomitants of one another.

For these reasons, God (Glory be to Him) describes the disbelievers as being ignorant: *And the servants of (God) Most Gracious are those who walk on the earth in humility, and when the ignorant address them, they say: Peace!*[3] *And when they hear vanity they withdraw from it and say: Unto us our works and unto you your works. Peace be unto you! We desire not the ignorant;*[4] *Keep to forgiveness (O Muḥammad), and enjoin kindness, and turn away from the ignorant.*[5] The Prophet (may God bless him and grant him peace) said after his people had immensely harmed him: 'O God, forgive my nation, for they have no knowledge.'[6]

The Prophet (may God bless him and grant him peace) said: 'Two characteristics—good manners and having *fiqh* of the religion—will never be coupled together in a hypocrite.'[7] Thus he made having *fiqh* of the religion incompatible with hypocrisy. Moreover, the Predecessors would not call someone a jurist unless his knowledge was accompanied by pious deeds. Saᶜd b. Ibrāhīm was asked 'Who had the most *fiqh* of those living in Medina?' He replied: 'The most pious amongst them (*atqāhum*).'

1 Q. xxx.29.
2 Q. ii.118.
3 Q. xxv.63 (Yusuf Ali translation).
4 Q. xxviii.55.
5 Q. vii.199.
6 Bukhārī 3477; Muslim 4646; Ibn Māja 4025; Aḥmad 4366.
7 Tirmidhī 2684; Tabrīzī 219. It is 'authentic' according to Albānī (*Silsilat al-aḥādīth al-ṣaḥīḥa* 278).

Farqad al-Sinjī asked al-Ḥasan al-Baṣrī about some matter whereupon he gave his opinion. Then [Farqad] said: 'But the jurists disagree with you.' So Ḥasan replied: 'May your mother be bereaved of you, Furayqid![1] Have you even seen with your own eyes a jurist? The jurist is one who abstains from this world, desires the Hereafter, is enlightened in his religion, perseveres in worshipping his Lord, does not backbite those who have a higher [religious status] nor mock those who have a lesser one, and does not desire compensation for [teaching others] the knowledge that God (Exalted is He) has taught him.'

Some of the Predecessors said that a jurist does not allow people to despair of the mercy of God, does not permit them to feel secure from the strategy of God, nor does he ever abandon the Qur'ān by desiring something else. Ibn Masᶜūd (may God be pleased with him) said: 'It is enough that through knowledge one fears God and it is sufficient that due to ignorance one becomes deluded away from God.'[2]

Thus this [first] group contends that the Qur'ān, the Sunna and statements of the Predecessors (both Companions and Successors) prove that knowledge and gnosis (*maᶜrifa*) inevitably result in guidance, and that the absence of guidance proves that one is ignorant and lacks knowledge. They added a rational argument maintaining that, as long as one remains rational, he will not prefer to be forsaken rather than saved, nor [will he prefer] eternal severe punishment over eternal bliss. And experience corroborates that. For this reason God (Glory be to Him) described those who disobey Him as being ignorant: *God shall only forgive those who do evil in ignorance (and) then turn quickly (in repentance) to God. These are they toward whom God relenteth. God is ever Knower, Wise.*[3] Sufyān al-Thawrī[4] said: 'Every

1 The diminutive (*taṣghīr*) of his name Farqad.

2 Ibn ᶜAbd al-Barr 1514.

3 Q. IV.17.

4 Sufyān b. Saᶜīd al-Thawrī (d. 161/778) was one of the prominent Successors and founder of a school of jurisprudence.

creature of God who sins is ignorant no matter if he is naive or a scholar. If he is a scholar, then who is more ignorant than him? If he does not know, then it is likewise due [to ignorance].' As for the Exalted's statement *then turn quickly (in repentance) to God. These are they toward whom God relenteth. God is ever Knower, Wise,*[1] [Sufyān] said this [repentance] must occur before death.

Ibn ʿAbbās (may God be pleased with him) said: 'The sins of a believer are due to his ignorance.' Qatāda[2] said: 'The Companions of the Messenger of God (may God bless him and grant him peace) unanimously maintained that everything done in disobedience to God is due to ignorance.' Suddī[3] said: 'Everyone who disobeys God is ignorant.'

This [first group] further defended their opinion as the correct one on the basis that if one's knowledge is perfect, then a servant will not sin. For instance, if one knew that another person was watching one through a window, one would not commit any wickedness. How can someone then commit a sin when he is completely aware that God is watching over him, has prohibited that sin, will punish him for doing it, as well as [knowing] the other evil ramifications that are associated with that sin? Thus, in that case, it is undeniable that one's heart is oblivious to that knowledge. His committal of that sin is due to ignorance, heedlessness and/or forgetfulness, which are all the opposite of knowledge.

Sins are a result of two types of ignorance: ignorance of the causes that would have otherwise warded off [that sin] and ignorance of the assured harms that will consequently occur due to it. Then there are many other forms that underlie these two types of ignorance. Thus disobedience to God is always due to ignorance, whereas

1 Q. IV.17.

2 Qatāda b. Diʿāma b. Qatāda al-Sadūsī (d. 117/735) was an exegete and one of the prominent Successors. Although born blind, he had an excellent memory and managed to become one of al-Ḥasan al-Baṣrī's students.

3 Ismāʿīl b. ʿAbd al-Raḥmān al-Suddī (d. 127/744) was a prominent Successor. He wrote an authoritative exegesis of the Qur'ān named *Tafsīr al-Suddī al-kabīr.*

obedience to Him is always accomplished using knowledge. These are some of the arguments this group has used.

The second group maintained that [complete] knowledge does not lead to guidance. Often times a person goes astray intentionally in spite of that person being certain. Moreover, he prefers to go astray and disbelieve even though he knows the evilness and shamefulness of [his ways]. They state that Iblīs—the enemy of God, caller to disbelief and leader of the wicked—knew well without a doubt of God's commandment to him to prostrate before Adam; but [Satan] chose instead to disobey God and be obstinate (*ʿānada*). Thus [Iblīs] willfully condemned himself to God's damnation and eternal punishment despite his knowledge and awareness.

Furthermore, [Satan] swore by the Almighty that he would lead astray all of His creation except for those who were sincere. Iblīs had no doubt about God and His Oneness (*waḥdāniyya*), being resurrected in the Hereafter, Paradise and Hellfire. In fact, his knowledge and recognition of all that is greater than what most people can ever hope to achieve. But he chose instead to be punished eternally in Hellfire and receive God's damnation and anger, and to be expelled from His Heaven and Paradise. Therefore [Iblīs'] disbelief was exclusively due to obstinacy rather than ignorance.

God (Exalted is He) said regarding the people of Thamūd: *And as for Thamūd, We gave them guidance, but they preferred blindness to the guidance.*[1] This indicates that God made the truth clear and known to them such that they acknowledged it and were certain of it; however, they freely chose to remain deluded. Thus their disbelief was not due to ignorance.

The Exalted related what Moses said to Pharaoh: *In truth thou knowest that none sent down these (portents) save the Lord of the heavens and the earth as proofs, and (for my part) I deem thee lost, O Pharaoh.*[2] The Exalted stated: *But when Our tokens came unto them, plain to see,*

1 Q. XLI.17.
2 Q. XVII.102.

they said: This is mere magic. And they denied them, though their souls acknowledged them, for spite and arrogance. Then see the nature of the consequence for the wrongdoers![1] Thus the Sublime confirmed that their denial and disbelief occurred despite their certainty, which is the strongest type of knowledge. So it was due to injustice and pride, and not to ignorance.

God (Exalted is He) said to His Messenger: *We know well how their talk grieveth thee, though in truth they deny not thee (Muḥammad) but evildoers flout the revelations of God.*[2] Ibn ʿAbbās (may God be pleased with him) and the exegetes state that this verse indicates that the disbelievers knew [Muḥammad] to be truthful, but they were obstinate and stubbornly rejected (*jaḥada*) the [message]. Qatāda said: 'They knew he was a messenger but they stubbornly rejected him.'

The Exalted also said: *O People of the Book, why disbelieve ye in the revelations of God when ye (yourselves) bear witness (to their truth)? O People of the Book, why confound ye truth with falsehood and knowingly conceal the truth?*[3] This indicates that they disbelieved in the Qur'ān and in [the Messenger] who conveyed it, despite the fact that they witnessed that it was the truth. Therefore their disbelief was due to obstinacy and stubborn rejection, not to their ignorance of [the message] or it being hidden from them.

God (Exalted is He) said regarding those Jews who practised magic: *And surely they do know that he who trafficketh therein will have no (happy) portion in the Hereafter.*[4] So, despite the fact that they knew that whoever accepted to practise magic would have no share in the Hereafter, they still did so.

The Exalted also said: *How shall God guide a people who disbelieved after their belief and (after) they bore witness that the Messenger is true and*

1 Q. XXVII.13–14.

2 Q. VI.33.

3 Q. III.70–71.

4 Q. II.102.

after clear proofs (of God's sovereignty) had come unto them? And God guideth not wrongdoing folk.[1] Ibn ʿAbbās (may God be pleased with him) said [this verse] describes the Banū Qurayẓa and Naḍīr[2] and those who professed the same. They disbelieved in the Prophet (may God bless him and grant him peace) even though they had awaited his coming and witnessed that he was a prophet. Their disbelief was, thus, due to their transgression and envy.

Moreover, Zajjāj said: 'God (Great and Glorious is He) has informed us that they have [rejected] all of the pathways of guidance. They deserve to remain astray due to their disbelief after receiving clear evidences.' The meaning of *how shall God guide* is that He will not guide them; that is because they acknowledged the truth, witnessed it, and were certain of it, yet intentionally disbelieved. On the other hand, one would hope that those who are astray due to ignorance may become believers once they encounter the guidance. As for those who acknowledge the truth and are certain of it, but then choose disbelief and going astray over [guidance], then why should God guide someone like them?

The Exalted said about the Jews: *And when there cometh unto them that which they know (to be the truth) they disbelieve therein. The curse of God is on disbelievers. Evil is that for which they sell their souls: that they should disbelieve in that which God hath revealed, grudging that God should reveal of His bounty unto whom He will of His servants.*[3] Ibn ʿAbbās (may God be pleased with him as well as his father) stated that their disbelief was not secondary to any doubts or uncertainties that they had, but rather was due to their transgression: they could not accept that a prophet would arise from an offspring of Ishmael. God stated thereafter: *And when there cometh unto them a messenger from God, confirming that which they possess, a party of those*

1 Q. III.86.

2 These were two of the three largest Jewish tribes living in Medina at the time of the Prophet.

3 Q. II.89–90.

who had received the Book fling the Book of God behind their backs as if they knew not.[1] Accordingly, although they knew its veracity, they cast it aside. So they disregarded it as if they were ignorant.

The Exalted said: *Then, if they turn away, thy duty (O Muḥammad) is but plain conveyance (of the message). They know the favour of God and then deny it. Most of them are ingrates.*[2] Suddī interpreted God's favour (*niʿmat Allāh*) as Muḥammad (may God bless him and grant him peace). This interpretation was also preferred by Zajjāj: "The [Jews] acknowledged the truth of Muḥammad's message, yet they rejected it." The beginning of the verse supports that opinion.

The Exalted said: *Recite unto them the tale of him to whom We gave Our revelations, but he sloughed them off, so Satan overtook him and he became of those who lead astray. And had We willed We could have raised him by their means, but he clung to the earth and followed his own lust. Therefor his similitude is as the similitude of a dog: if thou attackest him he panteth with his tongue out, and if thou leavest him he panteth with his tongue out. Such is the similitude of the people who deny Our revelations.*[3] Is there any greater proof than this verse? This person was given guidance by God but he cast it away, preferred to go astray and be seduced. It is even mentioned that he knew [God's] greatest Name, yet that knowledge did not benefit him. So if knowledge and gnosis necessarily resulted in one being guided, it would have inevitably occurred for this person.

They also maintain that the Exalted's notification about the disbelievers on the Day of Resurrection is sufficient [to prove their viewpoint]: *If thou couldst see when they are set before the Fire and say: Oh, would that we might return! Then would we not deny the revelations of our Lord but we would be of the believers! Nay, but that hath become clear unto them which before they used to hide. And if they were sent back they would return unto that which they are forbidden. Lo! they are liars.*[4] Is there

1 Q. II.101.
2 Q. XVI.82–83.
3 Q. VII.175–176.
4 Q. VI.27–28.

any greater knowledge than that possessed by those who have been resurrected, seen with their own eyes the Day of Judgment and experienced it, and been exposed to [the impending] punishment? Even if they were to be sent back to this world, they would again choose to be astray rather than being guided.

The Exalted said: *And though We should send down the angels unto them, and the dead should speak unto them, and We should gather against them all things in array, they would not believe unless God so willed. Howbeit, most of them are ignorant.*[1] Is there anything greater than seeing angels who have been sent down, having the dead speak to them to affirm the truthfulness of the Messenger, and having the truth and guidance presented clearly to them in this world? In spite of all that, they would still not have faith, submit to the truth, nor believe in the Messenger. Whoever reads the biography of the Messenger [Muḥammad] (may God bless him and grant him peace) will realize that his people [the Quraysh] and the Jews were absolutely certain of his truthfulness, yet they chose to remain astray and disbelieve instead of becoming faithful.

For instance, Umayya b. Abī al-Ṣalt was one of those who was endlessly waiting for a [prophet] and had knowledge of his coming. Once, while he was travelling with Abū Sufyān, the latter told him about the Messenger of God (may God bless him and grant him peace). Although [Umayya] became certain about [Muḥammad's] truthfulness, he still said: 'I will never believe in a prophet that comes from [a tribe] other than Thaqīf.' Furthermore, consider the case of Heraclius, who was certain that [Muḥammad] was a messenger of God, but preferred to remain astray and disbelieve in order to maintain his kingdom.

In addition, after the Jews asked the Messenger of God about the nine clear signs [of prophethood] and he informed them, they then kissed his hand and said: 'We witness that you are a prophet.' Thereafter the Prophet said: 'What prevents you from following

1 Q. VI.111.

me?' They replied: 'David supplicated to his Lord for the prophets to be from his lineage. We fear that our fellow Jews will kill us if we follow you.'[1] Thus, in spite of affirming his prophethood and attesting to it, they preferred disbelief and being astray.

Of note, such people did not become Muslims by solely testifying [that he was a prophet]. Rather, one is obligated to also obey and follow [Muḥammad in order to be considered a Muslim]. So if one says, 'I know that he is a prophet, yet I will not follow him or profess his religion', then he is one of the worst types of disbelievers. This is agreed upon by the Companions, the Successors and the Sunni Imams, who argue that it is not sufficient to articulate some statements deemed consistent with belief without full recognition (*maʿrifa*) in one's heart. Rather, one must also manifest actions of the heart [for faith to be accepted of one], like loving God and His Messenger and submitting to His religion, as well as commit oneself to obeying Him and following His Messenger. Faith is more than just recognition of the heart and affirmation by it.

The [second group] further maintain that the Qur'ān has revealed that disbelief is of many types. Firstly, it is due to the disbelievers being ignorant, astray and following their forefathers. This type of disbelief accounts for most of the masses. The second type of disbelief is due to stubborn rejection, obstinacy and intentionally opposing the truth. This is represented by the disbelief of those who were previously mentioned. It applies most often to those disbelievers who are in leadership positions because of their knowledge, power, provisions or wealth. They fear that they will lose their leadership position [if they enter the faith], so they intentionally prefer disbelief over faith. Thirdly, there is a disbelief that entails completely turning away without even considering what the Messenger has conveyed. Such people remain ambivalent and do not show either support or hostility to the Prophet. They simply shun [the message].

1 Tirmidhī 2733; Nasā'ī 4083. It is 'weak' according to Albānī (*Ḍaʿīf Sunan al-Tirmidhī* 2733).

Most philosophers deny the latter two types, and only affirm disbelief as a result of the first [that is, due to ignorance]. Yet those who deeply reflect on the Qur'ān, the Sunna and the biographies of the prophets realize with certainty that the claim of the philosophers is wrong. Furthermore, they realize that the disbelief of these nations generally occurred despite their certainty, knowledge and recognition of the veracity of the prophets and their mission and message. The Qur'ān repeatedly affirms that the idolaters still used to believe in God's existence and that He alone is their Lord and Creator. Thus how can it be maintained that these people never affirmed that they had a Lord and Creator? To claim so is a staggering misrepresentation. Therefore disbelief is more than just sole ignorance. Indeed, the worst types of disbelief are those which [the philosophers] have denied.

The [second group] also said that the heart has two classes of obligations, and if either of them is absent one cannot become a believer: [first] the obligation of recognition and knowledge; and [second] the obligation of love, obedience and submission. Just as one cannot be a believer if one does not attain knowledge and faith, one cannot be a believer if one does not manifest love, obedience and submission [to God]. Moreover, if one abandons the second obligation in spite of his knowledge and recognition, he is a greater disbeliever than one who disbelieves due to ignorance alone. This is because the one who is ignorant may become obedient once he recognizes and knows the truth, whereas there is no remedy for one who is obstinate. The Exalted said: *How shall God guide a people who disbelieved after their belief and (after) they bore witness that the Messenger is true and after clear proofs (of God's sovereignty) had come unto them. And God guideth not wrongdoing folk.*[1]

The [second group] maintained that love of God and His Messenger—actually that God and His Messenger are more beloved to the servant than anything else—is something that is necessary for

1 Q. III.86.

a person to be considered a Muslim. There is no doubt that love [of God] is a greater matter than knowledge. Also not everyone who affirms the [truthfulness of the] Messenger loves him (as has been shown earlier).

They also said that an envious person is led by his hatred of the envied person to be hostile to him and to pursue injuring him by any possible means, even if he knows the latter to be virtuous. The former's hostility is not due to ignorance of the latter's virtue and perfection, but is due to his evil intentions and desires. This describes [the reason for the envy and hostility displayed] against the messengers and their successors by some rulers who were deprived of their positions of leadership [after the messengers came]; and their attempts to prevent others from following [the messengers] in the erroneous hope that they would be able to retain their position of leadership. Yet the methodology (*sunna*) of God is to deprive such people of their leadership positions and disgrace them in their fellows' view. *And thy Lord is not at all a tyrant to His servants.*[1]

These are the arguments of both groups and they end here. Be as fair as a judge would be and decide by what you know [to be true]. The arguments of each group do not disprove the other. Do you have any other evidence by which you can ascertain the correct viewpoint and elucidate it whereby both groups will be content and the disagreement will cease? Whoever recognizes one's own worth and knows the value of others will prosper. God is the One Who opens [the doors to success] and He is the Most Knowledgeable.

We state, while relying on God: both groups have not departed from what knowledge would require nor have they deviated from true principles. Instead the disagreement and disparity between them is due to their use of generalities and not agreeing on the particulars. Nonetheless, once we specify the exact meaning of the wording, then the difference of opinion will cease, and it will become apparent that the two groups actually agree with one another.

1 Q. XLI.46.

The exposition of this is that prerequisites (*muqtaḍā*) are of two types. [Firstly], a prerequisite that always results in that which it obligates (*mūjibuh*) and requires (*muqtaḍāh*). This is like when a complete cause leads to its effect by necessity. The [second] prerequisite is not a complete one. That which it requires may fail to occur because of some inadequacy [that characterizes it], because a condition that would have led to the effect lapses, or because of the occurrence of an impediment.

If it is maintained that knowledge must necessarily result in guidance, whereby [knowledge] is claimed to be a complete prerequisite that necessarily results in [guidance], then the second group, who opine that knowledge does not necessarily lead to guidance, is correct. On the other hand, if it is intended that through knowledge one becomes suitable to being guided, but that [guidance] may fail to occur because of some inadequacy of one's [knowledge] itself, the lapse of some condition or the occurrence of an impediment, then the correct viewpoint is that of the first group. The explanation follows.

Knowledge is a causative factor leading to the well-being of the servant, his pleasure and joy, but it may fail to be effective for many reasons. The first is if one's knowledge is weak. The second is that one is not suitable. So his knowledge may be complete, but its effectiveness is conditional upon the purity of the place [i.e. his soul] and its ability to accept purification (*tazkiya*). If [his soul] is not pure nor capable of being purified, he will be like a barren land that cannot sprout vegetation, no matter how much rain falls upon it or how many seeds are planted in it. Similarly, if his heart is hard like a stone, he will not be able to benefit from any of his knowledge.

The Exalted has said about this type of people: *Those for whom the word of thy Lord (concerning sinners) hath effect will not believe, though every token come unto them, till they see the painful doom.*[1] The Exalted also said: *And though We should send down the angels unto them, and the*

1 Q. x.96–97.

dead should speak unto them, and We should gather against them all things in array, they would not believe unless God so willed. Howbeit, most of them are ignorant.[1] The Exalted also said: *Say: Behold what is in the heavens and the earth! But revelations and warnings avail not folk who will not believe.*[2] There are many other verses with a similar meaning in the Qur'ān. Thus if the heart is rock hard and obstinate, or if it is diseased and irresolute, then knowledge will be of no avail.

The third reason is an impediment like animosity, arrogance or pride. This is what prevented Iblīs from obeying [God's] command. It is the sickness of the ancient as well as future nations, except for those whom God has protected. It is also the reason that the Jews [of Medina] were not guided even though they encountered the Messenger of God (may God bless him and grant him peace) and acknowledged his prophethood. This is also what prevented ʿAbd Allāh b. Ubayy b. Salūl, Abū Jahl and other polytheists from becoming guided. Such people did not doubt [the Prophet's] authenticity or that he possessed the truth, but rather it was their pride and animosity that led them to disbelieve. Likewise for Umayya and others similar to his sort, who had knowledge of Muḥammad's coming and prophethood.

The fourth reason is the impediment of a leadership position or a kingdom, even if that person's pride does not prevent him from following the truth. Since he cannot reconcile submission [to God and following the Prophet] with maintaining his leadership position or kingdom, he shuns the former in order to maintain the latter. Such was the situation of Heraclius and other kings who disbelieved: they recognized the truthfulness of [Muḥammad's] prophethood and affirmed it albeit internally. Indeed they would have liked to enter into the religion [of Islam], but they were afraid that they would lose their kingdom. In fact, only a few of this type were able to be saved from this disease [and impediment]—only those whom God protected.

1 Q. VI.111.
2 Q. X.101.

It is likewise the disease of Pharaoh and his people. For this reason they said: *Shall we put faith in two mortals like ourselves, and whose folk are servile unto us?*[1] Thus they refused to believe, or follow Moses and Aaron, or obey them since the Israelites were their slaves. It is said that Pharaoh had actually considered following Moses and consulted his minister Hāmān. However, the latter advised him: 'You are now a deity who is worshipped, but you will become a servant worshipping another [if you follow Moses].' Hence Pharaoh refused to worship [God] and instead chose to maintain his leadership position and [his status as a false] deity.

The fifth reason is the impediment of temptations and wealth. This prevented many of the People of the Book from believing [in Islam]. They were afraid of losing the sustenance and wealth that they obtained from their people. The disbelievers of Quraysh would similarly dissuade a person from believing—each according to his desires. Thus they would say to a person who loves fornication that Muḥammad has forbidden that or say [to the drinker that] alcohol has been forbidden. It was in this manner that they dissuaded the poet Aʿshī away from Islam.

I debated many of the People of the Book regarding the truth of Islam. Afterwards, one of them said to me: 'I will not abandon [drinking] alcohol and I would rather drink it safely [as a non-Muslim *dhimmī*]. If I were to become a Muslim you would bar me from that and would whip me if I drank.' Another one said: 'I have many relatives who are rich. If I become a Muslim, I would not inherit anything from them, but I hope to do so.' There is no doubt that this type of thinking occurs in the minds of many disbelievers. Therefore the strength of the appeal of their temptations and wealth, along with the weakness of the calling of their faith, leads them to respond to the former and say that they do not want to distance themselves from their fathers and forefathers.

1 Q. xxiii.47.

The sixth reason is love of one's family, relatives and clan. Some feel that if one follows the truth and opposes their [relatives'] wishes, they will distance themselves from him or expel and banish him from amongst them. This is a major reason that many remain disbelievers.

The seventh reason is love of one's home and country. Even if his clan or relatives are not present, such a person may still feel that if he follows the Messenger, he will have to leave his home and country for a foreign and remote land. Thus he refrains [from believing] and stays in his country.

The eighth reason is their sense that following Islam and the Messenger disgraces, dishonours and defames their fathers and grandfathers. This is what prevented Abū Ṭālib and those like him from following Islam. They felt that if they became Muslim, they would essentially be affirming that their fathers and grandfathers were foolish, astray and guilty of the abominations of disbelief and polytheism. This is why the enemies of God said to Abū Ṭālib as his death was approaching: 'Do you desire anything other than the religion of ʿAbd al-Muṭṭalib?' His last words thereafter were that he would remain on the religion of ʿAbd al-Muṭṭalib. The enemies of God approached him in this manner because they knew of the high esteem he held his father, ʿAbd al-Muṭṭalib, and that he derived much honour and pride from that.

Of note, Abū Ṭālib had said at an earlier point: 'If it was not for the fact that [my becoming a Muslim] represents a cursing [of the tribe of] Banū ʿAbd al-Muṭṭalib, I would have affirmed it just for you [Muḥammad]' or something like that. Here is his poem that clearly shows that he knew the veracity of the prophethood of Muḥammad (may God bless him and grant him peace):

And I know that the religion of Muḥammad
Is the best religion of all for creation.
If it was not for my fear of being criticized or cursed
You would have found me rushing to accept it.

[He further said] in his poem *al-Lāmiyya*:

I swear by God that if it were not for the curses
That would be said by our leaders in their assemblies;
I swear and I am not joking that
We would have forever followed him wherever
[he led us].
They knew that our son [Muḥammad] is not a liar
Nor is he concerned with spreading falsehood.

The ninth reason occurs when their enemy ends up following the Messenger and enters into the religion earlier, and this then prevents them from following the guidance. So their opposition and enmity towards that person leads them to be hostile to the truth and its followers, even if they have no history of enmity per se for the latter. This is what occurred to the Jews in regards to the Anṣār [of Medina]: they were enemies and the Jews used to always promise and warn them of the Prophet's coming, and that they would follow and fight alongside him against them. But when the Anṣār surprised them by rushing to become Muslims, [the Jews'] enmity towards them caused the Jews to remain disbelievers.

The tenth reason is being impeded by one's customs, habits and upbringing. In truth, habits can become so strong that they overcome what is natural, to the point that they then become second nature. So a man might be raised upon a certain teaching from childhood, with his heart and soul raised on it in similar fashion to how his body grows up with his traditional food, to the point that he does not know anything else. But then knowledge comes upon him in a quick instant to do away with [the religion he was brought up on] and take its place; however, it becomes too difficult for him to change. Although this reason may be, conceptually, the weakest of all of the reasons, it is one of the most common. In fact, the religion of habits is the most prevalent one for most people. To change one's [habits or religion] is like changing from one nature to a second.

May God bless and grant peace to all His prophets and messengers, and specifically Muḥammad, who is the most perfect and best of them. They modified the habits of deviant nations, converted them to faith, and dislodged their evil habits and customs. One does not appreciate how difficult that is to do. Only those who are able to convert one man from his [false] religion and teachings to the truth [can recognize that]. May God recompense the messengers with the greatest of rewards—above that of anyone else of mankind!

Here an intricate question arises which decides the debate: Can a barrier effectively overcome some prerequisite condition and weaken it to such a degree that its requisite is negated? Put another way in order to address our concern here: Is it possible that an impediment, due to its strength, can overcome and weaken knowledge to such a degree that it is not effective at all? This gets to the essence of the issue at hand. The Qur'ān points to the fact that some impediments can completely block or alter the effectiveness of knowledge on one's heart.

The Exalted said: *And (remember) when Moses said unto his people: O my people, why persecute ye me, when ye well know that I am God's messenger unto you? So when they went astray God sent their hearts astray. And God guideth not the evil-living folk.*[1] Thus the Sublime punished them by turning their hearts away from the truth after they initially deviated. A parallel of that is His statement: *We confound their hearts and their eyes. As they believed not therein at the first, We let them wander blindly on in their contumacy.*[2] Thus it is said that those who have been exposed to the truth, but thereafter reject it, are punished such that their hearts, intellects and opinions become corrupt. Due to this, it is said that the opinions of one who follows his desires [and falsehood] are not legitimate, since they led him to deny the truth. The Exalted said: *Then because of their breaking of their covenant, and their disbelieving in the revelations of God, and their slaying of the prophets wrongfully, and their saying: Our hearts are covered (ghulf)—nay, but God set a seal upon them for their disbelief.*[3] The Sublime

1 Q. LXI.5.

2 Q. VI.110.

3 Q.IV.155. Of note, Pickthall translates *ghulf* as *hardened*.

thus notified us that their disbelief, after knowing the truth, was the reason that God sealed their hearts.

The word 'covered' (*ghulf* is the plural of *aghlaf*) represents a heart that has been encased with coverings. It is like saying a sword is within its sheath (*ghilāf*). It is also said 'A man is *aghlaf* and *aqlaf*' if he is not circumcised. To paraphrase, they mean to say: 'Our hearts are enclosed with a covering and therefore we cannot comprehend anything, O Muḥammad. We do not know what you are saying.'

We do not accept, for many reasons, the opinion of those who contend that the meaning of *ghulf* is that their hearts are containers filled with knowledge and wisdom. One is that *ghulf* is the plural of *aghlaf*, like *qulf* and *aqlaf* (uncircumcised), *ghulb* and *aghlab* (majority) and other parallels. The heart that is *aghlaf* is one that is encased within a covering (*ghilāf*); this is what is well known in linguistics. Second, there is no well-known or allowable usage of *ghilāf* to denote that the heart of a person is a container for such-and-such. This does not exist in any prose of [Arabic] literature, poetry, nor is there any parallel to that in the Qur'ān. It is only a distortion and therefore the verse should not be construed as such.

Third, a parallel is the statement of other disbelievers: *They say: Our hearts are under veils (concealed) from that which thou dost invite us.*[1] Here *akinna* has a [similar meaning] to covering (*ghulf*), which their hearts are within. Also derived [from this] is the usage of *kināna* for the quiver. Fourth, the context of the verse is not appropriate for the meaning that they contend, as He stated: *Nay, but God set a seal upon them for their disbelief.*[2] It is only appropriate that He would take away from them any knowledge or wisdom which they claimed[3].

1 Q. XLI.5 (Yusuf Ali translation). Pickthall translates *akinna* as *hardened.*

2 Q. IV.155.

3 Ibn al-Qayyim's viewpoint is corroborated by Biblical verses such as Deuteronomy 10.16: *Circumcise therefore the foreskin of your heart, and be no more stiffnecked.* Also consider Jeremiah 4.4: *Circumcise yourselves to the Lord, and take away the foreskins of your heart, ye men of Judah and inhabitants of Jerusalem: lest my fury come forth like fire, and burn that none can quench it, because of the evil of your doings.*

When they claimed that their hearts were encased in coverings and veils, and therefore could not understand his words, they were informed [first] that God recompensed them by sealing their hearts because of their disbelief, betrayal of their covenant and their killing of the prophets. There is no doubt that once a heart is sealed any knowledge within it becomes darkened, obliterated and is no longer effective.

It may even be that a cause that typically leads to guidance can result in one going astray. The Exalted said: *He misleadeth many thereby, and He guideth many thereby; and He misleadeth thereby only miscreants: those who break the covenant of God after ratifying it, and sever that which God ordered to be joined, and (who) make mischief in the earth—those are they who are the losers.*[1] Thus the Exalted notified us that the Qur'ān becomes [paradoxically] a cause for this group of people to go astray, despite the fact that He has guided His messengers and believing servants through it. It is for this reason that the Sublime states that only those who follow God's pleasure will be guided. The Exalted said: *And whenever a sūra is revealed there are some of them who say: Which one of you hath thus increased in faith? As for those who believe, it hath increased them in faith and they rejoice (therefor). But as for those in whose hearts is disease, it only addeth wickedness to their wickedness, and they die while they are disbelievers.*[2] What is more evil [in their regard] than the fact that knowledge, which is a source of guidance, [paradoxically] leads them to go astray!

Furthermore, some of the Predecessors used to say: 'Knowledge calls out to action: if the latter reacts, then the former remains; otherwise [knowledge] departs.' They also would say: 'We used to rely on [performing good] deeds in order to retain knowledge.' Thus one of the strongest causes for losing or forgetting knowledge is the abandonment of acting accordingly. For example, if a traveller does not follow a guide, he will not benefit from the latter's guidance. In that

1 Q. II.26–27.
2 Q. IX.124–125.

case, the traveller becomes like someone who is ignorant. Therefore actions must follow knowledge. A person who is knowledgeable but does not act is actually like one who is ignorant. Another example can be seen in someone who has gold and silver yet remains hungry and naked because he did not use either to buy enough to eat or clothe himself: he is no different than one who is poor and destitute. It has been said:

Whoever abandons spending when in need
Out of fear of poverty lacks [an intellect].

The Arabs sometimes term 'indecency' (*fuḥsh*) or 'obscenity' (*badhā'*) as 'ignorance' (*jahl*). That is because they are effects resulting from ignorance. Therefore they are named in accordance with what caused them. It is for this reason that Moses said to his people after they said: *Dost thou make game of us? He answered: God forbid that I should be among the foolish!*[1] Thus he equated mocking the believers with foolishness or ignorance. Similarly, the Exalted related Joseph saying: *If Thou fend not off their wiles from me I shall incline unto them and become of the foolish.*[2]

The Exalted also said: *Keep to forgiveness* (O *Muḥammad*), *and enjoin goodness, and turn away from the ignorant.*[3] What is meant is not 'shun those who are ignorant', for this would result in [the Prophet] not teaching or instructing them to be righteous; rather, the meaning is 'shun the impetuosity of those who act foolishly and do not respond to them in like fashion or criticize them'. Muqātil, ʿUrwa, and Ḍaḥḥāk[4] advised one to 'protect oneself from responding to their foolishness'. Another place that term is used is in the *ḥadīth*: 'If one is fasting, he should not raise his voice, nor act foolishly (*yajhal*).'[5]

In addition, a 'sin' (*maʿṣiya*) is also named 'ignorance'. Qatāda said

1 Q. II.67.

2 Q. XII.33.

3 Q. VII.199.

4 Ibn Muzāḥim al-Hilālī al-Ḍaḥḥāk (d. 102/720) was one of the prominent Successors, traditionists and exegetes.

5 Bukhārī 1904; Muslim 2706; Nasā'ī 2218; Ibn Māja 1691; Aḥmad 7340.

that the Companions of Muḥammad all agreed that anyone who disobeys God is ignorant (*jāhil*). What is intended here is not that he is ignorant regarding the prohibition, since if he is in fact so then he is not sinful—as one is not legally punishable in this world, nor in the Hereafter if one is ignorant regarding some prohibition; rather, the sin itself is named as 'ignorance'. It is either named that because it is the cause itself or to portray [the sinner] as being like one who is, in fact, ignorant.

Second, once those [Jews mentioned in Q.iv.155] rejected the truth and desired [falsehood], they were punished with the sealing [of their hearts], being overcome (*rayn*) [by their sins], and having their ability to comprehend and understand taken away from them. The Exalted said similarly about the Hypocrites: *That is because they believed, then disbelieved, therefor their hearts are sealed so that they understand not.*[1]

Third, they did not attain any benefit from their knowledge nor did it lead to their salvation and success. Therefore they were denied the essence [of knowledge]. The presence of something can be precluded because of the absence of beneficial effects or purposes. The Exalted states about the denizens of Hellfire: *Lo! whoso cometh guilty unto his Lord, verily for him is Hell. There he will neither die nor live.*[2] Thus God negates life therein because of the absence of life's beneficial nature or its purpose. It is also said, 'It is as if no money exists unless it is spent and no knowledge exists unless it is benefitted from.'

There is no contradiction in [God] using knowledge to establish the evidence, but then taking it away or negating it by sealing or stamping the hearts of those who fail to follow or act upon what the evidence obligates. The Exalted said: *And when thou recitest the Qur'ān we place between thee and those who believe not in the Hereafter a hidden barrier; and We place upon their hearts veils lest they should understand it, and in their ears a deafness; and when thou makest mention of thy Lord*

1 Q. lxiii.3.
2 Q. xx.74.

alone in the Qur'ān, they turn their backs in aversion.[1] Thus the Sublime notified us that He prevented them from comprehending His Book or benefitting from it. This does not impede them from being aware of the evidence against them, since had they not been aware of it in general, they would not have turned their backs away in aversion; but since they turned away upon hearing the remembrance of God's Oneness, this proved in fact that they understood the sermon. They were then recompensed with a veil over their hearts since they covered their ears.

The Exalted said similarly: *They could not bear to hear, and they used not to see.*[2] He negated their ability to hear despite the vigour and completeness of their senses. Since they had excessive hatred and aversion to it and His Book, they became like those who could not hear nor see.

Another statement is similar: *And they say: Our hearts are protected from that unto which thou (O Muḥammad) callest us, and in our ears there is a deafness, and between us and thee there is a veil.*[3] They meant that they refused to accept anything from him, hated hearing what he conveyed, and they preferred to shun it. They became like those who could not comprehend, nor hear, nor see the one speaking to them. The [following verse] applies to them: *Had we been wont to listen or have sense, we had not been among the dwellers in the flames.*[4] God recompensed them with Hellfire for those sins. The Exalted therefore said: *So they acknowledge their sins; but far removed (from mercy) are the dwellers in the flames.*[5]

Moreover, God (Exalted is He) sometimes negates their intellect, hearing and vision altogether, sometimes just hearing and intellect, sometimes hearing and vision, sometimes intellect and vision, and sometimes He negates only one of the aforementioned. Thus nega-

1 Q. XVII.45–46.
2 Q. XI.20.
3 Q. XLI.5.
4 Q. LXVII.10.
5 Q. LXVII.11.

tion of all three nullifies all of the perceptive faculties that allow one to attain knowledge. So negation of one nullifies that specific [instrument], but the others are also negated by necessity. For example, if the heart is corrupt, then hearing and vision also become so and vice versa.

If someone turns away from hearing the truth, or hates or does not like to see a particular person, then the guidance will not reach his heart, and he therefore becomes corrupt. Thus the Qur'ān negates something in particular here, while the others follow suit by necessity. Through this detailed exposition the manner by which the two group's viewpoints conform has become clear.

Now we will consider His statement: *Those unto whom We have given (ātaynāhum) the Book recognize (this revelation) as they recognize their sons*;[1] as well as other parallels as evidence. When God (Exalted is He) says *Those unto whom We have given the Book*, this only refers to the praiseworthy believers. But when God wants to criticize [at least some of] them and notify us of their obstinacy and preference for being astray, He uses the phrase 'those who had been given' (*ūtū*), based upon the passive participle.

The first example is represented by the Exalted's statement: *Those unto whom We have given the Book before it, they believe in it. And when it is recited unto them, they say: We believe in it. It is the Truth from our Lord. Even before it we were of those who surrender (unto Him). These will be given their reward twice over, because they are steadfast and repel evil with good, and spend of that wherewith We have provided them.*[2] It is also represented by His statement: *Shall I seek other than God for judge, when He it is Who hath revealed unto you (this) Book, fully explained? Those unto whom We have given the Book (aforetime) know that it is revealed from thy Lord in truth. So be not thou (O Muḥammad) of the waverers.*[3] This usage praises and cites them. The Exalted also cites them in the verse: *Say:*

1 Q. II.146.
2 Q. XXVIII.52–54.
3 Q. VI.114.

God, and whosoever hath knowledge of the Book, is sufficient witness between me and you;[1] and *Ask the followers of the Remembrance if ye know not!*[2]

The Exalted also said: *Those unto whom We have given the Book, who read it with the right reading, those believe in it. And whoso disbelieveth in it, those are they who are the losers.*[3] There is a difference of opinion regarding the personal pronoun *it* in *who read it with the right reading*. Some maintain that the pronoun refers to the Book [Torah or Gospel] which was revealed unto them. Ibn Masʿūd said: 'They enjoin what is permissible and forbid what is prohibited. They read [the Torah or Gospel] as it was revealed without altering [its words] in any way from their intended meanings.'[4] Others maintain that it was revealed regarding the People of the Book [who became Muslim]. It is alternatively said that *it* refers to the Qur'ān being read by the Muslims; but this is inconsistent and does not correspond with His statement: *Those unto whom We have given the Book recognise (this revelation) as they recognise their sons. But lo! a party of them knowingly conceal the truth.*[5]

Now God notified us that initially they recognized the Prophet Muḥammad (may God bless him and grant him peace) and his religion just as they knew their sons and therefore they accepted it. Thus He praised and cited them [as evidence] over those who disbelieved. It is for this reason that the exegetes mentioned that this group included ʿAbd Allāh b. Salām[6] and those like him. At the end of the verse though He selected another group for criticism; so this proves that the former group is not being criticized.

1 Q. XIII.43.

2 Q. XVI.43.

3 Q. II.121. Of note, *ātaynāhum* is translated here as *have* been given and *ūtū* is translated as *had* been given. No Qur'ānic English translation incorporates adequately what Ibn al-Qayyim discusses, and therefore these phrases were used.

4 See Q.IV.46 and Q.V.13.

5 Q. II.146.

6 ʿAbd Allāh b. Salām (d. 43/663) was a Jewish rabbi living in Medina. After the Prophet's emigration there he converted to Islam. Q. XLVI.10 most likely refers to him as being the one who attested to the veracity of the Qur'ān and became a believer.

The Exalted said in Q.vi: *Do ye in sooth bear witness that there are gods beside God? Say: I bear no such witness. Say: He is only One God. Lo! I am innocent of that which ye associate (with Him). Those unto whom We have given the Book recognize it as they recognize their sons.*[1] It is said that *it* [in this verse] refers to the Messenger and his truthfulness. Others maintain that *it* refers to His Oneness. The two viewpoints are actually necessary concomitants. In fact, this verse cites them as evidence against the polytheists; it does not criticize those who have been given the Book.

As for the second instance, [it reads]: *Those who have been given the Book know that (this revelation) is the Truth from their Lord. And God is not unaware of what they do. And even if thou broughtest unto those who had been given the Book all kinds of portents, they would not follow thy qibla.*[2] This [second verse] represents the testimony of the Sublime regarding [the disbelief] of those who *had been given* (*ūtū*) the Book. On the other hand, the first [verse] was for those who *have been given* (*ātaynāhum*) the Book and who are believers.

The Exalted also said: *O ye unto whom the Book had been given, believe in what We have revealed confirming that which ye possess, before We destroy countenances so as to confound them;*[3] *And say unto those who had received the Book and those who read not: Have ye (too) surrendered?*[4] Thus these verses are directed at those who had not yet believed. The Prophet (may God bless him and grant him peace) was not commanded to say this to those who had already believed and become Muslims.

Now He (Glory be to Him) only mentions those who *had been given a portion* (*ūtū naṣīban*) of the Book in derogation, like in His statement: *Hast thou not seen those unto whom a portion of the Book had been given, how they believe in idols and false deities;*[5] *Seest thou not those*

1 Q. vi.19–20. Pickthall translates *it* as *this revelation*.

2 Q. ii.144–145.

3 Q. iv.47.

4 Q. iii.20.

5 Q. iv.51.

unto whom a portion of the Book had been given, how they purchase error, and seek to make you (Muslims) err from the right way?[1] He also said: *Hast thou not seen how those who had been given a portion of the Book invoke the Book of God (in their disputes) that it may judge between them; then a faction of them turn away, being opposed (to it)?*[2]

To summarize, there are four categories. [Firstly], those who *have* been given the Book—they are not mentioned except in a praiseworthy manner. [Secondly], those who *had been given a portion of the Book*—they are never [mentioned] except in derogation. [Thirdly], those who *had* been given the Book—this is a more general label, and it may include both [good and bad], but it [mostly concerns the blameworthy], while the praiseworthy ones [who converted to Islam] are never singled out alone. Finally, [the term] 'People (*ahl*) of the Book' includes all of them in general; it addresses both the praiseworthy and blameworthy ones. This [last group] is represented in His statement: *They are not all alike. Of the People of the Book there is a staunch community who recite the revelations of God in the night season, falling prostrate (before Him)*;[3]and His statement that criticizes them: *Those who disbelieve among the People of the Book and the idolaters could not have left off (erring) till the clear proof came unto them.*[4]

The above exposition is very beneficial in answering one of the biggest issues about the principles of Islam: the issue of faith and the different opinions that Muslims hold in regards to it. We recounted many good anecdotes that have clarified the truth in this matter. And God knows best.

1 Q. IV.44.
2 Q. III.23.
3 Q. III.113.
4 Q. XCVIII.1.

CHAPTER SIX

Knowledge Leads to Spiritual Bliss and Elevates One's Rank

[Point 82: Knowledge is the greatest factor that differentiates humanity.]

Regarding [the ranks of] humanity, God (Glory be to Him) has differentiated between the best of humanity and the most evil to such an extent that one would not consider them to be members of the same race, due to the vastness of the spectrum of human beings, from the best of them to the worst.

God (Glory be to Him) created the angels with an intellect but they do not experience temptations, whereas He created animals with desires but no rational thinking. However, He created humans with both rational thought and a susceptibility to temptations. Thus whosoever's rationality overcomes his desires is better than the angels, and whosoever's temptations overwhelm his intellect is worse than the animals.

The Sublime also differentiated humanity with regards to knowledge. He made the most knowledgeable of humanity an instructor of the angels. The Exalted has said: *He said: O Adam, inform them of their names.*[1] Indeed there is no level higher than that. On the other hand, the most ignorant person is such that even Satan does not consider him to be acceptable or useful. Satan said to those who were ignorant followers of his: *I am quit of thee.*[2] The Devil also said

1 Q. II.33.
2 Q. LIX.16.

to those who were ignorant and disobeyed the Messenger:[1] *I am guiltless of you.*[2] By God, how vast is the difference between these two individuals! The angels prostrate to the first [namely Adam] and he teaches them from what God has taught him, whereas the second is not even considered by Satan to be an acceptable ally.

This great differentiation is due to knowledge itself and its effects. If there had been no benefit to knowledge except that it allows one to become proximate to the Lord of the universe, part of the world of the angels and the highest elite, then that would have been sufficiently eminent. In fact, attaining honour in this world and the Hereafter is dependent and conditional upon it.

[POINTS 83–84: THE MOST HONOURABLE PARTS OF THE HUMAN BEING ARE THOSE THAT CONDUCT KNOWLEDGE TO HIM.]

83. The most honourable part of a human is the location of his knowledge, which is his heart. Since the heart is the place of knowledge, whereas hearing is the messenger and vision is the vanguard, [the heart] is the ruler over all the other organs. It commands and directs them using that knowledge, and they follow and submit to it in obedience. The scholar's place relative to people is analogous to the heart compared to the organs.

Just as the goodness of the citizens is dependent upon the goodness of their ruling king (or their evilness is based upon the latter's evilness), people are dependent upon their scholars and rulers. The Predecessors have said: 'If two classes are good then the rest of the people will be good, whereas if they are evil then people will become evil—they are the scholars and rulers.' ʿAbd Allāh b. Mubārak has said:

1 This refers to the disbelievers who fought against the Messenger in the Battle of Badr, and thus disobeyed him. The full verse is: *And when Satan made their deeds seem fair to them and said: No-one of mankind can conquer you this day, for I am your protector. But when the armies came in sight of one another, he took flight, saying: I am guiltless of you. I see that which ye see not. I fear God and God is severe in punishment.*
2 Q. VIII.48.

Who has corrupted the religion except for the kings,
Evil bishops and rabbis?[1]

Since hearing and vision can perceive what other organs cannot, they were placed on the noblest part of the human being: the face. These two are the best and most beneficial organs. Nonetheless, there is a difference of opinion as to which one is superior. One group, including Abū al-Maʿālī[2] and others, said that hearing is better. They maintained that success in this world and the Hereafter is attained by following the messengers and accepting their message, and this occurs through hearing. Furthermore, those who do not hear do not know what the messengers conveyed. In addition, the most glorious Words of God (Exalted is He) are perceived through hearing. Indeed the eminence of God's Words is incomparable to those of His creation, just like He is incomparable to them. Moreover, the sciences can only be acquired by back and forth discussion, which can only be accomplished through hearing. Likewise, hearing can perceive universals and particulars, what is apparent or present and what is hidden or absent. On the other hand, vision can only perceive some of that which is apparent. What is more, hearing can sense all types of knowledge, so there is no comparison between the two.

For instance, let us suppose that there are two individuals: one can hear the words of the Messenger but cannot see his figure, whereas another individual can see him but cannot hear him speaking due to being deaf. Are they equal? In addition, while those who are blind cannot perceive some particulars, they can recognize them roughly by having them described. On the other hand, the knowledge that eludes those who lack hearing cannot be attained by eyesight. In addition, God (Exalted is He) has criticized the disbelievers in the

1 Ibn ʿAbd al-Barr 1100.

2 Abū al-Maʿālī Ḍiyāʾ al-Dīn ʿAbd al-Malik b. Yūsuf al-Juwaynī (d. 478/1085) was born in Juwayn (in present-day Iran). He later taught in Mecca and Medina (thus becoming known as *Imām al-Ḥaramayn*) before moving to Nishapur. He was a major proponent of Ashʿarī thought.

Qur'ān due to their lack of hearing more than their lack of vision. Moreover, when He criticized them due to their lack of vision it was only in connection with their lack of intellect and hearing.

Another group, including Ibn Qutayba, opined that vision is better, since the noblest and greatest pleasure is seeing God in Paradise, and this is only attainable by eyesight; that alone is a sufficient reason for favouring it. In addition, it is in the forefront of the heart and its vanguard, and thus it is closer to the heart than hearing. It is for this reason that they are juxtaposed when mentioned in the Qur'ān, like His statement: *So learn a lesson, O ye who have eyes!*[1] Deriving a lesson is by use of the heart, while seeing it is with one's eyes. The Exalted also said: *We confound their hearts and their eyes as they believed not therein at the first.*[2] He did not mention their hearing here. The Exalted said: *For indeed it is not the eyes that grow blind, but it is the hearts, which are within the bosoms, that grow blind;*[3] *He knoweth the traitor of the eyes, and that which the bosoms hide.*[4] He said concerning His Messenger: *The heart lied not (in seeing) what it saw;*[5] then He said: *The eye turned not aside nor yet was overbold.*[6]

These [aforementioned proofs] point to the fact that there is a strong relationship and connection between the heart and vision. It is also for this reason that people can often deduce what is in a person's heart from their eyes. Literature, whether prose or poetry, is replete with such examples; yet these instances are too numerous to be recounted here. They said it is for this reason that the heart trusts vision in ways that it never would trust hearing. Moreover, if [the heart] has any doubt about something, it checks it with what was visualized to either verify or repudiate it. Therefore vision is its judge. They said that this is corroborated by the *ḥadīth* related by

1 Q. LIX.2.
2 Q. VI.110.
3 Q. XXII.46.
4 Q. XL.19.
5 Q. LIII.11.
6 Q. LIII.17.

Aḥmad in his *Musnad*: 'The one who is notified [of some matter] is not like the one who saw it.'[1]

They said it is also for this reason that when God (Glory be to Him) notified Moses that his people were seduced in his absence and worshipped the calf, Moses' reaction was mild compared to when he saw and witnessed that. It was only at that point that he dropped the tablets, which then broke. Similarly, Abraham, the friend of God, asked his Lord to show him how He resurrects the dead. Although [Abraham] was certain of that already, he wanted to attain the highest level, which is contentedness of the heart.

They maintained that certainty is composed of three levels: the first is for hearing. The second is for witnessing, which is called (*ʿayn al-yaqīn*), and it is better and more perfect than the first level.[2] They said also that the eyes conduct to and away from the heart, thus the eyes are the mirror of the heart. They make manifest whether the heart loves or hates, loyally supports or opposes something, as well as showing joy or sadness. On the other hand, the ears do not transmit anything away from the heart at all—they only deliver to it.

Yet the truth is that each rationale has its particular superiority over the other. What is perceived by hearing is more generalized and universal, whereas what is sensed by vision is more complete and perfect. Thus hearing entails universals, while vision entails what is apparent, complete, perfect and encountered. There are two types of bliss enjoyed by the inhabitants of Paradise: one is to see God and the other is to hear His Words and speech.

A tradition states: 'Once the believers listen to the Qur'ān from the Beneficent, (Almighty and Most Glorious) on the Day of

1 Aḥmad 1842; Ibn ʿAdī, vol. vii, p. 551. It is 'authentic' according to Albānī (*Ṣaḥīḥ al-Jāmiʿ al-ṣaghīr* 5373).

2 No mention is made of the third level here but it is mentioned later in the book as 'true certainty' (*ḥaqq al-yaqīn*). See page 212 below.

Resurrection it will be as if they had never heard it before.'[1] It is also well known that meeting God and hearing His greetings and speech (as mentioned in Tirmidhī[2] and others) will not be similar to anything else whatsoever. There will be nothing more pleasurable to them than that. For this reason, the Sublime mentioned, as a warning to His enemies, that He will not speak to them. He also mentioned that He will be veiled away from them and that they will not see Him. Thus [hearing] His speech is the highest bliss enjoyed by the inhabitants of Paradise. And God knows best.

84. God (Glory be to Him) recounts in the Qur'ān His blessings upon His servants. Among those [blessings] is that He gave them the instruments to attain knowledge, including the heart, hearing and vision. In one instance, the tongue is mentioned as the heart utilizes it to expound [its thoughts].

In *Sūrat al-Niᶜam* or *al-Naḥl*, the Exalted recounts His blessings, both their foundations and branches, as well as what leads to them becoming complete and perfect. Furthermore, He mentioned how He made Himself known to them through [His blessings] and He dictated that they should thank Him accordingly. It starts with the bases of His blessings and ends with what leads to them becoming perfect. The Exalted said: *And God brought you forth from the wombs of your mothers knowing nothing, and gave you hearing and sight and hearts that haply ye might give thanks.*[3] Thus the

1 Al-Muttaqī al-Hindī 39,342. It is 'weak' according to Albānī (*Ḍaᶜīf al-Jāmiᶜ al-ṣaghīr* 4157).

2 Bukhārī 7518; Muslim 7140; Tirmidhī 2555; Aḥmad 11,835. Tirmidhī's version is: Abū Saᶜīd al-Khudrī narrated that the Messenger of God said: 'Indeed God will say to the people of Paradise: "O people of Paradise!" They will say: "We respond to You, O our Lord and we are at Your service." Then He will say: "Are you pleased?" They will say: "Why should we not be pleased when You have given us what you have not given anyone from Your creation." So He will say: "I shall give you what is greater than that." They will say: "And what is greater than that?" He will say: "I shall cover you in My Pleasure and I shall never become angry with you henceforth."'

3 Q. XVI.78.

Sublime mentioned how He blessed them by bringing them forth without them having any knowledge and then bestowed upon them hearing, vision and a heart so that they could attain as much knowledge as possible, in order for them to thank Him.

The Exalted also said [regarding the disbelievers]: *And had assigned them ears and eyes and hearts; but their ears and eyes and hearts availed them naught since they denied the revelations of Allah; and what they used to mock befell them;*[1] *Have We not made for him a pair of eyes and a tongue and a pair of lips, and shown him the two highways?*[2] Thus He mentioned here the two eyes through which one sees and observes. He also mentioned being guided to *najdayn*, which are the two paths of either good or evil, according to the majority of exegetes. This is also corroborated by another verse: *We have shown him the way, whether he is grateful or disbelieving.*[3] The tongue and lips are mentioned here since these two are the instruments for teaching, and He made them part of His signs that prove His existence, His Power, His Oneness and His Blessings. Since these three organs are the most eminent organs, God (Great and Glorious is He) mentioned them specifically in relation to what one will be questioned about. The Exalted said: *The hearing and the sight and the heart —of each of these it will be asked.*[4]

Thus the bliss of an individual is dependent on the rightness of these three organs: ears, eyes and the heart. God (Exalted is He) has bestowed upon the servant: [first] hearing to listen to the commandments, prohibitions and covenants of His Lord; [second] his heart to understand and comprehend them; and [third] his eyesight to witness His signs that prove His Oneness and lordship. Therefore the purpose of His bestowal of these instruments is to attain knowledge, which will then result in beneficial effects.

1 Q. XLVI.26.
2 Q. XC.8–10 (Yusuf Ali translation).
3 Q. LXXVI.3.
4 Q. XVII.36.

[Point 85: On the extrinsic, intrinsic and spiritual bliss that a human being experiences.]

There are three types of bliss that a soul wishes for. First is one that is extrinsic to the person's being. It is temporary as it is derived from the presence of another entity. [For example,] this is the bliss associated with wealth. A person could find himself fortunate and highly regarded by people, but all of a sudden he could become completely humiliated [if all his wealth is lost]. His condition thereupon becomes analogous to one whose skull is fractured by a stake driven into it by a stone. Another example of this first type [of bliss] is the beauty people derive from clothes or ornaments: if you look past their dress, you will find nothing else.

Some scholars told us a story about one of them being amongst some merchants on a boat that broke down and sunk. They [managed to survive but the merchants] became humiliated and poor after being proud and wealthy. On the other hand, the scholar, after reaching their destination, was respected, treated well, and given many gifts and honours. When they wanted to return to their home country, [the merchants] asked him: 'Do you have any request or message you want us to relay to your people?' He replied: 'Yes. Tell them that if you want a treasure that will never sink, then carry knowledge.'

Likewise, there was once a scholar who met with a handsome man dressed in beautiful clothes. He tried hard to learn something useful from the latter, but could not. Some asked [this scholar]: 'What did you think of that man?' He replied: 'It was as if I saw a beautifully decorated home, but nobody was living there.'

The second bliss involves the body and form. It includes good health, a balanced temperament, a good and well-proportioned build, and pure skin. This is associated with the person to a greater degree than the first. In reality, though, it remains extrinsic to his very soul and essence. A person is a human due to his spirit and heart, not his body and form. It has been said:

O you who serve the body and labour in doing so,
You are, because of your spirit not body, a human being.

The comparison of this [second bliss] to one's spirit and heart is like [the first bliss that involves contrasting] his clothes and dress to his body. The body is separate from the spirit and is an instrument of it. The body's bliss is dependent on the spirit's health and goodness since it is extrinsic to his soul and essence.

The third bliss is the true one and it involves the soul, spirit and heart. It is the bliss that results from beneficial knowledge. It is what remains present despite changing circumstances. It accompanies a person as he passes through the three abodes: this world, the grave and the Hereafter. One is also elevated to the most distinguished and perfect level [by virtue of this spiritual bliss].

The first [type of bliss] only accompanies him while he has wealth or fame. The second type is liable to disappear or change when his body weakens. Thus there is no real bliss except this third one. Furthermore, [the third] becomes stronger and greater with the passage of time. Even if one's wealth and fame no longer exist, it remains as his real treasure and honour. In addition, only once the spirit departs from the body and the first two types of bliss end does its real virtue become apparent. In fact, it is only through knowledge that one can recognize this bliss and pursue it. Thus the true bliss is derived from knowledge and what it results in. God grants success to those whom He wills. There is no denying that which He bestows, nor can anyone bestow that which He has blocked.

Nevertheless, most people dislike acquiring (*iktisāb*) this [spiritual] bliss due to the path's ruggedness, the bitter [pill] one has to swallow in the beginning, and because it cannot be attained except by striving vigorously. In contrast, one can attain the first one by being lucky, like hitting a jackpot, or gain it through inheritance, a gift or something similar. On the other hand, the bliss of knowledge cannot be inherited. It can only be attained by striving vigorously and pursuing it with a pure intention. A poet said correctly:

Say to the one who aspires for lofty matters
Without striving hard, you desire the impossible.

Another said:

If it was not for the difficulties, all people would reign supreme
But generosity [may] make one poorer and courage [may lead to] one's death.

Whosoever is determined and aspires to lofty matters is required to firmly love the religious path, which is the real bliss. In the beginning, it is intertwined with a variety of hardships and suffering. Yet if one forces oneself, whether willingly or unwillingly, to endure the difficulties along the path, then one will eventually arrive at an astonishing garden, an honourable seat and a noble status. Furthermore, one then finds that all the other pleasures are insignificant, like child's play. A poet said:

I saw that my desires took me afar
To an end beyond which I could not go further.
But once we met and I saw with my own eyes its beauty
I became certain that I was only playing.

So the honourable [aspirations] are surrounded by aversions. Bliss cannot be reached except over a bridge of hardships, and thus one can only reach it on a vessel made of hard work and diligence. Muslim related in his *Ṣaḥīḥ* that Yaḥyā b. Abī Kathīr said: 'Knowledge cannot be attained by relaxation of one's body.'[1] It is also said that 'Whoever wishes to relax [in Paradise] must abandon relaxation [in this world].'

The path to one's beloved
Is impossible without [enduring] hardship.

Had most people not been ignorant of the sweetness of this pleasure and its high status, they would have fought for it with swords.

1 Muslim 1390.

Instead, though, it is enclosed within a veil of hardships, and it has been hidden from them due to their ignorance. God has selected those whom He wills of His servants for it. God is the Possessor of great bounty.

[Point 86: A person's level and perfection is concordant with his knowledge and actions.]

God (Exalted is He) created everything in existence and allowed each to attain their noble objective. However, if one cannot reach the [level of] perfection, he will be moved to a lower level and used there. If he is incapable [of fulfilling the requirements of that level], then he is moved to a lower one. This continues until every last possible virtue is absent from him, and he becomes like a thorn or firewood that is not beneficial except to be used as fuel.

For example, if a horse's qualities are complete, it is used to carry kings and likewise treated with honour. Yet if it is inadequate in some fashion, it is used to transport those of a lower status. If it is even more inadequate, then it is used by soldiers. If it is lower still, then it is used similar to how a donkey is used: either to rotate a millstone, conduct rubbish, or something like that. After that, if no utility whatsoever exists for it, then it is slaughtered like a sheep.

Another example is metal: if it is not proper for a sword, then it is made into an axe or saw. A final example is a great and beautiful stately home: if it becomes ruined and destroyed, then it is instead used as a shed for sheep, camels or other animals.

The same applies to the descendants of Adam. If they are appropriate to being selected by God for His message and prophethood, then they become a messenger or prophet. The Exalted has said: *God knoweth best with whom to place His message.*[1] But if one's quiddity is lacking for this level, but [he is] appropriate to be a successor to prophethood, then God will prepare and bring him up for that. If he is inadequate for that, but appropriate for the level of sainthood being

1 Q. vi.124.

supported by Him (*wilāya*), then He will prepare him for that. If he is appropriate for deeds and worshipping rather than gnosis and knowledge, he is made to be of that level. And so on until the level occupied by the general believers is reached. If he is completely lacking and is not receptive to any goodness, then he becomes the fuel for Hellfire.

In an Israelite tradition Moses asked his Lord about the nature of those who will be punished. God said: 'O Moses, sow a plant!' and so he did. Then He inspired him to harvest it. Then He inspired him to pulverize it and then leave it alone, and so he did. Then he separated out the grain alone, leaving the stem and straw aside. Then He inspired to him: 'I will forsake those who have no goodness in them for Hellfire, like these stems and thorns, for they are not appropriate for anything except the fire.'[1]

A human being is promoted from one level of perfection to a higher one until he reaches a level appropriate to him. There is such a vast difference between one being [created from] a sperm [and an egg], and then being transformed into a human being who is greeted by the Lord in Paradise and able to see God's Countenance in the morning and evening. The Prophet (may God bless him and grant him peace) initially said when the angel [Gabriel] came to him and asked him to read: 'I do not know how to read.'[2] In the end, God said to him: *This day have I perfected your religion for you and completed My favour unto you.*[3] And God specifically said to him: *God revealeth unto thee the Book and wisdom, and teacheth thee that which thou knewest not. The grace of God toward thee hath been infinite.*[4]

It has been said that a group of Christians were talking amongst themselves when one of them said: 'How insignificant are the minds of the Muslims? They follow their prophet who was a shepherd of sheep! How can a shepherd of sheep be appropriate for prophethood?' But another one from amongst them replied: 'I swear to God

1 See Abū Nuʿaym, *Ḥilya*, vol. IV, p. 286.

2 Bukhārī 3; Muslim 403; Aḥmad 25,959.

3 Q. V.3.

4 Q. IV.113.

that they are more reasonable than us. God, in His wisdom, allows a prophet to herd unintelligible animals until he does so well, then He moves him from that to caring for a speaking animal. This wisdom is from God and a gradual progression for His servant. We, on the other hand, approached an infant who came forth from a woman who eats, drinks, urinates and cries and said he is our god who created the heavens and earth.' They thereafter stopped [discussing this further with] him.

Thus how can one who has a strong will and has his inadequacies removed from him by God, and is knowledgeable about what leads to bliss and wretchedness, be content with becoming an animal rather than being a king: *Firmly established in the favour of a Mighty King.*[1] In this way, the angels will be in his service entering from all gates [saying]: *Peace be unto you because you have persevered! How excellent this fulfillment is in the Hereafter!*[2]

This perfection is only attained via knowledge, caring for it, and carrying out its obligations. Thus the issue returns again to knowledge and its effects. And only God (Exalted is He) grants success.

The greatest loss and most intense regret is that of a person who is capable of achieving perfection but lets it slip away. Some of the Predecessors have said: 'If the paths to good are many, then those who fail to follow them are the most regretful.' One also said truthfully:

> I did not observe any worse fault done than
> The missed [opportunities] by those otherwise capable of attaining perfection.

Thus it has been established that there is nothing more repugnant for a human than to be heedless of the religious virtues, beneficial types of knowledge and good deeds. Those who are neglectful of all of that are foolish riff-raff. Their lives are not praiseworthy, and when they die they will not be missed. In fact, their absence is a relief for all; the heavens do not cry for them, nor does the earth miss them.

1 Q. LIV.55.
2 Q. XIII.24.

CHAPTER SEVEN

Knowledge Allows One to Protect Oneself from Doubts, Temptations and Evil

[POINT 87: ON DOUBTS, TEMPTATIONS AND OTHER COMPOSITE DISEASES OF THE HEART THAT ARE CAUSED BY IGNORANCE.]

The heart is exposed to two diseases: temptations (*shahawāt*) and doubts (*shubuhāt*). They alternate in coming at it. Once they become entrenched within the heart, it becomes ruined and dead. And only those whom God has cured from these ailments are exempt. God (Exalted is He) has mentioned these two diseases in His Scripture.

As regards to the disease of doubts, which is more destructive to the heart, it is exemplified in His statements regarding the hypocrites: *In their hearts is a disease, and God increaseth their disease;*[1] *And that those in whose hearts there is disease, and disbelievers, may say: What meaneth God by this similitude?*[2] The Exalted also said: *That He may make that which the Devil proposeth a temptation for those in whose hearts is a disease, and those whose hearts are hardened.*[3]

As regards to the disease of temptation it is in His statement: *O ye wives of the Prophet, ye are not like any other women. If ye keep your duty (to God), then be not soft of speech, lest he in whose heart is a disease aspire (to you).*[4] This indicates that they should not soften their words so that they may avoid the desires of those who have wickedness in

1 Q. II.10.
2 Q. LXXIV.31.
3 Q. XXII.53.
4 Q. XXXIII.32.

their hearts and [desire] fornication. It is mentioned that a woman speaking to a foreign man should speak in a harsh and strong manner, and should not soften nor weaken her voice so that any doubts or covetous desires are distanced.

Nonetheless, there are other diseases of the heart, like ostentatiousness (*riyāʾ*), arrogance (*kibr*), pride (*ʿujb*), envy (*ḥasad*), boastfulness (*fakhr*), haughtiness (*khaylāʾ*) and, finally, love of power and reigning over others. This last disease is a composite of both elements of doubts and temptations since it inevitably results from false misconceptions about oneself and vain desires, which then lead to pride, boastfulness, haughtiness and arrogance. These in turn lead to one fancying oneself to be great and superior, and desiring that people should aggrandize and praise one. Ultimately, all of these diseases originate from ignorance and their remedy is knowledge.

When a person who had a skull fracture died after being advised by some of the Companions to wash it, the Prophet (may God bless him and grant him peace) said: 'They killed him! May God kill them! They should have asked if they did not know. The cure of the helpless is to inquire.'[1] Thus the Prophet considered helplessness, which includes both the inability to attain knowledge or to express it, to be a disease which can only be cured by asking the scholars.

Now the diseases of the heart are more difficult to treat than those of the body because, at worst, bodily diseases lead to a person's death, whereas a diseased heart results in a person becoming eternally wretched. It is for this reason that God (Exalted is He) described His Book as a cure for the diseases of the heart. The Exalted said: *O mankind, there hath come unto you an exhortation from your Lord, a balm for that which is in the breasts, a guidance and a mercy for believers.*[2]

The impact of scholars on the heart is like that of doctors on the body. In fact, scholars are the doctors of the heart. Many towns

1 Abū Dāwūd 336; Ibn Māja 572; Ibn ʿAbd al-Barr 526. It is 'sound' according to Albānī (*Ṣaḥīḥ al-Jāmiʿ al-ṣaghīr* 4362).

2 Q. x.57.

dispense without physicians; and a person may live his whole life or most of it and never need a physician. On the other hand, those scholars who are knowledgeable about God and His commandments are the life and spirit of all that exists. We cannot dispense with them for even a moment. Indeed the heart's need for knowledge is greater than the body's need for air.

Moreover, the parallel of knowledge with the heart is like light for an eye, sound for an ear, or speech for the tongue. If such matters do not exist, then it becomes as if the eye is blind, the ear is deaf, or the tongue is mute. Therefore the Sublime characterizes those who are ignorant as blind, deaf and dumb. The Exalted said: *Whoso is blind here will be blind in the Hereafter, and yet further from the road.*[1] Now what is intended here is blindness of the heart in this world. The Exalted also said: *We shall assemble them on the Day of Resurrection on their faces, blind, dumb and deaf; their habitation will be Hell.*[2] Since that was their state in this world, they will be resurrected in that same state.

There is a difference of opinion about the nature of this blindness in the Hereafter. Some have said that it is a blindness of enlightenment, since the Exalted has informed us that the disbelievers will still be able to see on the Day of Resurrection, as they will be able to see the angels and Hellfire. Others have said that it refers to [physical] blindness. The latter is more likely due to the above verses and because of His statement: *He will say: My Lord! Wherefore hast Thou gathered me (hither) blind, when I was wont to see?*[3] This refers to [physical] blindness since the disbeliever was never able to see with enlightenment His [religious] evidences.

Farrā'[4] and others responded to the latter viewpoint by saying that God will resurrect them from their graves to the standing place

1 Q. XVII.72.

2 Q. XVII.97.

3 Q. XX.125.

4 Abū Zakariyya Yaḥyā b. Ziyād al-Farrā' (d. 207/822) was a notable grammarian and author of a grammatical commentary on the Qur'ān, entitled *Maʿānī al-Qur'ān*.

of the resurrection able to see, but they will become blind from there to the Hellfire.

[Point 88: Knowledge allows one to protect oneself from the six ways the Devil tries to corrupt one.]

God (Glory be to Him) in His wisdom has brought to bear an enemy [the Devil] who is knowledgeable about the many pathways that can lead to a person's destruction. The Devil bombards a person with a multitude of evils, and Satan remains resolved and never rests no matter whether the person is awake or asleep.

Without fail, the Devil manages to garner one of six things. First, he ultimately wants to prevent a person from attaining knowledge or faith so as to force him into disbelief. If the Devil achieves that, then he is finished with him and will rest. If he cannot do that, and the person is guided to Islam, then [second] he resolves to make him innovate [a blameworthy practice in the religion]. This is more desirable to the Devil than sinfulness, since one may seek forgiveness from a sin, but not from an innovation as one thinks oneself to be rightly guided. In some narrations, Iblīs says: 'I have destroyed the progeny of Adam by [whispering to] them to sin, but they have ruined my [plans] by asking for forgiveness and by [saying] there is no deity [worthy of worship] but God. Once I saw that, I spread amongst them whims [and blameworthy innovations] such that they sin but do not ask for forgiveness, because they think they are doing good deeds.'[1]

Upon failing, the Devil works to make a person commit major sins, which is the third, or minor sins, the fourth. If he fails to achieve that, then he preoccupies the person with deeds that are less superior, so that he cannot discern the best course of action—this is the fifth. If the Devil is unsuccessful in that, then he will pursue the sixth, which is to charge his followers to harm, curse, slander and falsely

1 Haythamī 17,574. It is 'fabricated' according to Albānī (*Silsilat al-aḥādīth al-ḍaʿīfa wa'l-mawḍūʿa* 5560).

accuse the person of [committing] major sins so as to grieve him, and distract his heart away from pursuing knowledge or having a strong will to carry out [righteous] deeds.

Now how can a person who has no knowledge of these matters protect and guard himself from his enemy, the Devil? Indeed one cannot escape from an enemy except by recognizing his methods and those of his gang, whom he depends on. One must know how to fight against the Devil and what to use against him, as well how to treat one's injuries [if they should occur]. But the ignorant are heedless and blind to this important aspect.

It is for these reasons that the enemy [Iblīs], his nature, as well as that of his followers and their deceptions are mentioned extensively in the Qur'ān. If it were not for this knowledge clarifying matters, no one would have been able to escape from the Devil. Hence salvation can only be attained through knowledge and its fruits.

[Point 89: On heedlessness and laziness being the most significant reasons for preventing one from goodness in this life and the Hereafter.]

The [two] greatest reasons that prevent a person from goodness in this world and bliss in the Hereafter are heedlessness, which is the opposite of knowledge, and laziness, which is the opposite of willpower and resolve. These are the origins for a person's suffering and deprivation.

As for those who are heedless, the Sublime has criticized such people and has forbidden us from being like them or obeying them. The Exalted said: *And be not thou of the neglectful;*[1] *And obey not him whose heart We have made heedless of Our remembrance;*[2] *Already have We urged unto Hell many of the jinn and humankind, having hearts wherewith they understand not, and having eyes wherewith they see not, and having ears wherewith they hear not. These are as the cattle—nay, but they are worse!*

1 Q. VII.205.
2 Q. XVIII.28.

These are the neglectful.[1] Moreover, the Prophet (may God bless him and grant him peace) advised: 'And do not become heedless, such that you forget about the mercy [of God].'[2]

Some of the scholars were asked about the excessive love (*ʿishq*) of bodily forms (*ṣuwar*)[3] and they said that it occurs to those who are heedless of the remembrance of God. Thus God has afflicted them by allowing them to revere others. The Devil finds shelter in a heedless heart. Satan is always trying to tempt with whisperings (*waswās*), but if one remembers God, then the Devil will withdraw (*khannās*).

ʿUrwa b. Ruwaym[4] said that the Messiah (peace be upon him) asked his Lord to see the position of the Devil relative to the offspring of Adam and he saw in a dream: 'Satan was represented as the head of a snake clutching onto a heart. If the servant remembers his Lord, it withdraws, but if one does not, then the snake clutches its head back on the heart.'[5] The Devil is always waiting for a person to become heedless so that he can plant seedlings consisting of whims, temptations or false fancies in his heart, which will in turn cultivate every type of bitter apple or thorn. The Devil will continue to send [those temptations] until one's heart is completely veiled [from any goodness] and is blind to it.

[Turning to] laziness, it brings about loss, neglect and severe regret. It is the opposite of strong will and resolve, which result from knowledge. Anyone who realizes that his perfection and bliss reside in some particular place will always resolutely pursue [knowledge] by using all his means. Everyone seeks perfection and pleasure, but most commit mistakes along the way due to their lack of knowledge.

1 Q. VII.179.

2 Tirmidhī 3583; Aḥmad 27,089. It is 'sound' according to Albānī (*Ṣaḥīḥ al-Jāmiʿ al-ṣaghīr* 4078).

3 This is a technical term that refers to a specific practice and belief, which is particularly prevalent amongst some Sufis.

4 Abū al-Qāsim ʿUrwa b. Ruwaym al-Lakhmī (d. 135/752) was one of the Successors.

5 Abū Nuʿaym, vol. VI, p. 123.

Willpower is preceded by knowledge and conception (*taṣawwur*); thus if the former does not occur, it is largely due to absence of the latter. If a servant is certain that his bliss, salvation and success will result from this pursuit, then why would he allow laziness to overcome him?

For this reason the Prophet (may God bless him and grant him peace) sought refuge with God from laziness: 'O God, I seek refuge with You from distress and grief, from helplessness and laziness, from miserliness and cowardice, from being heavily in debt and from being overcome by men.'[1] Thus he sought protection from eight things, represented in pairs. The harm that afflicts a heart is either due to what has occurred or what will occur; hence the reason for the different pairings [in the *ḥadīth*].

The first pairing is grief (*ḥuzn*) and distress (*hamm*). You could say that grief is due to a harm that has already occurred or one that cannot be repelled, while distress is due to an anticipated harm that one may be able to fend off. Incapacity (*ʿajz*) and laziness (*kasal*) are paired since if a servant fails to attain well being, perfection or pleasure, it is because either he is [truly] incapable or he is capable but is held back due to a lack of willpower, i.e. laziness. And the [lazy] person is more blameworthy than one who is [truly] incapable.

We must consider, though, that some may actually be initially capable of doing something, but then their laziness weakens their willpower to such a degree that it ultimately renders them incapable. As such, they are blameworthy for [both of these] traits in this case. This is the type of incapacity that God has criticized in the *ḥadīth* of the Prophet (may God bless him and grant him peace): 'God is critical of incapacity.'[2] If one is truly powerless, though, then his incapacity is not worthy of blame.

1 Bukhārī 2893; Muslim 6873; Tirmidhī 3484; Abū Dāwūd 1540; Nasāʾī 5464; Aḥmad 12,616.

2 Abū Dāwūd 3627; Aḥmad 23,983; Bayhaqī (*Sunan*) 20,725. It is 'weak' according to Albānī (*Ḍaʿīf al-Jāmiʿ al-ṣaghīr* 1759).

Some knowers (*ʿārifūn*) have said in their wills: 'Avoid laziness and exasperation (*ḍajar*). Laziness prevents one from rising up to carry out noble deeds, while exasperation prevents one from being patient in performing them.' Exasperation arises from laziness and incapacity, so the Prophet did not mention it by name separately in this *ḥadīth*.

Then he mentioned cowardice (*jubn*) and miserliness (*bukhl*), since a servant may be expected to be benevolent with either his wealth or his body. Thus the miserly person prevents his wealth from benefitting others, while the coward prevents his body from doing so. It is thought by many that miserliness necessitates cowardice, as it is not possible to be otherwise, because those who are benevolent by expending their bodies must be also generous with their wealth. What they have claimed though is not necessarily true. Bravery and generosity, and their opposites, are characteristics and natural dispositions (*gharā'iz*) that may be found together in a person. Yet a person may be endowed with one but not the other. People have witnessed others who are audacious, brave and courageous, but are the most miserly of people. This predominantly occurs amongst the Turks. One of them is braver than a lion but more miserly than a dog. Therefore a person may liberally expend his body, yet he is stingy with his wealth, whereby he will even fight to the death to preserve the latter. Such a person would rather sacrifice himself than his wealth. However, some people are benevolent with both themselves and their wealth. Yet others are benevolent with their wealth, but are reluctant to give of themselves. So these are the four types of people that exist.

Finally, the Prophet mentioned being strained under excessive debt (*ḍilʿ al-dayn*) and overcome by men (*ghalabat al-rijāl*), since subjugation of people occurs in [one of] two ways. Legitimate subjugation can happen when one succumbs to excessive debt, while unjust subjugation occurs when one is overpowered by others. May God bless and grant peace to the Prophet, who has been bestowed comprehensive maxims that encompass the treasures of knowledge and wisdom!

To return, heedlessness and laziness, which are the fundamental reasons for one's deprivation, are attributable to lack of knowledge and resolve. Therefore only [one possessed of knowledge and willpower] will attain perfection. People in this regard are divided into four groups. The first group has been blessed with knowledge and firm resolve to perform good deeds—this group is the elite of creation. They are described in the Qur'ān by His statement: *Those who believe and do good works;*[1] *And make mention of Our servants, Abraham, Isaac and Jacob, men of parts and vision;*[2] *Is he who was dead and We have raised him unto life, and set for him a light wherein he walketh among men, as him whose similitude is in utter darkness whence he cannot emerge?*[3] This last verse indicates that it is through life that resolve is attained and through light that knowledge is acquired. At the forefront of this group are the messengers endowed with firm resolve (*ulū al-ʿazm min al-rusul*).

The second group consists of those who have been deprived of both [knowledge and willpower]. They are characterized by His saying: *Thou canst not make the dead to hear, nor canst thou make the deaf to hear (the call when they have turned to flee);*[4] and *Thou canst not reach those who are in the graves.*[5] This group represents the worst of humanity. They fleece others and oppress them.[6] Although they consider themselves to be knowledgeable, their knowledge only extends to apparent [matters] of this worldly life, but they are

1 Q. XVIII.107.

2 Q. XXXVIII.45.

3 Q. VI.122.

4 Q. XXVII.80. The dead are those whose hearts are devoid of knowledge, and thus are spiritually dead. The deaf are those who have no understanding. By extension, these two groups have no ability or resolve to do any good.

5 Q. XXXV.22.

6 Thus they either force others to succumb to excessive debt or they unjustly subjugate people.

heedless of the Hereafter.[1] This harms them [spiritually] and is of no benefit to them. Even though they speak, their speech only emanates out of their desires and ignorance. Even though they may believe, it only includes faith in evil entities that are worshipped or obeyed (*al-jibt wa'l-ṭāghūt*).[2] Even though they may worship, they only worship others besides God who do not harm nor benefit them. Even though they debate, it is only with falsehood to try to weaken the truth.[3] They scheme and plot by night only in a manner displeasing to Him.[4] They may supplicate to God, but they include supplications to other deities, even though they are advised that they do not derive benefit [from such a practice]. If they worship, they are inattentive during their prayers and are ostentatious. They also avoid almsgiving.[5] They may judge but they only desire

1 This is derived from Q. xxx.7: *They know only some appearance of the life of the world, and are heedless of the Hereafter.*

2 This is derived from Q. iv.15: *Hast thou not turned thy vision to those who were given a portion of the Book? They believe in sorcery and evil.* This is per Yusuf Ali's translation, where *jibt* is translated as *sorcery*, which is the interpretation of Ibn ʿAbbās, Shuʿbī, Mujāhid, ʿAtā', and others. Of note, this is the only verse in the Qur'ān where *jibt* occurs, whereas *ṭāghūt* occurs in seven other verses. Pickthall translates *jibt* as *false idols* and *ṭāghūt* as *evil*. Qatāda said that *jibt* refers to Satan, while *ṭāghūt* refers to fortune-tellers. Ibn Masʿūd, Abū al-Ḥasan, and ʿIkrima interpreted *jibt* and *ṭāghūt* in this verse as two people: Ḥuyay b. al-Akhṭab and Kaʿb b. al-Ashraf. *Ṭaghūt* has also been interpreted as idols or Satan or fortune-tellers. It has also been said that *jibt* refers to Satan, while *ṭāghūt* refers to Satan's followers. *Lisān al-ʿArab* (on baheth.info) states that *jibt* and *ṭāghūt* encompass anything worshipped other than God. Some have said they refer to anybody who commands others to disobey God and His Prophet. In conclusion, any evil entity that is worshipped or obeyed is conveyed in the translation rendered above.

3 This is derived from Q. xviii.56: *Those who disbelieve contend with falsehood in order to refute the Truth thereby.*

4 This is derived from Q. iv.108: *He is with them when by night they hold discourse displeasing unto Him.*

5 This is derived from Q. cvii.5–7: *Who are heedless of their prayer; who would be seen (at worship) yet refuse small kindnesses!*

rulings based on the times of [pagan] ignorance.[1] They may write, but they *Write the Book with their hands and then say: This is from God, that they may purchase a small gain therewith. Woe unto them for that their hands have written, and woe unto them for that they earn thereby.*[2] They say: *We are peacemakers only. Are not they indeed the mischief-makers? But they perceive not.*[3]

Although they may appear to be humans, they are devils in reality. The majority of them, if you think about it, are donkeys, dogs or wolves. Without doubt, Baḥtarī's poetry characterizes them well:

> There is nothing left remaining of humanity in
> the majority
> That one can even imagine except their appearances.

Another said:

> Let not beards and appearances deceive you
> Nine tenths of those whom you see are cattle.
> To the lotus tree they are similar:
> Although pretty, it bears no fruit.

Nonetheless, better than all that is the Exalted's statement: *And when thou seest them their figures please thee; and if they speak thou givest ear unto their speech. (They are) as though they were blocks of wood in striped cloaks.*[4] In truth, they are [portrayed] as below:

> Like camels carrying books (*asfār*)[5] they only know of
> The excellence [of those books] that camels know.
> I swear by your lifespan that a camel does not know
> when going back and forth
> With its loads that figs are in the sacks.

And even more emphatic, more succinct, and rhetorically supe-

1 This is derived from Q. v.50: *Is it a judgment of the time of (pagan) ignorance that they are seeking?*

2 Q. ii.79.

3 Q. ii.11–12.

4 Q. lxiii.4.

5 The first line of poetry according to *Lisān al-ʿArab* actually begins: *Zawāmil li'l-ashʿār* ('camels carrying poems').

rior is the statement of the Exalted: *As the similitude of the ass carrying books. Wretched is the similitude of folk who deny the revelations of God. And God guideth not wrongdoing folk.*[1]

In the third group the door of knowledge has been opened but that of resolve has been locked. They occupy the same status as those who are ignorant or are even more evil. In the traceable *ḥadīth* [it is said]: 'Amongst the most punished people by God on the Day of Judgment are scholars who derived no benefit from their knowledge.'[2] It would have been better for these people if they had remained ignorant—then their punishment would have been less. In fact, their knowledge did not result in them attaining anything except evilness and punishment. There is no hope of salvation for someone like this. If someone is lost, it is hoped that he may return to the path once he sees it; but if someone already knows the path yet intentionally deviates away from it, how can it be hoped that he will be guided? The Exalted said: *How shall God guide a people who disbelieved after their belief and (after) they bore witness that the Messenger is true and after clear proofs (of God's sovereignty) had come unto them. And God guideth not wrongdoing folk.*[3]

The fourth group includes those who have been blessed with strong resolve and willpower, but have a lesser share of knowledge and recognition. If such a person is aided to find one who calls to God and His Messenger, and thereafter emulates him, then he will be one of those described by God as: *Whoso obeyeth God and the Messenger, they are with those unto whom God hath shown favour, of the prophets and the truly faithful ones and the martyrs and the righteous. The best of company are they! That is bounty from God, and God sufficeth as Knower.*[4] May God

1 Q. LXII.5.

2 Bayhaqī (*Shuʿab*) 1642; Haythamī 872; Mundhirī 219; Abū Nuʿaym, vol. x, p. 114 (whereby it states: 'The most punished person on the Day of Judgment is an imam who transgresses.'). It is 'very weak' according to Albānī (*Silsilat al-aḥādīth al-ḍaʿīfa* 1634).

3 Q. III.86.

4 Q. IV.69–70.

bless us with His grace and may He not deprive us due to our sins! God is the Most Forgiving and Most Merciful.

[Point 90: A list of characteristics that God has commended in the Qur'ān, which are a result of knowledge, as well as others which are criticized as they are mainly due to ignorance.]

Every characteristic that God has commended the servants with in the Qur'ān is due to knowledge and its consequences, while every one that He has criticized is a result of ignorance and its consequences. He commended them for their faith, which is the apex of knowledge and its core, and for their good deeds, which are the fruits of beneficial knowledge. He has commended them for: having gratitude and patience, hastening to do good deeds, loving Him and fearing Him, having hope and repenting to Him, forbearance, dignity, intelligence, reason, chastity, generosity, and preferring [God and His Messenger's commandments] over their desires, advising His servants and showing mercy to them, kindness, humility to them, forgiving those who harm them and pardoning the perpetrators, expending benevolence to all of them, doing good after making a mistake, enjoining good and forbidding evil, being patient in those circumstances that require patience, being content with their destiny, gentleness with the loyal supporters and strength against their enemies, being true to their promises, fulfilling their oaths, avoiding the ignorant ones, and accepting advice from those giving it. [God also commended them] for certainty, reliance [on Him], tranquility, calmness, perseverance, empathy; being just in statements, actions and characteristics; strength in carrying out His commandments, enlightenment in His religion, carrying out and accomplishing His rights, removing those who bar His cause, calling [others] to Him and His pleasure and to His Paradise, warning others of the inroads of those who are astray, elucidating the paths of seduction and the state of those who follow [to prevent others from falling into it], exhorting others to the truth and to patience, urging others to feed the poor, reverence for their parents, bonding with their relatives, expending salutations to all the believers, in addition to all the other praiseworthy characteristics and pleasing actions that God (Glory be to Him) has bore witness to.

The Exalted said: *Nūn. By the pen and that which they write (therewith), thou art not, for thy Lord's favour unto thee, a madman. And thine verily will be a reward unfailing. And thou art of a tremendous nature.*[1] ᶜĀ'isha (may God be pleased with her) once said after being asked about the character of the Messenger of God (may God bless him and grant him peace): 'His character was the Qur'ān.'[2] The questioner sufficed with that and said: 'I understood from her what I needed to do and that I should not ask about anything more.' These characteristics and other similar ones represent the fruits from the tree of knowledge.

On the other hand, the tree of ignorance simply yields all types of repugnant effects, such as disbelief, corruption, polytheism, injustice, oppression, enmity, apprehension, anxiety, ungratefulness, haste, immaturity, agitation, indecency, obscenity, stinginess and miserliness. For this reason, it is said that miserliness is ignorance combined with a bad opinion of people, which results in cheating them and being arrogant over them. Moreover, [other effects] include boastfulness, haughtiness, pride, ostentatiousness, seeking fame, hypocrisy, lying, breaking promises, harshness with people, taking revenge [without right], doing evil to those who do good, commanding evil and prohibiting the good, and not accepting [good] advice from others.

[Ignorance] also includes loving, attaching hopes or relying on others besides God, preferring their pleasure rather than God's contentment, and submitting to their commands rather than God's commandments. [The ignorant] are moribund when it comes to

1 Q. LXVIII.1–4.

2 Muslim 1739; Abū Dāwūd 1342; Ibn Māja 2333; Nasā'ī 1602; Aḥmad 24,601.

God's rights, yet firmly uphold their own claims. If they are infringed upon, they will become angered and their wrath will not end until they take more revenge than what they are entitled to. But if the inviolable rights of God are violated not even [one bead of] sweat flows from them in anger. They are weak in carrying out religious matters, and they are not enlightened.

In addition, some of the effects [of ignorance] are to call to the Devil's ways and oppress others. They follow their own desires thus preferring temptations over pious deeds. They gossip, ask too many [unnecessary] questions, squander money, bury infant girls, disobey their mothers, cut off their relatives, mistreat their neighbours, and do that which is shameless and dishonourable.

In conclusion, goodness is the fruit harvested from the tree of knowledge, while evil is simply thorns incurred from the tree of ignorance. If the projection of knowledge could be seen by eyesight, its beauty would be better than the sun or the moon, whereas if ignorance could be seen, its appearance would be the most repugnant. Moreover, all [spiritual] goodness in the world is a consequence of the knowledge that the messengers have conveyed. The same can be said of all goodness that occurs until the Hour and afterwards on the Day of Resurrection. On the other hand, any evil or mischief that has occurred in this world until the Hour, and afterwards on the Day of Resurrection, is caused by violating what was conveyed by the messengers.

The intellect, through its rationality, directs one to obey the messengers. The intellect directs the heart, body and soul to submit to the [messengers] and follow God's commandments. God (Glory be to Him) has praised the intellect and those who are rational in many places in His Book, while He has criticized those who lack intelligence and informed us that they are the denizens of Hellfire. The intellect is the instrument to acquire all knowledge, the method by which one differentiates truth from falsehood and good from bad, and how one recognizes what takes precedence over another. If one's intellect is not utilized to derive the majority of one's characteristics, thus allowing one to be good, then evilness will predominate and one will become ruined.

There are two types of intelligence: the first is innate, while the other is acquired. If a servant has both, it is from the grace of God Who bestows it upon whom He wills. One thus becomes upright and steeped in all types of bliss. On the other hand, if a person is deprived of either one of them, then a grazing animal is in a better state than him. Some people give preference to the possessor of the innate intellect, while others to the one with an acquired intellect. This issue is decided by realizing that the possessor of the innate intellect who lacks knowledge and experience will be undermined by many inadequacies. He will refrain and desist from taking advantage of opportunities because of the absence of an acquired intellect. But one who only has an acquired intellect is undermined by his audacity. His knowledge of opportunities and the means to them lead him to impulsively undertake them, while his innate intellect cannot hold him back.

If the innate intellect is blessed with an [acquired] religious intellect, derived from the lamp of prophethood, [then one can become blissful]. But if the acquired intellect is a worldly one filled with hypocrisy, [then one will become wretched]. The latter imagine themselves to [be good], but they are only deluded. They only see the intellect as [the means] to please people, remain safe, and gain their affection and love even though there is no way they can achieve that. Furthermore, they prefer relaxation and indifference, instead of enduring the stress of the burdens for God's sake, allying with others only for His sake, and having enmity only for His sake. Although [being a hypocrite] may be more secure for this person in the short term, it will ultimately bring about his ruin in the long term. Moreover, a person has not tasted the sweetness of faith until he allies himself [with the believers] and shows enmity towards [the disbelievers] only for God's sake. Thus the true intellect is that which leads one to seek the contentment of God and His Messenger. Only God grants success and support.

In a traceable *ḥadīth* [it is said]: 'God inspired an Israelite prophet to tell a specific worshipper: "Your asceticism of this world was in order to expedite relaxation and your solitude allowed you to acquire glory, but you have failed to do something that I have obligated upon you." The worshipper then said: "What did You oblige me to do?" God subsequently said [through the prophet]: "To ally yourself with a loyal supporter of Mine or to show enmity against an enemy of Mine."'[1] It has also been mentioned that God inspired Gabriel to destroy such-and-such a town upon which [Gabriel] said: 'My Lord, there is so-and-so worshipper there.' God replied: 'Begin with him as his face never showed anger (*lam yatamaʿʿar*) for My sake, not even for one moment.'[2]

1 Abū Nuʿaym, vol. x, p. 316; al-Khaṭīb al-Baghdādī (*Tārīkh*) 1014. It is 'weak' according to Albānī (*Silsilat al-aḥādīth al-ḍaʿīfa* 3337).

2 Tabrīzī 5152. It is 'very weak' according to Albānī (*Silsilat al-aḥādīth al-ḍaʿīfa* 1904).

CHAPTER EIGHT

The Superiority of Knowledge over Waging Battle for His Sake and over Supererogatory Deeds

[POINT 91: THE GATHERINGS OF REMEMBRANCE ARE JOINED BY THE ANGELS.]

Ibn ʿUmar narrated that the Prophet (may God bless him and grant him peace) said: 'Feast when you pass by the gardens of Paradise.' They said: 'And what are the gardens of Paradise?' He replied: 'They are the gatherings of remembrance. God has angels who are continually moving to seek out the gatherings of remembrance; when they arrive, they line up.'[1] ʿAṭā' said: 'The assemblies of remembrance are those where there is [a discussion of] what is permitted and what is forbidden, how to buy and sell, and [the legal rulings of] fasting, prayer, almsgiving, marriage and divorce, and pilgrimage.' This was also mentioned by Khaṭīb[2] in his book *al-Faqīh wa'l-mutafaqqih*.

[POINTS 92-96: POSSESSING FIQH IS BETTER THAN WORSHIP.]

92. Ibn ʿUmar narrated a traceable tradition: 'Attending an assembly of *fiqh* is better than worshipping for sixty years.'[3]

1 Tirmidhī 3510; Aḥmad 12,523; Abū Nuʿaym, vol. VI, p. 268; Haythamī 521; al-Khaṭīb al-Baghdādī (*Faqīh*), vol. I, p. 93. It is 'sound' according to Albānī (*Silsilat al-aḥādīth al-ṣaḥīḥa* 2562).

2 Abū Bakr Aḥmad b. ʿAlī, known as al-Khaṭīb al-Baghdādī (d. 463/1071), was a great traditionist, jurist and historian. He is famous for writing *Tārīkh Baghdād* as well as *Faqīh wa'l-mutafaqqih*.

3 Al-Khaṭīb al-Baghdādī (*Faqīh*), vol. I, p. 97; Zabīdī, vol. V, p. 173.

93. ʿAbd al-Raḥmān b. ʿAwf[1] narrated a traceable tradition: 'Having even a meagre understanding of *fiqh* is better than much worship.'[2]
94. Anas narrated a traceable tradition: 'The jurist is considered by God to be superior to a thousand worshippers.'[3] It appears that these[4] are all statements of the Companions and those who came after them.
95. Ibn ʿUmar also narrated [that the Prophet said]: 'The best type of worship is through *fiqh*.'[5]
96. Nāfiʿ[6] related that Ibn ʿUmar narrated a traceable tradition: 'God is best worshipped utilizing *fiqh* of the religion.'[7]

[Points 97–103: Statements from the Companions and Successors that scholarship and fiqh are better than supererogatory worship.]

97. Khaṭīb also narrated that ʿAlī said: 'The scholar has a greater reward than someone who is fasting, praying at night and fighting for the sake of God.'[8]

1 ʿAbd al-Raḥmān b. ʿAwf (d. 31/652) was one of the first eight people to become Muslim in Mecca. His wealth and generosity were well known. He was one of ten Companions promised Paradise by the Prophet (may God bless him and grant him peace).

2 Al-Khaṭīb al-Baghdādī (*Faqīh*), vol. I, p. 98; Haythamī 481 (who said it is 'very weak'); al-Muttaqī al-Hindī 28,921.

3 Al-Khaṭīb al-Baghdādī (*Faqīh*), vol. I, p. 105.

4 This is a reference to numbers 92–94.

5 Al-Khaṭīb al-Baghdādī (*Faqīh*), vol. I, p. 114; Haythamī 479; Mundhirī 2691; al-Muttaqī al-Hindī 28,763. It is 'weak' according to Albānī (*Ḍaʿīf al-Jāmiʿ al-ṣaghīr* 1024).

6 Nāfiʿ, the *mawlā* of Ibn ʿUmar (d. 117/735), was a prominent transmitter of *ḥadīth*.

7 Al-Khaṭīb al-Baghdādī (*Faqīh*), vol. I, p. 124; Haythamī 487; al-Muttaqī al-Hindī 28,811; Ibn ʿAbd al-Barr 125. It is 'fabricated' according to Albānī (*Silsilat al-aḥādīth al-ḍaʿīfa* 4461).

8 Al-Khaṭīb al-Baghdādī (*Faqīh*), vol. II, p. 197.

98. It has been reported that Abū Hurayra and Abū Dharr[1] both said: 'It is more beloved for us to learn a branch of knowledge than to pray one thousand supererogatory prayers. It is also more beloved to me to then teach that branch of knowledge, whether or not others apply it, than to pray one hundred supererogatory prayers.'[2] They also said: 'We heard the Messenger of God (may God bless him and grant him peace) say: "If the student of knowledge dies while he is in that state [of pursuing knowledge], he dies a martyr."'[3] I [Ibn al-Qayyim] state that this statement is corroborated by a previously mentioned *ḥadīth* narrated by Anas: 'Whoever goes out to seek knowledge, he remains in God's cause until he returns.'[4]

99. Abū Hurayra said: 'It is more beloved to me to implement something that I know regarding what is commanded or forbidden than to wage seventy battles for the sake of God.'[5] If this is a sound attribution, then it means that it is more beloved to him than waging seventy battles without knowledge. In truth, deeds done without knowledge can be a source of great corruption. Alternatively, he could have intended that because he taught this knowledge to others, he would obtain a reward similar to those who act according to it until the Day of Resurrection. And such [a reward] does not occur from waging battle alone.

100. Khaṭīb reported that Abū al-Dardā' said: 'Discussing knowledge for an hour is better than praying for a whole night.'[6]

1 Abū Dharr Jundub b. Junāda b. Sufyān al-Ghifārī (d. 32/652) was one of the first five people to accept Islam. He subsequently conveyed Islam to his tribe Ghifār whereupon half of them became Muslim. The other half accepted Islam with the coming of the Prophet. He was well known for his extensive knowledge.

2 Ibn ʿAbd al-Barr 115.

3 Al-Khaṭīb al-Baghdādī (*Faqīh*), vol. 1, p. 101; Haythamī 508; Ibn ʿAbd al-Barr 582; Zabīdī, vol. 1, p. 97. It is 'very weak' according to Albānī (*Silsilat al-aḥādīth al-ḍaʿīfa* 2126).

4 Tirmidhī 2647. It is 'weak' according to Albānī (*Ḍaʿīf al-Jāmiʿ al-ṣaghīr* 5570).

5 Al-Khaṭīb al-Baghdādī (*Faqīh*), vol. 1, p. 102; Zabīdī, vol. 1, p. 97.

6 Al-Khaṭīb al-Baghdādī (*Faqīh*), vol. 1, p. 102.

101. Khaṭīb also reported that Ḥasan said: 'It is more beloved to me to learn a branch of knowledge and teach it to another Muslim than being given the world to use for the sake of God.'[1]
102. Makḥūl[2] said: 'God is best worshipped by utilizing *fiqh*.'
103. Saʿīd b. al-Musayyab[3] said: 'Worshipping God is not solely achieved by fasting and praying, rather it is through *fiqh* of His religion.' This statement indicates two things: first of all, [worshipping God] does not occur through fasting and praying if they are devoid of knowledge, as it is only through *fiqh* that one knows how to fast and pray. Secondly, fasting and prayer are not the sole components of religion; rather, *fiqh* of His religion is one of the best means by which one can worship Him.

[POINTS 104–107: THE SCHOLARS AND JURISTS OCCUPY THE CLOSEST LEVEL TO THAT OF THE PROPHETS.]

104. Isḥāq b. ʿAbd Allāh b. Abī Farwa[4] said: 'The closest people to the level of prophethood are the scholars and warriors.' The scholars point out to people what the messengers have conveyed. A discussion has already preceded as to whether the scholar or the martyr is superior.
105. Sufyān b. ʿUyayna said: 'God considers the highest rank to be occupied by those who are in between Him and His servants [i.e. they convey the message]. They are the messengers and scholars.'
106. Muḥammad b. Shihāb al-Zuhrī[5] said: 'God is best worshipped

1 Ibid., vol. 1, p. 102.

2 Abū ʿAbd Allāh Makḥūl al-Azdī (d. 113/731) was one of the prominent Successors. He lived in Damascus.

3 Saʿīd b. al-Musayyab (d. 96/715) was one of the prominent Successors. He famously refused to marry his daughter (born out of his marriage to one of Abū Hurayra's daughters) to the son of the Caliph ʿAbd al-Malik and was punished for that. He lived until the Caliphate of ʿUmar b. ʿAbd al-ʿAzīz.

4 Isḥāq b. ʿAbd Allāh b. Abī Farwa (d. 144/762) was a *mawlā* of the family of ʿUthmān b. ʿAffān.

5 Muḥammad b. Muslim b. ʿUbayd Allāh b. Shihāb al-Zuhrī (d. 124/742) was one of the prominent Successors. He was a pivotal scholar and narrator of *ḥadīth*.

by utilizing *fiqh*.' These and other similar statements indicate that seeking *fiqh* of the religion is itself [a form of] worship.

107. Sahl b. ʿAbd Allāh al-Tustarī[1] said: 'Whoever wants to look upon the assemblies of the prophets should look to those of the scholars.' This is because the scholars are the successors of the prophets in their communities and the heirs of their knowledge.

[Point 108: Narrations regarding the superiority of knowledge over supererogatory prayers and waging battle.]

Many of the imams have clearly stated that pursuing knowledge is the best deed one can do. Shāfiʿī said: 'There is nothing that is better, after performing the obligations, than pursuing knowledge.' Sufyān al-Thawrī and the followers of the Ḥanafī school have reported that Abū Ḥanīfa said something similar.

As for Imam Aḥmad, there are three narrations [from him on the matter]: one of them is that knowledge is the best. He was asked: 'What is more beloved to you: to sit at night writing [*ḥadīth*s] or to pray the supererogatory prayers?' He replied: 'By writing you learn the precepts of your religion, and therefore it is more beloved to me.' Khallāl[2] mentioned in his book *al-ʿUlūm* many reports [from Imam

1 Abū Muḥammad Sahl b. ʿAbd Allāh al-Tustarī (d. 283/896) was a student of Dhū al-Nūn al-Miṣrī and a Sufi ascetic. He also wrote an exegesis entitled *Tafsīr al-Qurʾān al-ʿaẓīm* or *Tafsīr al-Tustarī*, which is considered to be the earliest extant Sufi commentary attributed to a single author.

2 Abū Bakr Aḥmad b. Muḥammad b. Hārūn b. Yazīd al-Baghdādī, better known as Khallāl (d. 311/923), was a prominent student of Imam Aḥmad who compiled the latter's jurisprudence in twenty volumes, entitled *al-Jāmiʿ li-ʿulūm Aḥmad b. Ḥanbal*.

Aḥmad stating] that knowledge is superior.[1]

The second narration is that [Imam Aḥmad] felt that, after the obligations, the supererogatory prayers are best, as the Prophet (may God bless him and grant him peace) said: 'Know that your best deeds are your prayers.'[2] In addition, after Abū Dharr asked him about prayer, the Prophet said: 'It is the highest objective.'[3] The Prophet also advised whoever asked to accompany him in Paradise: 'Increase your prostrations,'[4] that is, [increase your] prayers. Likewise, the Prophet said: 'Multiply your prostrations since every prostration you perform to God results in God elevating your level and absolving you of a sin.'[5]

The third narration is that [Aḥmad preferred the superiority of] waging battle, as he said: 'There is no equal to waging battle and only a few can endure it.'

As regards [to the opinion of] Mālik, Ibn al-Qāsim said that he heard Mālik saying: 'A group of people sought worship but neglected knowledge; thus they fought against the Community of Muḥammad with their swords. Had they sought knowledge, it

1 Ibn al-Qayyim mentions in a subsequent section: 'Isḥāq b. Manṣūr [mentioned] in his book that he asked Aḥmad b. Ḥanbal: "What type of knowledge did you mean when you said 'Studying knowledge for part of the night is more beloved to me than praying it?'" [Imām Aḥmad] replied: "Any knowledge which is beneficial to the Muslims in their religious matters." I asked: "Do you mean [*fiqh* of] ablution, prayer, fasting, pilgrimage, laws about divorce, and likewise?" He replied yes. Isḥāq [b. Manṣūr] said that Isḥāq b. Rāhawayh added: "The reality is what Aḥmad has mentioned."' Ibn ʿAbd al-Barr 108. See Ibn al-Qayyim, *Miftāḥ*, p. 212. Isḥāq b. Manṣūr al-Kawsaj (d. 251/865) was a Ḥanbalī from Khorasan. He wrote *Kitāb al-masāʾil ʿan-imāmay ahl al-Ḥadīth: Aḥmad b. Ḥanbal wa-Isḥāq b. Rāhawayh*. Isḥāq b. Ibrāhīm b. Mukhlid al-Ḥanẓalī, known as Isḥāq b. Rāhawayh (d. 238/853), was a prominent traditionist and scholar from Khorasan. He was a contemporary of Aḥmad b. Ḥanbal and one of the teachers of Bukhārī.

2 Ibn Māja 277; Aḥmad 22,436. It is 'authentic' according to Albānī (*Ṣaḥīḥ al-Jāmiʿ al-ṣaghīr* 952).

3 Aḥmad 21,546. It is 'sound' according to Albānī (*Ṣaḥīḥ al-Jāmiʿ al-ṣaghīr* 3870).

4 Muslim 1094; Abū Dāwūd 1320; Nasāʾī 1138.

5 Muslim 1093; Ibn Māja 1422; Aḥmad 22,377.

would have barred them from that.' Mālik also reported: 'Abū Mūsa al-Ashʿarī wrote to ʿUmar b. al-Khaṭṭāb that a number of people had memorized the Qur'ān, so ʿUmar wrote back to him to allocate [some money] from the treasury for them. The next year he wrote back that even more had memorized the Qur'ān. ʿUmar responded by writing back to remove them from the accounting books of the treasury. He was afraid that they would rush to memorize the Qur'ān without attaining a deep understanding [of the meaning of what they had memorized], and would thus interpret it incorrectly.' Ibn Wahb said: 'I was with Mālik b. Anas when I put aside my notebook and stood up to pray [a supererogatory prayer]. He then said: "What you have stood up for is not superior to what you have left."'[1]

Our Shaykh [Ibn Taymiyya] said: 'Each one of the Imams debated whether prayer, knowledge or waging battle is superior. ʿUmar b. al-Khaṭṭāb (may God be pleased with him) referred to them when he said: "If it were not for three [matters], I would not have liked to remain alive in this world: holding [arms] or preparing an army for God's sake, enduring the night [in prayer], and sitting amongst others to have the most pleasant discussions just like one would select the most delicious dates."' Thus the first is fighting, the second is praying at night and the third is discussing knowledge. The Companions of the Prophet, due to their perfection, fulfilled all three of these, but those after them could not accomplish [all three together].

[Point 109: Further ḥadīths and statements from the Companions regarding the superiority of knowledge over supererogatory deeds.]

Abū Nuʿaym and others related from some of the Companions that the Messenger of God (may God bless him and grant him peace) said: 'Knowledge is superior to supererogatory deeds. The highest reli-

1 Ibn ʿAbd al-Barr 116.

gious objective is piety.'[1] This [report] provides the definitive answer to the question. Now if the type of knowledge and the deed are both supererogatory and voluntary, then the supererogatory types of knowledge are better than those deeds of worship. This is because the benefit of knowledge extends beyond the person himself to others, whereas worshipping only benefits that specific person alone. In addition, the benefit of one's knowledge carries on beyond one's death, whereas that of worshipping ceases [in such a case].

[Point 110: A statement by Muᶜādh b. Jabal on the greatness of knowledge and that it encompasses all types of good deeds.]

Muᶜādh b. Jabal (may God be pleased with him) said:

> Acquiring knowledge for God's sake is piety (*khashya*), pursuing it is [a form of] worship (*ᶜibāda*), studying it represents glorification [of God] (*tasbīḥ*), seeking it out is [a form of] striving (*jihād*), teaching it to those who are unaware is charity (*ṣadaqa*), and expending it for one's family is a pious deed (*qurba*). God is only recognized and worshipped through [knowledge]; and one can only know what is permissible or forbidden and establish ties with relatives through it. It is also one's companion when one is alone. It guides one to prosperity (*sarrā'*) and supports one in times of hardship (*ḍarrā'*), aids one's friends, and allows one to become a friend to strangers. It is a luminary along the path to Paradise. Through it God elevates some people, thus making them leaders and guides to what is good, who are to be emulated and well regarded. The angels wish to befriend and anoint them with their wings. Everything, whether living or not, will ask for them to be forgiven, including the fish of the sea, the predatory beasts

1 Ḥākim, 317; Abū Nuᶜaym, vol. II, p. 211; Haythamī 478; al-Muttaqī al-Hindī 28,915. It is 'authentic' according to Albānī (*Ṣaḥīḥ al-Jāmiᶜ al-ṣaghīr* 4214).

> and cattle, the heavens and the stars. Knowledge enlivens the heart, gives light to the eyes and strength to the body. Therefore it prevents one from becoming ignorant, blind or weak. It allows the servant to reach the highest ranks of the righteous and elite. Contemplating what one knows is tantamount to fasting and studying it is like praying at night. It leads to good deeds and they follow it. The blissful ones are inspired with it, whereas the wretched are forbidden from attaining it.[1]

This tradition is well known to have been said by Muᶜādh. Abū Nuᶜaym reported it in his *Muᶜjam* [*Ḥilya*] as a *ḥadīth* narrated by Muᶜādh traceable to the Prophet (may God bless him and grant him peace). However, it is not authentically [attributable to the Prophet]; but it is adequately affirmed as a saying of Muᶜādh.

[Point 111: The revival of Islam occurs through knowledge.]

The Messenger of God (may God bless him and grant him peace) is reported to have said: 'Whoever dies while pursuing knowledge so as to revive Islam will only be separated from the prophets due to the latter's status of prophethood.'[2] Even though its chain of narration is not sound, the meaning is not far from being correct. This is because whoever pursues knowledge so that he may revive Islam is one of the truly faithful ones, and therefore his level follows that of the prophets.

[Point 112: Knowledge is the good (ḥasana) referred to in the verse: Our Lord! Give unto us in the world that which is good.]

Ḥasan [al-Baṣrī] interpreted *good* in the statement of the Exalted,

1 Abū Nuᶜaym, vol. 1, p. 238.

2 Ibn ᶜAbd al-Barr 219; al-Muttaqī al-Hindī 28,829; Dārimī 336. It is 'weak' according to Albānī (*Mishkāt* 249).

Our Lord! Give unto us in the world that which is good, as referring to knowledge and worship, and *in the Hereafter that which is good*[1] as referring to Paradise. This is one of the best interpretations. The most eminent type of righteousness in this world is beneficial knowledge and pious deeds.

[Points 113–114: Further statements regarding the superiority of knowledge over waging battle and supererogatory deeds.]

113. Ibn Masʿūd said: 'Take possession of knowledge before it is lifted away. This occurs when the scholars die. I swear [by God] in Whose hands is my soul that those who have been martyred in the path of God would wish to be resurrected by God as scholars due to the favours that the latter will receive. No one is born a scholar; but rather knowledge is [attained] by learning.'

114. Ibn ʿAbbās, Abū Hurayra and Aḥmad b. Ḥanbal all said: 'Discussing knowledge for part of the night is more beloved to us than staying up to pray.'

[Point 115: God protects those who pursue knowledge and will invite them to make amends if they sin.]

ʿUmar (may God be pleased with him) said: 'O people, acquire knowledge as God (Glory be to Him) has a cloak loved by Him that He uses to gown whoever pursues knowledge. But if one sins, God invites him to make amends (*yastaʿtibuh*) so as to not rid him of His cloak, and to prevent him from dying [with that sin].'[2] The meaning of God's *istiʿtāb* is that He invites His servant to make amends. Once one repents, asks for forgiveness, returns [to God] and requests the Lord's contentment (*aʿtaba Rabbah*), God withdraws His rebuke from him.

When an earthquake hit Kufa, Ibn Masʿūd said: 'Your Lord is inviting you to make amends (*yastaʿtibukum*), so request His con-

1 Q. II.201.

2 Ibn ʿAbd al-Barr 300.

tentment and make amends (*aʿtibūh*).' This type of *istiʿtāb* is negated by the Sublime in the Hereafter: *Therefor this day they come not forth from thence, nor can they make amends.*[1] This means that He will not invite them to request that He remove His rebuke from them. It is only withdrawn if repentance occurs, but they cannot do so in the Hereafter.

The Exalted also said: *And though they are resigned, yet the Fire is still their home; and if they ask for favour* (*yastaʿtibū*), *yet they are not of those unto whom favour can be shown* (*muʿtabīn*).[2] The meaning of this verse is that they will not be invited to make amends in the Hereafter. Also the disbelievers are not the type of people who will be allowed to have His rebuke withdrawn from them.

[Points 116–119: A further discussion regarding the superiority of a scholar over a worshipper, and that there is no benefit to one's existence if one does not continually increase in knowledge.]

116. ʿUmar (may God be pleased with him) said: 'The death of a thousand worshippers is less significant than the death of a single scholar enlightened with the knowledge of what is permitted by God and what is forbidden.'[3] The scholar, because of his knowledge and right guidance, destroys all that Iblīs tries to build. On the other hand, the worshipper's benefit is limited to himself.

117. Some of the Predecessors said: 'If a day comes upon me in which I do not increase my knowledge in a manner that brings me closer to God, then I have derived no benefit from the sun's rising that day.' Others said: 'If a day passes by but I do not gain any guidance or knowledge, then it is like I was not alive that day.'

118. Some of the Predecessors said: 'Faith is naked but its clothes

1 Q. XLV.35.
2 Q. XLI.24.
3 Ibn ʿAbd al-Barr 126.

are piety, its adornments are timidity and its effects are knowledge.'

119. It has been said in some reports: 'The scholar and the worshipper are separated by one hundred levels, and between each is the distance a race horse travels in seventy years.'

[POINT 120–122: GOD FORGIVES THE SCHOLARS WHO HAVE PURSUED KNOWLEDGE FOR HIS SAKE; BUT THOSE WHO PURSUE IT FOR WORLDLY GAIN ARE DEEMED TO BE MOST VILE.]

120. Ḥarb[1] reported in his *Masā'il* a tradition traceable to the Prophet (may God bless him and grant him peace): 'God (Exalted is He) will gather the scholars on the Day of Resurrection and say: "O community of scholars, I have only endowed you with My knowledge because I knew of your [righteousness]. I have not bestowed you with My knowledge to punish you. Therefore go forth as I have forgiven you."'[2]

121. Ibn al-Mubārak was asked: 'Who are the [real] people?' He replied: 'The scholars.' They asked: 'Who are the kings?' He replied: 'The ascetics.' They asked: 'Then who are the vile people?' He stated: 'Those who use the religion to enrich themselves.'[3]

122. Those who have attained knowledge will not be harmed by whatever eludes them. It is one of the greatest endowments and gifts. But if knowledge eludes one, one will never benefit from any fortune one acquires. Instead it will result in ill effects for him and be a cause for his ruin. Some of the Predecessors said: 'What can one gain if knowledge eludes one, and what escapes one if one has attained knowledge?'

1 Abū Muḥammad Ḥarb b. Ismāʿīl b. Khalaf al-Kirmānī (d. 280/893) was traditionist and Ḥanbalī scholar. His book *al-Masā'il* encompasses the viewpoints of Imam Aḥmad b. Ḥanbal and Isḥāq b. Rāhawayh, whom Ḥarb encountered directly. Only sections of it remain preserved and published. The above tradition is not present within what is extant. Ḥarb also wrote *Kitāb al-Sunna*, which has been published.

2 Haythamī 528. It is 'fabricated' according to Albānī (*Ḍaʿīf al-Targhīb* 62).

3 Abū Nuʿaym, vol. VIII, p. 167.

[Point 123: The heart dies if it does not pursue knowledge and wisdom.]

One of the knowers said: 'Does not an ill person die if food, drink and medicine are withheld from him?' It was said yes. They continued: 'Similarly, the heart will die if knowledge and wisdom are withheld from it for three days.' They have spoken the truth. If the heart is deprived of knowledge it dies, but one may not feel the death of the heart. One who is intoxicated and whose mind is incoherent experiences something similar.

Likewise, the senses of one who loves [excessively] or one who is meditating may become numb to a wound sustained while in that state. However, once he awakens [from that state], he will realize his pain. Similarly, once a person's death releases him from the burdens of this world and its distractions, then he will be able to clearly recognize his loss and ruin.

> Will you not awaken as the end is near?
> Will you not recognize that your heart is intoxicated?
> You will only awaken when the veil is lifted away.
> You will only remember this when reminders will be of no benefit to you.

So they will only realize that their ignorance was darkness once the veil is lifted away; what is hidden and concealed becomes known, secrets are laid bare, the dead are resurrected and what is in their hearts is retrieved. Furthermore, those who remained idle despite possessing knowledge will only experience regret.

[Points 124–126: Further statements by Abū al-Dardā'.]

124. Abū al-Dardā' said: 'Whoever thinks that seeking out knowledge is not [a form of] striving (*jihād*) has a deficient intellect and opinion.'[1]

125. Abū al-Dardā' also said: 'Learning one matter is more beloved to me than standing the night in prayer.'

1 Ibn ʿAbd al-Barr 159.

126. Abū al-Dardā' also said: 'The scholars and students both share in the reward, while the remainder of people are riff-raff devoid of goodness.'[1]

[POINT 127: PURSUING KNOWLEDGE IS LIKE WAGING BATTLE IN THE PATH OF GOD.]

Abū Hurayra narrated that he heard the Messenger of God (may God bless him and grant him peace) say: 'Whoever enters this mosque of ours to learn goodness or to teach it is like one who battles in the path of God. And whoever enters it otherwise is like an onlooker upon that which does not pertain to him.'[2]

[POINT 128: GOD PROTECTS THOSE WHO TAKE PART IN GATHERINGS OF KNOWLEDGE.]

Three men approached the Messenger (may God bless him and grant him peace) while he was sitting in a gathering [of knowledge]. One of them shunned [the gathering], another was timid and sat behind them, while the third sat in an opening in the circle. The Prophet (may God bless him and grant him peace) then said: 'One of them sought refuge with God so God protected him, while another was timid so God accepted (*istaḥyā*) him [and did not punish him], but the last shunned and thus God shunned him.'[3] Had there been no benefit to the student of knowledge except that God protects him and does not shun him, then that would have been sufficient.

1 Ibn ʿAbd al-Barr 133.

2 Aḥmad 8603; Ḥākim 310; al-Muttaqī al-Hindī 28,857. It is 'sound' according to Albānī (*al-Taʿlīqāt al-ḥisān* 87).

3 Bukhārī 66; Muslim 2176; Tirmidhī 2724.

CHAPTER NINE

An Exposition of a Tradition by ʿAlī Discussing the Characteristics of the True Scholars and Students of Knowledge

[POINT 129: AN EXPOSITION OF A WELL-KNOWN TRADITION BY ʿALĪ (MAY GOD ENNOBLE HIS FACE) REGARDING THE CHARACTERISTICS OF THE TRUE SCHOLARS AND STUDENTS OF KNOWLEDGE.]

Kumayl b. Ziyād al-Nakhaʿī[1] reported that ʿAlī b. Abī Ṭālib (may God be pleased with him) took him by his hand to a section of the cemetery. When it was dawn [ʿAlī] took deep breaths and said:

> O Kumayl b. Ziyād, hearts are like containers and the best of them have the most capacity. Memorize what I am telling you. People are divided into three classes: scholars of the Lord (*rabbānī*), students on the path of salvation, and finally riff-raff and foolish simpletons. The [last of these] follow any shepherd [who calls them], sway [wherever] any wind [blows], are not enlightened by the light of knowledge, nor do they seek refuge in a strong fortress.
>
> Knowledge is better than wealth since knowledge preserves you while you must work to protect wealth. Knowledge grows with expenditure—and in another nar-

1 Kumayl b. Ziyād al-Nakhaʿī (d. 82/701) was born in Yemen, and accepted Islam at the hands of ʿAlī. He later became a loyal supporter of ʿAlī despite all of the tribulations that occurred during the latter's Caliphate. Both Kumayl and Saʿīd b. Jubayr (d. 95/714) were ultimately martyred by Ḥajjāj after the Battle of al-Jamājum.

ration 'with good deeds'—while money decreases with spending. Knowledge judges upon other things, while wealth is judged. Love of knowledge is [part of] the creed that one must profess.

Knowledge earns obedience for the scholar during his lifetime and good remembrance after his death, while any benefit resulting from money disappears once it vanishes. Those who hoard wealth are [spiritually] dead, even if they are still alive [in this world], whereas scholars remain [spiritually] alive for the remainder of eternity. Although their [bodily] selves have ceased to exist, their embodiment exists within the hearts.

I promise you that here is knowledge—and he signalled to his chest. Oh, if only I could allot it to those who would uphold it! Instead it has fallen upon untrustworthy people who have hastily gathered it in order to use this religion as an instrument for their worldly affairs. [First, there are] those who use the evidences of God and His blessings to overrule His Book and rise above His creation. [Second, there are] those who yield [blindly] to the true scholars; however, they are not enlightened enough to revive (*iḥyā'*) [the religion], so the slightest uncertainty (*shakk*) or doubt (*shubha*) will pierce (*yanqadiḥ*) their hearts and never subside. [Third, there are] those who are insatiably preoccupied (*manhūm*) with their pleasures and are docile to their temptations. [Fourth, there are] those who are seduced with gathering and hoarding wealth. All of these types are excluded from being callers to this religion; and they are instead more like grazing cattle.

Knowledge fades away with the death of those who uphold it. Yet by the will of God this earth will not be devoid of [scholars] who remain steadfast for God's sake and convey His evidences. In that manner, they prevent the evidences and signs of God from falling into disuse. They are the least in number, but they occupy the greatest rank in God's sight. God defends His evidences by using them; they convey them to their colleagues and peers, and plant them in their hearts. This knowledge allows them to charge forth [and understand] the realities of the matter. It has also allowed them to find [the path] easily manageable, whereas the wanton (*mutrafūn*) find it rugged and difficult. They feel comfort [while on this path], while the ignorant ones feel loneliness. These [scholars] have bodies that are in this world, but their spirits are attached to the heavenly congregation. They are the viceroys of God on His earth and His callers to His religion. I promise you that I have a longing to see them. I ask God to forgive both you and me. If you want, you may leave now.[1]

Abū Bakr al-Khaṭīb [al-Baghdādī] said: 'This is a beautiful tradition. It has some of the best meanings and it is the most eloquent. The Emir of the Believers' division of people in the beginning is entirely correct. A person is not exempt from being included in one of the three groups he mentioned. They can either be scholars or students if they are of a perfect intellect and have no deficiencies. Otherwise, they can only be considered heedless of knowledge and its pursuit.'

We will now allude to some of the lessons present in this tradition. ʿAlī's statement (may God be pleased with him) 'Hearts are like containers' compares the heart to a container (*wiʿā'*), vessel (*inā'*) or valley (*wādī*). It can be a container for either good or evil. In some reports it is stated: 'God has vessels on this earth, which are the hearts. The best of them are the most compassionate, strongest and purest.' Some of the Predecessors said: 'The hearts of the righteous are ebullient with goodness, while the hearts of the wicked boil with wickedness.'

1 Abū Nuʿaym, vol. 1, pp. 79–80; al-Khaṭīb al-Baghdādī (*Faqīh*), vol. 1, p. 182.

The Exalted said: *He sendeth down water from the sky, so that valleys flow according to their measure.*[1] Thus God likened knowledge to water that falls from the sky and He likened hearts to valleys. A big heart will hold a vast amount of knowledge like a large valley will contain a vast amount of water, whereas a deprived heart can only hold a little knowledge like a small valley can only contain a little water. The Prophet (may God bless him and grant him peace) said: 'Do not call grapes *karm*... since *karm* is only the heart of the believer.'[2] They used to call grape trees *karm* due to their abundant benefits and goodness. Thus he informed them that the believer's heart is more entitled to this naming because of the great goodness within it and benefit from it.

ʿAlī's statement 'The best of them have the most capacity' is alluding to either those that fill up the quickest and are the most stable once filled or those that are filled with the best contents.

The intellect (*ʿaql*) is so named because it grasps the [knowledge] that has reached the heart and then holds on to it so that it does not escape. It is said 'one detains a camel' (*ʿaqala al-baʿīr*), and *al-ʿiqāl* is the cord used to restrain it. The mind is also called *ʿaql* because it restrains one from following seduction and becoming ruined. It is also named as such because it protects its owner just like a stone [wall] protects what it surrounds. Therefore comprehending (*ʿaql*) is more than just knowing or recognizing something.

Perception (*idrāk*) encompasses many things. First is awareness, which is followed by understanding, recognition, knowledge and, finally, comprehension. Thus the best hearts are those that contain good and continue to hold onto it. They are not hardened, stone-like hearts that do not accept [good in the first place]; nor are they foolish, whereby they can receive [knowledge] but not memorize or hold it. The best hearts are those that are both pliable (*layyin*) and strong; they accept what is stamped within them due to their pli-

1 Q. XIII.17.

2 Bukhārī 6183; Muslim 5868; Aḥmad 9977.

ability and are able, due to their strength, to memorize that image.

ʿAlī's statement 'People are divided into three classes: scholars of the Lord (*rabbānī*), students on the path of salvation, and finally riff-raff and foolish simpletons' represents a division specific to humanity. The reality is that a person has either attained perfection in knowledge and deeds or not. The former is a scholar of the Lord (*rabbānī*). If one is a student on the path of salvation,then he is trying to attain [that perfection]. Finally, the third are the riff-raff and foolish simpletons; they are completely deprived [of good].

As for a scholar of the Lord,[1] Ibn ʿAbbās (may God be pleased with both him and his father) said: 'He is an instructor. The wording is derived from *tarbiya*, which means to raise people up with knowledge just like parents would raise their child.' Saʿīd b. Jubayr said: 'It refers to one who is a knowledgeable and wise jurist.' Sībawayh[2] said: 'The letters *alif* and *nūn* are added at the end of *rabbānī* in order to emphasize that they have been selected by the Lord (Most Blessed and Exalted is He) and endowed with His knowledge. It is similar to saying *shaʿrānī*, i.e. a large amount of hair, or *liḥyānī*, i.e. a great beard.'[3]

Wāḥidī[4] opined: 'The scholar of the Lord is selected by the Lord to be endowed with knowledge of Him, His Divine Law and His

1 Al-Khaṭīb al-Baghdādī mentioned: 'The scholar of the Lord is the most virtuous person. Furthermore, the level of a scholar is higher than even that of a jurist who issues independent legal verdicts (*mujtahid*). The Exalted said: *Be ye* (*rabbāniyyīn*) *faithful servants of the Lord by virtue of your constant teaching of the Book and of your constant study thereof* [Q. III.79].' See al-Khaṭīb al-Baghdādī, *Faqīh*, vol. 1, p. 182.

2 Abū Bishr ʿAmr b. ʿUthmān b. Qanbar (d. 180/796) was more commonly known by his original Persian name, Sībawayh. He was a great Arabic linguist. Although not a native speaker, he wrote the first book on Arabic grammar, which he named *al-Kitāb*.

3 Ibn al-Anbārī (d. 328/940) also maintained that the *rabbānī* are ascribed to the Lord and that the letters *alif* and *nūn* are added at the end to emphasize their close relationship to Him. See Ibn al-Qayyim, *Miftāḥ*, p. 150.

4 Abū al-Ḥasan ʿAlī b. Aḥmad al-Wāḥidī (d. 468/1075) was a scholar and author of a commentary on the Qur'ān titled *Asbāb al-nuzūl*.

Attributes (Most Blessed and Exalted is He).' It should be noted that *rabbānī* is different from *ribbiyyūn* in His statement: *And with how many a prophet have there been a number of devoted men (ribbiyyūn) who fought (beside him).*[1] *Ribbiyyūn* here means 'a group' according to the consensus of the exegetes. Finally, one is not a scholar of the Lord unless he acts in accordance with his knowledge and then instructs others.

The second group consists of students on the path of salvation. They intend, by virtue of their knowledge, to attain salvation. They acquire knowledge with sincerity, learn only what is beneficial, and act on what they know. Only if these three conditions are fulfilled can one be considered a student on the path of salvation. So if one learns what is harmful, he is not on the path of salvation. Similarly, if he only learns for [worldly reasons] and not to attain salvation, then he will not be considered a student. Also if he learns something but does not act upon it, then he will not attain salvation.

In addition, one should not learn so as to argue with fools, debate the scholars, or garner people's attention. Those who do so will be denizens of Hellfire. The Prophet (may God bless him and grant him peace) said: 'The pursuit of knowledge should only be for the sake of God. Whoever learns it to gain some worldly thing will not smell the scent of Paradise.'[2] Thus these types of people are not on the path of salvation, but instead are on the path of their ruin. May God protect us from being forsaken!

The third group consists of those who are forsaken and who shun knowledge. They are neither scholars nor students, but rather riff-raff (*hamaj*) and foolish simpletons. The riff-raff are ignorant, foolish simpletons. *Hamaj* is the plural of *hamja*, which is a small fly, like a gnat; thus he likened the riff-raff and rabble of people to it. *Hamaj* can also be a verbal noun, which means that one mismanages his affairs and livelihood.

1 Q. III.146.

2 Abū Dāwūd 3664; Ibn Māja 252; Aḥmad 8457; Ḥākim 288; Abū Nuʿaym, vol. IV, p. 84; Ibn ʿAbd al-Barr 1143; al-Khaṭīb al-Baghdādī (*Faqīh*), vol. II, p. 175. It is 'authentic' according to Albānī (*Ṣaḥīḥ al-Jāmiʿ al-ṣaghīr* 6159).

ʿAlī's statement that they 'follow any shepherd [who calls them]' means that they follow anyone who screams or calls them, whether to guidance or to error. This is due to their ignorance. They will respond to this calling regardless of whether it is to the truth or falsehood—in fact, the religion is most harmed by this type of people. They are the most numerous, yet they are considered by God to be most vile. They are the wood used to set ablaze every discord and strife. Every conflagration is fired up by those who spread falsehood and it is taken up by the riff-raff and foolish simpletons. Their caller is named a *nāʿiq* so as to liken them to sheep that are screamed at by the shepherd, because they follow him wherever he takes them. The Exalted said: *The similitude of those who disbelieve (in relation to the Messenger) is as the similitude of one who calleth unto that which heareth naught except a shout and cry. Deaf, dumb, blind, therefore they have no sense.*[1]

Then ʿAlī (may God be pleased with him) stated that they 'sway [wherever] any wind [blows]' and in another narration 'with every screamer'. Thus he likened their weak intellects to weak [tree] branches; and he likened their desires and whims to the wind, as the branch sways with the wind wherever it blows it. Had their intellects been perfect, they would have been like a massive tree that cannot be moved by the wind.

This should be contrasted with the analogy that the Prophet (may God bless him and grant him peace) drew for the believers: 'The similitude of a believer is that of a fresh, tender plant, which the wind bends sometimes and at other times it makes it straight. And the example of a hypocrite is that of a pine tree which keeps straight till it is uprooted suddenly.'[2] This analogy refers to the violent winds of tribulation, harm, injury and fear that the believers must face. They remain between well-being and tribulation, blessings and tests, health and sickness, safety and fear. They succumb at times and are

1 Q. II.171.
2 Bukhārī 5643; Muslim 2810; Aḥmad 15,769.

able to overcome these in other instances. Consequently, these tribulations expiate their sins and purify them. On the other hand, the disbelievers are filthy and are only suitable as fuel [for Hellfire].

The afflictions affecting a disbeliever do not contain mercy, nor do they lead him to become wiser. This is in contrast to the adversities encountered by the believers [wherein there is mercy and wisdom that can be gained]. A poet portrayed the believer's response to desires and callers to discord, strife, error and innovations in religion as follows:

> The towering mountains would vanish while his heart
> Remains upon the covenant—not wavering nor changing.

ʿAlī (may God be pleased with him) then said that they were 'not enlightened by the light of knowledge, nor do they seek refuge in a strong fortress'. He explained the reason that the [third group] found themselves in such a condition was because they did not attain enough knowledge or enlightenment to differentiate between the truth and falsehood. The Exalted said: *O ye who believe, be mindful of your duty to God and put faith in His Messenger. He will give you twofold of His mercy and will appoint for you a light wherein ye shall walk;*[1] *Is he who was dead and We have raised him unto life, and set for him a light wherein he walketh among men, as him whose similitude is in utter darkness whence he cannot emerge?*[2] The Exalted also said: *Whereby God guideth him who seeketh His good pleasure unto paths of peace. He bringeth them out of darkness unto light;*[3] *But We have made it a light whereby We guide whom We will of Our servants.*[4]

If the heart is devoid of light, it becomes confused and does not know how to proceed. Due to this confusion and ignorance, it follows any calling that it hears. But if the truth is entrenched within

1 Q. LVII.28.
2 Q. VI.122.
3 Q. V.16.
4 Q. XLII.52.

one's heart, it strengthens one, and one is able to prevent things that would otherwise harm or destroy one. For this reason, God specifies that knowledge-based evidence is a powerful authority (*sulṭān*)—this was previously discussed.

Attaining bliss is predicated on two fundamentals: knowledge and power. The Sublime described Gabriel, the most distinguished instructor (may God's peace and blessings be upon him), saying: *It is naught save an inspiration that is inspired, which one of mighty powers hath taught him.*[1] The Exalted also said in *Sūrat al-Takwīr*: *That this is in truth the word of an honoured messenger, mighty, established in the presence of the Lord of the Throne.*[2] Thus God characterized Gabriel with knowledge and power.

To return, there is a better meaning that ʿAlī (may God be pleased with him) may have intended, and it is that they were not enlightened by the light of knowledge, nor did they search out an enlightened scholar to emulate or follow. A person can either be enlightened, [spiritually] blind yet following one who is enlightened, or blind and travelling alone without a guide.

ʿAlī's (may God be pleased with him) statement 'Knowledge is better than wealth since knowledge preserves you, while you must work to protect wealth' indicates that knowledge preserves and protects its owner from the causes that lead to disaster and ruin. A human being would not purposely hurl himself into a disaster if he is fully rational, nor would he subject himself to ruin unless he was ignorant. For example, if one knows that a food is poisoned, he will avoid eating it because of that knowledge. On the other hand, one who is ignorant will die due to his ignorance. Similarly, the expert physician, due to his knowledge, will be able to [practise preventative medicine] thus allowing him to avoid many diseases and illnesses. Likewise, one who is knowledgeable about the possible perils that could destroy him along the path will be more cautious.

1 Q. LIII.4–5.
2 Q. LXXXI.19–20.

The scholar who has knowledge of God and His commandments and is knowledgeable about the enemy [Iblīs], his tricks, and the manner by which he intrudes upon people will be protected by this knowledge from Satan's whisperings and sowing of temptations, doubts, uncertainties and disbelief. He will have a guardian consisting of knowledge and faith that will repel Satan every time the latter approaches, and make [the Devil] retreat in disgrace.

A servant can secure the above as causes, [but more importantly] God is behind his preservation, guarding and protection. If God leaves him be, for even a moment, he will be snatched away by his enemy. The knowers (*ʿārifūn*) are in agreement that success (*tawfīq*) indicates that God has not left you to your own devices. They are also in agreement that becoming forsaken (*khudhlān*) occurs when God leaves you to your own devices.

Then ʿAlī said: 'Knowledge grows with expenditure while money decreases with spending.' So every time the scholar uses his knowledge to [educate] people, it becomes greater, stronger and more manifest. By teaching others he is able to memorize what he has taught them and also attain new knowledge. [With regards to the latter,] it may have been that there was some issue that was not unveiled to him yet, but after discussing it, it became clear to him. Subsequently, the door to further knowledge is opened up to him, and he then becomes more enlightened.

Since recompense is in accordance with the deed, and just as he taught people whilst they were ignorant, God will recompense him by teaching him what he is ignorant of. ʿUyāḍ b. Ḥimār narrated that the Prophet (may God bless him and grant him peace) said: 'God said to me: "Spend, for I will bestow upon you."'[1] This includes the expenditure, application and use of knowledge. Gaining knowledge occurs in two ways: one is by teaching it and the other is by acting upon it. Thus acting on one's knowledge allows it to develop and grow; and it opens up many doors that were [previously] closed.

1 Bukhārī 7496; Muslim 2309; Ibn Māja 2123; Aḥmad 7298.

ʿAlī's statement that 'money decreases with spending' does not contradict the statement of the Prophet (may God bless him and grant him peace): 'Giving charity does not diminish wealth.'[1] This *ḥadīth* indicates that when you donate charity, [that contribution] will be substituted. As for knowledge, it is like a brand of fire: even if the scholar uses it, it will not decrease. Instead, knowledge will increase afterwards. It can also be likened to a well: every time it is drawn from, its fountainhead becomes stronger and rises forth.

The superiority of knowledge over wealth can be known by many ways:

1. Knowledge is our inheritance from the prophets, while money is what the kings and wealthy bequeath.
2. Knowledge preserves one who possesses it, while one who is wealthy has to guard his assets.
3. Money decreases with disbursements, while knowledge increases with usage.
4. When a wealthy person dies, he becomes separated from his wealth. On the other hand, knowledge accompanies one into his grave.
5. Knowledge rules over wealth, while wealth cannot judge over knowledge.
6. Wealth can be acquired by the believer and disbeliever, the righteous and the wicked, whereas beneficial knowledge is only attained by the believer.
7. The scholar is needed by kings and those of lesser status, while the poor and the destitute are the ones most in need of those who are wealthy.
8. The self becomes more distinguished and purified by gathering and attaining knowledge, and this leads to it becoming perfect and eminent. Although wealth may be amassed, it will never perfect a person nor will it make his character perfect. Often times, the self becomes more stingy, miserly and greedy [as it amasses more wealth]. Thus striving for knowledge signifies [the soul's] perfection, while

1 Muslim 6592; Tirmidhī 2029; Aḥmad 9008.

greediness for wealth is an indication of its deficient nature.

9. Wealth induces one to be unjust to others, and to be boastful and haughty, while knowledge calls one to be humble and uphold worship [of God]. Wealth leads to many attributes of the kings, while knowledge calls one to the characteristics of the worshippers.

10. Knowledge attracts one to the bliss that he has been created for, while money is a barrier between one [and Paradise].

11. Abundance of knowledge is more eminent since being wealthy is extrinsic to the human essence. It is possible that one could lose all his wealth in one moment, thus becoming poor and destitute. On the other hand, someone who is knowledgeable is not worried about privation, but rather he is always learning more. It has been said:

> I have become prosperous and independent from all
> people without money, for to be
> Prosperous and of high status one must be independent
> from something, not through it.

12. Money enslaves the owner who worships it. The Prophet (may God bless him and grant him peace) said: 'Let the slave of the dinar and dirham perish.'[1] Knowledge, on the other hand, enslaves him to his Lord and Creator. Thus [knowledge] only calls him to the servitude of God.

13. The love of knowledge is the basis for every piety. On the other hand, love of this world and money are the roots of all evil.

14. The value of an affluent person is in his wealth, whereas the value of a scholar is in his knowledge. If the former's wealth becomes non-existent, his worth follows suit. Yet the value of the scholar never diminishes, but instead is perpetually multiplying and increasing.

15. The essence [of the value] of wealth is similar to that of the material body, while the essence of knowledge is like that of the spirit. Yūnus b. Ḥabīb said: 'Your knowledge is connected to your spirit, while your wealth is associated with your body. The differ-

1 Bukhārī 2887; Ibn Māja 4135.

ence between the two is, therefore, like the difference between the spirit and the body.'

16. Had the scholar been offered this world instead of his share of knowledge, he would never accept the former as a substitute. On the other hand, had the heedless wealthy person known of the eminence and superiority of knowledge, the delight that one would experience, and the perfection that one would attain with knowledge, he would wish to trade all his wealth for the [scholar's] knowledge.

17. Obedience to God cannot be accomplished without knowledge, whereas the majority of those who disobey Him do so [for the sake of making] money.

18. The scholar calls people to God using his knowledge, whereas the wealthy one uses his status and wealth to make people [desire] this world.

19. Affluence may often cause one who is wealthy to perish. Some excessively love [wealth] and, therefore, once they see that someone has more than them, they may strive to destroy him. This is seen in actuality. On the other hand, the one who has abundant knowledge brings about a [spiritual] life for himself as well as others. Once people see that the scholar has their best interests at heart, they will love, help and revere him.

20. The pleasure that results from wealth is either an imaginary pleasure or an animalistic one. Thus if one derives pleasure from amassing it, then that is an imaginary (*wahmiyya*) and delusional (*khayāliyya*) pleasure. If one is pleased as a result of spending it in pursuit of his temptations, then it is an animalistic one. On the other hand, the pleasure of knowledge is an intellectual and spiritual pleasure that resembles the delight and pleasure of the angels.

21. The sages of all nations agree in criticizing the one who avariciously and greedily amasses money. They also disregard him and deem him to be deficient. On the other hand, they agree in venerating the one who enthusiastically gathers knowledge. They also praise, love and consider him to be perfect.

22. They similarly agree in venerating the one who abstains from wealth, shuns collecting it, shows no regard for it, and prevents his heart from being enslaved to it. They also criticize those who avoid learning and do not eagerly pursue it.
23. A person who is wealthy is only praiseworthy if he restrains himself from using his [wealth for himself] and spends it instead on others. On the other hand, the more one is characterized with knowledge and exhibits it, the more praiseworthy one is.
24. An affluent and wealthy individual is characterized by fear and sadness: he is sad before attaining it and then fearful after amassing it; and the greater [his wealth], the stronger his fear [of losing it]. On the other hand, the one who has abundant knowledge feels secure, happy and joyous.
25. An affluent and wealthy individual will inevitably become separated from his wealth. At that point, he will suffer due to its loss. On the other hand, someone who has abundant knowledge will never see it vanish, nor will he suffer or encounter pain. Thus the pleasure of an affluent and wealthy person is fleeting, temporary and followed by pain, while the pleasure of one who has abundant knowledge is permanent and perpetual, and will not be followed by pain.
26. The pleasure and/or perfection that the self experiences with wealth is like the perfection and beauty a naked person seeks when he wears clothes that are borrowed and will inevitably have to be returned to its owner one day. On the other hand, the beauty and perfection associated with knowledge becomes an established and ingrained trait that one is never separated from.
27. The essence of an affluent and wealthy person is one of deprivation, while the prosperity resulting from knowledge is real and true.
28. A person who is favoured and honoured because of his wealth will find that vanish if his wealth disappears. On the other hand, those who are favoured and honoured because of their knowledge will find themselves increasingly treated as such.
29. Someone being favoured [only] due to his wealth is a sign that

he is deficient. Had it not been for his wealth, he would have been deserving of disgrace. On the other hand, someone being favoured and honoured because of his knowledge is a sign of his perfection. It acknowledges that this characteristic is intrinsic to him, and is not something extrinsic.

30. Those who seek perfection by becoming wealthy are trying to reconcile two opposites, so they seek something that is unattainable. This is substantiated by what follows. Power is an attribute of perfection and attributes of perfection are loved for themselves. Independence from others is also an attribute of perfection that is loved for itself. There also is a natural inclination towards generosity, giving charity and being magnanimous. These are perfections desired by those who are rational, and they are loved by people.

But if one realizes that it requires spending a great deal of money, that one's power may abate, and that one may be in need of others in the future, then one will flee from those traits; and one will think that perfection lies in holding on to one's money. This affliction is a known occurrence to the general populace and few are exempt.

Nonetheless, a person's heart will waver between these two demands, each trying to win him over, and he will remain unsettled. Some people will prefer donating and being magnanimous, while others will prefer to hold onto their power and affluence. These are the two options available to those who are rational.

But others will be so ignorant and foolish that they will want to try to accommodate both alternatives. Thus they will promise others that they will donate and be generous in the hope of gaining their compliments and commendations; but when the time comes, they will not fulfill what they had vowed. At that point, they will instead be criticized. They will also make pledges, but their hearts and hands will not fulfill them. They will, thus, fall into repugnance and ignominy. If you notice the state of [many of] those who are wealthy, you will find that they are held captive to this affliction, and therefore they whine and complain most of the time.

On the other hand, those who have abundant knowledge will not be exposed to any of this; but rather the more they expend, the greater their happiness, joy and delight is. Although some of the pleasures and enjoyments that the wealthy experience as a result of their money will elude [the scholars], it must be acknowledged that the pleasure and delight that the scholars experience, due to their knowledge, have been relinquished by the former.

In addition, the fatigue and suffering that the scholar [endures] to attain knowledge, in order to gather and organize it, is often less than that of those who accumulate wealth. The Exalted said to the believers in order to comfort them when they encounter suffering and fatigue along the path to obeying and pleasing Him: *If ye are suffering, they suffer even as ye suffer and ye hope from God that for which they cannot hope. God is ever Knower, Wise.*[1]

31. The pleasure that is felt [by an avaricious person] from wealth and affluence only happens when it is continuously renewed. So when the wealth of such people remains the same, the pleasure either goes away or decreases, as their nature is to always be greedy for more money; hence they remain in a continual state of feeling impoverished. Even if such [covetous] people were to own all the vaults on this earth, their [sense of] poverty, need to pursue [money] and greediness will remain. They are always insatiable (*manhūmūn*) and are never satisfied with their current level of wealth.

In contrast, those who have abundant knowledge and faith experience the same amount of pleasure whether it only persists or is renewed—it can even increase [in either of those states]. They also avidly seek [knowledge and faith] because of many additional pleasures, such as delight and happiness, which occur upon reaching their aspirations and goals.

32. Affluent people are often called upon to grant favours to people and to be benevolent with them. They will either refuse or oblige. If they refuse [and chose to limit their wealth] to themselves, others

1 Q. IV.104.

will hate, criticize and despise them. Moreover, whosoever is hated and despised by people will encounter evil and harm faster than even a fire setting a piece of dry wood ablaze or a torrential flood going downhill. In addition, once he realizes that people detest, hate and disregard him, he will suffer greatly and be consumed by worry, grief and sadness.

But if he tries to oblige all [people] by being benevolent and giving, he will never be able to fulfil them all, as he will inevitably find that he can only benefit some, and not all. This opens up the door to enmity and criticism from those whom he has excluded and even those to whom he has shown compassion. As for those who are excluded, they will say to themselves: 'Why would he donate to others while being miserly with us?' As for the group that receives from him, they will [initially] be pleased and happy with what good they have been given, but they will covet more gifts; and since it is difficult to continue in most instances, this ultimately leads to intense hatred and criticism. For this reason, it has been said: 'Be fearful of the evil done by those whom you have been benevolent with.'

On the other hand, these deficiencies cannot occur to those who have abundant knowledge. The scholar can expend it for the whole world and they can all join in. Knowledge will never vanish.

33. There are three instances wherein the accumulation of wealth is associated with harm: one before [acquiring it], one at the time of acquiring it, and one after it is lost. As for the first instance, it includes the inevitable difficulties, hardships and pains by which it is amassed.

The second instance includes the difficulties associated with preserving and protecting it. In addition, one's heart becomes attached to it, such that one is always anxious and worried about [losing it]. He becomes like someone who excessively loves his beloved, and yet he notices [others'] eyes from every direction staring at them and desiring to injury him. What kind of life or joy is there for one whose condition is like this? He knows that his enemies and those who are jealous will never stop trying to separate him from his beloved [money]. If they cannot win [that wealth] from him, their purpose becomes to at least try to rid him of it so as to bring him down to their level. Thus [in the first case] they succeed in attaining it, but if not then [in the second case at least] they will both become equally deprived.

If they were able to accomplish the same with a scholar, they would do so. But since they know that there is no way to deprive him of his knowledge, they instead resort to rejecting and denying [his scholarship] in order to prevent others from loving, favouring and commending him. And if his knowledge shines astoundingly clear, they will slander him and attribute every repugnance and major evil to him, claiming he is a deceiver (*talbīs*) and a fraud (*tadlīs*), or that he is simply duplicitous (*zawkara*)[1]. They will also allege that he is ostentatious, snobbish or desiring fame. This degree of opposition to the scholars by those who are ignorant and unjust is inevitable, just like hot and cold weather. Those [scholars] who are of sound mind should not be troubled by such actions as there is no way that they can stave it off. Instead, they should prepare themselves, just like one would do to endure the winter's cold or the summer's heat.[2]

The third instance of harm that wealth may bring occurs after the person loses it, due to his heart being attached to it. And we have not even discussed here that one will be held accountable [in the Hereafter] for one's revenues and expenditures, and how one acquired [wealth] and spent it. Those who have abundant knowl-

1 In many editions of the *Miftāḥ* the word *zawkara* is instead rendered as *dawkara*. This and other typographical as well as some editorial errors were pointed out in an article by Shaykh ʿAbd al-Raḥmān Qā'id, found at <http://ahlalhdeeth.com/vb/showthread.php?t=255994> (last accessed on 25 May 2016).

2 Ibn al-Qayyim has written: 'The Shaykh of Islam, Ibn Taymiyya (may God, Exalted is He, have mercy upon him) once told me: "Afflictions and trials are like hot and cold weather. If one realizes that they are inevitable, then one will not become angered, stricken with anxiety, or grieved upon encountering them."' See Ibn al-Qayyim, *Madārij*, vol. III, p. 361.

edge and faith are free from all of these harms. Despite the fact that [knowledge] can only be attained by crossing a bridge of fatigue, patience and difficulty, they are still guaranteed every type of pleasure, happiness and joy.

34. In order to derive the pleasure associated with wealth one must mingle with others. Had such a person been alone and isolated, he would derive no benefit from his money, nor could he enjoy it completely. His relationship with others, though, becomes the source of much harm and pain. Since peoples' natures and desires differ such that what is good for one is bad for another, he becomes afflicted by them. Hatred and enmity will inevitably occur between them all.

Pleasing all of them is impossible; it is like trying to reconcile between two opposites. Pleasing some while displeasing others leads to evil and enmity. Furthermore, the greater one's mingling, the more reasons for enmity and malice. For this reason, the evil that occurs from one's relatives and friends is many times more than the evil that occurs from other foreign or distant acquaintances. Again, this only occurs in the case of one who is affluent. After he is no longer of any benefit to them, they will avoid mingling and interacting with him. It is only at that point that he will find respite from their harm. On the other hand, these harms rarely occur for those with abundant knowledge.

35. Money is not specifically desired for itself, as no benefits accrue from it alone. It does not satisfy one's hunger or thirst, warm one, nor does it lead to joy. Rather, it is desired as a means to such ends.

It is well known that the ends are more eminent than the means. Many sages have said that there is no reality to these ends, which are imperfect, but rather they are only pursued to avoid pain. Therefore the means to them [i.e. wealth] must be even more flawed. For instance, [they say that] clothes are worn to defend against the pain of heat, cold or wind and that one derives no additional pleasure from them. Similarly, [they state that] food is eaten to stave off the pain of hunger. It is also well known that pain occurs while pursuing and even after attaining those ends, but this harm and pain is less than that which is avoided. Thus the human being will endure the lesser of two evils in order to avert the greater of the two. It has been related that it was said to a sage after drinking a distasteful glass of medicine: 'How do you feel now?' He replied: 'I am living in an abode of tribulations whereby I avert one ill by enduring another.' In reality, the pleasures of this world, including foods, drinks, clothes, homes and marriage, are all of this kind.

In fact, there are only two real pleasures that one experiences: eating and intercourse. There is no third type of pleasure whatsoever. Everything else is a means to these two [ends]. However, even these pleasures torment one from many aspects: [first,] by imagining that these desires will dissipate and cease; and [second,] because they are infused with harm, saturated with pain, and surrounded by fear. The pain endured is often not worth the benefit.

[Third,] consider that the vile and downcast can enjoy them just as much as the sages. The participation of the vile and contemptible people—to the degree that they can even exceed the sages—is another reason one should avoid and shun them. Many have recognized this and later became ascetics for that reason. There are many examples of this in poetry and prose:

> I will abandon loving it—not because of hate
> But because there are too many other participants.
> If a fly lands on some food
> I will hold my hand back even though my self will desire it.
> Likewise, lions will avoid a watering place
> If dogs had lapped it.

It was said to an ascetic: 'Why have you renounced this world?' He replied: 'Because its participants are contemptible, the loyal are few and the rude are many.'

[Fourth,] the pleasure that one achieves is dependent on the degree of need for it and the pain incurred while seeking it. The stronger the desire to win something over, the greater the resulting pleasure is when it comes into existence. The need and extent of pleasure occurring in the present balances out the pain required to attain it in the past. They neutralize each other and, therefore, it is almost as if the pleasure never existed. It is similar to the example of one who was whipped ten times and compensated with ten dirhams. Most of the temptations of this world are nothing but that. Such a thing cannot really be considered a pleasure, bliss or perfection. Instead, they are like the performance of a necessity, such as urination or a bowel movement. A human is burdened by these, but when he performs his need, he becomes relieved; however, this relief is not considered to be delightful or pleasurable.

[Fifth,] there is no way to attain either of these two desires [food and intercourse] except through encountering the impurity and pain that is associated with them. Take the example of the pleasure associated with eating: if an intelligent person would consider the state of his food after being mixed with his saliva, he will become disgusted with it. Furthermore, upon that bite being swallowed, he would naturally become nauseated if it came back up. Then once it settles in his stomach, it becomes totally foul. Finally, if one eats more than what one needs, one will incur a variety of different types of diseases. Had it not been that his survival was dependent upon eating, it would have been better and more appropriate for him to abstain.

As for the pleasure of intercourse, the impurities that are involved are obvious enough that its deficiencies need not be mentioned. Briefly, one is embarrassed to see or mention the organs involved in this pleasure. Covering the genitals is a matter that God has made His creation innately disposed to. However, the pleasure of intercourse cannot occur without uncovering and seeing them, and encountering the impure fluids that emanate from them. Furthermore, the time frame of the pleasure of intercourse is so fleeting. Is it worth all the difficulties, length of time needed to cajole, and fatigue involved just to experience a momentary pleasure that is like the blink of an eye? This also proves that this pleasure is not a necessary type of goodness, bliss or perfection that people were created for. Instead, people have been equipped for other matters; however, they do not fulfill them due to their heedlessness and laziness. A poet said:

> You were prepared for a [great] matter if you would only realize
> So hold yourself in high esteem and avoid grazing with untended cattle.

In addition, one becomes weak in body, heart and soul after the pleasure of intercourse. Sages from all nations agree in criticizing those who are insatiably preoccupied with [intercourse]. They have a low opinion of them and consider them to be like animals. Had it been goodness [in and of itself] or perfection, then those who directed their efforts solely to it would have been considered the most perfect of people.

Furthermore, the heart that directs its intentions and desires to these pleasures remains entrenched in much anxiety, grief and sadness. Again, whatever pleasures are experienced, when compared to the pain required, is like a drop in the ocean. It has been said: 'The enjoyment is the weight of a seed while the sadness is that of a *qinṭār*.'[1] Moreover, if one cannot attain it, then one will endure pain and suffering. Yet if one can reach it, then one will endure the pain involved in the process of attaining it; that is, the fatigue, hardship and competition with others for it. He will also endure pain once he attains it because he shall be afraid that he will become separated from it either temporarily or permanently. Thus it becomes known that this heart is perpetually drowning in oceans of anxiety, grief and sadness. His self fools him and satisfies him with an atom's

1 This refers to a heavy weight which in some countries equals 256.4 kg. Therefore the meaning is that a great sadness results from following one's temptations.

weight of pleasure, but hides from him the tremendous amount of pain and suffering.

Finally, if he is prevented from some pleasure and there is no way to reach it, then his pain will become absolute and crush him entirely. Thus if that is the extent of these animalistic pleasures, which are the end objectives of gathering wealth, then what would you presume about the value of the means?

On the other hand, the pleasure of those who have abundant knowledge and faith is continuous; and their joy and delight is complete. This state does not cease and, therefore, they do not encounter sadness or pain. God (Exalted is He) said: *There shall no fear come upon them neither shall they grieve.*[1]

36. Those who are affluent hate death and meeting God. Due to their love of money, they dislike being separated from it and would love to remain [in this world] so that they can enjoy it fully. This is the reality. On the other hand, knowledge makes one love to meet his Lord and allows one to abstain from this transient life.

37. Reminiscing over the wealthy will end when they die, whereas the scholar will remain in our thoughts. The Emir of the Believers [ʿAlī] said: 'Those who hoard wealth are [spiritually] dead, even if they are still alive [in this world], whereas scholars remain [spiritually] alive for the remainder of eternity.' Thus the hoarders of wealth are like the living dead, whereas the scholars, even after their death, remain alive.

38. Knowledge relative to the spirit is like the spirit compared to the body. The spirit is enlivened through knowledge just like the body is alive by virtue of the spirit. One who is affluent is intent on increasing the lifespan of his body. On the other hand, knowledge is the life of the hearts and spirits, as was firmly established previously.

39. The heart is [like] the king of the body, and knowledge is its adornment and instrument by which its kingdom is established. The greatest that can be said about money is that it adorns and beauti-

1 Q. v.69.

fies the body if one spends it in that way. But if one hoards it and does not spend, it then it can do none of that. Instead, it becomes a shortcoming and a curse.

40. One should only [pursue] as much wealth as one needs to sustain oneself. This amount will allow him to prepare his provisions for the journey to the Lord (Great and Glorious is He). Anything above that preoccupies a person and prevents him from preparing and packing his provisions for that trip. Thus the harm [of surplus wealth] is greater than its benefit. The more wealth increases, the greater a person's attachment [to this world], and the more he is distracted from preparing for what is ahead of him.

On the other hand, the more beneficial knowledge one has, the more one prepares the provisions and readies the equipment for the trip ahead. God is the Facilitator and we rely on Him. There is no might or power save in Him. The Exalted said: *And if they had wished to go forth they would assuredly have made ready some equipment, but God was averse to their being sent forth and held them back and it was said (unto them): Sit ye with the sedentary!*[1]

ʿAlī then said: 'Love of knowledge'—or 'the scholars'—'is [part of] the creed that one must profess.' Since knowledge is the inheritance bequeathed by the prophets, love of knowledge and the scholars represents love of the inheritance of the prophets. Love of knowledge is one of the signs of being blissful, whereas hatred of it indicates wretchedness. All of this only pertains to the knowledge conveyed by the messengers and passed on to their community, not to every type of knowledge.

In addition, love of knowledge leads one to learn, teach and follow it—indeed this is [part of] the religion. Hating it prevents one in this regard and indicates that one is wretched and astray. In addition, God (Glory be to Him) is the Most Knowledgeable and He loves all those who are knowledgeable. He places His knowledge [and wisdom] in only those whom He loves. Those who love knowledge

1 Q. IX.46.

and the scholars love what God loves. This is what one must profess.

Then ʿAlī said: 'Knowledge earns for the scholar obedience during his lifetime and good remembrance after his death.' Here *yuksabu* means that 'he has earned it' or that 'it is allotted to him'. A statement of Khadīja (may God be pleased with her) substantiates this [understanding]: 'You keep good relations with your kith and kin, help the poor and the destitute, serve your guests generously and assist (*tuksibu*) the deserving, calamity-afflicted ones.'[1] It has been narrated with both a *fatḥa* and a *ḍamma* on the *tā'*. The latter (*tuksibu*) means 'to provide money or glory for them'. This is the correct interpretation. Those who stated it was [*taksibu*] with a *fatḥa*, said it means: 'You profit from the destitute due to your knowledge and mastery of trading.' We seek refuge in God from this understanding! Khadīja is too noble to say something like that in such a critical situation. She could not have implied to the Messenger of God (may God bless him and grant him peace): 'Receive glad tidings because I swear by God that God will not forsake you, since you profit with many dirhams and dinars and are good at trading.' The likes of this misinterpretation is only mentioned so as to prevent some from being deceived when interpreting the words of God and His Messenger.

The point is that ʿAlī's statement that 'knowledge earns for the scholar obedience during his lifetime' means that it will bring about obedience to him. Everyone, including the kings and those below them, needs to obey the scholar, since he commands them to obey God and His Messenger. It is only for that reason that creation is obligated to obey [the scholar]. The Exalted said: *O ye who believe, obey God, and obey the Messenger and those of you who are in authority* (*ulī al-amr*).[2] *Ulī al-amr* has been interpreted by some as 'the scholars'. Ibn ʿAbbās said: 'They are the jurists (*fuqahā'*) and scholars who teach

1 Bukhārī 3 and 6982; Muslim 403; Aḥmad 25,959.
2 Q. IV.59.

people the religion.' This is also the opinion of Mujāhid,[1] Ḥasan [al-Baṣrī], Ḍaḥḥāk, and one of the two narrations from Aḥmad. Another interpretation of *ulī al-amr* is 'the rulers', and it is the opinion of Ibn Zayd and the other of two narrations from Ibn ʿAbbās and Aḥmad. However, the verse intends all of them [that is, jurists, scholars and rulers]. One who has knowledge regarding what the Messenger conveyed, and then fulfills those precepts, should be the most obeyed person on this earth.

ʿAlī then said that 'any favour due to money disappears once it vanishes'. This indicates that any favour done to [a wealthy person], such as honouring or loving him, serving or fulfilling his needs, giving him esteem or appointing him to a position of power and otherwise, is only out of regard for his affluence. Thus once his money vanishes, those favours also disappear. It may even be that those people who used to devote themselves to his service and strove to benefit him will no longer even greet him [once the money has gone]. This is often referred to in poetry and prose, as some have said: 'Fair-weather friends abandon you once the wind changes.'

It is also said: 'Do not be surprised if others honour you because of your wealth or power—[but know that] this honouring will cease if the latter vanish. However, you should be astonished if others respect you due to your knowledge or religion.' Sometimes people will give [high] regard to someone due to the [distinguished] clothing he wears, but they would withdraw such esteem if he were to take them off. Mālik said: 'I heard that Abū Hurayra was invited to a banquet, but when he arrived, they barred him from entering. He went back home and wore a different set of clothes upon which he was allowed to enter. When the food was served, he put the food in his sleeves. They questioned him and he said: "It was these clothes that allowed me to enter; therefore they will [be the ones to] eat."'

1 Mujāhid b. Jabr al-Makhzūmī (d. 104/722) was one of the Successors. He studied the exegesis of the Qur'ān with Ibn ʿAbbās and was a source for the exegesis of Sufyān al-Thawrī and Ṭabarī.

This was narrated by Ibn Muzayn al-Ṭulayṭalī[1] in his book [*Tafsīr al-muwaṭṭa'*]. This is in contrast to the favours that occur due to knowledge as they never cease. Instead, they are always increasing as long as knowledge is not taken away from that scholar.

In addition, the favours due to wealth are in exchange [for something else], while those due to knowledge and religion are out of love, kindness and piety. Furthermore, the favours due to wealth can be granted to the righteous and the depraved, the believers and disbelievers alike, whereas those due to knowledge and religion only occur to those worthy of them.

Alternatively, this [statement of ʿAlī] can indicate that those who have benefitted from your gifts will consider your favours null if your wealth subsequently vanishes. On the other hand, those who have benefitted from your knowledge and guidance will always recognize that good will.

The explanation of ʿAlī's statement, 'Those who hoard wealth are [spiritually] dead, even if they are still alive [in this world], whereas scholars remain [spiritually] alive for the remainder of eternity', has already preceded. His statement, 'Although their [bodily] selves have ceased to exist, their embodiment exists within the hearts', indicates that even if their [bodily] selves have passed on, their image and knowledge remains within the hearts. This existence is an intellectual and cognitive one. People's love of them, as well as emulating them and deriving benefit from their knowledge, necessitates that [those scholars] remain in the forefront of their thoughts. One [of the poets] said:

> It is amazing that the lover complains of being distant!
> Can the beloved become hidden from the loving heart?
> Your shadow is in my eyes, your remembrance is in
> my speech

1 Yaḥyā b. Ibrāhīm b. Muzayn al-Ṭulayṭalī (d. 259/873) was a Mālikī judge of Toledo, Spain, during Muslim rule. His *Tafsīr al-muwaṭṭa'* only exists in manuscript form in Qayrawān, Tunisia.

And your dwelling is in my heart—so how will you
become concealed?

ʿAlī's statement, 'I promise you that here is knowledge'—and he signalled to his chest— proves the permissibility of informing another of the knowledge and goodness one possesses so that they can emulate and benefit from one. Derived from that is the statement of Joseph the truthful (peace be upon him): *Set me over the storehouses of the land. I am a skilled custodian.*[1] Thus whoever informs others regarding something about himself so that he can propagate the good which is beloved to God and His Messenger is deserving of praise. This is different from one who informs people so as to make demands and become aggrandized by them. God will recompense the latter with people's hatred and belittlement. Actions are [recompensed] according to intentions.

In addition, [it is permitted] for someone to commend himself to avoid some injustice or harm, to justly obtain something rightfully his, or to fend off the greedy aspirations of vile people. It is also permissible in the case of getting engaged if [the other family] does not know him well. However, it would be better to delegate this to someone else who knows him. One really should minimize self-commendation as it is often blameworthy and can lead one to become boastful or proud.

Then ʿAlī mentions four types of people who are not suitable to carry this knowledge. First are those who are untrustworthy. Even though they are intelligent and have good memories, their insight is marginal. Also they use this knowledge, which is an instrument of the religion, for worldly [matters]. They use this knowledge to gain and petition for [worldly benefit], and trade it like they would another commodity. These people are untrustworthy and God will never allow them to become leaders. A trustworthy person is not biased, nor does he desire anything but to follow the truth and conform to it; and he does not ask to be given power or authority. But

1 Q. XII.55.

those [untrustworthy] people use what is intended for the Hereafter instead as a commodity and trade for their worldly benefit. They have betrayed God, His servants and His religion.

ʿAlī then said [that they] 'use the evidences of God and His blessings to overrule His Book and rise above His creation'. This is one characteristic of these traitors. The meaning is that they use their knowledge to arbitrate; they give preference [to their desires] and advocate [their opinions] over [the Book]. This is the condition of many as they turn their back on the Book of God and subordinate it to their knowledge. This is not the condition of the true scholars as they will use the Book of God to overrule everything else. They arbitrate using the Book of God, making it the supreme standard, just as God (Exalted is He) has commanded. Those who do so are successful and blissful, but those who follow [their opinions] are forsaken and wretched.

The second type consists of those who yield [blindly to the true scholars]. Their hearts have not truly felt delight with this [knowledge]—nay, their insight is weak. This is the state of those who blindly imitate the truth. These people, although they may be saved, are not the [leading] callers to this religion. Instead, they are considered to be part of the troops rather than the princes and knights.

ʿAlī then said that 'the slightest uncertainty or doubt will pierce their hearts'. This is so due to their weak knowledge and lack of insight. On the contrary, he who is deeply rooted in knowledge will remain firmly certain, even if he encounters doubts to the tune of the number of the waves of the ocean. He cannot be agitated by doubts; instead he will be able to repudiate and deflect them by using knowledge, which is his guardian and army. Moreover, he will become more certain because he is able to recognize the invalidity of those [doubts] and rebut them. But if a person does not have true knowledge and is unable to repel [these uncertainties], then manifold doubts will successively come upon his heart until he is riddled with them and becomes a sceptic.

There are two armies of falsehood that come upon the heart: sinful temptations and false doubts. The Shaykh of Islam [Ibn Taymiyya] (may God be pleased with him) once told me after I asked him one question after another: 'Do not allow your heart to succumb to thoughts and doubts like a sponge. In that case, it would become saturated [with evil] only to later spew that out. Rather, consider it to be like a solid glass [diamond]: although doubts may pass by its surface, they will not become settled in it. [Then your heart] sees them for what they are due to its clarity and repels them due to its firmness.' I do not know of any advice that I have benefitted from more in repelling doubts than this.

Doubts have been named *shubha* because they make falsehood bear a resemblance (*ishtibāh*) to the truth. [In such cases,] however, the clothing of truth is dressed over a body of falsehood. Most people notice the superficial good and upon seeing that goodness will think that it is correct. But the [true] possessor of knowledge, who has certainty, will not be deceived by such [appearances]. Instead, he will see what is hidden beneath the surface; thus its reality will become elucidated to him. An example of this is counterfeit money: the ignorant one is deceived and only sees that it is coated with silver, while an accountant realizes its counterfeit nature.

If the intelligent and rational person reflects and ponders the aforementioned, then he realizes that most people will accept a doctrine if it is expressed in a [personally agreeable] fashion, but will reject it if it is phrased differently. I have seen, according to God's will, [the truth of] this in many people's books: they rejected the truth and misrepresented it by sugar-coating what is repugnant. Many of the Sunni Imams, such as Imam Aḥmad and others, have said in this regard: 'We do not do away with some Attribute of God's Attributes just because of some misrepresentation. For example, the Jahmiyya call the affirmation of God's perfect Attributes—whether His [eternal] life, knowledge, speech, hearing, vision, and all that He has characterized Himself by—to be anthropomorphism (*tashbīh wa-tajsīm*). They also consider whoever affirms such [Attributes] to be an anthropomorphist (*mushabbih*)!'

Only those who have a scanty or deficient intellect or are weak-sighted would abandon the true meaning due to this type of false characterization. Every sect portrays their doctrines in the best possible fashion, whereas they depict those of their opponents in the worst way that they can. But those who have been blessed by God and are enlightened can elucidate the truth from falsehood, and they are not deceived by the manner of expression.

If you want to find out the true meaning [of a doctrine] and whether it is true or false, then strip it of its clothing, which are the phrases, divest your heart from any antipathy or bias, and then adequately inspect it in an objective manner. Do not be like one who [favourably] considers the opinions of his colleagues and those whom he thinks well of completely with all his heart, but then looks harshly or critically at those of his opponents or those whom he thinks ill of. Those who look antagonistically at someone may see the good as evil, whereas the one who has some predilection towards a person may see evil as good. No one has been protected from this except those whom God has willed to bestow honour upon and is pleased with [such as to allow them to] accept the truth. It has been said:

> The pleased eye is blunted from [recognizing] faults
> Just like the displeased one sees [only] evil.
> Another said:
> They looked with an eye of antagonism. Had they [considered it]
> Favourably they would have thought well of it instead of thinking it to be repugnant.

If this [aforementioned discussion] concerns issues that one can see and perceive with one's own eyes, which includes what is tangible and cannot be distorted, then what do you think about the reflections of the heart, which perceive meanings that are susceptible to being misjudged? We rely on God [to guide us] to recognize and accept the truth, and to repudiate falsehood and not be deceived by it. God loves those who have knowledge and always return to Him. They should never rush, but rather should stand firm until they gain knowledge and certainty regarding what has been presented to them.

One should not be hasty or reckless before perfectly consolidating [one's knowledge] as the former are traits from the Devil. If one does not stand firm in the face of the initial shock of encountering basic doubts, then one will only be left with regret in the end. Imam Aḥmad and Nasā'ī[1] related a supplication of the Prophet (may God bless him and grant him peace): 'O God, I ask You to allow me to stand firm in my affairs and I ask You to make me determined to remain upon guidance.'[2] These two [firmness and determination] comprise all success. The servant fails only because he neglected both or one of them. Haste, recklessness, being startled by basic doubts, indifference, being moribund and neglecting opportunities all lead to failure. If a person first stands firm and secondly remains determined, then he will be completely successful. God is the One Who ensures success.

The third type of person [depicted in ʿAlī's statement] is one who is insatiably preoccupied with attaining his pleasures. He follows the calling of temptations wherever they lead him. This [type of] person will never be able to become an heir of the Prophet. He will not be able to attain knowledge except if he abandons those pleasures and forgoes relaxation. Yaḥyā b. Abī Kathīr said: 'Knowledge cannot be attained by relaxation of one's body.'[3] Ibrāhīm al-Ḥarbī said: 'The sages of every nation unanimously agree that the blessed abode is

1 Abū ʿAbd al-Raḥmān Aḥmad b. Shuʿayb b. ʿAlī al-Nasā'ī (d. 303/915) was an Imam of *Ḥadīth* and was a student of Abū Dāwūd (d. 275/889). His compilation *Sunan al-Nasā'ī* includes 5761 *ḥadīth*s with repetition. Incidentally, *Sunan Abī Dāwūd* contains 5274.

2 Tirmidhī 3407; Nasā'ī 1305; Aḥmad 17,114; Ibn Ḥibbān 935. This section of the *ḥadīth* is 'sound' according to Albānī (*Silsilat al-aḥādīth al-ṣaḥīḥa* 3228).

3 Muslim 1390.

not reached by living in luxury. Whoever prefers relaxation should [know that] those who follow their desires cannot become heirs of the prophets.'

The heart can really only have one [ultimate] objective and it must be free to pursue it. If one's goal is to satisfy one's pleasures and temptations, then one will neglect learning. If the pleasure associated with attaining knowledge does not supersede the pleasures of the body and temptations of his self, then he will never be able to reach a [high] level of knowledge. But if someone's desire for knowledge takes precedence, it is hoped that he will be amongst the group he aspires to join.

The pleasure of knowledge is an intellectual and spiritual pleasure that is similar to that of the angels. Yet the pleasures associated with temptations, like food, drink and intercourse, are animalistic ones that humans share with animals. Finally, the pleasure associated with doing evil, perpetrating injustice, spreading corruption, and being vainglorious above others on this earth are satanic ones—they share those [traits] with Iblīs and his demon followers.

Nonetheless, all pleasures become null once the spirit separates from the body except for the pleasure of knowledge and faith. At that point, it becomes even more perfect since the body can no longer distract [the spirit from true bliss]. Whoever wishes for the ultimate pleasure and prefers the eternal bliss, will find it in knowledge and faith.

In addition, those [animalistic and satanic] pleasures abate quickly—once they end, distress and sorrow follow. Then the sinner may need to treat that [distress or sorrow] by repeating [the sin] so as to avoid that pain. It may be that this habitual return is painful and disliked by him, but he is induced to do so to prevent the distress and sorrow from occurring. There is such a vast difference between all that and the pleasures associated with knowledge, faith in God, loving Him, drawing near to Him, as well as the felicity associated with His remembrance—those are the true pleasures.

The fourth type [of person mentioned in ʿAlī's statement] relates to those who are seduced with gathering, investing and hoarding wealth. They are so infatuated and consumed that they do not see any other pursuit more agreeable besides it. There is such a vast difference between this type of person and those who seek knowledge.

Again, these four types are not callers to this religion, leading scholars or sincere students pursuing knowledge. Those possessing a semblance to those [who are scholars or students] only dubiously do so. They claim that they have reached the status [of nobility], but instead they are cut off. Some may compare them [to the true scholars] because of some knowledge that they may see. They justify it saying: 'We are not better than them and we do not give preference to ourselves over them.' Those who are seduced consider these imitators to be sources of evidence. Some of the Companions said: 'Beware of the discord resulting from the wicked scholar and the ignorant worshipper. Their discord is a tribulation for every seduced one.'[1]

ʿAlī's statement essentially compares such people to grazing cattle. This comparison is derived from the statement of the Exalted: *They are but as the cattle—nay, but they are farther astray.*[2] The Sublime did not stop by comparing them just to cattle, but instead described them as further astray. Here *sā'ima* means 'grazing' (*rāʿīya*), and the Emir of the Believers compared them to [grazers] because their sole endeavour is the pursuit of this world and its rubble.

God (Exalted is He) sometimes likens those who are ignorant or astray to cattle and, on other occasions, to donkeys. This latter analogy is for those who have learned knowledge but do not comprehend or act upon it. Finally, sometimes [they are likened] to dogs, and this applies to those who abandoned knowledge and instead pursued their temptations and whims.

ʿAlī's statement, 'Knowledge fades away with the death of those

1 Ibn ʿAbd al-Barr 1161. In this reference it was said by Ibn al-Mubārak.

2 Q. xv.44.

who uphold it', is based on the *ḥadīth* of the Prophet (may God bless him and grant him peace) narrated by ʿAbd Allāh b. ʿUmar and ʿĀ'isha (may God be pleased with them): 'Indeed God does not take away knowledge by removing it from the hearts of people, but instead He seizes that knowledge by taking the scholars. Once no scholar remains, people begin to ask ignorant leaders, who give their verdicts without knowledge. They are misguided and they lead people further astray.'[1] Thus the fading away of knowledge is due to the passing of the scholars.

Ibn Masʿūd said on the day that ʿUmar (may God be pleased with him) died: 'I consider that nine-tenths of knowledge has been lost today.' It was previously mentioned that ʿUmar (may God be pleased with him) said: 'The death of a thousand worshippers is less significant than the death of a single scholar enlightened with the knowledge of what is permitted by God and what is forbidden.'[2]

ʿAlī's statement, 'Yet by the will of God this earth will not be devoid of [scholars] who remain steadfast for God's sake and convey His evidences', is derived from the authentic *ḥadīth* of the Prophet (may God bless him and grant him peace): 'There will always exist a group from my Community upon the truth. They will not be harmed by those who have forsaken or opposed them until God's decree comes and they are in this manner.'[3] Anas also narrated that the Messenger of God (may God bless him and grant him peace) said: 'My Community is like the rain: it is not known whether the first [of the rain] is better or the last.'[4] ʿAmmār and ʿAbd Allāh b. ʿAmr said: 'Had it not been for the fact that there exist those in the last of this Community who remain steadfast conveying God's evidences and formulating independent legal verdicts, they would not have been described with that goodness.'

1 Bukhārī 24; Muslim 6796; Tirmidhī 2652; Ibn Māja 9; Aḥmad 6511.

2 Ibn ʿAbd al-Barr 126.

3 Muslim 4950; Tirmidhī 2229; Abū Dāwūd 4252; Ibn Māja 10.

4 Tirmidhī 2869; Aḥmad 12,327. It is 'authentic' according to Albānī (*Silsilat al-aḥādīth al-ṣaḥīḥa* 2286).

In addition, this Community is the most perfect and the best to ever exist in humanity; and its prophet is the Seal of the Prophets. Since there is no prophet who will come after [Muḥammad], God provided it with scholars. Every time a scholar dies another succeeds him. In that manner, the distinguishing characteristics of this religion (*maᶜālim al-dīn*) do not go into oblivion, nor do its guideposts (*aᶜlām*) become unknown. As for the Israelites, every time a prophet would die another prophet would succeed him. Thus they were always led by prophets. The scholars of this Community are like the prophets for the Israelites.

Khawlānī narrated that the Messenger of God (may God bless him and grant him peace) said: 'God will continue to sprout up for this religion new plants that He will use to serve Him.'[1] The plants of God (*ghars Allāh*) are those who are knowledgeable and act righteously. Therefore, if the earth had become devoid of scholars, these plants of God would likewise be absent.

Now some people have added fabrications to this tradition of ᶜAlī or claimed that it is a proof of the 'awaited one' (*muntaẓar*).[2] This statement of ᶜAlī is well known and only those who are liars have added to it. Furthermore, the evidences of God are not upheld by someone who is unknown and hidden. Those who are ignorant cannot hear any news or learn anything from [that type of person], and those who are astray cannot be guided by him. Those who are fearful cannot become secure and those who are subjugated cannot become empowered through [such a hidden one]. What kind of evidence of God is upheld by someone whose body cannot be seen, his speech cannot be heard, and his whereabouts remain unknown, especially by those whose principles maintain that claim?

They were prompted to make such a claim by using the [following principle]: 'It is necessary that God's evidence be severed

1 Ibn Māja 8; Aḥmad 17,787. It is 'sound' according to Albānī (*Silsilat al-aḥādīth al-ṣaḥīḥa* 2442).

2 Here Ibn al-Qayyim briefly discusses the Twelver Shiᶜi belief of occultation.

[temporarily] from those charged with obligations out of divine providence for them.' O God, how amazing is this providence that has occurred as a result of this non-existent—even infallible [as they claim]—person! And what types of the Lord's evidences have they substantiated predicated on this false principle? Since there is no way whatsoever for them to meet this non-existent person (*maʿdūm*) and become guided by him, is [God's providence] displayed best by charging them with something unbearable [that is, waiting for his coming], and by making them excused [from other obligations] due to their lack of evidence [and the awaited one's absence]? They have tried to escape from one thing, but have only fallen into something more evil. It has been said:

> The one who seeks protection with ʿAmr when [afflicted] with troubles
> Is like one who seeks protection from the sun-baked ground with fire.[1]

God has promised to disgrace those who diminish the Companions for the latter are the best of this Community and are at the forefront of it. [God has also promised that] people will see the faults [of those who denigrate the Companions] and He will expose them. We seek protection with God from being forsaken. This poet says it best:

> Is it not time that the cellar [in Samarra] brought forth [the Twelfth Imam]
> Which you have assumed and claimed? Is it not time?
> Your rationale is faulty since you have considered him to be
> The third of a group which includes griffons (*ʿunaqāʾ*) and ghouls (*ghīlān*)

The evidences held by this 'hidden one' have become completely lost and null. In reality, they have invalidated the evidences of God, not preserved them. This tradition of the Emir of the Believers [ʿAlī] (may God be pleased with him) is forthright [in stating] that one who

1 This is akin to the English idiom 'Jump out of the frying pan into the fire.'

upholds the evidences of God on this earth is one who relays and conveys them from God to His servants. ʿAlī (may God be pleased with him) exemplifies such characteristics, as do his brothers, the Rightly-Guided Caliphs, and those who will follow them until the Day of Resurrection.

ʿAlī's statement, 'In that manner, they prevent the evidences and signs of God from falling into disuse', illustrates that it is impossible for them to become null. If it is said: What is the difference between evidences (*ḥujaj*) and signs (*bayyināt*)? The answer is that *ḥujaj* are the evidences of knowledge that can be heard by one's ears and understood by one's heart. God (Exalted is He) mentioned Abraham debating and showing his people the invalidity of their position by using evidences of knowledge: *That is Our argument. We gave it unto Abraham against his folk. We raise unto degrees of wisdom whom We will. Thy Lord is Wise, Aware.*[1] Ibn Zayd interpreted *argument* to be 'knowledge of evidences'.

In addition, *ḥujja* can also indicate 'argument' (*mukhāṣima*), as per the statement of the Exalted: *Unto this, then, summon (O Muḥammad). And be thou upright as thou art commanded, and follow not their lusts, but say: I believe in whatever Book God hath sent down, and I am commanded to be just among you. God is our Lord and your Lord. Unto us our works and unto you your works; there is no argument between us and you.*[2] This indicates that once the truth has become evident, clear and manifest, then no further arguments or debates should occur. The purpose of debating (*jidāl*) is only to manifest the truth. Once the truth becomes evident, then there is no further benefit in arguing and debating. Further arguments and debates just become troublesome, so one should dispense with them. This is the meaning of this verse.

Many of those who are ignorant have the erroneous impression that one should not debate others because the Divine Law and the Prophet (may God bless him and grant him peace) did not use evi-

1 Q. VI.83.

2 Q. XLII.15.

dence against his opponents or debate them. Some ignorant logicians and followers of Greek philosophy [go even further] and claim [first of all] that the Divine Law only addressed the masses and that evidence cannot be deduced from it. [Secondly, they argue] that the prophets only called the masses by using sermons, while the [true] evidences are only for the elite. [Thirdly, they argue] that only they and those who follow their methods truly adhere to the proofs. All of this is due to their ignorance of the Divine law and the Qur'ān. The Qur'ān is replete with all types of evidences and proofs with regards to issues of His Oneness, His creation of this universe, the resurrection and His sending of the messengers.

The speculative theologians (*mutakallimūn*) and others do not render definitive proofs of the above [issues] except that the Qur'ān provides them with more eloquent expressions, clearer signs and more complete meanings that are far removed from any uncertainty or need for [further] questioning. Indeed many of the master speculative theologians, whether ancient or modern, have acknowledged this [fact].

Abū Ḥāmid [al-Ghazālī][1] mentioned in the beginning of the *Iḥyā'*:

> Some [may object] by asking: Why did I not discuss the branches of speculative theology and philosophy, and clarify whether they are either blameworthy or praiseworthy? My reply is: Know that all the beneficial proofs found in speculative theology are encompassed within the

1 Abū Ḥāmid Muḥammad b. Muḥammad al-Ghazālī (d. 504/1111) is considered by many to be the Renewer (*mujaddid*) of his century and the Proof (*ḥujja*) of Islam. He wrote many significant books, including the *Iḥyā' ʿulūm al-dīn* [The Revival of the Religious Sciences], which bridged the gap between orthodox practice and Sufism, and is considered to be his greatest work. He also wrote *Tahāfut al-falāsifa* [The Incoherence of the Philosophers], which successfully refuted Greek philosophy and its supporters amongst the Arab philosophers, such as Fārābī and Ibn Sīnā (Avicenna). He also provided the Islamic creed for the schools built by Niẓām al-Mulk, which led to a Sunni revival. His theology was Ashʿarī, while his jurisprudence was Shāfiʿī.

> Qur'ān and the Traditions of the Prophet. Whatever is not included in either [the Qur'ān or the Traditions of the Prophet] is not there because they are either blameworthy debates, which are innovations as I will show subsequently; or they are controversial and contradictory; or they are long-winded farces (*tarahāt*) and senseless jibber-jabber (*hadhayānāt*) that our natures would belittle and our understanding would reject; or they are statements that are not even relevant to the religion. None of this existed in the first period [of Islam] whereby it was considered an innovation to take [speculative theology] up in its entirety.[1] The ruling regarding this has changed now, though, since innovations have occurred that turn people away from the requisites of the Qur'ān and the Sunna. A group has emerged[2] that has fabricated doubts and arranged false statements [to embolden them]. Thus that which was previously forbidden has now become permissible due to its necessity.[3]

Rāzī said in his book *Aqṣām al-ladhdhāt* [The Types of Pleasure[4]]: 'I considered the books of speculative theology and philosophical methodologies, but I did not feel that it satisfied one's thirst, nor did it cure one's ailment. Instead, I saw the closest methodology to be that of the Qur'ān. One can read [verses] that [definitively] affirm: *Unto Him good words ascend;*[5] and *The Beneficent One, Who is established*

1 This sentence is present in Ghazālī's book but the latter part is missing in the text used for this translation.

2 This phrase is also included in Ghazālī's book but is missing in the text used for this translation.

3 Ghazālī, *Iḥyā'*, vol. 1, p. 22.

4 This book is also entitled *Dhamm ladhdhāt al-dunyā* [Censure of the Pleasures of this World]. Regarding this text, see Shihadeh, *The Teleological Ethics of Fakhr al-Dīn al-Rāzī*, pp. 187–188. The paragraph as rendered by Ibn al-Qayyim is somewhat summarized.

5 Q. xxxv.10.

on the Throne.[1] One can also read [verses] that [definitively] negate: *Naught is as His likeness.*[2] Whoever has experienced what I have will recognize what I have.' Rāzī is only pointing out the definite proofs of the Qur'ān that he understands. Once one deeply understands the proofs of the Qur'ān, which are transmitted, rational, definitive, based on evidence and certain, no doubts can intervene between him and them, and nothing tenable can take their place. In that case, one's heart will never abandon the Qur'ān.

The firmly-rooted (*rāsikhūn*) scholars are knowledgeable regarding [these proofs]. Firm knowledge makes the heart content, puts the self at ease, increases one's intellect and enlightenment, and allows evidences to become strengthened. There is no way for anybody in the world to repudiate the [scholar] who uses this knowledge based on evidence. Whoever argues using these evidences will tear apart the doubts his opponents try to instill in people. It is only through [firm knowledge] that the hearts become receptive and responsive to God and His Messenger.

One speculative theologian said: 'I spent my whole life in speculative theology seeking proofs, but I found that I only became more distant from them. I therefore went back to the Qur'ān to ponder and contemplate it. I found that I had the true evidence all along without realizing it. I thought to myself: By God, I am like the one depicted by the poet: "One of the most amazing and astonishing things is a crowd / Near one who is beloved yet they cannot reach him / It is like a stallion in the desert dying from thirst / Even though it carries water on its back."'

He continues to say: 'Once I returned to the Qur'ān, I found the rulings and proofs. I also found God's evidences and signs such that if every correct thing the speculative theologians had written in their books was accumulated, one of the *sūra*s of the Qur'ān would still be more complete in comparison. Furthermore, [the Qur'ān's] phrases

1 Q. xx.5.
2 Q. xlii.11.

are more beautiful and eloquent, and they conform to [reality] in detail, take care [of our needs], allude to matters where doubts may occur, and guide one on how to respond to them. It is just as has been said: "[The Qur'ān] is sufficient and it cures anything in the heart / It has not omitted any need whether major or minor." The [doubts] of speculative theology kept on swarming upon my heart, but I rejected them and did not allow them to enter. Thus these [doubts] were turned away.'

The point is that the Qur'ān is full of all of the types of evidences, proofs and correct types of deductions by analogy (*aqyisa*). Furthermore, God (Exalted is He) commanded His Messenger (may God bless him and grant him peace) to uphold them and debate others: *And reason with them in the better way;*[1] *And argue not with the People of the Book unless it be in (a way) that is better.*[2] Only those who are extremely ignorant would deny that [command].

To return, the point is to differentiate between 'evidences' (*ḥujaj*) and 'proofs' (*bayyināt*). I say that 'evidences' are substantiations based on knowledge (*al-adilla al-ʿilmiyya*), while 'proofs' is the term used for anything that reveals the truth, whether it is a manifest token (*ʿalāma manṣuba aw imāra*) or a proof based upon knowledge. The Exalted said: *We verily sent Our messengers with clear proofs* [(*bayyināt*)], *and revealed with them the Book and the Balance.*[3] Thus 'proofs' are the signs (*āyāt*) that God uses to prove the truthfulness of the [messengers], and they include inimitable prophetic miracles (*muʿjizāt*). The Book [in this verse is distinct from those signs and it] is what actually calls [people to the guidance].

The Exalted said: *The first Sanctuary appointed for mankind was that at Becca, a blessed place, a guidance to the peoples; wherein are clear signs (of God's guidance, such as) the place (maqām) where Abraham stood up to pray.*[4]

1 Q. XVI.125.
2 Q. XXIX.46.
3 Q. LVII.25.
4 Q. III.96–97.

The Place of Abraham is a sign that can be seen and it is one of God's signs in this world. Also consider the verse in which Moses said to Pharaoh and the latter's people: *I come unto you (lords of Egypt) with a clear proof from your Lord. So let the Children of Israel go with me. (Pharaoh) said: If thou comest with a sign, then produce it, if thou art of those who speak the truth. Then he flung down his staff.*[1] The flinging of the staff and its turning into a serpent was the proof (*bayyina*) described here. These are the types of signs that God (Exalted is He) spoke about when He said: *Naught hindereth Us from sending signs (āyāt) save that the folk of old denied them.*[2]

It is due to the Sublime's mercy and benevolence that He did not respond to the request of the disbelievers [of Quraysh]. His methodology (*sunna*), which cannot be altered, is that if the [disbelievers] ask for a sign and He responds to them but yet they still do not believe, then He will punish them by wiping them out (*isti'ṣāl*). Since the Sublime knew that they would not believe even if they were given all of the signs, He did not answer their request. As a result, they were not deserving of that particular punishment. Instead, the offspring [of those same rejectors] subsequently believed in Him. They believed without needing these signs that were proposed by their [fathers]. Therefore the fact that these requested signs were not sent down was due to the Lord's perfect wisdom, mercy and benevolence.

On the other hand, evidences continued to be revealed in an increasing fashion. The Messenger of God (may God bless him and grant him peace) died while leaving behind a vast number [of evidences]; and they will all remain until the Day of Resurrection.

ʿAlī's statement, 'They are the least in number, but they occupy the greatest rank in God's sight', indicates that this group of people represent the fewest number in creation, and so they are considered to be strangers. The Prophet (may God bless him and grant him

1 Q. VII.105–107.

2 Q. XVII.59.

peace) said: 'Verily Islam started as something strange (*gharīb*) and it will again revert to being strange just as it began. So blessed are the strangers (*ghurabā'*).'[1] Thus the believers are few when compared to all of humanity, the scholars are a small subset of the believers, and these [strangers] are only a minority of the scholars. Do not succumb to a thought which deceives those who are ignorant: 'Had these people been on the truth, they would not have been the minority opposed by the majority.' Know that these [strangers] are the true [and elite] of humanity, and that those who oppose them are only human beings [in form].

Ibn Masʿūd said: 'Let none of you be characterless (*imʿa*) by saying "I only want to follow the [majority of] people." Rather, you should settle on believing even if all other people have disbelieved.'[2] The Sublime has criticized the majority in many places: *If thou obeyedst most of those on earth they would mislead thee far from God's way;*[3] *And though thou try much, most men will not believe;*[4] *Few of My servants are thankful;*[5] *Many partners oppress one another, save such as believe and do good works, and they are few.*[6] One of the knowers said: 'Your loneliness on the path is proof of the righteousness you seek.'

> Do not be afraid of the desolation along the path
> you are taking.
> Instead, walk [knowing] that the truth is guarding you.

Then ʿAlī said: 'God defends His evidences by using them; they convey them to their colleagues and peers and plant them in their hearts.' This is because God (Glory be to Him) has ensured the preservation of His evidences and signs. The Prophet (may God bless him and grant him peace) notified us that, 'There will always

1 Muslim 372; Ibn Māja 3986; Aḥmad 3784.
2 Haythamī 851.
3 Q. VI.116.
4 Q. XII.103.
5 Q. XXXIV.13.
6 Q. XXXVIII.24.

exist a group from my Community upon the truth. They will not be harmed by those who have forsaken or opposed them until the Hour occurs.'[1]

The plants of God, which He uses for His religion, will continuously implant knowledge into the hearts of those whom God is pleased with and has deemed fit for that. Thus the evidences of God and those who uphold them will always remain present on this earth. Some of the Predecessors used to supplicate: 'O God, make me one of Your plants who obey You by doing righteous deeds in accordance with Your will.'

Those whom God has supported to preserve this religion did not die except after they had spread their knowledge and wisdom, either to their peers or by authoring books that people could benefit from. It is for this reason and others [previously mentioned] that the scholars are superior to the worshippers.

Then ʿAlī said: 'This knowledge allows them to charge forth [and understand] the realities of the matter. It has also allowed them to find [the path] easily manageable, whereas the wanton (*mutrafūn*) find it rugged and difficult. They feel comfort [on this path] while the ignorant ones feel loneliness.' The path to the Hereafter is rugged and difficult for most people. This is due to the fact that their temptations, wishes and habits conflict with it; therefore few undertake it. It is also due to the paucity or absence of their knowledge regarding the journey's end, what they were created for and what has been prepared for them. They also found following their temptations and desires easier than being sincere and pious. Thus they inclined towards indifference (*daʿa*) and relaxation, and they preferred this immediate life (*ʿājil*) over the Hereafter (*ājil*). Those who are deluded away from God and obstinately reject His greatness and His lordship will say allegorically: 'Take hold of what you see and leave those things which you have only heard about.'

1 Tirmidhī 2192; Ibn Māja 6; Aḥmad 15,597 and 20,361. It is 'authentic' according to Albānī (*Silsilat al-aḥādīth al-ṣaḥīḥa* 403).

Those who uphold the evidences of God clearly see what the ignorant—who are dim-sighted—cannot. The flag post of bliss was raised up and so they raced towards it. They are certain of the Lord's promise; thus they abstained from everything else and only aspired to His [reward of Paradise]. They knew that this lowly world is a transient abode, not a permanent one; a passing stopover, not a resting place to delight in; and that its inhabitants are like travellers sitting underneath the shade of a tree only to soon leave it and move on. They are certain that it is like a dream during one's sleep or like a shadow that will vanish. Therefore their hearts have abandoned [this world] and they have turned their backs on it. Their hearts hurry towards the Hereafter empowered by their firm resolve. They abandoned their dreams and the pleasures associated with them, for the lover [of the Hereafter] does not actually sleep at night. They knew that the path was long and that their stay [in this world] was short— only [intended] to be a stopover for supplying provisions.

These all are the fruits of certainty. If the heart is certain of what is forthcoming of God's generosity and what He has prepared for His loyal supporters, he can almost witness [His Paradise] beyond the veil of this lowly world. He knows that once that veil is removed he will be able to see it directly. This [certainty] leads to the dissipation of any loneliness and he will be able to manage the [path] easily.

This is the first level of certainty. Here what is known is unveiled [only] to the heart. It witnesses it and has no doubts about it. This is followed by the second level, which is witnessed certainty (*ʿayn al-yaqīn*). This is seen [directly] by one's eyes, whereas the first is only witnessed by the heart. This is then followed by the third level, which is true certainty (*ḥaqq al-yaqīn*). This is to touch (*mubāshara*) and to grasp (*idrāk*) what is known. For example, the first [level of certainty] is your knowledge that there is water in a certain valley, while the second is if you can see it, and the third occurs once you drink it.

It is in this light that the *ḥadīth* of Ḥāritha should be understood. The Prophet (may God bless him and grant him peace) said: 'How do you view yourself, Ḥāritha?' He said: 'I view myself as a true believer.' The Prophet said: 'There is a reality to every statement, so what is the reality of your faith?' He said: 'I have abstained from this world and its temptations by praying at night and fasting during the day. I feel as if I am clearly looking at the Throne of my Lord. It is also as if I can see the inhabitants of Paradise visiting each other and the denizens of Hellfire crying out for relief [from the punishment].' The Prophet said: 'Here is a servant whose heart has been enlightened by God.'[1] This is how knowledge allows one who has it to charge forth and understand the realities of the matter.

In a well-known tradition [the Prophet said]: 'Once [the spiritual] light enters the heart, it opens up and rejoices.' It was said: 'What is the sign of that?' The Prophet said: 'Shunning this deceptive abode, seeking out the eternal abode, and preparing for death before it comes.'[2]

The Companions could reach this state when they were with the Prophet (may God bless him and grant him peace), as he would remind [and describe for] them Paradise and Hellfire. Hanẓala al-Usaydī, one of the scribes of the Prophet (may God bless him and grant him peace), once went crying with Abū Bakr (may God be pleased with him) to the Messenger of God. The Messenger of God (may God bless him and grant him peace) said when he saw him: 'What is the matter, Hanẓala?' He said: 'Hanẓala has become a hypocrite, O Messenger of God! You remind us of Hellfire and Paradise when we are with you, and it is as if we can see them with the naked eye. But when we leave, we forget so much because we become busy with our wives and livelihood.' The Messenger of God said: 'If you were to remain in the same state that you are in when

1 Bayhaqī (*Shuʿab*) 10,108; Haythamī 190 (who said it is 'weak').

2 Bayhaqī (*Shuʿab*) 10,068; Hākim 7863. It is 'weak' according to Albānī (*Mishkāt* 5228).

you are with me, the angels would shake your hands while you are in your gatherings, on your travels and on your beds. But Hanẓala, there is a time for this and a time for that.'[1]

The point again is to say that what allows the heart to charge forth into the reality of faith, to easily manage what others find difficult, and to feel comforted whereas others would feel loneliness, is the perfect knowledge and pure love it possesses. Love is concordant with knowledge and [love] becomes stronger as [one's knowledge becomes] greater, and vice versa. The lover does not find the path to be rugged or difficult as he actually reaches his beloved, nor does he feel loneliness along it.

Then ʿAlī said: 'These [scholars] have bodies that are in this world, but their spirits are attached to the heavenly congregation.' The spirit is a heavenly essence made of heavenly matter, but for now it is required to live in this earthy body. Yet every spirit continuously aspires for its home in the heavens and longs for it like a bird for its nest. However, because it is excessively distracted [with our daily lives], it wants to remain forever on this earth and it forgets its [real] abode and home. But it cannot rest anywhere else, just like there will be no rest for the believer until he meets his Lord.

This lowly world is truly [the believer's] prison. Therefore you will notice that the believer's body is in this lowly world, while his spirit is amongst the heavenly congregation. In a traceable *ḥadīth* narrated by Tammām[2] [we read]: 'If the servant sleeps while he is prostrating, God will mention his magnificence to the angels saying: "Look at My servant! His body is on the earth while his soul is with Me."'[3] This meaning is also portrayed by a saying of some of the Predecessors: 'The hearts are always roaming: one is around rot-

1 Muslim 6966; Tirmidhī 2514; Ibn Māja 4239; Aḥmad 17,609.

2 Abū al-Qāsim Tammām b. Muḥammad al-Rāzī (d. 414/1023) was a traditionist and author of *Fawā'id al-Ḥadīth*.

3 Tammām 1670; Zabīdī, vol. 1, p. 420. It is 'weak' according to Albānī (*Silsilat al-aḥādīth al-ḍaʿīfa* 953).

ten [actions and people] (*hushsh*) while another is circumambulating with the angels around [God's] Throne.'

The greatest punishment for the spirit is being entrenched and concealed in the depths of the body, because it is distracted by [the body's] pleasures, cut-off from noticing what it was created for, and [distracted] away from its [eternal] abode, place of comfort and high level. But the intoxication (*sukr*) induced by following temptations veils it from being cognizant of that pain and suffering. Then once it awakens from its intoxication and [becomes free of] adversities, all types of regret will descend upon it. At that point, [the spirit] will lament missing out on the generosity of God, proximity to Him and the feeling of comfort in His [presence]. It has been said:

> Allow your heart to travel wherever it desires
> Yet its love is only for its first love.
> How many residences on this earth is a young man fond of
> But he will always be nostalgic for his first home!

The believing servant in this world is [like someone who has been taken] captive away from Paradise to this abode of hardship and toil wherein he is enslaved. How can he be blamed for longing for the abode [of Paradise] when he has been separated from those whom he loves and [instead] gathered together with his enemies? I have written some poetry in this regard:

> Welcome to the Gardens of Eden as it is
> Your first home and settlement.
> But we have been taken captive by the enemy. Do you think
> That we will be able to return to our homeland and be safe?

It has been said [by Mutanabbī]:

> It is wished [by the enemy] that our hearts forget [Paradise]
> But our natures reject that disrupter.

For this reason, the believer is a stranger in this abode. No matter where he lives he remains in a strange abode. The Prophet (may God bless him and grant him peace) said in this regard: 'Be in this world as if you were a stranger or a passer-by.'[1] The Prophet (may God bless him and grant him peace) used to be amongst his Companions in body but his heart and spirit were with his Lord, Who provided him with [spiritual] sustenance.

Abū al-Dardā' said: 'If a servant sleeps, his spirit ascends to beneath the Throne. If it is pure, then it is allowed to prostrate, but if not then it is not allowed to do so.' This, and God knows best, is the reason that one who is in a state of ritual impurity should make ablution before going to sleep, as this ascendance occurs in the state of sleep. The spirit can also be free of the body due to other reasons. In those cases, it is able to rise and ascend to the degree that it is free. It may be that the love of the beloved is such that only his body is present amongst people, while his spirit is with his beloved.[2] This is well described in poetry and prose.

ʿAlī then said: 'They are the viceroys[3] of God on His earth.' Those who view that it is permissible to say that one is 'the viceroy of God on this earth' use this statement as evidence. Some of the Companions also used the following verses of God as evidence: *And when thy Lord said unto the angels: I am about to place a viceroy in the earth*;[4] *He it is Who hath made you viceroys in the earth*;[5] *Is not He (best) Who answereth the wronged one when he crieth unto Him and removeth the evil, and hath made you viceroys of the earth?*[6]

1 Bukhārī 6416; Tirmidhī 2333; Ibn Māja 4114; Aḥmad 4764.

2 Ibn al-Qayyim has mentioned further *ḥadīths* in this regard and describes the different types of strangeness: 'The righteous are strange [or few] in comparison to people in general, the ascetics are strange relative to the righteous, and the knowers are strange when compared to the ascetics.' See Ibn al-Qayyim, *Madārij*, vol. III, pp. 184–195.

3 The Arabic term for 'viceroys' is *khulafā'*, sing. *khalīfa*.

4 Q. II.30.

5 Q. XXXV.39.

6 Q. XXVII.62.

Moses said to his people: *It may be that your Lord is going to destroy your adversary and make you viceroys in the earth, that He may see how ye behave.*[1] The Prophet (may God bless him and grant him peace) also said: 'Indeed God will establish you and make you viceroys on this earth so that He may see how you behave. So guard yourselves against this world and [the seduction] of women.'[2] They also pointed to the statement of the shepherd speaking to Abū Bakr (may God be pleased with him) as evidence:

O viceroy of the Beneficent, we are a true people
Prostrating in the early morning and late afternoon.
We give our earnest money as we realize that God
has revealed
That a portion of our wealth be distributed as almsgiving.

But a second group opposed using that term and maintained it should not be said that someone is the 'viceroy of God'. This is because the word 'viceroy' denotes someone who has taken the place of another who is absent; but God (Exalted is He) is always present and never absent, near and never distant, and He is All-Seeing and All-Hearing. Thus it is impossible for another to succeed Him. Instead, He (Glory be to Him) is the One Who always succeeds His believing servants.

The Prophet (may God bless him and grant him peace) said in an authentic *ḥadīth* regarding the Antichrist (*Dajjāl*): 'If he appears while I am amongst you, then I will be his adversary on your behalf. But if he appears and I am not amongst you, then each man will have to fend for himself. God is my Successor[3] in taking care of every believer.'[4] ʿAbd Allāh b. ʿAmr narrated that the Messenger of God used to say when he would travel: 'O God, You are the Companion on a journey, and the Successor who takes care of one's family and

1 Q. VII.129.

2 Muslim 6948; Tirmidhī 2191; Ibn Māja 4000; Aḥmad 11,169.

3 Although the Arabic *khalīfa* is used in this context, it is inappropriate to refer to God as a 'Viceroy'.

4 Muslim 7373; Tirmidhī 2240; Abū Dāwūd 4321; Ibn Māja 4075; Aḥmad 17,629.

those left behind.'[1] In another authentic *ḥadīth* the Prophet (may God bless him and grant him peace) said: 'May God have mercy on Abū Salama and elevate his status amongst the guided ones. May He be his Successor in taking care of his family.'[2]

Abū Bakr al-Ṣiddīq (may God be pleased with him) disagreed with those who would call him 'the viceroy of God' (*khalīfat Allāh*), and he would say: 'I am not the viceroy of God, but rather the viceroy of the Messenger of God and this is sufficient for me.'

The [second group] also said there is no disagreement that the statement of the Exalted, *I am about to place a viceroy in the earth*,[3] refers to Adam and his offspring. Furthermore, all of the exegetes, Predecessors and later scholars are in agreement that He made Adam a successor to those who preceded him on this earth. It has been said that the jinn were its inhabitants [previously] and that the angels inhabited it after the jinn. This is mentioned in the exegeses.

The [second group] also maintained that the intended meaning of the Exalted's statement, *He it is Who hath made you viceroys in the earth*,[4] is that He made each generation succeed another such that every time one passes another succeeds it until the end of time—not that they are the viceroys of God.

Some have also maintained that this is specifically addressed to the Community of Muḥammad (may God bless him and grant him peace), indicating that He made them succeed the prior nations. Although there is no doubt that it is directed to this Community specifically, it also includes all of humanity. God made their father [Adam] succeed those before him and then made his offspring into successors, one generation after another, until the Hour arises. Therefore this succession is one of His signs: *Is not He* (*best*) *Who*

1 Muslim 3275; Tirmidhī 3439; Abū Dāwūd 2598; Aḥmad 6311.
2 Muslim 2130; Abū Dāwūd 3115; Ibn Māja 1447; Aḥmad 26,534.
3 Q. II.30.
4 Q. XXXV.39.

answereth the wronged one when he crieth unto Him and removeth the evil, and hath made you viceroys of the earth?[1]

As for the statement of Moses to his people, *It may be that your Lord is going to destroy your adversary and make you viceroys in the earth, that He may see how ye behave,*[2] it does not refer to them succeeding God, but rather that they will succeed Pharaoh and his people whom He destroyed. Similarly, the statement of the Prophet (may God bless him and grant him peace), 'God will make you viceroys on this earth', indicates that they will be successors to the prior nations that have been destroyed.

As for the poetry of the shepherd, it was said in the absence of the truly faithful one [Abū Bakr]. It is not known whether it actually reached Abū Bakr or not; and if it did reach him, then it is unknown whether he permitted this term or not.

My opinion is that, if what is intended by 'viceroy of God' is to claim that one succeeds God, then the group who prohibited this is correct. But if the intention of this attribution is that God made one a viceroy to succeed others who had preceded, then it is not forbidden. In this manner, the answer becomes clear regarding the statement of the Emir of the Believers [ʿAlī] that the [scholars] are 'the viceroys of God on His earth', whereby He made them succeed others.

If it is said that this attribution does not denote praise, since it is applicable to the entire Community, the response is that it connotes selecting and distinguishing this [elite group of scholars]. It is similar to the attribution of being His servant in the statement of the Exalted: *As for My servants, thou hast no power over any of them;*[3] *The (faithful) servants of the Beneficent are they who walk upon the earth modestly;*[4] and other like examples. It is well known that all of crea-

1 Q. XXVII.62.
2 Q. VII.129.
3 Q. XV.42.
4 Q. XXV.63.

tion are His servants. Thus the [term] 'successors' is like 'servant' in His statements: *God is Seer of His servants*[1] and *God willeth no injustice for (His) servants*;[2] and 'viceroys of God' is analogous to *servants* in: *Lo! as for My servants, thou hast no power over any of them.*[3]

Finally, ʿAlī said that they are 'His callers to His religion.' Here *al-duʿāt* is the plural of caller (*dāʿin*), like judge (*qāḍin*) and [the plural] *quḍāt* or thrower (*rāmin*) and [the plural] *rumāt*. Their attribution to God [as His callers] also connotes that they were selected specifically [for that purpose]. They call others to His religion in order to worship and love Him. They are the elite of God's creation, and they are bestowed the highest status by God (as will be proven by the next point).

1 Q. III.15.
2 Q. XL.31.
3 Q. XV.42.

CHAPTER TEN

Knowledge is Essential to Attaining Certainty and to Calling to God

[Point 130: One of the highest ranks is calling to God, and this requires extensive knowledge.]

The Exalted said: *And who is better in speech than him who prayeth unto his Lord and doeth right, and saith: I am of those who are Muslims (surrendering unto Him).*[1] Ḥasan [al-Baṣrī] said: 'This refers to a believer who has responded to God's calling. He then calls people to it and does righteous deeds accordingly.' God loves such a person, and he is one of His loyal supporters. Being a caller to God is one of the highest ranks that a servant can reach. The Exalted said: *And when the servant of God stood up in prayer to Him, they crowded on him, almost stifling;*[2] *Call unto the way of thy Lord with wisdom and fair exhortation, and reason with them in the better way.*[3]

The Sublime has made the status of the recipients dictate the manner of calling (*daʿwa*). [Firstly], those who are rational, accept [the message] and do not stubbornly reject the truth are called to it through wisdom. [Secondly], those who are receptive but are unmindful or hesitant for some reason are called by good advice. This is through enjoining them to [good] and forbidding them from [evil]. It also involves making them yearn [for Paradise] and

1 Q. XLI.33.
2 Q. LXXII.19.
3 Q. XVI.125.

fear [Hellfire].[1] [Thirdly], those who stubbornly reject and are obstinate are debated only in an amicable way. This is the correct [interpretation] of this verse.

It does not mean, as is claimed by those who are held captive by Greek philosophy, that wisdom is the demonstrative syllogism (*qiyās al-burhān*) used to call the elite; good advice is the rhetorical syllogism (*qiyās al-khiṭāba*) used to call the masses; and debating with that which is better is the dialectical syllogism (*qiyās al-jadalī*) used to refute those who try to provoke discord (*shaghab al-mashāghib*) by debating with analogies composed of agreed-upon premises. This is falsehood[2] and it is built upon the premises of philosophy. It is in opposition to the principles of the Muslims and the rules of the [Islamic] religion in many aspects, but this is not the place to discuss this.

The Exalted said: *Say: This is my way. I call on God enlightened with sure knowledge. I and whosoever followeth me.*[3] Kalbī said: 'It is incumbent upon everyone who follows [the Prophet] to call to that which he called to, to remind [people] with the Qur'ān and give them [good] advice.' A person cannot truly be one of the Prophet's followers until he calls to what the [Messenger] has called to; and calling others perfectly requires extensive knowledge. As such, this is sufficient to show the eminence of knowledge. God blesses with His grace those whom He wills.

1 Ibn al-Qayyim adds in a subsequent section that is not translated in the main text: 'It is for this group that the allegories were drawn, the evidences were established, and the opposing views and responses to them were mentioned.' See Ibn al-Qayyim, *Miftāḥ*, p. 204.

2 Ibn al-Qayyim states in another section that has not been translated in the main text: 'These interpretations are from the likes of the Qarāmiṭa, Bāṭiniyya and extremist Ismāʿīlīs. They interpret the Qur'ān so as to make it comply with their false doctrines. The Qur'ān is free and infallible from all of these falsehoods and madnesses.' See Ibn al-Qayyim, *Miftāḥ*, p. 205.

3 Q. XII.108.

[POINT 131: KNOWLEDGE IS ESSENTIAL TO ATTAINING CERTAINTY.]

If there was no benefit to knowledge except that it engenders certainty, [then that would be sufficient]. Certainty is the greatest source of life for the heart; and contentment, power and ability all occur as a result of it. It is for this reason that God (Glory be to Him) praised and commended those who possess it in His Book: *And are certain of the Hereafter;*[1] and *We have made clear the revelations for people who are sure.*[2] He said regarding His friend Abraham: *Thus did We show Abraham the kingdom of the heavens and the earth that he might be of those possessing certainty.*[3]

God criticized those who do not have certainty by saying: *Because mankind had not faith in Our revelations.*[4] ʿAbd Allāh b. Masʿūd narrated a *ḥadīth*: 'Do not try to please others in ways which are displeasing to God. Do not praise someone else for what God has given you, nor criticize him for what He has withheld from you. The bounties of God cannot be granted to you [if not willed by God] even by the most intent person, nor can they be withheld from you [if willed by God] by the hatred of your enemies.'[5]

God (Exalted is He), due to His justice and wisdom, made spirituality, ease and joy result from contentment and certainty, while He made distress and grief result from discontent and doubts. Thus if the heart is touched by certainty, it becomes filled with light and all uncertainties and doubts become expelled from it. In that manner, it becomes cured from its deadly diseases. As a result, one becomes thankful to God and remembers, loves and fears Him alone.

Faith is built upon pillars—two of them are certainty and love. They lead to all other [good] deeds, whether from the heart or the

1 Q. II.4.
2 Q. II.118.
3 Q. VI.75.
4 Q. XXVII.82.
5 Haythamī 6291; Mundhirī 2648; Abū Nuʿaym, vol. IV, p. 121. It is 'fabricated' according to Albānī (*Ḍaʿīf al-Targhīb* 1064).

body. But if they are weak, then actions are likewise weak. All stations of the [pious] travellers (*manāzil al-sā'irīn*) and ranks of the knowers (*maqāmāt al-ʿārifīn*) are achieved through [certainty and love]. They result in every good deed, beneficial knowledge and straight guidance.

The masters mentioned that excellent certainty (*al-jayyid al-yaqīn*) occurs when knowledge is firmly established in the heart, never becoming overturned, transformed or changed. Sahl [al-Tustarī] said: 'It is sinful for a heart that has smelled the scent of certainty to find tranquillity in anything other than God.' It has also been said: 'Some of the signs [of certainty] are: seeking God's assistance in every matter, turning to Him whenever any misfortune [strikes], and aspiring to His Countenance through action or inaction.'

Sirrī[1] said: 'Tranquillity, which occurs despite all of the [evil] thoughts that run through your heart, is a result of your certainty that any action on your part will not benefit you nor repel what is decreed.' I say that this applies only if one is not commanded to undertake a particular action, for if one is so ordered then one's certainty requires one to strive with all of one's abilities. It has been said that if the servant truly perfects his certainty then every tribulation will become a blessing, and every hardship (*miḥna*) will become a favour (*minḥa*). Knowledge leads to the first level of certainty. It has also been said: 'Your knowledge leads to your actions, while certainty carries you [in times of hardship].' Thus certainty is one of the greatest blessings of the Lord.

One cannot become truly content except by climbing upon the step of certainty. The Exalted said: *No calamity befalleth save by God's leave. And whosoever believeth in God, He guideth his heart.*[2] Ibn Masʿūd stated that this [verse] describes a servant who is content and at peace when afflicted by a calamity, because he knows it is from God. His

1 Abū al-Ḥasan Sirrī b. al-Maghallis al-Saqaṭī, known as Sirrī (d. 251/867), was a prominent Sufi of Baghdad. He was the student of Maʿrūf al-Karkhī. He later taught the prominent Sufi Junayd, who was his nephew.

2 Q. LXIV.11.

heart's contentment and submission (*taslīm*), along with [God's] guidance, only occurred because of his certainty.

[POINT 132: AN EXPOSITION OF THE DIFFERENT TYPES OF KNOWLEDGE AND A CRITIQUE OF GREEK LOGIC.]

Abū Yaʿlā al-Mawṣilī[1] related in his *Musnad*: Anas b. Mālik narrated that the Prophet (may God bless him and grant him peace) said: 'Pursuit of knowledge is obligatory upon every Muslim.'[2] Every Muslim is obligated to have faith; and one cannot envision faith without knowledge and deeds.

Moreover, the Divine Law of Islam is obligatory upon every Muslim, and it cannot be fulfilled until one recognizes and knows it. God (Exalted is He) brought forth His servants from the wombs of their mothers without any knowledge; therefore pursuing knowledge is obligatory upon every Muslim. In addition, is it possible to worship God, which is His right over all of His servants, except through knowledge? And can knowledge be attained except by pursuing it?

Furthermore, there are two types of knowledge that one is obligated to learn. The first is obligatory for each individual (*farḍ ʿayn*)—no Muslim should be ignorant of this type. It encompasses many subtypes: [the first is] knowledge of the five prescripts of faith, which are faith in God, His angels, His Books, His messengers and the Last Day. If someone does not believe in these he cannot be considered to have faith nor does he deserve to be named 'a believer'. God (Exalted is He) said: *But righteous is he who believeth in God and the Last Day and the angels and the Book and the prophets*;[3] *Whoso disbelieveth in God and His angels and His Books and His messengers and the Last Day,*

1 Abū Yaʿlā Aḥmad b. ʿAlī b. al-Muthanna al-Mawṣilī (d. 307/919) was a traditionist who collected a *Musnad* containing 7555 *ḥadīths*.

2 Bayhaqī (*Shuʿab*) 1546; Haythamī 472; Abū Nuʿaym, vol. VIII, p. 323; Ibn ʿAdī, vol. III, p. 249. It is 'authentic' according to Albānī (*Ṣaḥīḥ al-Jāmiʿ al-ṣaghīr* 3913).

3 Q. II.177.

he verily hath wandered far astray.[1] In addition, when Gabriel asked the Messenger of God (may God bless him and grant him peace) about faith the Prophet said: 'To believe in God, His angels, His Books, His messengers and the Last Day.'[2] [Gabriel] then said: 'You have spoken the truth.'

The second subtype concerns knowledge of the Divine Law of Islam. The servant is obligated to know ablution, prayer, fasting, pilgrimage and almsgiving. He must also know what they entail, their requirements and what nullifies them.

The third subtype concerns the five universal prohibitions conveyed by all the messengers and present in the Divine Laws and Books. They are mentioned in the statement of the Exalted: *Say: My Lord has indeed forbidden indecencies whether apparent or secret, sin and wrongful oppression, that ye associate with God that for which no warrant hath been revealed, and that ye say concerning God that which ye know not.*[3] These have been forbidden by all of the messengers upon all people and at all times; and they are never permissible. Hence God used the word *innamā* to denote absoluteness. In contrast, there are other things which are forbidden at some times and permitted in others; for example, [the prohibition of eating] a dead animal, blood and pork, which are not absolutely forbidden [in all circumstances].

The fourth subtype concerns knowledge of the laws of interactions and dealings that occur between oneself and others, specifically and generally. Such obligations vary according to how each person's conditions and status differ. Thus what is obligatory for the Imam in regards to his followers is different than what is obligatory for a man with his family or neighbours. Likewise what is obligatory for someone who is a merchant and who must learn the rulings regard-

1 Q. IV.136.

2 Bukhārī 50; Muslim 99; Tirmidhī 2610; Abū Dāwūd 4695; Nasā'ī 4993; Ibn Māja 63; Aḥmad 191.

3 Q. VII.33.

ing his trade is different than someone who does not sell but only buys things out of necessity.

Now obligatory knowledge cannot be precisely delineated due to people's differences and reasons for it. This all returns to three principles: belief, action and relinquishment (*tark*). Belief obligates one to follow the essence of the truth. Actions obligate one to recognize the truth, such that one's freely-chosen movements, whether apparent or hidden, are consistent with what the Divine Law commands and makes permissible. And relinquishment obligates one to recognize what one should abstain from; and then one should do so with tranquillity for the sake of pleasing God. Knowledge of the movements of both the heart and body is applicable here.

As for the obligations that are sufficed if only performed by some (*farḍ kifāyah*), I do not know of a correct general rule, since every one includes what he thinks is obligatory. Some will include within it the knowledge of medicine, mathematics, engineering and land surveying, while some will add to those the branches of industry like farming, weaving, metallurgy, sewing and the like. Others will add knowledge of [Greek] logic (*manṭiq*) and even consider it to be obligatory for each individual (*farḍ ʿayn*). By this the correct faith of the blind imitators is destroyed. This [stance] is delusion and madness—there are no obligations except those commanded by God (Glory be to Him) and His Messenger.

Had [Greek] logic been a correct [branch] of knowledge, then it ultimately would be like land surveying, engineering and the like. Instead, though, its falsehoods are many times greater than its truths. Some who have read through it and devoted themselves to it are surprised at the corrupt nature of its principles and fundamentals, its variance with pure reason, its inclusion of precepts that are baseless and without proof, and its attempt to differentiate between two equals or equate between two disparate entities. I asked some of its leaders and scholars about it and one of them thought about it and said: 'This knowledge represents a type of mental training (*ṣaqalath al-adhhān*) that has existed from ancient times and, therefore, we should just accept it. It is the best we have in the field of logic.'

I became acquainted with the works of the linguist Abū Saᶜīd al-Sirafī and the rebuttals of many of the speculative theologians and scholars of Arabic to the corruptions and contradictions [of Greek logic]. They included Abū Bakr b. al-Ṭayyib,[1] ᶜAbd al-Jabbār,[2] [Abū ᶜAlī] al-Jubbā'ī and his son [Abū Hāshim], Abū al-Maᶜālī, Abū al-Qāsim al-Anṣārī[3] in addition to many others. Finally, I read the Shaykh of Islam [Ibn Taymiyya's] response to them (may God sanctify his spirit). He wrote two books—one longer and one shorter[4]—that included wonderful marvels, which exposed their secrets, unveiled their deceptive façade and disgraced them. I then wrote some poetry regarding it:

How bewildering is the logic of the Greeks!
It contains many untruths and slanderous lies
It results in the best of minds becoming mad
And it corrupts people's innate disposition.
Its principles and foundations are shaky
For they are built on the edge of a crumbling cliff.
Although one is in dire need and submissive

1 Abū Bakr Muḥammad b. al-Ṭayyib al-Bāqillānī (d. 402/1013) learned directly from the students of Ashᶜarī. Ibn Taymiyya said about him that he was the 'best of the Ashᶜarī speculative theologians'.

2 Abū al-Ḥasan ᶜAbd al-Jabbār b. Aḥmad al-Hamādhānī al-Asadābādī (d. 415/1025) was a prominent Muᶜtazilī scholar and chief judge of the province of Rayy (in present-day Iran). His major work on Muᶜtazilī thought was named *al-Mughnī fī-abwāb al-tawḥīd wa'l-ᶜadl*.

3 Abū al-Qāsim Salmān b. Nāṣir al-Naysābūrī al-Anṣārī (d. 512/1118) was an Ashᶜarī scholar and Sufi. He was a student of Juwaynī and wrote a commentary on the latter's work named *Sharḥ al-Irshād*. His most famous student was Abū al-Fatḥ al-Shahrastānī.

4 Ibn Taymiyya wrote two books repudiating Greek logic: the longer one was *al-Radd ᶜala'l-manṭiqiyyīn* and the shorter one was entitled *Naqd al-manṭiq*. Of note, the first was abridged by Jalāl al-Dīn al-Suyūṭī and translated into English by Wael Hallaq, under the title *Ibn Taymiyya against the Greek Logicians* (Oxford: Clarendon Press, 1993).

It still betrays him both in secret and in public.
One walks in the [town] squares, his tongue scattering
[its untruths]
Walking on the bricks he necessarily
Moves languidly and stumbles continuously.
It appears like a mirage in an abyss
To the thirsty and confused eye.
It leads him on with assumptions and expectations.
Although he desired to quench his thirst
He never finds anything but deprivation.
He returns in disappointment and loss;
He yields only regret and bewilderment.
He wasted his life instead of being secure;
He will find only little on his Scale [in the Hereafter].

Did Shāfiʿī, Aḥmad or the rest of the Imams of Islam or exegetes ever consider the parameters or positions of [Greek] logic? Or were they able to attain their knowledge without it? Indeed they were more distinguished and rational than to waste their time thinking about the madness of the [Greek] logicians. [Greek] logic has not entered into any [branch of] knowledge except that it has corrupted it and muddled its principles.

Some say that the sciences of the Arabic language, including grammar, linguistics, etc., are all obligations that suffice if performed by some, since understanding the Words of God and His Messenger are dependent upon them. Others think that learning jurisprudence (*uṣūl al-fiqh*) is an obligation that is accomplished if performed by some, since it is through this knowledge that one can recognize the correctness of proofs and the methodology of how to derive them. The aforementioned are not obligations incumbent upon everyone, whereas knowledge about [the pillars of] faith and the [obligatory aspects of the] Divine Law of Islam are.

In general, if a servant is dependent on some [branches] of knowledge and deeds then those required from and obligated upon him are considered to be just like the necessity of the means [to the ends]. It is well known that this dependence differs accordingly for each individual, the times, and the linguistic and intellectual [ability of each]; thus there is no definite amount, and God knows best.

[Point 133: The most knowledgeable of God's servants are never satisfied with their knowledge and therefore avidly seek more.]

In the *Ṣaḥīḥ* of Ibn Ḥibbān, Abū Hurayra narrated that the Prophet (may God bless him and grant him peace) said:

> Moses asked his Lord about seven characteristics, six of which he thought he possessed, and the last was one he disliked. He said: 'O my Lord, who is the most pious of Your servants?' God said: 'The one who remembers [Me] and does not forget.' Moses asked: 'Who is the most guided of Your servants?' God said: 'The one who follows the guidance.' Moses asked: 'Who is the wisest of Your servants?' God said: 'The one who judges others as he would [want] himself [to be judged].' Moses asked: 'Who is the most knowledgeable of Your servants?' God said: 'A scholar who is never satiated with knowledge. He is always adding the knowledge of others to his.' Moses asked: 'Who is the mightiest of Your servants?' God said: 'The one who forgives even if he is able [to attain his rights].' Moses asked: 'Who is the most affluent of Your servants?' God said: 'He who is content (*yarḍā*) with what has been bestowed.' Moses asked: 'Who is the poorest of Your servants?' God said: 'The one who is deprived [of knowledge and religion].'[1]

Thus God has informed us in this *ḥadīth* that the most knowledge-

1 Ibn Ḥibbān 6217; *Bidāya*, vol. 1, p. 291. It is 'sound' according to Albānī (*Silsilat al-aḥādīth al-ṣaḥīḥa* 3350).

able of His servants is one who is never satiated with his knowledge, so he is always adding the knowledge of others to his. There is no doubt that if one is described as being from amongst the greatest of God's servants, then one must possess the loftiest characteristics of perfection.

Moses travelled a great distance so that another learned man [Khiḍr] could teach him what God had taught him. Although the Beneficent spoke to Moses and he was the most honourable of humanity in God's sight during his time (and the most knowledgeable), his avidity and insatiable preoccupation with knowledge led him to travel to another learned man. Had it not been for the fact that knowledge is the most eminent thing that one's soul should strive for, Moses would have preferred to remain to take care of the needs of his community and avoid the hardship and fatigue associated with that journey. Yet this noble prophet (may God bless him and grant him peace) knew the value of knowledge and its possessors.

[POINT 134: ONE CAN ONLY ATTAIN PERFECTION BY ACTING UPON KNOWLEDGE OF WHAT GOD LOVES AND IS PLEASED WITH.]

God (Glorious and Exalted is He) originated the creation to worship Him. This [servitude] includes loving Him and giving preference to what pleases Him. It is for this reason that He sent His messengers, revealed His Books and prescribed His Divine Laws. In order to attain perfection a person must make all his movements concordant with what God loves and is pleased with. For this reason He made following the Messenger a sign of [the servant] loving Him. The Exalted said: *Say, (O Muḥammad, to mankind): If ye love God, follow me; God will love you and forgive you your sins. God is Forgiving, Merciful.*[1]

Thus the sincere and loving person considers himself to be a traitor if he moves in any freely-chosen manner that is not consistent with the pleasure of his Beloved. If he even performs an act that is permissible on account of his nature or his desire, he repents from

1 Q. III.31.

it just as he would repent from a sin. This adherence continues to become stronger until all of his permissible actions become [a form of] worship. Consequently, he hopes to be rewarded for his sleeping, eating and relaxation just as he would hope for the reward of his praying at night, fasting and striving. He is always between either joy, for which he is thankful to God, or hardship, for which he is patient. He is perpetually moving towards God, whether in sleep or while awake.

Some of the scholars have said: 'The habits of the masters are like the worship of the simpletons, while the worship done by the simpletons are just habits.' Some of the Predecessors said: 'It may be that the sleep and eating of the masters are better than the night prayers and [supererogatory] fasting of the simpletons.' When the sincere and loving person speaks he does so for God's sake and using what God [has revealed]. When he is quiet it is for God's sake, when he moves it is with the commandment of God, and when he is tranquil his tranquillity is to ready himself to later work for the pleasure of God.

It is well known that a [student who has lofty aspirations] is in great need of knowledge. This is because it is only through knowledge that he can differentiate between what movements and types of tranquillity are beloved to God [and those that are not]. Thus his need for knowledge is not like that of others who just pursue knowledge for itself or because it is in itself a characteristic of perfection. Instead, he needs it to make his substance become upright. Therefore the masterly knowers stridently advised their students towards knowledge and its pursuit.

They also maintained that whoever does not pursue knowledge will not be successful, and considered them as riff-raff (*sifla*). Dhū al-Nūn [al-Miṣrī][1] was asked: 'Who are the riff-raff?' He responded:

1 Thawbān b. Ibrāhīm Dhū al-Nūn al-Miṣrī (d. 245/859) was a prominent Egyptian Sufi whose works are not extant. His most famous student was Sahl al-Tustarī, who was mentioned earlier.

'Those who do not know the path to God (Exalted is He), nor could they ever find it.' Abū Yazīd[1] said: 'If you see that a person has been given many miracles—even if he were to fly in the air—do not be deceived. You must observe whether he is acting in accordance with [God's] commandments and prohibitions, guarding the limits [imposed by God], and acknowledging the Divine Law.' Abū Ḥamza al-Bazzāz[2] said: 'Those who know the path of truth will find ease in following it. There is no guide for this path except the Messenger. One must follow his statements, actions and affairs.'

The Sufi ascetic Muḥammad b. al-Faḍl[3] said: 'The deterioration of Islam will occur due to four kinds of people: those who do not act according to what they know; those who act without knowledge; those who are inactive and do not have knowledge; and those who prevent others from learning.' My opinion is that the first kind is the most harmful [in the eyes of] the masses. They use it as an excuse when any disaster or calamity strikes. People think highly of the second kind—the ignorant worshipper—because of their worship and righteousness. Therefore people imitate such worshippers despite the latter's ignorance. These first two kinds are mentioned by some of the Predecessors, who said: 'Beware of the discord caused by the wicked scholar and the ignorant worshipper. Their discord is a tribulation for everyone they seduce.'[4] Since people emulate their scholars and worshippers, if the scholars are wicked and the worshippers are ignorant, then the devastation becomes generalized to all. Subsequently, the discord becomes great for both the elite and masses.

The third kind does not possess knowledge, nor do they perform actions; and they are like the grazing cattle. The fourth kind are

1 Abū Yazīd b. Tayfūr b. ʿĪsā al-Bisṭāmī (d. 261/875) was a famous Sufi ascetic.

2 Abū Ḥamza Muḥammad b. Ibrāhīm al-Baghdādī al-Bazzāz (d. 289/901) was a jurist and Sufi. He was a contemporary of Junayd and Imam Aḥmad.

3 Abū ʿAbd Allāh Muḥammad b. al-Faḍl b. al-ʿAbbās al-Balkhī (d. 317/929) was a Sufi ascetic. This saying can be found in Dhahabī, *Siyar ʿalām al-nubalā'* (Beirut: Mu'assasat al-Risāla, 1985), vol. XIV, p. 525.

4 Ibn ʿAbd al-Barr 1161. In this reference it was said by Ibn al-Mubārak.

[human devils], agents of Iblīs, on this earth. They hold people back from pursuing knowledge and gaining *fiqh* of this religion. They are more harmful than the jinn demons, since they intervene directly between people's hearts and God's guidance and His path.

These four kinds mentioned by this knower (may God's mercy be upon him) are all on the edge of a crumbling cliff and on the path of destruction. Any harm or enmity that occurs to a scholar who calls to God and His Messenger is because of them. Ultimately, God puts into operation those whom He wills to perpetrate that which displeases Him, just like He employs those whom He loves to pursue what pleases Him. God is the Most Knowledgeable and He is the Seer of what His servants do. It is only through knowledge that the manner and secret by which these groups work becomes unveiled. Thus all goodness is derived from knowledge and what is in accordance with it. Likewise all evil is due to ignorance and what results from it.

[Point 135: Those who are knowledgeable have been entrusted to preserve, defend and call to this message. They are the saints supported by God.]

God (Glory be to Him) made the scholars trustees of His religion and revelation. He is pleased that they preserve it, act upon it uprightly and defend it. This alone is an honourable status and great virtue. The Exalted said: *Such is the guidance of God wherewith He guideth whom He will of His servants. But if they had set up (for worship) aught beside Him, (all) that they did would have been vain. Those are they unto whom We have given the Book and command and prophethood. But if these disbelieve therein, then indeed We shall entrust it to a people who will not be disbelievers therein.*[1]

Some have said that those *people* are the prophets. Others have opined that they are the Companions of the Messenger of God (may God bless him and grant him peace). Yet others maintain that

1 Q. VI.88–89.

they include all of the believers. These are the main opinions but there are secondary [opinions], such as: they are the Anṣār from Medina, or both the Anṣār from Medina and the Muhājirūn from Mecca, or a group of people from amongst the Persians. Ibn Jarīr [al-Ṭabarī][1] opined: 'It refers to the eighteen prophets that God named in the preceding verses.'[2]

[The correct] opinion is that this *sūra* was revealed in Mecca and the statement *if these* signifies those who disbelieved from [the Prophet's] people [of Quraysh] principally, but also includes those who will show enmity to [the Muslims] in the future. Thus everyone who disbelieves in what the Prophet conveyed is included [in *these*]. Those who are entrusted with it principally are the prophets; and the believers who followed them are so [secondarily]. Accordingly, everyone who acts to preserve, defend and call to it is included [amongst those entrusted]. Those most deserving to be included amongst the followers of the Messenger [Muḥammad] are those who are his successors and heirs, since they are the ones entrusted with it. God knows best wherein to place His guidance and He selects those whom He wills for it.

This verse signals and gives glad tidings that the message will always be preserved and never lost. Furthermore, it indicates that if [Quraysh] neglects it or does not accept it then another people will accept, preserve, care for and defend it. Thus the former's disbelief does not result in any loss or harm. Rather, others will come who are suitable and deserving of it.

One should reflect on the eminent and dignified nature of this meaning. It induces His believing servants to take the initiative and quickly accept it. It also makes them take notice of His love and preference for them by virtue of this blessing over His disbelieving

1 Abū Jaʿfar Muḥammad b. Jarīr al-Ṭabarī (d. 310/923) was a prominent polymath and exegete, who authored the magisterial *Tafsīr al-Ṭabarī* and *Tārīkh al-Ṭabarī*, amongst other works.

2 See *Tafsīr al-Ṭabarī*, vol. XI, p. 518. The preceding verses, which mentioned the eighteen prophets, are Q. VI.83–86.

enemies. The latter are disparaged and are contemptible—He cares not for them nor is He concerned with them. [It is as if God is saying to the disbelievers:] 'If you do not believe then My believing servants, who are entrusted with it, will still be numerous indeed.' The Exalted said: *Say: Believe therein or believe not, those who were given knowledge before it, when it is read unto them, fall down prostrate on their faces, adoring, saying: Glory to our Lord! Verily the promise of our Lord must be fulfilled.*[1]

If a king were to say to his subjects 'If there are some who reject my goodwill, disobey my commandments and neglect their oaths to me, I have others yet who will obey my orders, honour their oaths to me and carry out their obligations towards me', then his loyal subjects will experience happiness and joy, as well as a vigour and zeal, that will thereafter result in them carrying out their obligations and honouring their master and king even more. This is something experienced and seen.

Now if it is asked: 'Is it correct to name one who has been entrusted by God as "the trustee of God" (*wakīl Allāh*), for it is just like saying someone is a saint supported by God (*walī Allāh*)?' My opinion is that it does not necessarily follow that entrusting someone with a [limited] matter can unrestrictedly result in formulating a subject noun that is absolute. Likewise, [as previously discussed], it does not necessarily follow that being a viceroy leads outrightly to saying that someone is the 'viceroy of God' (*khalīfat Allāh*).

Some of the Predecessors interpreted *We shall appoint it to a people* as: 'We have bestowed it upon them.' Therefore it cannot be said that one is the entrusted deputy of God just because he has been bestowed or favoured with it. This is different than the derivation of *walī Allāh* from 'friendship' (*muwālāh*), for it is a result of [His] love and proximity to [Him]. Just as it is said one is God's servant or His beloved (*ḥabībuh*), it is said he is supported by Him (*waliyyuh*).

God (Exalted is He) supports His servant due to His benevo-

1 Q. XVII.107–108.

lence; and it is a consolation and mercy for him. This is different than what occurs amongst people, as one will be loyal to another in order to strengthen oneself through group association. In the latter situation, the action is due to the vulnerability and neediness of the persons involved. But the Almighty and Self-Sufficient (Glorious is He) is not supportive of anyone due to any dependence or need. The Exalted said: *And say: Praise be to God, Who hath not taken unto Himself a son, and Who hath no partner in the sovereignty, nor hath He any protecting friend through dependence. And magnify Him with all magnificence.*[1] Thus He did not negate His support generally or absolutely; rather, He negated that His support of them is due to any dependence. He affirmed that He supports them with His statements: *Verily the friends of God are (those) on whom fear (cometh) not, nor do they grieve;*[2] and *God is the Protecting Guardian of those who believe.*[3]

[POINT 136: THOSE WHO ARE KNOWLEDGEABLE AND UPRIGHT WILL BE ABLE TO REPUDIATE ANY DISTORTIONS, ANY ATTEMPTS TO BREAK UP THIS RELIGION AND ANY MISINTERPRETATIONS.]

It has been related through many chains of narration that the Prophet (may God bless him and grant him peace) said: 'This knowledge [inherited from the Prophet] will be conveyed by the successors [of this Community] who are upright and trustworthy. They will repudiate the distortions of the extremists, those who attempt to break up [the religion] by negating [its precepts], and the misinterpretations of those who are ignorant.'[4] The conveyance that is being referred to in this *ḥadīth* is [carried out] by those who are entrusted, as was mentioned in the prior verse [Q. VI.89]. In this manner, the Prophet's knowledge will never become lost nor vanish.

1 Q. XVII.111.

2 Q. X.62.

3 Q. II.257.

4 Bayhaqī (*Sunan*) 20,911; Ibn ʿAdī, vol. 1, p. 211; Haythamī 601; al-Khaṭīb al-Baghdādī (*Sharaf*), pp. 47–52; Tammām 899; al-Muttaqī al-Hindī 28,918; *Bidāya*, vol. x, p. 337. It is 'authentic' according to Albānī (*Mishkāt* 248).

Everyone who conveys the knowledge [and accomplishes what] the Prophet referred to must inevitably be upright and trustworthy. Their integrity is evident to such a degree that no doubts, disputes or uncertainties can exist to disparage them. The Imams are well known amongst this Community to transmit the Prophetic knowledge and inheritance [in such a fashion]—they are all upright and trustworthy by the declaration of the Messenger of God (may God bless him and grant him peace). Thus it is not acceptable to defame them.

On the other hand, those who are innovators and whose religion is suspect are well known to be disparaged and defamed by this Community. They are not considered by this Community to be conveyors of this [Prophetic] knowledge.

Some may make a mistake, though, regarding this term 'upright and trustworthy' by assuming that this uprightness alludes only to those who have no sins; but that is not the case. Instead, it refers to those who can be entrusted with this religion, even if they do some things which they must repent to God for. These [sins] do not negate them being upright and trustworthy, just like the presence [of sins] does not negate one being a believer or being supported [by Him].

[Point 137: The preservation of this religion and our worldly affairs occurs through the safeguarding of knowledge.]

Awzāʿī[1] related that Ibn Shihāb al-Zuhrī said: 'Adhering to the Sunna leads to the safeguarding of knowledge. Otherwise, it will be quickly withdrawn. The widespread presence of knowledge leads to the maintenance of both the religion and [our] worldly affairs. If knowledge vanishes then [the goodness present in] both of those also fades away.'

1 Abū ʿAmr ʿAbd al-Raḥmān b. ʿAmr al-Awzāʿī (d. 158/774) was a prominent Successor to the Successors. He was the founder of the Awzāʿī school of jurisprudence, which thrived in the 8th and 9th centuries CE, becoming dominant in Andalus and north-west Africa (until the Mālikī school replaced it), as well as in Syria.

CHAPTER ELEVEN

God Commended Muḥammad, Abraham, the Messiah and many other Prophets due to their Knowledge

[Point 138: Stories which exemplify that knowledge, more than anything else, elevates those who possess it both in this world and the Hereafter.]

Knowledge raises the one who possesses it in this world and the Hereafter more than any power, wealth or anything else. Thus knowledge makes the honourable one more distinguished and it raises a servant to the point that he may sit amongst the council of kings.

Nāfiᶜ b. ᶜAbd al-Ḥārith came to ᶜUmar b. al-Khaṭṭāb at ᶜUsfān, [after] ᶜUmar had appointed him to rule the people of Mecca. ᶜUmar said to him: 'Who have you designated to lead the people of the valley [in your absence]?' He replied: 'Ibn Abzī.' ᶜUmar said: 'Who is Ibn Abzī?' He said: 'He is one of the people of clientage (*mawlā*).' ᶜUmar said: 'Have you appointed a *mawlā* over them?' He said: 'He has memorized the Book of God and has knowledge of the obligations.' ᶜUmar said: 'Your Prophet (may God bless him and grant him peace) said: "God will raise some people through this Book, while He will lower others due to [their rejection of] it."'[1]

Abū al-ᶜĀliya said: 'I would go to Ibn ᶜAbbās while he [was sitting] on his dignified seat surrounded by Quraysh. He would take me by the hand and seat me next to him. Quraysh once made a signal to me [to move], and Ibn ᶜAbbās noticed that. He said:

1 Muslim 1897; Ibn Māja 218; Aḥmad 232.

"This knowledge makes the honourable one more distinguished and allows a slave to assume a lofty position."'

Ibrāhīm al-Ḥarbī[1] said that ʿAṭā' b. Abī Rabāḥ was the black slave[2] of a woman in Mecca and his nose was like a small bean (*bāqilāt*) [or a collection of small beans]. On one occasion, Sulaymān b. ʿAbd al-Malik,[3] the Emir of the Believers, came along with his two sons to ʿAtā'. They sat down with him while he was praying. Once ʿAtā' finished, he turned to them, and they asked him about many of the rituals of pilgrimage. After he turned his back towards them, Sulaymān told his sons to get up, and so they did. He then said: 'My sons, do not distance yourself from the pursuit of knowledge, as I will never forget our humbleness in this situation.'

Ḥarbī said Muḥammad b. ʿAbd al-Raḥmān al-Awqas had a neck that appeared to be broken [and sunken] within his trunk and his two arms were [scrawny] like lancers (*zujjān*). His mother said to him: 'O my son, do not be ridiculed and made fun of by people. You must pursue knowledge as it will elevate you.' He was thereafter appointed as a judge in Mecca for twenty years. It was said that the plaintiffs and defendants would tremble when in front of him until he left. One time a woman passed by him while he was saying: 'O my Lord, free my neck from Hellfire.' She then said: 'O my son, do you even have a neck?'

Yaḥyā b. Aktham[4] said that the Rashīdī [Ma'mūn] said to him:

1 Abū Isḥāq Ibrāhīm b. Isḥāq al-Ḥarbī (d. 285/898) was a traditionist and scholar who lived in Baghdad.

2 In order to accurately convey the intent of the speaker, the translation here departs from translating *ʿabd* as 'servant', and here renders it as 'slave'.

3 Sulaymān b. ʿAbd al-Malik b. Marwān (d. 99/717) was the seventh Umayyad caliph after Muʿāwiya b. Abī Sufyān, Yazīd b. Muʿāwiya, Muʿāwiya b. Yazīd, Marwān b. al-Ḥakam, ʿAbd al-Malik b. Marwān and al-Walīd b. ʿAbd al-Malik. He ruled for only two years, 715-717 CE, and named ʿUmar b. ʿAbd al-ʿAzīz b. Marwān, his second cousin (considered to be the fifth Rightly-Guided Caliph), to succeed him before passing away.

4 Yaḥyā b. Aktham (d. 242/856) was chief justice during the Abbasid Caliphate under the rule of al-Ma'mūn b. Hārūn al-Rashīd and later Mutawakkil.

'What is the most distinguished level?' He said: 'Yours, O Emir of the Believers.' He said: 'Do you know of anyone nobler than me?' I said no. He said: 'But I know of a man who in his gathering relates [*ḥadīth*s along with] their chains of narration from the Messenger of God.' [Yaḥyā continues:] 'I said: "O Emir of the Believers, how can this man be better than you? You are the cousin of the Messenger of God, and you have been delegated the affairs of the believers." He said: "Woe unto you! He is better than me because his name is associated with the name of the Messenger of God (may God bless him and grant him peace). [The Prophet's name] never dies; yet we die and pass away. The scholars remain despite the passing of the ages."'

Muzanī[1] related that he heard Shāfiʿī say: 'Whoever learns the Qur'ān will have an exalted standing, whoever learns *fiqh* will attain a nobler status, whoever learns linguistics will become more gentle in nature, whoever learns mathematics will become sounder in judgment, and whoever records the *ḥadīth*s will possess stronger evidences. But whoever does not live chastely will never benefit from his knowledge.'[2]

ʿAbd Allāh b. Dāwūd mentioned that he heard Sufyān al-Thawrī say: '*Ḥadīth* is power. Whoever desires it for this world will find it to be so, and whoever pursues it for the Hereafter will discover it to be so.'

Al-Naḍr b. Shumayl[3] said: 'Whoever desires to become more distinguished in this world and the Hereafter should learn knowledge. One can attain no further bliss than being entrusted in [matters concerning] the religion of God, and being in between God and His servants [by relating the message].'

1 Abū Ibrāhīm Ismāʿīl b. Yaḥyā al-Muzanī (d. 264/878) was a jurist and prominent student of Shāfiʿī who wrote *Mukhtaṣar al-Muzanī fi-furūʿ al-Shāfiʿiyya.*

2 Ibn ʿAbd al-Barr 822.

3 Abū al-Ḥasan al-Naḍr b. Shumayl al-Māzinī (d. 204/820) was one of the Successors to the Successors. He was a contemporary of Aḥmad b. Ḥanbal and was summoned to testify as to the nature of the Qur'ān during the Inquisition (*Miḥna*).

In his book *al-Jalīs wa'l-anīs*, Abū al-Faraj al-Muʿāfā b. Zakariyya al-Jarīrī[1] mentioned that ʿUtbā's father said:

> Muʿāwiya built a council in Abṭiḥ, and sat there along with [his wife Fākhita] the daughter of Qaraẓa. A caravan group stopped over and a young man raised his voice singing:
>
> Whoever wants to compete with me will do so to no avail
> He will fill the bucket until the knot of the rope.
>
> He asked: 'Who is this?' They replied: "ʿAbd Allāh b. Jaʿfar.'[2] He said: 'Let him go.' Then amongst another group there was a boy singing:
>
> The women said: Do you know this young man?
> They said: Yes, [of course]
> We recognize him! Can the moon be hidden?
>
> Muʿāwiya asked: 'Who is this?' They said: "ʿUmar b. Abī Rabīʿa.'[3] He said: 'Open the way for him so that he can leave.' Then amongst another group there was a man being questioned about the rituals of the pilgrimage, which were unclear to the questioners. One said: 'I threw [the seven stones] before I shaved.' [Another said:] 'I shaved before I threw.' [Someone answered these questions correctly, so] Muʿāwiya asked: 'Who is that [answering]?' They replied: "ʿAbd Allāh b. ʿUmar.' So he turned to the daughter of Qaraẓa and said: 'He and your father are honourable. By God, [knowledge leads to] honour in this world and the Hereafter.'

1 Abū al-Faraj al-Muʿāfā b. Zakariyya al-Nahrawānī al-Jarīrī (d. 390/1000) was a scholar and author of *al-Jalīs al-ṣāliḥ al-kāfī wa'l-anīs al-naṣiḥ al-shāfī* (Beirut: Dār al-Kutub al-ʿIlmiyyah, 2005), which includes discussions regarding the proper conduct of kings and rulers. See vol. 1, p. 505 of Jarīrī's book for this story. It is also mentioned by Ibn ʿAbd al-Barr 333.

2 ʿAbd Allāh b. Jaʿfar b. Abī Ṭālib (d. 60/680) was a Companion. He was the son of Jaʿfar b. Abī Ṭālib (the older brother of ʿAlī), who was one of the chief commanders in the Battle of Mutah when he was martyred. His early childhood was spent in Abyssinia, as his parents had migrated there.

3 ʿUmar b. Abī Rabīʿa al-Makhzūmī (d. 100/719) was a notable poet of Quraysh.

Sahl al-Tustarī said: 'Whoever wants to behold the councils of the prophets should observe those of the scholars. So-and-so would be asked "What would you say about a man who swore upon his wife [that he would divorce her because of] such-and-such statement?" and he would respond: "He has divorced his wife." Then another would opine: "That statement has not broken his oath." Only a prophet or a scholar could differentiate. So recognize them for that.'

[POINT 139: ONE SHOULD NOT HOLD THE IGNORANT IN ESTEEM.]

It is well known by the elite and the masses that the ignorant ones who have no knowledge are dressed with a clothing of humiliation, denigration and diminution.

Muᶜāwiya related: 'I heard Aᶜmash say: "I wish I could smack those who do not know any *ḥadīth*s with my sandals."' Hishām b. ᶜAlī said: 'I heard Aᶜmash say: "If you see a shaykh[1] who cannot read the Qur'ān and does not record *ḥadīth*s, then smack him because he is one of the *qamarā'* shaykhs."' Abū Ṣāliḥ [Hishām] said: 'I asked Abū Jaᶜfar [al-Aᶜmash]: "Who are the *qamarā'* shaykhs?" He said: "They are atheistic (*dahriyyūn*) shaykhs who get together on nights with a full moon to discuss the history of past nations, yet not one of them can even perform ablution for prayer."'

Muzanī said that when Shāfiᶜī would see a shaykh he would ask him about a *ḥadīth* or *fiqh*. If he knew nothing, then Shāfiᶜī would say: 'May God not reward you on behalf of Islam as you have lost yourself and lost your Islam!'

One of the Abbasid Caliphs was playing chess and his uncle asked to come in, whereupon he covered up the chessboard. Once the latter sat down he said: 'My uncle, did you read the Qur'ān?' He replied no. He asked: 'Did you record anything of the Sunna?' He responded no. He said: 'Did you look into *fiqh* and scholarly debates of it?' He replied no. He finally asked: 'Did you look into the

1 Such instances use 'shaykh' in conformity with its original Arabic usage of 'old man'.

Arabic language and the history of the past nations?' He responded no. The Caliph then said: 'Unveil the chessboard and continue playing,' for his bashfulness and timidity ceased. His opponent said to him: 'O Emir of the Believers, how can you uncover it, and yet one is amongst us who you should be bashful of?' He said: 'Be quiet! No one is with us.'

Human beings are differentiated from all other animals due to being selected with knowledge, reason and understanding. If these are absent, then nothing remains except that which is jointly common between them and all livestock animals. Now people will not be timid in front of such a person, nor will they avoid doing something [shameful] in their presence, which they would otherwise be bashful of doing in the presence of those who are virtuous and scholarly.

[Point 140: The knowledgeable would not wish to be wealthy if it required them to give up their knowledge.]

Anyone who possesses some commodity other than knowledge will abandon it once he knows of other goods that are better. Only those who have knowledge would not [abandon their commodity], since they would not love to have a share of anything else [besides knowledge].

Abū Jaʿfar al-Ṭaḥāwī[1] said: 'I was with Aḥmad b. Abī ʿImrān[2] when a man who has been given [the wealth of] this world passed by us. I looked at him and was distracted away from what we were discussing. He said to me: "It is as if you are thinking about that man's possessions?" I replied yes. He said: "Should I point you to a

1 Abū Jaʿfar Aḥmad b. Muḥammad al-Ṭaḥāwī (d. 321/933) was a traditionist and prominent scholar. His uncle was Muzanī (a leading student of Shāfiʿī), but he later became a student of Aḥmad b. Abī ʿImrān and adhered to the Ḥanafī school. He wrote a well-known book on creed named *al-ʿAqīda al-Ṭaḥāwiyya* or *Bayān Ahl al-Sunna wa'l-Jamāʿa*. He also authored some renowned books on *fiqh*, such as *Sharḥ maʿānī al-āthār* and *Ikhtilāf al-fuqahā'*.

2 Abū Jaʿfar Aḥmad b. Abī ʿImrān (d. 280/893) was a Ḥanafī scholar, who later became the chief judge of Egypt.

way in which God will transfer His money to you and transfer the knowledge you possess to him? Thereafter, you will live as a wealthy but ignorant man, and he will live as a poor scholar." I said: "No. I would not choose that. Knowledge is affluence without money, might without a clan and a powerful authority without men.'"

It has also been said:

> Knowledge is a treasure and provision that does not run out.
> It is truly a wonderful friend if it befriends you.
> A person may amass money but become deprived of it after a short time,
> Thus becoming subject to humility and combat.
> But those who accumulate knowledge will always be exultant with it.
> They do not fear that it will become lost or taken away.
> O ye who possess knowledge, what a great treasure you have collected:
> No accomplishment or amount of gold is ever equivalent to it.

[Point 141: God will recompense those who are righteous with knowledge and wisdom.]

God (Glory be to Him) informed us that He will recompense those who are righteous with a reward far greater than what they deserve. The Sublime also informed us that He will recompense righteousness with knowledge. This is proof that [knowledge] is one of the greatest types of reward.

As for the first, it is mentioned in the Exalted's statement: *And whoso bringeth the truth and believeth therein—such are the dutiful. They shall have what they will of their Lord's bounty. That is the reward of the good: That God will remit from them the worst of what they did, and will pay them for reward the best they used to do.*[1] As for the second, Ḥasan

1 Q. xxxix.33–35.

[al-Baṣrī] said: 'Whoever excels in worshipping God in his youth, God will bestow upon him wisdom in adulthood. This is due to His statement: *And when he reached his prime We gave him wisdom and knowledge. Thus We reward the good.*'[1]

[Point 142: Luqmān on the heart's need of knowledge being like the earth's need of rain.]

God (Glory be to Him) has made knowledge for the heart just as important as rain for the earth. Thus, just as life could not exist on this earth without rain, life cannot exist within the heart without knowledge. In the *Muwaṭṭa'*, Luqmān[2] is said to have told his son: 'My son, sit amongst the scholars and keep company with them. God (Exalted is He) enlivens dead hearts with the light of wisdom just as He enlivens the dead earth with abundant rain.'[3]

Nonetheless, the earth only needs rain sometimes; and it is [harmful if it becomes] continuous. Yet one needs knowledge with every breath; and greater knowledge only results in more righteousness and benefit.

[Point 143: The importance of avoiding timidity when pursuing knowledge.]

Many of the characteristics that are not praiseworthy, and which one could be criticized for [in other circumstances], such as flattery, avoidance of timidity, submissiveness towards scholars, frequently going to them and the like, are instead praiseworthy in the pursuit of knowledge. To this point, Ibn Qutayba mentioned a tradition: 'Flattery is not a characteristic of the believers except in the pursuit

1 Q. XII.22.

2 The 31st *sūra* of the Qur'ān is named 'Luqmān' after him. It contains more of his advice to his son. He is considered by most scholars to be a wise man, but not a prophet.

3 Mālik, Chap. 59, *ḥadīth* 1; Ibn ʿAbd al-Barr 676.

of knowledge.'[1] This has also been said by some of the Predecessors.

Ibn Isḥāq mentioned: "ʿAlī said something great. If you were to ride a mount in pursuit of a saying like it, the mount would have died before you could find anything close to it. [ʿAlī said]: "One should not put one's hope in anyone other than God, should not fear anything except one's sins, should pursue learning if one does not know and should not be timid. If one is asked about something which he does not know, he should say: 'I do not know.' One should realize that patience relative to faith is like the position of the head on top of the body: if the head is cut off, the body dies. Likewise, if patience dissipates, faith can no longer exist.""

Some scholars have said: 'Knowledge cannot be acquired by one who is timid or one who is arrogant. The former's timidity prevents him, while the latter's arrogance hinders him.' Therefore the characteristics [mentioned at the beginning of this point] are only praiseworthy in the pursuit of knowledge because they enable one to attain [knowledge]. Thus these characteristics are part of one's perfection and they enable one to attain perfection.

Ḥasan [al-Baṣrī] said: 'Whoever uses his timidity as an excuse preventing him from pursuing knowledge will wear the clothing of ignorance. Therefore cut up the clothing of timidity. And whoever allows himself to be subservient [to the scholars] will attain more advanced knowledge.' ʿAlī (may God, Exalted is He, be pleased with him) said: 'Seeking prestige results in failure, and being timid leads to deprivation.' Ibrāhīm [al-Ḥarbī] said to Manṣūr: 'Ask questions as if you are a simpleton, and memorize like those with great intelligence.'

Asking anything from others is a blemish, deficiency and submissiveness for the person [asking] and is inconsistent with one's sense of honour except [when inquiring about] knowledge. In that case it is exactly consistent with one's perfection, honour and power. Some scholars have said: 'The best characteristic a person can have is

1 Bayhaqī (*Shuʿab*) 4521; Ibn ʿAdī, vol. III, p. 119; Ibn ʿAbd al-Barr 859. It is 'fabricated' according to Albānī (*Silsilat al-aḥādīth al-ḍaʿīfa wa'l-mawḍūʿa* 381).

inquiring to gain knowledge.' It has also been said: 'If you sit with a scholar then ask him questions to understand, not to cause vexation.' Ru'ba b. al-ʿAjjāj said: 'I went to al-Nasāba al-Bikrī whereupon he said: "I may be mistaken, but I have heard that you may be like some who if I am quiet do not ask, and if I speak do not heed." I said: "I hope that I will not be like that." He then said: "Who are the enemies of honour?" I said: "Inform me." He said: "The associates of evil: if they see goodness, they cover it; and if they see evil, they spread it." He added: "Knowledge can be associated with ruin, misfortune and shortcoming. Its ruin is forgetting it, its misfortune is [that people] lie using it, and its shortcoming is that it is spread amongst those who are not suitable for it."'[1]

Ibn al-Aʿrābī hymned:

How close is a thing when fate foreordains it!
And how remote is it if it is not predestined!
Ask a jurist and you will become a jurist like him.
Whoever is vast in knowledge strives adeptly.
Ponder on the knowledge that you will [use to] deliver a legal opinion
As there is no goodness in knowledge that one does not ponder.
It may be that the person procures [his aim] yet he is inadequate
And it may be that his diligence will fail even though he was not incapable.
The men whose actions should be emulated have vanished
And those who are ignorant of every matter have become disguised.
I live amongst [blind] followers who embellish one another.
They reject one faulty person [only to favour] another lame one.

1 Ibn ʿAbd al-Barr 702.

There are six levels for [attaining] knowledge: first, asking well; second, listening well and paying attention; third, understanding well; fourth, memorizing; and fifth, teaching others. Finally, the sixth is the result of [knowledge]: it is to act upon it and comply with its legal limits.

Some people are deprived of [knowledge] due to their inability to ask questions well. This is either because they do not ask at the right time or they ask about [non-essential] things while neglecting other more important ones. Others are deprived due to their inability to listen, as speaking and debating is more preferable and beloved to them than listening. This is a hidden deficiency in most people who pursue knowledge, and it prevents them from attaining more advanced knowledge.

Ibn ʿAbd al-Barr mentioned that one of the Predecessors said: 'The goodness of one who understands well will not be able to rectify the badness of being a poor listener.'[1] ʿAbd Allāh b. Aḥmad mentioned in [his narration of Imām Aḥmad's] book *al-ʿIlal*: "ʿUrwa b. al-Zubayr[2] loved debating with Ibn ʿAbbās, and so the latter would avoid him. On the other hand, ʿUbayd Allāh b. ʿAbd Allāh b. ʿUtba would ask him gently, and therefore [Ibn ʿAbbās] would generously teach the latter from his knowledge.'[3] Ibn Jurayj said: 'I did not extract knowledge from ʿAṭā' except by being kind to him.'[4] Some of the Predecessors said: 'If you sit amongst the scholars then be more avid to listen than to speak.'

God (Exalted is He) said: *Therein verily is a reminder for him who*

1 Ibn ʿAbd al-Barr 699.

2 ʿUrwa b. al-Zubayr b. al-ʿAwwām (d. 94/713) was one of the Successors. He was the son of al-Zubayr b. al-ʿAwwām (one of the ten promised Paradise by the Prophet) and Asmā' bint Abī Bakr al-Ṣiddīq. He heard therefore many *ḥadīth*s from his aunt ʿĀ'isha, which he later transmitted. His older brother was ʿAbd Allāh b. al-Zubayr, who was martyred by Ḥajjāj.

3 Aḥmad, *al-ʿIlal wa-maʿrifat al-rijāl li-Aḥmad: riwāyat ibnih ʿAbd Allāh* (Riyadh: Dār al-Khānī, 2001), p. 156.

4 Ibn ʿAbd al-Barr 625.

hath a heart, or giveth ear with full intelligence.[1] Deeply reflect upon the treasures of knowledge contained within this verse. By taking care to understand, many doors of knowledge and guidance will be opened for the servant. The Sublime commanded His servants to ponder His signs, which are read and heard, along with those that are seen and witnessed (*mashhūda*), so that they will be a reminder for those who have a [spiritual] heart. Those whose hearts are deprived of attentiveness, and thus are away from God, will not benefit from any sign that passes by them, even if all signs did. The uninterrupted sequence of His signs [for those who are heedless] can be compared to the rising of the sun, moon and stars, and their setting upon those who are blind.

Ultimately, one who possesses an [enlightened] heart will not benefit unless two things are present. The first is that he is attentive and witnesses that which he encounters. If one is distracted and yields to aspirations, temptations and fantasies then one will not benefit. He will also not benefit unless he devotes himself entirely to listening to what he is advised and rightly-guided towards.

There are three issues here: the first is the integrity, well-being and acceptance of the heart. Second is its presence and avoidance of being absent-minded (*shurūd*) or scattered (*tafarruq*). Third is attentively listening and being inclined to it. Furthermore, it includes being devoted to the reminder. God (Exalted is He) mentioned all three in this [aforementioned] verse.

Ibn ʿAṭiyya[2] states: 'Here the heart connotes the intellect. The meaning is that [the reminder] benefits only one who has an atten-

1 Q. L.37.

2 This refers to ʿAbd al-Ḥaqq b. Ghālib b. ʿAbd al-Raḥmān, who was also known as Ibn ʿAṭiyya (d. 541/1147). He was an exegete who lived in Muslim Spain, and he wrote *al-Muḥarrar wa'l-wajīz fi-tafsīr al-Kitāb al-ʿazīz* or also referred to as simply *Tafsīr Ibn ʿAṭiyya*.

tive heart.' He also mentioned that Shiblī[1] states: 'It represents a heart that is always aware of God and is never heedless, not even for a moment.' The meaning of His statement *or who gives ear and earnestly witnesses (the truth)*[2] is that he directs his hearing to this news and advice and has understood it. It is like His statement *And I endued thee with love from Me,*[3] which means it became established upon him. Some of the exegetes said that the meaning of His statement *and earnestly witnesses (the truth)*[4] is that he witnesses it and directs his attention to it, rather than being distracted or thinking about something else.

The author of *al-Kashshāf* [Zamakhsharī][5] interpreted *for him who hath a heart* to mean '[he whose heart is] attentive'. Those whose hearts are inattentive are like those who do not have hearts. *Gives ear* means 'inclined to listen' (*iṣghā'*). *Earnestly witnesses (the truth)* indicates that they are cognizant, for if they are unmindful they may as well be absent. Alternatively, it may indicate a believer who attests that it is a revelation from God in truth. [This believer] is included amongst the witnesses in His statement *that ye may be witnesses against mankind.*[6]

There are four different opinions regarding the witness (*shahīd*). The first is that it is derived from *mushāhada*, i.e. witnessing by being attentive (*ḥuḍūr*). This is the most correct viewpoint and nothing else is appropriate in the context of this verse. The second [opinion] is that it is derived from testimony (*shahāda*). It is that he attests that he is truthfully certain. The [third opinion] is that he is one of those

1 Abū Bakr Dulaf b. Jaḥdar al-Shiblī (d. 334/945) was a prominent Sufi and student of Junayd. He was initially wealthy, and worked in a governmental capacity; but he later abandoned his position in order to pursue the spiritual path with full dedication.

2 Q. L.37 (Yusuf Ali translation).

3 Q. XX.39.

4 Q. L.37.

5 Maḥmūd b. ʿUmar al-Zamakhsharī (d. 539/1144) was a Muʿtazilī scholar. He authored the exegesis *al-Kashshaf ʿan-ḥaqā'iq al-tanzīl wa-ʿuyūn al-aqāwīl fi-wujūh al-ta'wīl* or better known as just *al-Kashshāf.*

6 Q. II.143.

who will be a witness over people on the Day of Resurrection. The [fourth opinion] is that it is a testimony (*shahāda*) by God that one [attests] to the veracity of the prophethood of His Messenger (may God bless him and grant him peace), due to what He has taught him of the previously-revealed Books.

To return to the reasons for one being deprived of knowledge, [let us remember that] the fifth is not spreading it or teaching it. God will afflict those who conceal their knowledge and do not propagate or teach it by causing them to forget and lose it. This is a recompense that is concordant with their deed. This matter is seen and experienced in reality.

As for the sixth [reason for being deprived of knowledge], acting upon [knowledge] necessarily results in one remembering it, deeply reflecting on it and caring for it. Some of the Predecessors said: 'We would rely on acting upon our knowledge in order to memorize it.' Other Predecessors also said: 'Knowledge shouts out to action and if the latter responds then the former will remain, otherwise it will leave.'[1] Finally, there is nothing better than actions to acquire and accrue abundant knowledge.

God (Exalted is He) said: *O ye who believe, be mindful of your duty to God and put faith in His Messenger. He will give you twofold of His mercy and will appoint for you a light wherein ye shall walk.*[2] He also said: *Observe your duty to God. And God is teaching you.*[3] The latter verse is composed of two independent clauses. The [first] is an invitation (*ṭalabiyya*) and it is a commandment to be pious. The [second] is an informative one: *God is teaching you* indicates that God will teach us what to avoid in order to achieve piety. It is not a response to the command for piety. Had it been intended as a consequence [of the first clause], then it would have been cut short and divested of the letter *waw* ('and') [in between the two clauses]. [In that case,] He would have said: 'If

1 Ibn ʿAbd al-Barr 1274 (attributed to Sufyān al-Thawrī).

2 Q. LVII.28.

3 Q. II.282.

you fear God then He will teach you' (*ittaqū Allāh yuʿallimukum* or *in tattaqūhu yuʿallimukum*). He said [in another verse]: *O ye who believe, if ye keep your duty to God, He will give you discrimination (between right and wrong).*[1] Deeply reflect upon that!

[Point 144: On ten instances in the Qur'ān where God negates any equivalence between knowledge and ignorance.]

God (Glory be to Him) negated that there is any equality between the scholar and others, just as He has negated equality between the good and evil person, the enlightened and the ignorant, light and darkness, being sheltered or exposed to a hot wind, the inhabitants of Paradise versus the denizens of Hellfire, the one who commands justice and is on the straight path versus the dumb person who is incapable of doing anything [good], between the believers and disbelievers, between those who believe and do righteous deeds versus those who are corrupters on this earth, and finally between the pious and the wicked. These are the ten instances in the Qur'ān where He has negated equivalence. This is sufficient to illustrate the eminence of knowledge and the scholars. Finally, if one looks closely at all of these [demarcations], then one finds that knowledge was the differentiating factor resulting in their inequality.

[Point 145: Knowledge saves one from punishment, as exemplified by the story of the hoopoe bird with Solomon.]

After Solomon promised the hoopoe bird that he would severely punish or slaughter it, the latter was only rescued due to its knowledge. It began by initially addressing him: *I have found out (a thing) that thou apprehendest not, and I come unto thee from Sheba with sure tidings.*[2] It was only emboldened because of its knowledge. The weak hoopoe

1 Q. viii.29.
2 Q. xxvii.22.

bird would not have otherwise spoken thus to King Solomon, who was [the epitome of] strength, had it not been for the powerful authority of knowledge.

In addition, there is well-known story along the same lines. One day, after being asked a question, a teacher said: 'I do not know.' One of his students said: 'I know [the answer to] this question.' The teacher became angered and disturbed. The student said: 'O my teacher, you are not more knowledgeable than Solomon, son of David, even if you were to reach the pinnacle of [your] knowledge, and I am not more ignorant than the hoopoe bird when it said to Solomon: *I have found out (a thing) that thou apprehendest not*.' Thereafter, the teacher held back from criticizing or reprimanding him any further.

[Point 146: On some examples of the prophets achieving honour and distinction due to their knowledge.]

Those who have achieved any honour in this life or the Hereafter did so through knowledge. Reflect on what occurred to Adam and how he was favoured over the angels by God's teaching him all of the names, whereby even the [angels] acknowledged [his distinction]. Furthermore, after he was afflicted, he was compensated with something better than living in the Garden: the Lord taught him His Words.

Also [reflect on] what occurred to Joseph: he was established over the land [of Egypt], and became powerful and great due to his knowledge of how to interpret dreams. In addition, God taught him how to extract his one brother from amongst the rest of them in such a manner that not only did they accept it, but they would have judged similarly [if given the chance]. Eventually their matter resulted in their empowerment and a praiseworthy ending—all because of [Joseph's] knowledge. The Sublime alluded to this in His statement: *Thus did We contrive for Joseph. He could not have taken his brother according to the king's law unless God willed. We raise by grades (of mercy) whom We will, and over every lord of knowledge there is one more knowing.*[1] The interpretation [of the latter verse] is: 'We will elevate those whom We desire with knowledge, just as We raised Joseph's status over his brothers through it.'

God also stated regarding Abraham (peace be upon him): *That is Our argument. We gave it unto Abraham against his folk. We raise unto degrees of wisdom whom We will.*[2] This elevation [of Abraham] occurred through knowledge of evidences, while that of [Joseph] was due to knowledge of administration.

Likewise [reflect on] what happened to Khiḍr as a result of his knowledge when he took as a student the one to whom the Beneficent spoke, [Moses]. The latter asked him kindly: *May I follow thee, to the end that thou mayst teach me right conduct of that which thou hast been taught?*[3]

Also [reflect on] what occurred to Solomon. He had knowledge of the language of the birds, which led to him subduing the kingdom of Sheba and attaining its treasures. Ultimately, Sheba submitted to his authority. For this reason he said: *O mankind! Lo! we have been taught the language of the birds, and have been given (abundance) of all things. This surely is evident favour.*[4]

Also [reflect on] what occurred to David. He had knowledge of making coats of armour as a protection from the enemies' weapons. The Sublime recounted the blessing of this knowledge upon His servants: *And We taught him the art of making garments (of mail) to protect you in your daring. Are ye then thankful?*[5]

Also [reflect on] what occurred to the Messiah because of his knowledge of the Book, wisdom, Torah and Gospel: God raised him up to Him, and favoured and honoured him.

Also [reflect on] what occurred to [Muḥammad], the master of

1 Q. XII.76.
2 Q. VI.83.
3 Q. XVIII.66.
4 Q. XXVII.16.
5 Q. XXI.80.

the offspring of Adam, regarding the knowledge that God mentioned as being a blessing when He said: *God revealeth unto thee the Book and wisdom, and teacheth thee that which thou knewest not. The grace of God toward thee hath been infinite.*[1]

[Point 147: A discussion of God's commendation of Abraham in a Qur'ānic verse.]

God (Glory be to Him) commended His friend Abraham when He said: *Abraham was a nation* (umma) *obedient to God, by nature upright, and he was not of the idolaters; thankful for His bounties; He chose him.*[2] There are four types of commendation present here.

God began [by saying] that he is an *umma*; that is, a leader whose example is to be followed. Ibn Masᶜūd said: '*Umma* is a teacher of good.' It is the verb derived from 'exemplar' (*i'timām*), [meaning] one who is to be emulated.

The difference between the words *umma* and *imām* are twofold: first, the *imām* is followed in everything, whether it is by his intention or not. Therefore the road can be referred to as an *imām*. The Exalted said: *And the dwellers in the wood indeed were evildoers. So we took vengeance on them; and they both are on a high road* (imām) *plain to see.*[3] On the other hand, a road is not called an *umma*. Second, *umma* includes an additional meaning: it encompasses the perfection of knowledge and deeds. Thus [Abraham] was one individual who possessed all of these characteristics, which otherwise would be distributed amongst many people.

1 Q. iv.113.
2 Q. xvi.120–121.
3 Q. xv.77–79.

Also in the *ḥadīth* [we read]: 'Zayd b. ʿAmr b. Nufayl[1] is to be resurrected on the Day of Resurrection by himself as one nation (*umma waḥda*).'[2] A nation is called an *umma* because it denotes one people who are gathered together on one religion.

The second [type of commendation] is present in His statement *obedient* (qānit) *to God*. Ibn Masʿūd said: '*Qānit* denotes "one who obeys."'[3] [The plural form of] *qunūt* can mean many things but they all come back to the fact that one is persistently obedient.

Third, He [commended him] by saying *by nature upright* (ḥanīf). Here *ḥanīf* indicates 'one who is devoted to God'. The meaning also necessitates that one lean away from and is averse to anything else. This meaning is essential—it is not just some linguistic detail.

Fourth, [God commended him in] His statement *thankful for His bounties*. Being [truly] thankful for a blessing is contingent upon three elements: acknowledging the blessing and that it is from the One Who blesses, using it for His pleasure, and performing good deeds accordingly. Thus the servant is not considered to be thankful unless he fulfills all three of these.

The point is that God praised His friend [Abraham] with four characteristics: knowledge, performing good deeds accordingly, teaching [knowledge], and spreading it.

1 Zayd b. ʿAmr b. Nufayl was the cousin of ʿUmar b. al-Khaṭṭāb who died before the Prophet began preaching Islam. Zayd had refused idol worship and criticized Quraysh for such a practice. He later travelled and inquired into Judaism and Christianity, but refused them also. Instead, he opted to remain a *ḥanīf* (which denotes one who is upon the religion of Abraham). Asmā' bint Abī Bakr narrated that she saw him leaning against the Kaʿba saying: 'O people of Quraysh! By God, none of you is upon the religion of Abraham except me.' Bukhārī 3828. It is also reported that Zayd said: 'O God, I make You my witness that I am upon the religion of Abraham.' Bukhārī 3827.

2 *Musnad al-Ṭayālisī* 231.

3 Ibn ʿAbd al-Barr 797.

[Point 148: An explanation of the Messiah's statement: And [God] hath made me blessed wheresoever I may be.]

The Sublime related that the Messiah said: *Lo! I am the servant of God. He hath given me the Book and hath appointed me a prophet, and hath made me blessed wheresoever I may be.*[1] Sufyān b. ʿUyayna interpreted *blessed wheresoever I may be* as 'always instructing goodness'.[2] This proves that God blesses one who teaches goodness to another person. Blessedness results from goodness occurring, multiplying and persisting. This really only occurs in the setting of teaching the knowledge inherited from the prophets.

It is for this reason also that the Sublime named His Book as 'blessed'. God (Exalted is He) said: *This is a blessed Reminder that we have revealed;*[3] *(This is) a Book that We have revealed unto thee, full of blessing.*[4] Thus the blessedness of His Book and His Messenger leads to knowledge, guidance and calling to God.

[Point 149: The servant is rewarded for any knowledge or goodness whether it is something that he directly pursued or that was indirectly engendered by him.]

Abū Hurayra (may God be pleased with him) narrated that the Prophet (may God bless him and grant him peace) said: 'When a person dies, his deeds are cut off except for three: charity that still exists, knowledge that others benefit from, and a righteous son who supplicates for him.'[5]

This is one of the greatest proofs for the eminence of knowledge and its great fruits. The reward [of knowledge] continues even after a person dies if it is being benefited from. It is as if he is still alive, since [the benefit derived from] his good deeds [and wealth] do not cease.

1 Q. xix.30–31.

2 Ibn ʿAbd al-Barr 798.

3 Q. xxi.50.

4 Q. xxxviii.29.

5 Muslim 4223; Tirmidhī 1376; Abū Dāwūd 2880.

He continues to be remembered and commended, and it is like he is living a second life.

The Prophet (may God bless him and grant him peace) specifically mentioned the reward of these three because that person was the cause for their occurrence, even though it is beyond what he [directly] strove for (*saʿy*) or acquired (*kasb*). But since he is the cause that originated the occurrence of a righteous child, continuous charity, or knowledge being benefitted from, the rewards and recompense flow to him. Thus the servant is rewarded for what he [directly] pursued or what is [indirectly] engendered by him.

The Exalted mentioned these two principles in *Sūrat al-Barā'a*: *That is because neither thirst nor toil nor hunger afflicteth them in the way of God, nor step they any step that angereth the disbelievers, nor gain they from the enemy a gain, but a good deed is recorded for them therefore. God loseth not the wages of the good.*[1] All of these occurrences [i.e. thirst, hunger and angering their enemy] are [indirectly] engendered by their actions, and are not within their power. Then He said: *Nor spend they any spending, small or great, nor do they cross a valley, but it is recorded for them, that God may repay them the best of what they used to do.*[2] Here, the spending [of their wealth] and traversing of the valley are [direct] actions, which are within their power.

In the first case, He said *a good deed is recorded for them*. Here, the action is not the sole independent cause that led to the occurrence of what is engendered; instead, it is only one of many. Since the thirst and fatigue [they endure] and the angering of their enemy are not a result of their [direct] actions, what is recorded for them is not the same exact [deed]; rather, it is recorded for them as a righteous deed. In the other case, regarding actions that are within their power, like spending and traversing the valley, they are righteous deeds in and of themselves; thus the exact same deed is recorded for them. They are empowered to carry them out and they occurred via their will

1 Q. IX.120.

2 Q. IX.121.

and capability. In conclusion, one is rewarded in return for [direct] actions that are within one's power, and also those which are [indirectly] engendered. We ask God for success.

[Point 150: A discussion on whether a scholar who has performed many righteous deeds is more likely to be forgiven for a sin than an ignorant person.]

Ibn ʿAbd al-Barr related that ʿAbd Allāh b. Dāwūd[1] said: 'On the Day of Resurrection, God (Glorious and Exalted is He) will separate the scholars away from being judged and will say: "Enter Paradise with what you have. I did not bestow My knowledge upon you except because I willed goodness for you."'[2] In another narration, God will say: 'O community of scholars, I would not have placed My wisdom in you had I willed to punish you. I know that you have sinful deeds mixed in, just as others have, but I have concealed them and forgiven you for all of them. I was worshipped as a result of your legal opinions and your teaching of My servants. You will not be held accountable [for your sins]. Enter Paradise.' [ʿAbd Allāh b. Dāwūd] then said: 'No one can bestow what He has denied nor can anyone deny what He has bestowed.' He also said that this meaning has been related via a traceable chain of narration that is connected [to the Prophet].[3]

Ibrāhīm [al-Ḥarbī] said: 'It has reached me that on the Day of Resurrection the good deeds of a person will be placed on one end of the Scale and his evil sins on the other. The latter will be heavier, such that he will become despondent thinking that he will be entered into Hellfire. Then something like a cloud will come and rain down good deeds of his until they are heavier than his evil sins.' It will be said to him: "Do you recognize these [good] actions of yours?" He

1 Abū ʿAbd al-Raḥmān ʿAbd Allāh b. Dāwūd b. ʿĀmir al-Khuraybī (d. 213/828) was a scholar and traditionist. Dhahabī states that he would not narrate *ḥadīth*s to Bukhārī out of a sense of caution.

2 Ibn ʿAbd al-Barr 231.

3 Ibn ʿAbd al-Barr 231; Haythamī 528 (who said it is 'very weak').

will say no. It will be said: "This is a result of the good you taught people, for they acted upon [your teachings].""[1]

Some argue that the principles of the Divine Law (*qawā'id al-Sharʿ*) necessitate that the ignorant person be pardoned and forgiven, while [forgiveness] for the scholar should not occur [for the same sin], since the scholar is more aware of the evidences of God than one who is ignorant. In addition, the scholar knows the repugnance of disobedience and God's hatred of it more than the ignorant one, and is aware of God's punishment for it. Finally, the scholar needs to acknowledge God's blessing in bestowing knowledge upon him (which is much greater than His blessing upon an ignorant person).

Those who have been blessed, favoured and distinguished by God, yet then wrong themselves by pursuing their temptations, indulging in destructive major sins, unashamedly violating that which is forbidden, thinking nothing of these sins and their consequences—they are punished and criticized to a far greater degree than those who are not of the same status. It is for this reason that the Exalted said: *O ye wives of the Prophet, whosoever of you committeth manifest lewdness, the punishment for her will be doubled, and that is easy for God.*[2] Moreover, for this reason, the legal punishment of a free person is twice that of a slave regarding fornication, slandering innocent women and drinking wine. The Prophet (may God bless him and grant him peace) also said: 'Amongst the most punished people by God on the Day of Resurrection are scholars who derived no benefit from their knowledge.'[3] Some of the Predecessors have said: 'The ignorant person is forgiven for seventy sins before the scholar is forgiven for one.' Some of them likewise said: 'God excuses those who are ignorant for things that He would not excuse the scholars for.'

1 Ibn ʿAbd al-Barr 234.

2 Q. xxxiii.30.

3 Bayhaqī (*Shuʿab*) 1642; Haythamī 872; Mundhirī 219. It is 'very weak' according to Albānī (*Silsilat al-aḥādīth al-ḍaʿīfa* 1634).

The reply to the above is that although what has been mentioned is true without a doubt, there are also principles of the Divine Law and wisdom establishing that whosoever has a great number of righteous deeds and has done many glorious deeds for [the sake of] Islam, then he will be pardoned for things that another would not be excused for.

The Prophet (may God bless him and grant him peace) said to ʿUmar: 'Perhaps God has looked favourably upon those who waged battle at Badr and said: "Do whatever you like, for I have forgiven you."'[1] This is what prevented him (may God bless him and grant him peace) from exacting punishment on someone who perpetrated a major sin, and had betrayed him and the Muslims. The Prophet informed them that [Ḥāṭib b. Abī Baltaʿa] had fought in [the Battle of] Badr. The aforementioned is proof that the prerequisites for [Ḥāṭib's] punishment had been established, but it was not carried out because he had fought in that great battle. Consequently, that major error was forgiven because it was comparatively small in relation to what he had done of righteous deeds. Similarly, the Prophet said after urging people to give charity and ʿUthmān (may God be pleased with him) contributed generously: 'Whatever ʿUthmān does after today will not harm him,' [and he repeated it two times].'[2] Also the Prophet said to Ṭalḥa[3] after the latter allowed him (may God bless him and grant him peace) to ascend on his back to the boulder: 'It [Paradise] is obligatory for Ṭalḥa.'[4]

As for Moses, the one to whom the Almighty, Most Beneficent

1 Bukhārī 3007; Muslim 6401; Tirmidhī 3305; Abū Dāwūd 2650; Aḥmad 600.

2 Tirmidhī 3701; Aḥmad 20,630. It is 'sound' according to Albānī (*Mishkāt* 6073).

3 Ṭalḥa b. ʿUbayd Allāh (d. 35/656) was the eighth to accept Islam. He was one of the ten Companions promised Paradise by the Prophet.

4 Tirmidhī 3738; Aḥmad 1417. It is 'sound' according to Albānī (*Silsilat al-aḥādīth al-ṣaḥīḥa* 945). The tradition is: 'On the day of [the Battle] of Uḥud, the Messenger of God wore two coats of mail. He tried to get up on a boulder, but was not able to. So Ṭalḥa squatted under him, lifting the Prophet upon it, such that he could sit on the boulder. So he said, "It [Paradise] is obligatory for Ṭalḥa."'

and Most Glorious, spoke: he dropped the tablets, upon which were the Words of God written by Him, on the ground such that they broke; he hit the Angel of Death in the eye and knocked it out; and he disagreed (*ʿātaba*) with His Lord on the night of *Isrā'* regarding the Prophet [Muḥammad] (may God bless him and grant him peace) saying: 'How is it that a young [prophet] sent after me has more of his community in Paradise than my community?' And he took Aaron's beard and dragged him by it despite the fact that the latter was a prophet of God. All of these do not diminish his high status in the sight of his Lord. In fact, his Lord (Exalted is He) honours Moses and loves him due to the immense nature of his actions against His enemy and those who emerged against him, the patience he exemplified and the harm that he withstood for [the sake of] God.

It is well known by people, and is established in their innate disposition, that those who have thousands of righteous deeds will be pardoned for one or two sins. It has been said:

> If one who is beloved has one sin
> Then his righteous deeds will provide him with a
> thousand intercessors.

Another said:

> If the offensive action is only one then his
> Actions, which made others joyous, are many.

God (Glory be to Him) will weigh the righteous deeds of the servant against his sins on the Day of Resurrection, and whichever will outweigh the other will dominate. Thus He will forgive and pardon those who have done many righteous deeds, who prefer what He loves and what pleases Him, yet sometimes succumb to the demands of their nature, in a manner that He would not deal with others.

In addition, if the scholar makes a mistake he is able to revert quickly, realize what has transpired, and correct his mistake. He is just like an expert physician who has insight into a disease, its aetiologies and its treatment: he is able to [identify and] cure it more quickly than one who is ignorant. Additionally, the scholar recognizes the commandments of God, attests to the veracity of His promise and His warning, is fearful of Him, finds fault in himself due to his perpetration [of that sin], believes that God has forbidden what he has done, but that also his Lord forgives sin. It also results in him doing [good deeds] which are beloved by the Lord [in order to make amends] and offset that sin, and weaken or eliminate its effect altogether.

On the other hand, one who is either completely or mostly ignorant of all of the above has nothing but the darkness of the sin, its repugnance and its evil consequences. Thus these two cases are unequal. This represents the definitive answer in this matter. Ultimately, the repugnance in both situations—whether [in relation to] a scholar or an ignorant one—results from ignorance and its consequences. This is clear proof of the eminence and excellence of knowledge. We rely on God for success.

[Point 151: Pursuing knowledge is an action of the heart as well as the means to actions of worship.]

The scholar, with his constant immersion in knowledge and learning, is in constant worship. Learning and teaching are both [forms of] worship. Ibn Masʿūd said: 'The scholar always remains in prayer.' Some asked: 'How is he [always] praying?' He replied: 'By remembering God in his heart and on his tongue.'[1]

Muḥammad b. ʿAlī al-Bāqir[2] said: 'A scholar who benefits others with his knowledge is superior to a thousand worshippers.' He also said: 'Narrating and transmitting *ḥadīth*s is better than the worship of a thousand worshippers.' Since the pursuit of knowledge,

1 Ibn ʿAbd al-Barr 259.

2 Muḥammad b. ʿAlī b. Ḥusayn b. ʿAlī b. Abī Ṭālib al-Bāqir (d. 114/733) was a prominent Successor and jurist of the *Ahl al-Bayt*. He lived in Medina. Due to his great depth of knowledge he was named al-Bāqir (the Revealer). He is considered by the Shīʿa to be the Fifth Imam and he is the father of Jaʿfar al-Ṣādiq, whom is considered the Sixth Imam.

researching and recording of it are actions of both the heart and body, they are the best types of actions. They involve sincerity, reliance [on God] in tribulation, repentance, piety, contentment, and are thus connected to actions of the heart.

If it is said that knowledge is only a means to action, and it is only desired so as to attain the latter; and actions are the end objective; and it is well-known that the ends are more eminent than the means; then how is it that the means [knowledge] are preferable to the ends [action]? The reply is that both knowledge and action are divided into two groups: one group represents the means and the other the end objectives. Thus not all types of knowledge are only considered to be the means. Instead, knowledge of God, His Names and His Attributes are absolutely the most eminent types of knowledge, and are pursued for themselves.

God (Exalted is He) said: *God it is Who hath created seven heavens, and of the earth the like thereof. The commandment cometh down among them slowly, that ye may know that God is Able to do all things, and that God surroundeth all things in knowledge.*[1] Therefore knowing that God is omniscient and omnipotent is the ultimate objective of creation.

The Exalted also said: *So know* (*O Muḥammad*) *that there is no god save God.*[2] Thus the knowledge of the Exalted's Oneness and that there is no god worthy of worship but Him is pursued for itself. These two issues—i.e. to know the Exalted Lord through His Names, Attributes, actions and judgments, and thereafter to worship Him according to those requisites and necessities—are essential. Thus, just as worshipping Him is desired and intended in and of itself, knowledge and recognition of Him is so too. Knowledge, as has been previously mentioned, is one of the best forms of worship, since it encompasses both the ends and the means.

As regards to the contention that actions are the end objec-

1 Q. LXV.12.
2 Q. XLVII.19.

tives, one must differentiate between those involving both the heart and the body and those only involving the body. If the former is what is intended, then that contention is true. This is proof that knowledge is the desired end objective, because it is an action of the heart (as has been mentioned previously). But if only the latter is intended, i.e. actions of the body alone, then that contention is not correct. In reality, actions of the body are means intended for other [more lofty end objectives]. One's reward or punishment, and being praiseworthy or blameworthy, are fundamentally due to [actions of] the heart. The foremost purpose of the body's actions is achieving righteousness, increase [in this], purification and uprightness of the heart, in addition to worshipping one's Lord and Owner. Therefore some actions are end objectives and some are means, just [as has been mentioned] in the case of knowledge.

In addition, if the types of knowledge which are solely a means are not followed by actions then that person will not have benefitted from [his knowledge]. In that case, the action [had it occurred] becomes nobler than [this knowledge]. On the other hand, it should not be said that isolated actions are more eminent than the types of knowledge which one aims for as an end. How can it be said that isolated bodily worship is superior to knowledge about God, His Names, His Attributes, His judgments for His creation and His commandments? How can [action] be better than the types of knowledge regarding actions of the heart, inadequacies of the soul, the manners by which actions are corrupted or prevented from being accepted by God, the tenets of faith and what strengthens or weakens it? Indeed whoever fulfills both types of action is higher in perfection. If the servant has a choice it would be better to spend his extra time learning the knowledge inherited from the prophets, rather than spending it in isolated worship. This is the definitive response to this question, and God knows best.

[Point 152: The most virtuous rank is occupied by those who use their knowledge and wealth to carry out pious deeds.]

Abū Kabsha al-Anmārī[1] narrated that the Messenger of God (may God bless him and grant him peace) said:

> The world includes only four types of people. [Firstly], a servant whom God has provided with both wealth and knowledge. He uses them to carry out pious deeds for his Lord's sake and nurtures the ties of kinship whilst knowing God's rights. This is the most virtuous rank. The next is a person whom God provides with knowledge, but He does not provide him with wealth. He says: 'If I had wealth I would carry out the same [pious] deeds as so-and-so.' Due to his [sincere] intention, their reward is the same. The [third] is a person whom God provides with wealth, but He does not provide him with knowledge. He spends his wealth rashly without knowledge. He is not fearful of his Lord, does not nurture the ties of kinship, nor does he recognize God's rights. This is the most despicable rank in God's sight. Finally, there is a person whom God does not provide with wealth or knowledge. He says: 'If I had wealth, then I would carry out the same [evil] deeds as so-and-so.' He has the same intention and so his sin is the same.[2]

Thus the Prophet (may God bless him and grant him peace) divided people into four groups. The best are those who have been given knowledge and wealth, and are benevolent to people as they use their wealth and [teach them their] knowledge. The next rank includes those who have been given knowledge but not wealth.

1 Saʿīd b. ʿAmr Abū Kabsha al-Anmārī (d. 40/660) was a Companion who narrated 11 *ḥadīths*.

2 Tirmidhī 2325; Ibn Māja 4228; Aḥmad 18,024. It is 'authentic' according to Albānī (*Ṣaḥīḥ al-Jāmiʿ al-ṣaghīr* 3024).

Even though they both have the same reward for their intentions, the almsgiver's rank is higher because of what he has donated and given in charity. The scholar who does not possess wealth has the same reward only because of his definitive intention and isolated statement, which are associated with his [limited] capability.

The third group is composed of those who have been given wealth but not knowledge. They are the worst people in God's sight, because their wealth has led to their destruction. It would have been better for them if they lacked that wealth. They were bestowed with the provisions necessary to reach Paradise, but instead they [squandered] them to go to Hellfire. The fourth group has neither wealth nor knowledge, but their intention would have been to disobey God if they were given the financial ability. This group's rank follows that of those who are wealthy yet ignorant, but their intention to be sinful is the same.

In conclusion, the Prophet divided those who are blissful into two groups, and he established that their knowledge and good deeds were the cause of their bliss. Then he divided those who are wretched into two groups, and made ignorance and its consequences the cause of their wretchedness.

CHAPTER TWELVE

The Importance of Contemplation and Reflection

[Point 153: Statements from the Predecessors regarding the importance of contemplation and that it leads to further knowledge.]

Some of the Predecessors have said: 'Contemplation (*tafakkur*) for an hour is better than worship for sixty years.' A man asked Umm al-Dardā' after [Abū al-Dardā's] death about his worship. She answered: 'He spent much of his day in contemplation.'[1] Ḥasan [al-Baṣrī] said: 'Contemplation for an hour is better than praying at night.' Fuḍayl [b. ʿIyāḍ] said: 'Contemplation is like a mirror: it reflects your benevolent deeds and evil sins back to you [so that you may recognize them for what they are].'[2] Sufyān [b. ʿUyayna] would often say:

> If a man would just contemplate
> He would learn a moral lesson from everything.[3]

Ḥasan also interpreted the Exalted's statement *I shall turn away from My revelations those who magnify themselves wrongfully in the earth*[4] as He will prevent them from contemplating about [His revelations].

Some of the knowers said: 'If the hearts of the pious rose to contemplate what they could of the Unseen and veiled goodness of the Hereafter, they would find no peace of mind or satisfaction in their lives.' Ḥasan also said: 'Solitude for long periods is better [to

1 Abū Nuʿaym, vol. I, p. 208.
2 Abū Nuʿaym, vol. VIII, p. 109.
3 Abū Nuʿaym, vol. VII, p. 306.
4 Q. VII.146.

improve one's] contemplation. Prolonging contemplation is proof that one is on the path to Paradise.' Wahb [b. Munabbih][1] said: 'If one contemplates deeply it will only increase his knowledge. If one is knowledgeable, then he will inevitably act.' ʿUmar b. ʿAbd al-ʿAzīz said: 'Contemplating about the blessings of God is one of the best types of worship.' ʿAbd Allāh b. Mubārak said to one of his companions who was deep in contemplation: 'Where did you reach?' He responded: 'The path.'

Bishr[2] said: 'If people were to really contemplate about the greatness of God they would not disobey Him.' Ibn ʿAbbās said: 'Praying two units of prayer well with good intention and with contemplation is better than praying at night without a [pious] heart.' Abū Sulaymān[3] said: 'Contemplating this world results in the occurrence of a barrier which obstructs [one from aspiring to] the Hereafter. It is a punishment for rulers. On the other hand, contemplating the Hereafter instills wisdom and piety in one's heart.'

Ibn ʿAbbās said: 'Contemplating goodness leads one to act upon it.' Shāfiʿī said: 'Depend on silence to improve your speech and depend on contemplation to improve your deductions.' Contemplation is an act of the heart, whereas worshipping is an act of the body. Since the heart is nobler than the body, its actions [which include contemplation] are better than the body's. In addition, contemplation allows one to [reach] levels of faith which are higher than isolated action alone.

Contemplation necessitates the unveiling (*inkishāf*) of matters and the manifestation of their realities. It differentiates their degrees of goodness or evilness, allows one to recognize the causes that lead to or prevent their occurrence, as well as what hinders their requisites from manifesting.

1 Wahb b. Munabbih (d. 110/728) was a prominent Successor and traditionist. He wrote *Kitāb al-Isrā'īliyyāt*.

2 Abū Naṣr Bishr b. Ḥārith al-Ḥāfī (d. 225/840) was a scholar and Sufi ascetic. He was a student of al-Fuḍayl b. ʿIyāḍ and a contemporary of Imam Aḥmad.

3 Abū Sulaymān ʿAbd al-Raḥmān b. Aḥmad b. ʿAṭiyya al-Dārānī (d. 215/830) was a famous Sufi ascetic.

It also differentiates between what is imaginary and delusional. These would otherwise prevent most people from taking advantage of opportunities despite their potential to do so. There is no greater impediment—that prevents the majority from attaining perfection, success and bliss both in this life and the Hereafter—than these imaginations and delusions. This impediment can only dissipate if correct thoughts, and a sincere and firm resolve, occur; these allow one to differentiate between imaginations and the truth. In fact, most people are drowning in these [delusions]. Also if one thinks about the evil end results of sins and temptations, he will think beyond the initial pleasure and instead will recognize the pain and sadness that will ultimately occur. Whoever contemplates those evil consequences will hardly ever go ahead with [sins].

Similarly, one may desire relaxation, indifference, laziness and idleness instead of performing pious deeds because of the hardships and difficulties associated with the latter. But once one contemplates the abundant and perfect pleasures, goodness and happiness to be attained [in the Hereafter], those [thoughts] will overcome the initial difficulties. The more deeply one thinks about those [outcomes] the greater one's pursuit will be and the easier it will be for one to endure [those hardships]. Such a person will become more energetic and have a stronger resolve.

If someone reflects on the depth to which his wealth, pursuit of power and illusions have enslaved him, he will become embarrassed that his reasoning and self allowed him to become so [misled]. It has been said:

> Had the excessive lover contemplated the end outcome
> of [pursuing] the
> Beauty that has captivated him, he would not have become beguiled.

One should not focus one's attention on this world, nor become content with it, get angry about things related to it, pursue it, toil for it, support or have enmity toward others due to it.

In the *Musnad* of [Imam Aḥmad] it is narrated that the Prophet (may God bless him and grant him peace) said: 'God has drawn [a parallel between] the food that the offspring of Adam eat and this world. Even if [food] is embellished and salted, one knows what happens to it.'[1] Thus, if someone who is [spiritually] free remembers that outcome when contemplating the end result of his affairs, he will hold himself in high enough esteem to refuse to become enslaved to what will end by becoming the most rotten and wicked thing.

Contemplation of two known things leads to the fruition of a third. For example, if one's heart recalls and is certain of what this immediate life encompasses, both in terms of its blessings but also its inadequacies and temporary nature; and then remembers the superior blessings, pleasures and infinite nature of [Paradise in] the Hereafter; then this leads to the fruition of a third type of knowledge, which is that the Hereafter and its superior and infinite bliss should take precedence in the mind of any intelligent and rational person over this temporary and loathsome worldly life.

Most people though are uncertain of the Hereafter and do not try to become more knowledgeable about it. They are pulled in two different directions: one being this worldly life, which is the stronger caller since they have merely heard about the Hereafter [and not seen it]. Thus, if they abandon this worldly life for the Hereafter, their selves will make them think that they are abandoning something definite for some notion or imaginary thing. It is like this [worldly life] says to him: 'Do not leave a coin weighing an atom for a pearl that is promised.' This evil has prevented many people from preparing for the Hereafter and working for it appropriately. Again, it is due to their weak knowledge and lack of certainty in [the Hereafter]. If they were absolutely certain of it and their hearts were not pervaded with doubts, they would not be negligent or indifferent in pursuing it.

1 Aḥmad 21,239; Ibn Ḥibbān 702; Haythamī 18,075. It is 'authentic' according to Albānī (*Silsilat al-aḥādīth al-ṣaḥīḥa* 382).

Thus it becomes known that one's preference for this worldly life and lack of preparation for the Hereafter is not at all concordant with perfection of one's belief and faith.

On the other hand, the second group are absolutely certain without any doubt that there is another abode, a Hereafter that they have been created for, and that this [worldly] abode is only one of the stages along which the traveller journeys on (*manzil min manāzil al-sā'irīn*) to the Hereafter. They know that the Hereafter is everlasting, and that its bliss or punishment does not abate. They also know that this world's luxury or suffering are nothing compared to the Hereafter's; they are only like [water] that clings to one's finger if one puts it into the sea and then removes it. Therefore this knowledge leads to the fruition of their preference, pursuit and complete preparation for the Hereafter.

One should seek out and endeavour to attain [what is beloved to God] through contemplation (*tafakkur*), recollection (*tadhakkur*), reflection (*naẓar*), deep reflection (*ta'ammul*), consideration (*iʿtibār*), pondering (*tadabbur*) and insight (*istibṣār*). These meanings are close to each other in some aspects but diverge in others.

'Contemplation' (*tafakkur*) is so called because it involves making use of one's thought with an attentive [heart]. 'Recollection' (*tadhakkur*) is so called because it involves remembering knowledge after having forgotten it. An example is in the statement of the Exalted: *Those who ward off (evil), when a thought of evil from the Devil troubleth them, they do but remember (God's guidance) and behold them they see (aright)!*[1]

'Reflection' (*naẓar*) is so called because the heart directs its attention to what is viewed. 'Deep reflection' (*ta'amala*) is so called because one repeatedly reflects on something time after time until it becomes elucidated and unveiled to one. 'Consideration' (*iʿtibār*)—which is the *iftiʿāl* derivation of 'traverse' (*ʿubūr*)—is so called because it allows one to traverse from one thing to another. One traverses from that

1 Q. VII.201.

which was just contemplated to recognition of a third [reality]; and this is the point of consideration. It is also for this reason that *ʿibra* is named 'a moral lesson'. God (Exalted is He) said: *Herein is indeed a lesson for him who feareth;*[1] *Herein verily is a lesson for those who have eyes.*[2]

'Pondering' (*tadabbur*) is so called because one considers the *adbār* of matters, which are the end outcomes and consequences of them. The Exalted said: *Have they not pondered the Word;*[3] and *Will they not then ponder on the Qur'ān? If it had been from other than God they would have found therein much incongruity.*[4] Pondering over a statement is to look at its beginning and its end, and then to repetitively look at it over and over again. For this reason it came in the *tafaʿʿul* derivation. 'Insight' (*istibṣar*)—which is the *istifʿāl* derivation of 'enlightenment' (*tabṣira*)—is so called because it indicates that an issue has become clear, unveiled and elucidated to one's penetrating vision (*baṣīra*).

Recollection and contemplation each have an additional meaning that the other does not. 'Recollection' connotes that the heart repetitively remembers what it knows and recognizes, so that it subsequently becomes entrenched and established within it. As a result, it cannot become erased from the heart. 'Contemplation' connotes that one's knowledge has increased, and that one has attained something not previously existent. Thus contemplation attains [knowledge] while recollection protects it. For this reason Ḥasan [al-Baṣrī] said: 'The knowledgeable scholars persist in using recollection for contemplation and using contemplation for recollection. They work on their hearts until wisdom emanates from them.' Thus contemplation and recollection are both the seeds and irrigation for knowledge. Conversing about and deliberating on [knowledge] lead to its propagation (*talqīḥ*). Some of the

1 Q. LXXIX.26.
2 Q. III.13.
3 Q. XXIII.68.
4 Q. IV.82.

Predecessors said: 'The assemblies of men lead to the propagation [of knowledge in] people's minds.'

Goodness and bliss are within a safe, and its key is contemplation. It is incumbent that one contemplates. Contemplated knowledge also allows the heart to reach a [higher] state (*ḥāl*). That state necessarily engenders a will, which inevitably results in the occurrence of an action. Thus here are five matters: [first] contemplation, which results in knowledge [the second]. The combined effect of both of them is [a third], the state that the heart reaches. The consequence of that [state] is [a fourth], the will. Finally, the fruit of that [will] is action. Indeed contemplation is the basis and key for all this goodness.

This unveils for you the excellence and eminence of contemplation. It is one of the best and most beneficial actions of the heart. It has even been said: 'Contemplation for an hour is better than worship for a year.' Contemplation allows one's mind to become alive with awareness (*ḥayāt al-yaqaẓa*) instead of being [spiritually] dead; prevents one from desiring [this world] avidly; allows one to abstain from it and be content [with whatever one has]; delivers one from the prison of this life to the expanse of the Hereafter; cures one from the diseases of temptations and doubts; and [bars one from] latching onto this abode of delusions—thus making one desire to return to God. It also remedies one from the afflictions of blindness, deafness and dumbness [i.e. ignorance]; and makes one [recognize] the blessings of God, such as vision, hearing, understanding, knowledge, certainty and delight.

Piety is a result of contemplation. Likewise, those who avoid contemplation will inevitably be disobedient [to the Lord]. Satan approaches an empty and void heart and plants within it seedlings of vile thoughts, which instigate a will and firm resolve to carry out [evil] actions. On the other hand, if [Satan] finds a heart which is preoccupied with contemplating about good and beneficial thoughts—like what one is created for and commanded to do or the everlasting bliss or the painful punishment that has been readied and prepared for one—then the Devil will not find a place to plant [evil thoughts].

Now contemplation is attached to four matters: first, a beloved and desired objective; second, the path to reach that objective; third, a disliked harm that one seeks to render null; fourth, the manner by which one can make that [harm] become null. The thoughts of those who are rational do not go beyond these four.

Any contemplation that is other than these is [to be considered] as vile thoughts, delusions or vain aspirations. Examples include one who is destitute yet imagines himself to be wealthy and powerful; one who is feeble yet dreams that he is a great king running a country; and the thoughts of a drunkard or a person intoxicated on drugs. Vile thoughts are the stock of despicable and contemptible types of people, since they are satisfied with delusions and content with impossibilities. These thoughts continue to strengthen until they necessarily result in vile effects, wicked thoughts and [spiritual] diseases that are difficult to eliminate.

The thoughts of people [attached to] this world, who will have no share [of Paradise] in the Hereafter, will have their result. Once the truth becomes verified, this world becomes null, and the Hereafter begins; and the winners will become clear from those who have been deceived [by this world]—at that time those who were vain will be lost.[1]

We will now elaborate—with the help of God and His grace—on the thoughts of those who believe in the Hereafter. Whoever pursues something is considered to be a lover of it, and his preference is to be near it. He takes the path towards it, and reaches it after strenuous striving. This necessitates that his thoughts be connected to the beauty, perfection and attributes of his beloved. His thoughts

1 Derived from the Q. XL.78: *But when God's commandment cometh (the cause) is judged aright, and the followers of vanity will then be lost.*

must also be attached to the goodness, happiness and enjoyment he will attain. His contemplation about the state of his beloved revolves around the latter's beauty and excellence, and his need to become righteous and benevolent. The stronger his love, the greater, more robust and magnified are his thoughts. His heart becomes wholly engrossed with [the beloved] and no part remains leftover [to think about] anyone else. He lives amongst the people in form, but his heart entirely dwells on his beloved.

If the beloved is the True Beloved [God]—and it is not proper to truly love anyone except Him, and no one else should be loved unless it is for His sake—then he is the most blissful of those who love Him, and he possesses an appropriate love. Furthermore, he has enabled himself to reach the perfection that he was created for. There is no way, at all, to attain perfection without [this love].

But if that love is for anything else—which inevitably is in vain and will cease to exist— then he has loved inappropriately and has wronged himself to the most repugnant degree. Consequently, he will only attain the utmost wretchedness and pain. If this is recognized then it becomes known that loving something else besides the True God represents the essence of the servant's wretchedness and loss.

The contemplation of one who loves the Beloved so completely that it dominates his heart does not go beyond thinking about his connection to his Beloved or [reflecting] on himself [and his relationship with his Beloved]. He must contemplate about his Beloved in two ways: first, [contemplating] His Beauty and Attributes; or second, [contemplating] His actions, benevolence, grace and kindness, which are all indicative of His perfect Attributes.

If one reflects on oneself, then it can only take the form of two manners. Firstly, it is either about those characteristics of his that are displeasing and disliked by his Beloved or [are a cause] for Him to disregard him. Now one should always be striving and contemplating on how to avoid and distance oneself from these [evil] things.

Secondly, one contemplates and works to attain those characteristics and actions that will bring one closer to God and make one more beloved by Him.

The first two thoughts result in his love becoming stronger and magnified. The second two thoughts result in the Beloved loving him, having regard for him, being compassionate with him, and preferring him over others. The first two thoughts concern knowledge of the Oneness of God, that He alone should be worshipped, [and concern] His Attributes (Glory be to Him) and His actions. The third and fourth concern the path that leads to Him, and they include [contemplating on how best to avoid] the evils that cut one off or prevent one from travelling along the path to Him.

When a person contemplates his own character it allows him to first distinguish those [traits] which are beloved to his Lord versus those which are disliked by Him. Second, he should ask himself whether he is characterized by them or not? Third, if a person is characterized by [something which is disliked or hated by God], then [he should think about] the manner by which he can rid and free himself of it. On the other hand, if he is not characterized by [something disliked] then he [should ask himself] what should he do to preserve his rightness, maintain his wellness and protect himself? If he is characterized by something which is beloved and pleasing to God then [he should contemplate on] how he can preserve it and ensure its continuity? If he is not characterized by it then by what manner can he adopt it and make it one of his attributes?

Then one must contemplate his actions accordingly. The ways of thinking about them are so numerous that they can barely be recounted. But [in general] they can be summarized into six types: apparent or hidden pious deeds; apparent or hidden evil deeds; and praiseworthy or blameworthy attributes and characteristics.

As for contemplating the Attributes of the One Who alone should be worshipped, as well as His actions and judgments, one must declare the Lord to be infallible from anything which is not befitting to Him. One should only characterize Him with the majesty and honour that He alone is entitled to. Furthermore, [such necessary decorum] also includes pondering His Words. God (Glory be to Him) has revealed to us His Names, Attributes and actions through the conveyance of His messengers. It includes also pondering about His decree and actions in relation to both His saints, whom He supports, and His enemies. In doing so one realizes that He is the True Manifest God and that it is not proper that anyone else be worshipped but Him. One also realizes that He is omnipotent and omniscient; that His punishment is severe; that He is the Most Forgiving, Most Merciful, Almighty and Most Wise; and that He does what He wills; that all of His actions revolve around wisdom, mercy, justice and that which is beneficial—nothing exists outside of these. There is no way to attain these fruits except by [first] pondering His Words and [second] observing the effects of His actions.

The Exalted charged His servants to do these two. He said regarding the first: *Will they not then ponder on the Qur'ān?*[1] *Will they then not meditate on the Qur'ān;*[2] *Have they not pondered the Word;*[3] *(This is) a Book that We have revealed unto thee, full of blessing, that they may ponder its revelations.*[4]

He said regarding the second: *Say: Behold what is in the heavens and the earth!*[5] *In the creation of the heavens and the earth and (in) the difference of night and day are tokens (of His sovereignty) for men of understanding, such as remember God, standing, sitting and reclining, and consider the creation of the heavens and the earth;*[6] *In the heavens and the earth are portents for believers. And in your creation, and all the beasts that He scattereth in the earth, are portents for a folk whose faith is sure.*[7] *Have they not travelled in the land to*

1 Q. IV.82.
2 Q. XLVII.24.
3 Q. XXIII.68.
4 Q. XXXVIII.29.
5 Q. X.101.
6 Q. III.190–191.
7 Q. XLV.3-4.

see the nature of the consequence for those who disbelieved before them?[1] *Say (O Muḥammad, to the disbelievers): Travel in the land, and see the nature of the consequence for those who were before you!*[2]

Most blessed is He Who has made His Words enliven and cure [our] hearts. In summation, there is nothing more beneficial for the heart than reading, pondering and contemplating the Qur'ān. It documents all of the stations of the [pious] travellers (*manāzil al-sā'irīn*), states of the doers (*aḥwāl al-ʿāmilīn*) and ranks of the knowers (*maqāmāt al-ʿārifīn*). It engenders one to love and have longing for God, fear Him, hope in Him, always return to Him, rely on Him, be content, entrust [oneself to Him], thank Him, have patience, in addition to all of the other states that describe a heart which is alive and perfect. It also drives one away from all of the blameworthy characteristics and actions which lead to one's heart becoming corrupt and ruined.

If people knew the benefit of pondering the Qur'ān, they would devote themselves to it exclusively. If one [is aware of] a verse that will cure his heart, and then reads it maybe one hundred times or for an entire night with contemplation, this will be better for him than reading the entire Qur'ān without pondering or understanding it. This will also allow one's heart to attain [a higher level of] faith and experience the beauty of the Qur'ān [to a greater degree]. This was the habit of the Predecessors, whereby one of them would repeat one verse until dawn. [In this practice,] they [were emulating] the Prophet (may God bless him and grant him peace), who once repeated the following verse until dawn:[3] *If Thou punish them, they are Thy servants, and if Thou forgive them (they are Thy servants). Thou, only Thou, art the Mighty, the Wise.*[4] Thus reading the Qur'ān with contemplation is the basis for righteousness of the heart.

1 Q. XL.21.

2 Q. XXX.42.

3 Aḥmad 21,538.

4 Q. V.118.

For this reason Ibn Masᶜūd said: 'Do not senselessly read the Qur'ān like it is poetry or prose. Grasp its marvels. Let your hearts be moved by it. Do not be anxious to just end [the mere reading of] a *sūra*.' Moreover, Abū Jamra said that he told Ibn ᶜAbbās: 'I am fast at reading the Qur'ān. I can read it in three days.' Ibn ᶜAbbās replied: 'It is more beloved to me to recite one *sūra* of the Qur'ān and ponder it for an entire night than to read the Qur'ān as you do.'

There are two ways by which contemplation of the Qur'ān occurs: [first] to understand what the Exalted Lord's will is for us; and [second] to contemplate the meanings of what He has charged His servants with. God has revealed the Qur'ān so that they may ponder and contemplate it, not so that they would simply recite and then subsequently shun it. Al-Ḥasan al-Baṣrī said: 'The Qur'ān was revealed so that it would be acted upon. Follow it by acting upon it.'

If you deeply reflect upon how God (Glory be to Him) has called His servants to contemplate His Book and signs, you will find yourself attaining knowledge of Him (Glorious and Exalted is He) and His Oneness; His Attributes of perfection and glorious characteristics; His omnipotence and omniscience; His perfect wisdom, mercy, benevolence, generosity, kindness and justice; what pleases Him and leads to His reward, as well as what is [deserving] of His wrath and leads to His punishment. God has made Himself known to His servants through the [Qur'ān] and charged them to contemplate His signs [so rise to that with a heart full of love for Him].

BIBLIOGRAPHY

Abū Khaliyl (tr.). *English Translation of Jāmiᶜ at-Tirmidhī*. Riyadh: Darussalam Publications, 2007. [=Tirmidhī, Abū ᶜĪsā Muḥammad b. ᶜĪsā al-Sulamī, al-. *Jāmiᶜ al-Tirmidhī*]

Abū Zayd, Bakr b. ᶜAbd Allāh. *Ibn Qayyim al-Jawziyya: ḥayātuh āthāruh mawāriduh*. Riyadh: Dār al-ᶜĀṣimah, 1995.

Albānī, Muḥammad Nāṣir al-Dīn, al-. *Silsilat al-aḥādīth al-ḍaᶜīfa wa'l-mawḍūᶜa wa atharuhā al-sayyi' fi'l-umma*. Riyadh: Maktabat al-Maᶜārif, 1992.

———. *Silsilat al-aḥādīth al-ṣaḥīḥa wa-shay' min fiqhihā wa fawā'idihā*. Riyadh: Maktabat al-Maᶜārif, 1995.

Ali, Abdullah Yusuf. *The Holy Qur'an: Text, Translation, and Commentary*. Lahore: Shaykh Muhammad Ashraf Publishers, 1938.

Al-Qoz, Anas Abdul-Hameed. *Men and the Universe: Reflections of Ibn al-Qayyem*. Riyadh: Darussalam, 2004.

Anjum, Ovamir. 'Sufism without Mysticism? Ibn Qayyim al-Ǧawziyyah's Objectives in *Madāriǧ al-Sālikīn*'. In Caterina Bori and Livnat Holtzman (eds.), *A Scholar in the Shadow: Essays in the Legal and Theological Thought of Ibn al-Qayyim al-Ǧawziyyah* (Oriente Moderno XC, no. 1. Rome: Istituto per l'Oriente C. A. Nallino, 2010), pp. 161–188.

Asad, Muhammad. *The Message of the Qur'ān*. Bristol: The Book Foundation, 2003.

Aṣbahānī, Abū Nuᶜaym Aḥmad b. ᶜAbd Allāh, al-. *Ḥilyat al-awliyā' wa ṭabaqāt al-aṣfiyā'*. Beirut: Dār al-Kutub al-ᶜIlmiyyah, 1988.

Azzam, Abdul Rahman. *Saladin: The Triumph of the Sunni Revival*. Cambridge: The Islamic Texts Society, 2014.

Baghdādī, Abū Bakr Aḥmad al-Khaṭīb, al-. *Al-Faqīh wa'l-mutafaqqih*. Ed. Abū ᶜAbd al-Raḥmān ᶜĀdil b. Yūsuf al-Gharāzī. Dammam: Dār Ibn al-Jawzī, 2000.

———. *Tārīkh Baghdād*. Ed. Bashshār ᶜAwād Maᶜrūf. Beirut: Dār al-Gharb al-Islāmī, 2002.

Bayhaqī, Abū Bakr Aḥmad b. al-Ḥusayn al-. *Al-Sunan al-kubrā li'l-Bayhaqī*. Ed. Muḥammad ᶜAbd al-Qādir ᶜAṭā'. Beirut: Dār al-Kutub al-ᶜIlmiyyah, 2003.

———. *Shuʿab al-īmān*. Ed. ʿAbd al-ʿAlī ʿAbd al-Ḥamīd Ḥāmid. Riyadh: Maktabat al-Rushd, 2003.

Bell, Joseph N. *Love Theory in Later Ḥanbalite Islam*. Albany: State University of New York Press, 1979.

Dārimī, Abū Muḥammad ʿAbd Allāh b. ʿAbd al-Raḥmān, al-. *Sunan al-Dārimī*. Ed. Ḥusayn Salīm Asad al-Dārānī. Riyadh: Dār al-Mughnī, 2000.

Dhahabī, Abū ʿAbd Allāh Shams al-Dīn Muḥammad b. Aḥmad, al. *Siyar aʿlām al-nubalāʾ*. Editor-in-Chief Shuʿayb al-Arnaʾūṭ. Beirut: Muʾassasat al-Risāla, 1985.

Fitzgerald, Michael Abdurrahman and Slitine, Moulay Youssef (trs). *Ibn Qayyim al-Jawziyya on the Invocation of God*. Cambridge: Islamic Texts Society, 2000. [=Ibn Qayyim al-Jawziyya, Abū ʿAbd Allāh Shams al-Dīn Muḥammad b. Abī Bakr. *al-Wābil al-ṣayyib min al-kalim al-ṭayyib* (extract)]

Ghazālī, Abū Ḥāmid Muḥammad b. Muḥammad, al-. *Iḥyāʾ ʿulūm al-dīn*. Beirut: Dār al-Maʿrifa, 2004.

Ḥākim, Abū ʿAbd Allāh Muḥammad b. ʿAbd Allāh, al-. *Al-Mustadrak ʿalaʾl-Ṣaḥīḥayn liʾl-Ḥākim*. Ed. Muṣṭafā ʿAbd al-Qādir ʿAṭāʾ. Beirut: Dār al-Kutub al-ʿIlmiyyah, 1990.

Hallaq, Wael. *Ibn Taymiyya against the Greek Logicians*. Oxford: Clarendon Press, 1993.

Haythamī, Abū al-Ḥasan Nūr al-Dīn ʿAlī, al-. *Majmaʿ al-zawāʾid wa manbaʿ al-fawāʾid*. Ed. Ḥusām al-Dīn al-Qudsī. Cairo: Maktabat al-Qudsī, 1994.

Holtzman, Livnat. 'Ibn Qayyim al-Jawziyyah'. In Joseph E. Lowery and Devin Stewart (eds.), *Essays in Arabic Literary Biography II: 1350–1850* (Wiesbaden: Harrassowitz Verlag, 2009), pp. 202–222.

Honerkamp, Kenneth (tr.). *The Book of Knowledge: Book 1 of The Revival of the Religious Sciences*. Louisville: Fons Vitae, 2016.

Hoover, Jon. 'God's Wise Purposes in Creating Iblīs: Ibn Qayyim al-Ǧawziyyah's Theodicy of God's Names and Attributes'. In Caterina Bori and Livnat Holtzman (eds.), *A Scholar in the Shadow: Essays in the Legal and Theological Thought of Ibn al-Qayyim al-Ǧawziyyah* (Oriente Moderno xc, no. 1. Rome: Istituto per l'Oriente C. A. Nallino, 2010), pp. 113–134.

Ibn ʿAbd al-Barr, Abū ʿUmar Yūsuf b. ʿAbd Allāh b. Muḥammad. *Jāmiʿ bayān al-ʿilm wa faḍlih*. Ed. Abū al-Ashbāl al-Zuhayrī. Dammam: Dār Ibn al-Jawzī, 1994.

Ibn ʿAdī, Abū Aḥmad. *Al-Kāmil fi-ḍuʿafāʾ al-rijāl*. Eds. ʿĀdil Aḥmad ʿAbd al-Mawjūd and ʿAlī Muḥammad Muʿawwaḍ. Beirut: Dār al-Kutub al-ʿIlmiyyah, 1997.

Ibn Ḥajar, Abū al-Faḍl Aḥmad b. ʿAlī. *Al-Durar al-kāminah fī aʿyān al-māʾata al-thāmina*. Hyderabad: Maṭbaʿat Majlis Dāʾirat al-Maʿārif al-ʿUthmāniyya, 1972.

Ibn Ḥanbal, Abū ʿAbd Allāh Aḥmad b. Muḥammad. *Al-ʿIlal wa maʿrifat al-rijāl li-Aḥmad: riwāyat ibnih ʿAbd Allāh*. Riyadh: Dār al-Khānī, 2001.

———. *Musnad al-Imām Aḥmad*. Eds. Shuʿayb al-Arnaʾūṭ and ʿĀdil Murshid. Beirut: Muʾassasat al-Risāla, 2001.

———. *Al-Radd ʿala'l-zanādiqa wa'l-Jahmiyya*. Ed. Daghash b. Shabīb al-ʿAjamī. Kuwait City: Ghirās, 2005.

Ibn Ḥazm, Abū Muḥammad ʿAlī b. Aḥmad b. ʿAbd Allāh b. Saʿīd. *Asmāʾ al-Ṣaḥāba al-ruwāt wa ma li-kulli waḥid min al-ʿadad*. Beirut: Dār al-Kutub al-ʿIlmiyyah, 1992.

Ibn Ḥibbān, Abū Ḥātim Muḥammad. *Ṣaḥīḥ Ibn Ḥibbān*. Ed. Shuʿayb al-Arnaʾūṭ. Beirut: Muʾassasat al-Risāla, 1988.

Ibn Ḥibbān, Abū Ḥātim Muḥammad and Albānī, Muḥammad Nāṣir al-Dīn, al-. *Al-Taʿliqāt al-ḥisan ʿala Ṣaḥīḥ Ibn Ḥibbān*. Jeddah: Dār Bawzīr, 2003.

Ibn Kathīr, Abū al-Fidāʾ Ismāʿīl ʿImād al-Dīn b. ʿUmar. *Al-Bidāya wa'l-nihāya*. Damascus: Dār al-Fikr, 1986.

Ibn Māja, Abū ʿAbd Allāh Muḥammad b. Yazīd and Albānī, Muḥammad Nāṣir al-Dīn, al-. *Ṣaḥīḥ Sunan Ibn Māja/Ḍaʿīf Sunan Ibn Māja*. Riyadh: Maktabat al-Maʿārif, 1997.

Ibn al-Qayyim, Abū ʿAbd Allāh Shams al-Dīn Muḥammad b. Abī Bakr. *Ḥādī al-arwāḥ ilā-bilād al-afrāḥ*. Beirut: Dār Ibn Ḥazm, 2011.

———. *Iʿlām al-muwaqqiʿīn ʿan Rabb al-ʿĀlamīn*. Beirut: Dār al-Kutub al-ʿIlmiyyah, 1991.

———. *Madārij al-sālikīn bayn manāzil iyyāka naʿbudu wa iyyāka nastaʿīn*. Beirut: Dār al-Kitāb al-ʿArabī, 1996.

———. *Miftāḥ dār al-saʿāda wa manshūr wilāyat al-ʿilm wa'l-irāda*. Eds. Sayyid b. Ibrāhīm b. Ṣādiq ʿImrān and ʿAlī Muḥammad. Cairo: Dār al-Ḥadīth, 1994.

———. *Miftāḥ dār al-saʿāda wa manshūr wilāyat al-ʿilm wa'l-irāda*. Ed. ʿAbd al-Raḥmān b. Ḥasan b. Qāʾid. Mecca: Dār ʿĀlam al-Fawāʾid, 2015.

———. *Al-Ṣawāʿiq al-mursala ʿala'l-Jahmiyya wa'l-muʿaṭṭila*. Riyadh: Dār al-ʿĀṣima, 1987.

———. *Shifāʾ al-ʿalīl fī masāʾil al-qaḍāʾ wa'l-qadar wa'l-ḥikma wa'l-taʿlīl*. Eds.

Aḥmad b. Ṣāliḥ b. ʿAlī al-Ṣamʿānī and ʿAlī b. Muḥammad b. ʿAbd Allāh al-ʿAjlān. Riyadh: Dār al-Ṣamayʿī, 2013.

———. *Ṭarīq al-hijratayn wa bāb al-saʿādatayn*. Ed. Aḥmad Ibrāhīm Zahwa. Beirut: Dār al-Kitāb al-ʿArabī, 2005.

Ibn Rajab, Zayn al-Dīn ʿAbd al-Raḥmān. *Dhayl ṭabaqāt al-Ḥanābila*. Ed. ʿAbd al-Raḥmān b. Sulaymān al-ʿUthaymīn. Riyadh: Maktabat al-ʿUbaykān, 2005.

Imām, Abdul Rāfi Adewale (tr.). *The Biography of Imām Ibn al-Qayyim*. Riyadh: Darussalam Publications, 2006. [=translation of a work on the life of Ibn al-Qayyim by Ṣalāhud-Dīn ʿAlī ʿAbdul-Mawjūd]

Jarīrī, Abū Faraj al-Muʿāfā b. Zakariyya al-Nahrawānī, al-. *Al-Jalīs al-ṣāliḥ al-kāfī wa'l-anīs al-nāṣiḥ al-shāfī*. Ed. ʿAbd al-Karīm Sāmī al-Jundī. Beirut: Dār al-Kutub al-ʿIlmiyyah, 2005.

Johnstone, Penelope (tr.). *Ibn Qayyim al-Jawziyya Medicine of the Prophet*. Cambridge: The Islamic Texts Society, 1998.

Khān, Muḥammad Muḥsin (tr.). *The Translation of the Meaning of Ṣaḥīḥ al-Bukhārī*. Riyadh: Darussalam Publications, 1997. [=Bukhārī, Abū ʿAbd Allāh Muḥammad b. Ismāʿīl, al-. *Ṣaḥīḥ al-Bukhārī*]

Khaṭṭāb, Nāṣiruddīn, al- (tr.). *English Translation of Ṣaḥīḥ Muslim*. Riyadh: Darussalam Publications, 2007. [=Naysābūrī, Abū al-Ḥusayn Muslim b. al-Ḥajjāj, al-. *Ṣaḥīḥ Muslim*]

——— (tr.). *English Translation of Sunan Ibn Mājah*. Riyadh: Darussalam Publications, 2007. [=Ibn Māja, Abū ʿAbd Allāh Muḥammad b. Yazīd. *Sunan Ibn Māja*]

——— (tr.). *English Translation of Sunan an-Nasā'ī*. Riyadh: Darussalam Publications, 2007. [=Nasā'ī, Abū ʿAbd al-Raḥmān Aḥmad b. Shuʿayb, al-. *Sunan an-Nasā'ī*]

Knysh, Alexander D. (tr.). *Al-Qushayrī's Epistle on Sufism*. Reviewed by Muhammad Eissa. Reading: Garnet Publishing, 2007. [=Qushayrī, Abū al-Qāsim al-. *Al-Risāla al-Qushayriyya fī- ʿilm al-taṣawwuf*]

Krawietz, Birgit and Tamer, Georges (eds.). *Islamic Theology, Philosophy and Law: Debating Ibn Taymiyya and Ibn Qayyim al-Jawziyya*. Berlin: De Gruyter, 2013.

Livingston, John W. 'Ibn al-Qayyim al-Jawziyyah: A Fourteenth Century Defense against Astrological Divination and Alchemical Transmutation.' *JAOS* 91 (1971), no. 1, pp. 96–103.

Mālik b. Anas. *Muwaṭṭa' al-Imām Mālik*. Ed. Muḥammad Fu'ād ʿAbd al-Bāqī. Beirut: Dār Iḥyā' al-Turāth al-ʿArabī, 1985.

Mundhirī, Abū Muḥammad ʿAbd al-ʿAẓīm b. ʿAbd al-Qawī, al-. *Al-Targhīb wa'l-tarhīb min al-Ḥadīth al-sharīf*. Ed. Ibrāhīm Shams al-Dīn. Beirut: Dār al-Kutub al-ʿIlmiyyah, 1996.

Mundhirī, Abū Muḥammad ʿAbd al-ʿAẓīm b. ʿAbd al-Qawī, al- and Albānī, Muḥammad Nāṣir al-Dīn, al-. *Ṣaḥīḥ al-Targhīb wa'l-tarhīb/Ḍaʿīf al-Targhīb wa'l-tarhīb*. Riyadh: Maktabat al-Maʿārif, 2000.

Mustafa, Abdul-Rahman. *On Taqlīd: Ibn al-Qayyim's Critique of Authority in Islamic Law*. New York: Oxford University Press, 2013.

Muttaqī al-Hindī, ʿAlā' al-Dīn ʿAlī b. Ḥusām al-Dīn, al-. *Kanz al-ʿummāl fi-sunan al-aqwāl wa'l-afʿāl*. Eds. Bakrī Ḥayānī and Ṣafwat al-Saqqā. Beirut: Mu'assasat al-Risāla, 1981.

Nasā'ī, Abū ʿAbd al-Raḥmān Aḥmad b. Shuʿayb, al- and Albānī, Muḥammad Nāṣir al-Dīn, al. *Ṣaḥīḥ Sunan al-Nasā'ī/Ḍaʿīf Sunan al-Nasā'ī*. Riyadh: Maktabat al-Maʿārif, 1999.

Pickthall, Muhammad Marmaduke. *The Meaning of the Glorious Qur'an*. London: Allen & Unwin, 1976.

Publisher. (ed. and tr.) *Provisions for the Hereafter* (*Mukhtaṣar Zād al-Maʿād*). Riyadh: Darussalam, 2003. [=At-Tamimi, Muhammad ibn Abdul Wahhab. *Zād al-Maʿād*]

Publisher. (tr.) *The Names and Attributes of Allah According to the Doctrine of Ahl-us-Sunnah wal Jamaʿah*. Suffolk: Jamʿiat Ihyaa' Minhaaj Al-Sunnah, 1999. [=a work by ʿUmar Sulaiman al-Ashqar]

Qadhi, Yasir. 'The *Unleashed Thunderbolts* of Ibn Qayyim al-Ǧawziyyah: An Introductory Essay'. In Caterina Bori and Livnat Holtzman (eds.), *A Scholar in the Shadow: Essays in the Legal and Theological Thought of Ibn al-Qayyim al-Ǧawziyyah* (Oriente Moderno xc, no. 1. Rome: Istituto per l'Oriente C. A. Nallino, 2010), pp. 135–149.

——— (tr.). *English Translation of Sunan Abu Dawud*. Riyadh: Darussalam Publications, 2008.

Rapoport, Yossef and Ahmed, Shahab (eds.). *Ibn Taymiyya and His Times*. Karachi: Oxford University Press, 2010.

Rāzī, Tammām b. Muḥammad, al-. *Fawā'id Tammām*. Ed. Ḥamdī ʿAbd al-Majīd al-Salafī. Riyadh: Maktabat al-Rushd, 1991.

Shāmī, Ṣaliḥ Aḥmad, al-. *Faḍl al-ʿilm wa'l-ʿulamā'*. Beirut: al-Maktab al-Islāmī, 2001.

Shihadeh, Ayman. *The Teleological Ethics of Fakhr al-Dīn al-Rāzī*. Leiden: Brill, 2006.

Sijistānī, Abū Dāwūd Sulaymān b. al-Ashʿath al-Azdī, al- and Albānī, Muḥammad Nāṣir al-Dīn, al-. *Ṣaḥīḥ Sunan Abī Dāwūd/Ḍaʿīf Sunan Abī*

Dāwūd. Riyadh: Maktabat al-Maʿārif, 1998.

Sliti, Abdullah. 'A Lost Legacy of Critical Engagement: Ibn al-Qayyim on Divine Determination (*qadar*).' PhD thesis, Durham University, 2015.

Suyūṭī, ʿAbd al-Raḥmān Jalāl al-Dīn b. Abū Bakr, al- and Albānī, Muḥammad Nāṣir al-Dīn, al-. *Ṣaḥīḥ al-Jāmiʿ al-ṣaghīr wa-ziyādatih/Ḍaʿīf al-Jāmiʿ al-ṣaghīr wa-ziyādatih*. Beirut: Al-Maktab al-Islāmī, 1988.

Tabrīzī, Muḥammad b. ʿAbd Allāh al-Khaṭīb, al-. *Mishkāt al-maṣābīḥ*. Ed. Muḥammad Nāṣir al-Dīn al-Albānī. Beirut: al-Maktab al-Islāmī, 1985.

Ṭayālisī, Abū Dāwūd Sulaymān b. Dāwūd al-Jārūd, al-. *Musnad Abī Dāwūd al-Ṭayālisī*. Ed. Muḥammad b. ʿAbd al-Muḥsin al-Turkī. Giza: Dār Hijr, 1999.

Tirmidhī, Abū ʿĪsā Muḥammad b. ʿĪsā al-Sulamī, al- and Albānī, Muḥammad Nāṣir al-Dīn, al-. *Ṣaḥīḥ Sunan al-Tirmidhī/Ḍaʿīf Sunan al-Tirmidhī*. Riyadh: Maktabat al-Maʿārif, 1998.

Zabīdī, Murtaḍā, al-. *Itḥāf al-sāda al-muttaqīn*. Beirut: Mu'assasat al-Tārīkh al-ʿArabī, 1994.

Zaghlūl, Muḥammad al-Saʿīd b. Basyūnī. *Mawsūʿat aṭrāf al-Ḥadīth al-Nabawī al-sharīf*. Beirut: Dār al-Kutub al-ʿIlmiyyah, 2008.

INDEX

Aaron, 110, 263
ʿAbd Allāh b. Aḥmad, 249
ʿAbd Allāh b. ʿAmr b. al-ʿĀṣ, 63, 70, 201, 217–18
ʿAbd Allāh b. Dāwūd, 241, 260
ʿAbd Allāh b. Jaʿfar, 242
ʿAbd Allāh b. Salām, 120
ʿAbd Allāh b. Ubayy b. Salūl, 109
ʿAbd Allāh b. ʿUmar, 55, 201, 242
ʿAbd al-Jabbār, 228
ʿAbd al-Raḥmān b. ʿAwf, 154
ablution, 216, 226, 243
Abraham, xii, xxii, 127, 204; debate with his father and his people, 14, 255; God's commendation of, 256–7; Place of Abraham, 208–209
abrogation (*naskh*), xxii
Abū al-ʿĀliya, 239–40
Abū Bakr b. ʿAyyāsh, 81
Abū Bakr al-Ṣiddīq, xxvi, 73, 81, 213, 217, 218, 219
Abū al-Dardā', 43–4, 155, 165–6, 216, 269
Abū Dharr, 155, 158
Abū Ḥanīfa, 157
Abū Hārūn, 68
Abū Hurayra, 54, 59, 192, 230, 258; guidance, 40; mosque, 52, 166; remembrance of God, 56; superiority of knowledge, 155, 162, 166; wisdom, 66–7
Abū Jahl, 109
Abū Jamra, 281
Abū al-Maʿālī, 125, 228
Abū Masʿūd al-Badrī, 64
Abū Mūsa al-Ashʿarī, 23, 159
Abū Nuʿaym, 159, 161
Abū Saʿīd al-Khudrī, 65, 68
Abū Saʿīd al-Sirāfī, 228
Abū Salama, 218
Abū Ṣāliḥ Hishām, 243
Abū Sufyān, 104
Abū Ṭālib, 111–12
action, 227, 265; contemplation and, 270, 275, 281; knowledge as an action of the heart, 266; knowledge calls out to action, 115–16, 252; necessity of applying knowledge, xix, 165, 172, 176, 233
Adam, xviii, 17, 18, 218; angels and, 16, 123; exit from the Garden, xviii, 1, 254; sin, xviii; superiority over angels due to his knowledge, 17, 18, 123, 124, 254; wisdom ensuing from the creation of, 17
Aḥmad b. Abī ʿImrān, 244–5
Aḥmad b. Shuʿayb, 46
ʿĀ'isha bint Abī Bakr, 59, 69, 75, 149, 201
al-Albānī, Nāṣir al-Dīn, xxviii
ʿAlī b. Abī Ṭālib, 37, 39, 69, 247; categorisation of humanity according to levels of perfection, 167, 169, 171; description of true scholars and students of knowledge, xix, xxiv, 167–220; four types of people who cannot be callers to religion, 168, 194–200; 'hearts are like containers', 167, 169; superiority of the scholar, 154, 167, 169; 'those who hoard wealth are spiritually dead', 168, 189, 193

Ali, Yusuf, xxvii
almsgiving, 145, 153, 217, 226, 268; see also charity
al-Aʿmash, Abū Jaʿfar, 243
ʿAmmār, 201
Anas b. Mālik, 67, 154, 155, 201, 225
angels, 16–17, 71, 123, 135, 160, 214; Adam and 16, 123 (Adam's superiority due to his knowledge, 17, 18, 123, 124, 254); Angel of Death, 263; bearing witness to God's Oneness, 6, 7; circumambulating God's Throne, 215; Divine teaching, 31; gatherings of remembrance, 153; *ḥadīth*, 42, 43–4, 45–6; as messenger, 72; pleasure of knowledge is similar to angels' delight and pleasure, 179, 199; the sincerest well-wishers of God's creation, 45; see also Gabriel; Isrāfīl; Michael; scholars and angels
animal, 14, 24, 123; grazing animal/livestock, 1, 35, 37, 76, 151, 168, 200, 244; knowledge differentiates humans from animals, 74–5, 76, 244; prayers for the scholar, 42, 47
Anjum, Ovamir, xv
al-Anmārī, Abū Kabsha, 267
annihilation (*fanā'*), xv
Anṣār, 112, 235
al-Anṣārī, ʿAbd Allāh al-Harawī, xiv–xv; *Manāzil al-sā'irīn*, xiv, xv
al-Anṣārī, Abū al-Qāsim, 228
Antichrist (*Dajjāl*), 217
antinomianism (*suqūṭ al-taklīf*), ix, xv
ʿ*aql*, see intellect
Arabic language, 228, 229, 241, 243
ʿ*ārifūn*, see knowers
arrogance (*kibr*), 75, 101, 109, 137, 247
Asad, Muhammad, xxvii
asceticism, xxvi, 164, 186, 233
Ashʿarī doctrine, xi, xxi
Aʿshī, 110
astrology, xxiii
ʿAṭā' b. Abī Rabāḥ, 48, 153, 240, 249
awliyā', see loyal supporters
al-Awqas, Muḥammad b. ʿAbd al-Raḥmān, 240
al-Awzāʿī, Abū ʿAmr, 238

badhā', see obscenity
al-Bāhilī, Abū Umāma, 42
Bakr Abū Zayd, xiii
Banū ʿAbd al-Muṭṭalib, 111
al-Bāqir, Muḥammad b. ʿAlī, 264
al-Baṣrī, Ḥamīd, 66
al-Baṣrī, Zakariyya b. ʿAbd al-Raḥmān, 45–6
Battle of Badr, 44, 48, 262
al-Bazzāz, Abū Ḥamza, 233
beauty, 60, 130; beauty of knowledge, 150, 180 (greater than physical beauty, 18); beauty of the Qur'ān, 280; brilliance and beauty of the face, 59, 60–1
believer, 121, 134, 210, 235; analogy of a tender plant, 173–4; praiseworthy believer, 119–20, 121, 122; a stranger in this abode, 215–16
Bell, Joseph, xiv, xvii
Bilāl b. al-Ḥārith, 68
Bishr, Abū Naṣr, 270
al-Bisṭāmī, Abū Yazīd, 233
blessing, 128–9, 258, 275
bliss, xix, 43, 44, 212; contemplation, 275; extrinsic bliss, 130, 131; intrinsic bliss, 130–1; knowledge and, xix, 131, 268; power and, 175; ranks of, 1, 2; seeing God and hearing His Words, 127–8; spiritual bliss, xix, 131–2
boastfulness (*fakhr*), 137, 149, 194

body, 84, 130–1, 143, 161, 214, 266; beauty of knowledge is greater than physical beauty, 18; body/spirit relationship, 214, 215, 216; face, 59, 60–1, 125; a spiritual grave, 5; tongue, 32, 103, 128, 129, 138, 229, 264; see also hearing/listening; senses; vision
breath, 80, 89, 138, 246
al-Bukhārī, Muḥammad, 35
bukhl, see miserliness

calling (*daʿwa*), 221; calling to religion, 221, 222, 235, 258; four types of people who cannot be callers to religion, 168, 194–200; God's calling, 221; manner of, 221–2; scholars as 'callers to His religion', 169, 220
certainty, 223, 275; doubt and, 223; excellent certainty, 224; fruits of, 212; God criticized those who do not have it, 223; God praised those who possess it, 223; heart, 212, 223; knowledge and, xviii, 195, 196, 223–5 (certainty as the strongest type of knowledge, 101); lack of certainty in the Hereafter, 272; leadership in religious affairs, xviii; levels of, 127, 212–13, 224 (witnessed by the heart, 212; witnessed certainty, 212); remembrance of God, xviii; signs of, 224
charity, 41, 181, 258, 259, 262, 268; 'giving charity does not diminish wealth', 177; *ṣadaqa*, 51, 160; see also almsgiving
chastity, 148, 241
Christians, 134–5; see also People of the Book
Community of the Prophet, 63, 201–202, 218; attachment to, 60, 62; Paradise, 263
Companions, 42, 52, 58, 59, 69, 98, 105, 200, 234; best of the Community, 203; privilege of the Prophet's company, 213–14; superiority of knowledge, 154–5, 159–61
consideration (*iʿtibār*), 273–4
contemplation (*tafakkur*), xx, 269–76; action and, 270, 275, 281; contemplation of our own character and actions, 278; contemplation of the True Beloved, 277–9; discerning good and evil, 270, 271; discerning the imaginary and the delusional, 271; excellence and eminence of, 275; goodness and bliss, 275; heart, 270, 273, 275; knowledge and, xx, 270, 274; one of the best types of worship, 270; piety, 275; Qur'ān, 280–1; Satan, 275–6; superiority over worship, 269, 270, 275; vile thoughts as the opposite of, 276; wisdom, 274
contentment (*riḍā'*), xii–xiii
corruption, 56, 84, 113, 119, 149, 227
cowardice (*jubn*), 142, 143
creation, xx, 31, 32, 86, 90–1, 231; affirmation of God's Oneness, 8; created through His knowledge, 92; creation of humanity, xviii, 16–17, 31, 56–7; the Creator, 90–1; knowledge of God as the objective of, 15, 56–7, 265; obligation to obey the scholar, 191; prayers for the scholar, 42, 43, 47; sign of God's omnipotence and omniscience, xx, 14, 32, 265
customs/habits, 112–13

al-Ḍaḥḥāk, Ibn Muzāḥim al-Hilālī, 116, 192
Dajjāl, see Antichrist
al-Dārānī, Abū Sulaymān, 270
David, 28, 29, 51–2, 105, 254, 255
daʿwa, see calling
Day of Judgment, 48, 53
Day of Resurrection, 12, 127–8, 138–9, 164, 252, 260, 263
death, 137, 165, 258; death of the heart deprived of knowledge, 165; death of the wealthy, 189; end of pleasures at death, 199; preparing for death before it comes, 213; seeking knowledge until, 66; spiritual death, 5, 20, 168; see also scholar, death of
debate, 73, 172, 203–204, 206, 208, 222, 249; purpose of, 204
debt, 142, 143
deep reflection (*ta'ammul*), 273
Devil, see Satan
al-Dhahabī, Muḥammad b. Aḥmad: *Siyar aʿlām al-nubalā'*, ix
dhikr, see remembrance of God
disbelief, 121, 149; disbelief after knowing the truth, 113–14; ignorance and, 97, 105; reasons of, 108–15; types of, 105–106; see also ignorance; obstinacy
disbeliever, 97, 174, 235–6; obstinacy, 101–104, 119; see also hypocrite; ignorant
discerning good and evil, xx–xxi; contemplation, 270, 271; innate disposition and reason to recognize the good, xx; intellect, xx–xxi, 150; knowledge as judge, 76–7, 81, 92, 160; rational moral values, xx–xxi; reason and, xxi; reason/revelation congruity on, xxiii; see also Ashʿarī doctrine
disobedience, 261, 275; ignorance and, 98, 99, 106, 117
distress (*hamm*), 142, 199, 223
Divine Attributes, ix, 57, 79, 85, 171–2, 279; All-Cognizant, 79; All-Seeing and All-Hearing, 217; anthropomorphism, 196–7; contemplation of, 277, 278–9; God loves those who love His Attributes, 72; hearing, 75, 76; knowing God through, 57; knowledge of, 15, 89, 281 (the most noble and best type of knowledge, xix, 89, 265); the Most Generous, 31; the Most Knowledgeable, 17, 18, 79, 107, 190, 234; the Most Wise, 17; the Omniscient, 85; Paradise, 72; remembrance of God, 71; see also Divine Names
Divine Law (*sharīʿa*), xxii, 22, 29, 91, 171; evidence, 205; guidance, 40; knowledge of, 225, 226, 229; recompense is in accordance with the deed, 40, 59; sin, 261, 262; teachings on what pleases or displeases God, xx
Divine Names, 57, 279; *al-Akram*, 31; knowing God through, 57; knowledge of, 89 (the most noble and best type of knowledge, 89, 265); see also Divine Attributes
doubt, 38, 168, 198, 206, 272; certainty, 223; contemplation, 275; falsehood, 196; heart, 38, 136, 196; the Qur'ān expels doubts, 39, 208; *shubha*, 196; weak knowledge, xxiv, 195; weak willpower, xxiv
drinking, 80, 110, 165, 199, 261

eating, 24, 175, 186, 187, 226, 232
envy (*ḥasad*), 40–1, 102, 107, 137

evidence, 3, 14, 33–4, 86, 117, 202–203; Divine Law, 205; evidence for God's existence and Attributes, 89; evidence/proof distinction, 204, 208–209; evidences of knowledge, 204; firm knowledge strengthens evidence, 207; knowledge-based evidence has *sulṭān*, 32–3, 175; Muḥammad's prophethood, 29; preservation of Divine evidences and signs, 210–11; Qur'ān, 57, 58, 205–208
evil/the repugnant, 100, 150, 181, 234; Divine Law on competing evils, xxii; due to privation of spiritual life and light, 20; ignorance and, 94, 234; innate disposition to recognize the repugnant, xx; punishment, xxi; see also discerning good and evil
existence, 92; grades of, 31–2

faith, 15, 24, 62, 105, 122; the best of deeds is faith in God, 78, 80–1; certainty and love, 223; five prescripts of faith, 225–6, 229; Ibn al-Qayyim, x; knowledge and, 24, 78, 148, 163–4, 225; the knowledgeable, 9; path/straight path, 23, 24; perfection of, 78; a spiritual light in the hearts of the believers, 22–4
Fākhita, daughter of Qaraẓa, 242
fakhr, see boastfulness
falsehood, xxv, 34, 76, 113, 196; discerning truth from falsehood, 197–8
family, 111, 160, 217–18, 226
fanā', see annihilation
faqīh, see jurist
Farqad al-Sinjī, 98
fasting, 81, 116, 153, 161, 213, 226, 232; knowledge and, 154, 156
fiqh, 35–6, 241, 243; good manners and *fiqh* will never be coupled together in a hypocrite, 67; learning and teaching *fiqh* is better than supplication alone, 70; superiority over worship, 153–4, 156–7; see also jurisprudence
fiṭra, see innate disposition
flattery, 246–7
food, 186, 272; need for knowledge is greater than need for food, 80, 89
foolishness, 19, 116, 135, 167
the forbidden, 26, 110, 117; knowledge and, 92, 153, 160, 163, 201, 226, 261
fornication, 61, 110, 137, 261
al-Fuḍayl b. ʿIyāḍ, 42, 82, 269
fuḥsh, see indecency

Gabriel, 49, 71, 83, 85–6, 134, 152, 226; knowledge and power of, 175; the most distinguished instructor, 175
al-Ghazālī, Abū Ḥāmid Muḥammad, 205–206; *Book of Knowledge*, xxiv; Ibn al-Qayyim/al-Ghazālī comparison, xxiv; *Iḥyā' ʿulūm al-dīn*, xxiv, 205; truly faithful, xxvi
gnosis (*maʿrifa*), 78, 98, 103, 105, 134
God, xv, 90; contemplation of, 277–9; God' s causality, denial of, ix, xvi; God's knowledge, 18, 83, 85; God's wisdom, ix, xvi, xxii, xxiii; knowledge as method to prove God, 32; knowledge of God, xix, 15, 89, 90, 281; love for God, xv, 90–2, 106–107, 148, 199, 223, 231, 281; Oneness, 6–8, 100, 121, 278, 281 (connection between knowledge and God's Oneness, xix, 265); trust in, xvii, 3; see also Divine Attributes; Divine Names
God-fearing, 12–13, 148, 223, 252–3

good deed, 53, 56, 223–4, 260–1, 268; actions must follow knowledge, 115–16; the best of deeds is faith in God, 78, 80–1; excellence of, 26–7; knowledge and, 35–6, 81–2, 115, 148, 161; prayer, 158; preference to knowledge over deeds, 64; see also pious deed; righteous deed
Gospel, 28, 120, 255
gratitude/thankfulness, 148, 223, 257
grief (*ḥuzn*), 142, 183, 188, 223
guidance, xx, 1, 39, 63; categories of, 86–8; excellence of, 39–40; God's guidance, 83–4 (asking for God's guidance, 83–5); the guide receives the same reward as the guided, 40, 68; Hereafter, 87–8; misguidance, 40; need of, 84–5; the Prophet, 63–4, 87; see also guidance and knowledge
guidance and knowledge, 94–100, 108; analogy of abundant rain and water, 36–9; ignorance and guidance, 98; knowledge is not enough to attain guidance, xix–xx, 100–107, 108–19; see also guidance

ḥadīth, xxiv, xxvii–xxviii; authentic *ḥadīth*, xxviii, 201, 217, 218; chains of narrators, xxvii, 161, 241, 260; evidence, 206; fabricated *ḥadīth*, xxviii, 63; *fiqh*, 35; '*Ḥadīth* is power…', 241; *ḥadīth qudsī*, 50; importance of understanding, memorizing and conveying *ḥadīth*s, 59–64, 264; knowledge of, 66, 241, 243; 'This knowledge will be conveyed by the successors…', xxv, 7, 237; memorization of, 59–61; Qur'ān, 23–4; sound *ḥadīth*, xxviii; understanding the *ḥadīth*s, 59–61; weak *ḥadīth*, xxviii
al-Ḥāfiẓ b. Busṭām, 66
hamaj, see riff-raff
hamm, see distress
Ḥanbalī school, ix, xiv, 157
ḥanīf, see upright
Hanẓala al-Usaydī, 213–14
Ḥarb, Abū Muḥammad, 164
al-Ḥarbī, Ibrāhīm, 198–9, 240, 247, 260–1
Ḥāritha, 213
ḥasad, see envy
Ḥasan al-Baṣrī, 66, 98, 161–2, 192, 221, 281; contemplation, 269–70, 274; knowledge, 156, 247; worship and knowledge, 83, 245–6
Ḥāṭib b. Abī Baltaʿa, 262
haughtiness (*khaylā'*), 137, 149
hearing/listening, 34, 74, 124, 125, 129, 144, 249; certainty and, 127; hearing as a blessing, 128–9, 275; hearing/vision comparison, 125–6, 127; heart, 250–1; ignorant/disbeliever, described as deaf, 9, 19, 34, 74, 95, 96, 118–19, 138, 173, 275; meanings of, 75–6; see also senses
heart, 61, 128–9, 170; analogy of the valley, 38; attentiveness, 250–1, 273; the best hearts, 170–1; blindness of the heart, 138–9; certainty, 212, 223; contemplation, 270, 273, 275; corruption of, 113, 119; death of the heart deprived of knowledge, 165; diseases of, 136–7 (cure for, 137); doubt, 38, 136, 196; faith, a spiritual light in the hearts of the believers, 22–4; *ghulf*, 113–14; hardness of, 108–109, 113, 170; heart/vision relationship, 126–7; hearts are always roaming, 214–15; 'hearts are like containers', 167, 169–70; as the intellect, 250–1; the king of the body, 189;

knowledge and, 38, 67, 106, 108–109, 161, 173–4, 189, 246, 250, 264–6; love, 106; obligations of, 106; as place of knowledge, 124, 129; Qur'ān, a spiritual light in the hearts of the believers, 21–4; scholar, the doctor of the heart, 137; sealed heart, 95, 96, 114–15, 117–18; temptation, 136, 196, 250
heedlessness, xxv, 99, 140–1, 144, 188
Hellfire, xix, 88, 91, 117, 119, 134
Heraclius, King, 104, 109
Hereafter, xix, 24, 272–3; blindness of the heart, 138–9; guidance in, 87–8; lack of certainty in, 272; preparation for the Hereafter, 273; this world, as a bridge to the Hereafter, 56
hijra (migration from Mecca to Medina), 26, 64
ḥikma, see wisdom
al-Hindī, al-Muttaqī, xxvii
al-Hindī, Ṣafī al-Dīn, xi, xxi
Hishām b. ʿAlī, 243
Holtzmann, Livnat, xiii
Hoover, Jon, xvi
Ḥudhayfa, 23
ḥujja, see legal conveyance
humanity, xviii–xix; creation of, xviii, 16–17, 31, 56–7; Divine teaching, 30–1; levels of perfection, 72–4, 77–8, 133–4, 135, 144–7, 167, 169, 171 (ʿAlī's categorisation of humanity, 167, 169, 171); knowledge differentiates humans from animals, 74–5, 76, 244; ranks of, 123–4, 267–8; wisdom in the creation of, xviii, 16–17; the worst of, 144–7
ḥuzn, see grief
hypocrite, 58, 76, 77, 117, 151, 173, 213; good manners and *fiqh* will never be coupled together in, 67, 97; Qur'ān, recitation of, 23–4; see also disbeliever

ʿibāda, see worship
Iblīs, see Satan
Ibn ʿAbbās, ʿAbd Allāh, 32, 99, 101, 102, 161, 239–40, 249; contemplation, 270, 281; scholars, 42–3, 54–5, 69, 171, 191–2
Ibn ʿAbd al-Barr, 43, 249, 260
Ibn Abī Uways, 45
Ibn Abzī, 239
Ibn ʿAdī al-Jurjānī, 59, 69
Ibn al-Aʿrābī, 248
Ibn ʿAṭiyya, 250–1
Ibn al-Faḍl, Muḥammad, 233–4
Ibn Ḥajar, xxviii
Ibn Ḥanbal, Aḥmad, 23, 66, 80, 157–8, 162, 192, 196, 229; doubt, 198; *Musnad al-Imām Aḥmad*, 127, 272
Ibn Ḥibbān, 230
Ibn Isḥāq, 247
Ibn al-Jawzī, ix
Ibn Jurayj, ʿAbd al-Malik, 48, 249
Ibn Kathīr, Ismāʿīl ʿImād al-Dīn, ix–x; *al-Bidāya wa'l-nihāya*, ix, xxvii; *Tafsīr*, ix
Ibn Māja, 70
Ibn Masʿūd, ʿAbd Allāh, 60, 120, 145, 162–3, 201, 210, 224, 256, 257, 264; envy, 40–1; knowledge and fear of God, 13, 98; Qur'ān, 281
Ibn al-Mubārak, ʿAbd Allāh, 66, 124–5, 164, 270
Ibn Muzayn al-Ṭulayṭalī, 193
Ibn al-Qāsim, 158
Ibn al-Qayyim al-Jawziyya, ix–xi; faith, x; Ibn al-Qayyim/al-Ghazālī comparison, xxiv; Ibn al-Qayyim/Ibn Taymiyya comparison, xv; Ibn al-Qayyim/Ibn

Taymiyya relationship, xi–xiii (indebtedness to Ibn Taymiyya, xi); imprisonment, xii; Kaʿba, x, xvii, 3; love for God, xv; love for Islam, xv; love for the Prophet, xv; physician, xvi; pilgrimage, x, xvii; prayer, x, xi; Qur'ān, ix, x; remembrance of God, x; Sunna, ix, x; teachers, xi; testimonials to, ix–x; worship, x–xi; see also the entries below for Ibn al-Qayyim

Ibn al-Qayyim on Knowledge, xix–xx, xxvii; methodology of the translation, xxvi–xxviii; see also *Miftāḥ dār al-saʿāda*

Ibn al-Qayyim, works by, ix, xii, xiii–xvi, xxviii; *Badāʾiʿ al-fawāʾid*, xvii; early period, xiii; *Hādī al-arwāḥ*, xvii, xviii; *al-Ijtihād wa'l-taqlīd*, 29; *Iʿlām al-muwaqqiʿīn ʿan-Rabb al-ʿālamīn*, xiii–xiv; jurisprudence, xiii–xiv; *Kitāb al-rūḥ*, xiii; late period, xiii, xvi; *Madārij al-sālikīn*, x–xi, xii, xiii, xiv, xv, xvi–xvii (purpose of, xv); middle period, xiii, xiv; originality, xvii; *al-Qaṣīda al-nūniyya*, x, xi; *al-Ṣawāʿiq al-mursala ʿala'l-Jahmiyya wa'l-muʿaṭṭila*, xi; *Shifāʾ al-ʿalīl*, xvi, xxii; Sufism, xiv, xv; *Ṭarīq al-hijratayn*, xiv, xv; theology, xiv; *al-Ṭibb al-nabawī*, xvi; *al-Ṭuruq al-ḥukmiyya*, xiv; *al-Wābil al-ṣayyib min al-kalim al-ṭayyib*, xiii; *Zād al-maʿād*, xiv, xvi, xvii; see also *Ibn al-Qayyim on Knowledge*; *Miftāḥ dār al-saʿāda*

Ibn Qutayba al-Dinawārī, ʿAbd Allāh, 15, 126, 246–7

Ibn Rajab, ʿAbd al-Raḥmān Zayn al-Dīn, x; *Jāmiʿ al-ʿulūm wa'l-ḥikam*, ix

Ibn Shihāb al-Zuhrī, 156–7, 238

Ibn Taymiyya, ix, 83; contentment, xiii; death, xxii; doubt, 196; Ibn al-Qayyim/Ibn Taymiyya comparison, xv; Ibn al-Qayyim/Ibn Taymiyya relationship, xi–xiii; imprisonment, xii; magnanimity, xii; *Naqd al-manṭiq*, xvi; *al-Radd ʿala'l-manṭiqiyyīn*, xvi; al-Rāzī, Fakhr al-Dīn, xxi; speculative theology, xv–xvi, 228; works by, xii

Ibn al-Ṭayyib, Abū Bakr, 228

Ibn ʿUmar, 153, 154

Ibn Wahb, 159

Ibn Zayd, 192, 204

idolatry, 106, 122, 256

idrāk, see perception

ignorance (*jahl*), 13; disbelief, 97, 105; a disease, 89; disobedience and, 98, 99, 106, 117; effects of, 149–50, 264, 268; evil as result of, 94, 234; God negates equivalence between knowledge and ignorance, 8, 253; ignorance and guidance, 98; innate disposition leads to hate ignorance, 20; repulsive nature of, 20, 34–5, 150; sin, 98–9, 116–17, 118, 261, 264; types of, 99

ignorant (*jāhil*), 4, 5; characteristics of, 149–50; comparison with different animals, 200; denizens of Hellfire, 34–5; described as blind, 8–9, 34, 86, 95, 96, 100, 118–19, 138, 140, 173, 212, 275; described as deaf, 9, 19, 34, 74, 95, 96, 118–19, 138, 173, 275; Divine command to avoid the ignorant, 9, 19–20; ignorant worshipper, 200, 233; the most ignorant person, 123; one should not hold the ignorant in esteem, 243–4; rebuke, 18–19, 116; see also riff-raff

incapacity, 1, 17, 142, 143
indecency (*fuḥsh*), 20, 116, 149
injustice, 4, 101, 194, 199, 220
innate disposition (*fiṭra*), 20, 85, 90, 228, 263
innovation, 4, 55, 68, 83, 139, 174, 206, 238
insight (*istibṣār*), 61, 73, 77, 194, 195, 273, 274
intellect (*ʿaql*), 34, 118, 126, 170; acquired intellect, 151; angels, 123; discerning good and evil, xx–xxi, 150; heart as, 250–1; human being, 123; innate intellect, 151; knowledge and, 150, 151
intercourse, 74, 186, 187–8, 199
Isḥāq b. ʿAbd Allāh b. Abī Farwa, 156
Ishmael, 102
Islam, 92, 110, 111, 210; four kinds of people who cause deterioration of, 233–4; Ibn al-Qayyim's love for, xv; pillars of Islam, xxi–xxii; requisites for being a Muslim, 105, 106–107; revival through knowledge, 161, 168
Isrāfīl, 83, 85–6
istibṣār, see insight
iʿtibār, see consideration

jāhil, see ignorant
jahl, see ignorance
Jahmiyya, 72, 196
al-Jarīrī, Abū al-Faraj al-Muʿāfā, 242
Jesus, 28, 141, 255, 258
Jews, 101–105, 109, 112, 117, 120, 202; see also People of the Book
jihād, see striving
jinn, 34, 49, 56, 140, 218, 234
Johnstone, Penelope, xvi
Joseph, 18, 28, 61, 116, 194, 254–5
al-Jubbāʾī, Abū ʿAlī, 228
al-Jubbāʾī, Abū Hāshim, 228
jubn, see cowardice
jurisprudence (*uṣūl al-fiqh*), 54, 229; Ibn al-Qayyim, xiii–xiv; *Iʿlām al-muwaqqiʿīn ʿan-Rabb al-ʿālamīn*, xiii–xiv; *al-Ṭuruq al-ḥukmiyya*, xiv
jurist (*faqīh*), 54, 97–8, 191–2

Kaʿb al-Aḥbār, 59
Kaʿba, x, xvii, 3, 14, 91
Kalbī, 222
kasal, see laziness
Khadīja, 191
khalīfat Allāh, see viceroy of God
Khallāl, 157–8
al-Khaṭīb al-Baghdādī, Abū Bakr, 154, 155–6, 169
Khawārij, 62
Khawlānī, 202
khaylāʾ, see haughtiness
Khiḍr, 25, 28–9, 231, 255
kibr, see arrogance
king, 76–7, 124–5, 135, 164, 236; needs to obey the scholar, 191; wealth, 177, 178; see also ruler
knowers (*ʿārifūn*), xxvi, 224, 280; see also scholar/student of knowledge
knowledge, 1, 2; active and passive nature of, 92–3; analogy of rain or water, 36–9, 170, 246; beauty of knowledge, 150, 180 (greater than physical beauty, 18); benefits of, xix, 88–9, 160–1; eminence of, 3, 6, 18, 24, 25, 37, 60, 64, 65, 79, 88–9, 258, 264; excellence of, 6, 18, 25, 26–7, 39, 64, 65, 79, 264; a great bounty, 15; importance of, xix, 1, 32, 238, 246; the inheritance of the prophets, 44, 51–2, 177, 190, 238; levels of, 60; as means to attain Paradise, xviii, xx, 160; merit of, 88–9, 258; as method to prove God, 32; mystical knowledge, xv;

obligatory knowledge, 225–7, 229 (subtypes, 225–7); pleasure of, 89, 91–2, 108, 179, 180, 182, 185, 189, 199; propagation of, 274–5; raises its possessor in this world and the Hereafter, 239–43, 254–5; reasons for being deprived of knowledge, 249, 252; reward of, 258–9, 267; safeguarding of, 238; types of, 89, 92–3; weakness of, xxiii, xxiv, 108; see also gnosis; guidance and knowledge; knowledge, pursuit of

knowledge, pursuit of, 67; appetite for knowledge must never be satisfied, 65–6, 230–1; attaining knowledge, six levels for, 249; avoiding timidity when pursuing knowledge, 246–8; Divine command to ask for more knowledge, 11; learning as a form of worship, 264; necessity of pursuing knowledge, xix, 163, 190, 225, 232; pursuing knowledge is an action of the heart and means of worship, 264–6; pursuing knowledge should be for the sake of God only, 172; seeking knowledge is a form of striving, 57, 58, 132–3, 165, 182, 185; seeking knowledge until death, 66; travelling to acquire knowledge, 25–6, 57 (Moses' travel to learn from Khiḍr, 25, 231, 255); see also knowledge

the knowledgeable, see scholar/student of knowledge

Kumayl b. Ziyād al-Nakhaʿī, 167

laziness (*kasal*), 1, 140, 141–3, 144, 188, 271; willpower, 142

leadership, xviii, 105, 107, 109, 110; knowledge and, 79–80, 81

legal conveyance (*ḥujja*), xx–xxi, 204

Livingston, John W., xxiii

love, 91, 223; heart, 106; knowledge and, 91–2, 214; knowledge, love for, 168, 178, 190 (as part of the creed one must profess, 168, 190–1); family, love for, 111; God, love for, xv, 90–2, 106–107, 148, 199, 223, 231, 281; power, love of, 137; Prophet, love for, 106–107

loyal supporters (*awliyā'*), 4, 28, 50, 77, 148, 152, 221

Luqmān, 246

Makḥūl al-Azdī, Abū ʿAbd Allāh, 156

Mālik b. Anas, 45, 158–9, 192

al-Mālikī, Aḥmad b. Marwān, 45–6

al-Ma'mūn b. Hārūn al-Rashīd, Caliph, 240–1

manāzil al-sā'irīn, see stations of the travellers

maʿrifa, see gnosis

martyr, xxvi, 59, 155; the best of God's creation, 17, 77, 78; scholar's superiority over, 77, 78

Mary, mother of Jesus, 28

al-Mawjūd, Salāhud-Din ʿAbd, xvii

al-Mawṣilī, Abū Yaʿlā, 225

Mecca, x, xxii, xxviii, 235

memorization, 36–7; *ḥadīths*, 59–61; Qur'ān, 10, 64, 159, 239, 241

messengers, 112–13, 133, 150, 279; angels as, 72; the best of God's creation, 17, 49, 72–3, 78, 144, 156

Michael, 83, 85–6

Miftāḥ dār al-saʿāda, xiii, xvi–xxiv, xxviii; al-Ghazālī, Abū Ḥāmid Muḥammad, xxiv; importance of, xvii; originality, xvii; repetition, xxviii; Volume I, xx, xxvii, xxviii; Volume II, xx, xxiii; see also *Ibn al-Qayyim on Knowledge*; Ibn al-Qayyim, works by

miserliness (*bukhl*), 142, 143, 149
al-Miṣrī, Dhū al-Nūn, 232–3
modesty, 20
monism (*waḥdat al-wujūd*), ix, xiv
Moses, 19, 116, 127, 134, 217, 230, 262–3; knowledge, 28; Pharaoh and, 86, 100, 110, 209, 219; Torah, 25, 29; travelling to learn from Khiḍr, 25, 231, 255
mosque, 52, 70, 91, 166
Muʿādh b. Jabal, 58, 160–1
Muʿāwiya b. Abī Sufyān, 35, 71, 242, 243
Muhājirūn, 235
Muḥammad, ʿAlī, xxvi
Mujāhid b. Jabr al-Makhzūmī, 192
Muqātil, 116
Muslim b. al-Ḥajjāj, 35, 132
Mustafa, Abdul-Rahman, xiii–xiv
Muʿtazila, xxi, xxii–xxiii, 46, 62
al-Muzanī, Abū Ibrāhīm, 54, 241, 243
al-Muzanī, Kathīr, 68
mysticism, xv

al-Naḍr b. Shumayl, 241
Nāfiʿ, 154
Nāfiʿ b. ʿAbd al-Ḥārith, 239
al-Nasāba al-Bikrī, 248
al-Nasāʾī, Abū ʿAbd al-Raḥmān, 198
naskh, see abrogation
al-Nawwās b. Samʿān, 22
naẓar, see reflection
nearness to God, xviii, 89, 124, 199
Noah, 19

obedience, 100, 105, 179, 257; knowledge earns obedience for the scholar, 168, 191–2
obscenity (*badhāʾ*), 116, 149
obstinacy, 75, 100–103, 105, 109, 119; no remedy for, 106
ostentatiousness (*riyāʾ*), 137, 149

Paradise, 91; access through the Prophet, 2; Community of the Prophet, 263; Divine Attributes and, 72; entering Paradise, xix, 88; hardships and tribulations as bridges to higher levels of, xx; knowledge, as means to attain Paradise, xviii, xx, 160; longing for, 215; scholar, 43, 44, 55, 59, 260; willpower, as means to attain Paradise, xviii, xx
path/straight path, 22–3, 37, 58, 278; companions, 2, 5; faith, 23, 24; hardship of, 211, 212, 214; knowledge and, 169; knowledge and willpower as door to, 1; loneliness on, 210, 212, 214; the Prophet as a guide on, 2; Qur'ān, 21, 24
patience, xviii, 148, 247; rank of those who are patient, xxvi, 27; willpower, xviii
People of the Book, 20–1, 101, 110, 120, 122, 208; see also Christians; Jews
perception (*idrāk*), 170
perfection, 181; knowledge and, 144, 147, 160, 161, 180, 181 (perfection is only attained via knowledge, 135, 231); levels of perfection, 72–4, 77–8, 133–4, 135, 144–7, 167, 169, 171 (ʿAlī's categorisation of humanity, 167, 169, 171); martyr, 17, 77, 78; messengers, 17, 49, 72–3, 78, 144, 156; perfection of faith, 78; prophets, 17, 49, 51, 72, 73, 78; requisites for, 90–1; the truly faithful, 17, 73, 78; willpower and, 144, 147; see also scholars' higher rank
philosophy, 106, 206; al-Ghazālī, Abū Ḥāmid Muḥammad, xxiv; Greek philosophy, 205, 222, 227–9; Ibn Taymiyya, xv–xvi

Pickthall, Muhammad Marmaduke, xxvii
piety, 56, 82, 97, 160, 164, 252; knowledge and, 178; a result of contemplation, 275; see also pious deed
pilgrimage, 91, 153, 226, 240, 242; Ibn al-Qayyim, x, xvii
pious deed, 12, 69, 82, 97, 150, 162, 271, 278; wealth and, 267; see also good deed; piety; righteous deed
pleasure, 132, 141, 149, 186–9, 215; animalistic pleasure, 179, 189, 199; eating, 186, 187; end of pleasures at death, 199; imaginary pleasure, 179; intercourse, 186, 187–8; pleasure of knowledge, 89, 91–2, 108, 180, 182, 185, 189; pleasure of knowledge is similar to angels' delight and pleasure, 179, 199; preoccupation with attaining pleasures, 198–9; satanic pleasure, 199; true pleasure, 199; wealth, pleasure from, 179, 180, 182, 185
polytheism, 109, 111, 121, 149
pondering (*tadabbur*), 273, 274, 279; pondering the Qur'ān, 280, 281
prayer, 54, 154, 226; asking for God's guidance, 83–5; contemplation, 270; God responds to, 76; Ibn al-Qayyim, x; importance of, 158; inattentive prayer, 145; knowledge and, 156; leading the prayers, 64; learning and teaching *fiqh* is better than supplication alone, 70; prayers for the scholar, 42, 43, 46–7, 69; praying at night, 154, 157, 159, 161, 165, 213, 232, 269, 270; prostration, 158, 214, 216, 217; the scholar always remains in prayer, 264; supererogatory prayer, 158; see also worship
Predecessors, 81, 98, 115, 135, 163–4, 211, 218, 232, 247, 249, 274–5; contemplation, 269–70, 280; jurist, 97–8; Qur'ān, 13, 22
pride (*ʿujb*), 101, 109, 111, 137, 149, 194
the Prophet, 2, 16, 213–14, 241; disbelief in, 101–105, 109; Divine command to ask for more knowledge, 11; Divine command to avoid the ignorant, 19; following the Prophet, 82, 105, 111, 231, 233, 235, 280; guidance, 63–4, 87; 'His character was the Qur'ān', 149; Ibn al-Qayyim's love for Prophet, xv; as intermediary between God and the people, 2; knowledge, 15–16, 28, 29–30; knowledge inherited from, 2, 44, 49; love for the Prophet, 106–107; preference to those with superior levels of knowledge, 64–5; prophethood, 29–30, 104–105, 109, 111–12, 252; revelation of the Qur'ān, 15–16, 134, 255–6; Seal of the Prophets, 202; wisdom, 15–16; *Zād al-maʿād*, xiv, xvi
prophets, 49, 106, 112–13, 133, 234; the best of God's creation, 17, 49, 51, 72, 73, 78; knowledge, inheritance of the prophets, 44, 51–2, 177, 190, 238; prophethood, 51–2
punishment, 113, 147, 209, 261; absence of punishment before the sending of a messenger, xxi; knowledge saves from punishment, 253–4; punishment for not teaching or spreading knowledge, 252; scholar, 261
purification (*tazkiya*), 43, 108, 266

Qatāda b. Diʿāma b. Qatāda al-Sadūsī, 99, 101, 116–17
qibla, xxii

Qur'ān, ix, xxiv, xxvii, 15, 21, 22–3, 24, 27, 82, 122, 258, 281; beauty of, 280; causality, xxii; contemplating the Qur'ān, 280–1; doubt, 39, 208; evidence, 57, 58, 205–208; Ibn al-Qayyim, ix, x; importance of teaching the Qur'ān, xix, 65; knowledge of, xix, 52, 64, 65, 120 (the noblest and most virtuous, 24); memorization of, 10, 64, 159, 239, 241; pondering the Qur'ān, 280, 281; praiseworthy characteristics commended by God and due to knowledge, 148–9; Q. III.18: xix, xxiv, xxv, 6, 8, 95; reading, 10, 13, 24, 120, 243, 280–1; recitation of, 23–4, 64; revelation to the Prophet, 15–16, 134, 255–6; similitudes in, 13, 39, 96; a spiritual light in the hearts of the believers, 21–4; *Sūrat al-ʿAlaq*, 30–1; *Sūrat al-Barā'a*, 259; *Sūrat al-Furqān*, 57; *Sūrat al-Ḥadīd*, 77; *Sūrat al-Ikhlāṣ*, 72; *Sūrat al-Naḥl*, 128; understanding the, 37, 280, 281
Quraysh, 104, 110, 209, 235, 239

al-Rabīʿ b. Anas, 57
Rāfiḍa, 62
Ramaḍān, 14
rancour, 60, 61–3
al-Rāzī, Abū Ḥātim, 45
al-Rāzī, Fakhr al-Dīn, 206–207; *ʿArbaʿīn*, xxi; *Muḥaṣṣal*, xxi
reading: Divine command to read, 31; Qur'ān, 10, 13, 24, 120, 243, 280–1
recollection (*tadhakkur*), 273, 274
reflection (*naẓar*), xx, 273, 277
remembrance of God (*dhikr*), 52, 56, 90–1, 199, 223; angels, 153; benefits of, xiii; certainty, xviii; Divine Attributes, 71; gatherings of remembrance as 'gardens of Paradise', 153; Ibn al-Qayyim, x; magnificence of, 71; nearness to God, xviii; as protection against Satan, 141; scholar, 264; *al-Wābil al-ṣayyib min al-kalim al-ṭayyib* (*The Invocation of God*), xiii
repentance, xix, xxvi, 98, 99, 148, 162–3, 265
the repugnant, see evil/the repugnant
riḍā', see contentment
riff-raff, 135, 166, 167, 171, 172–3, 174; *hamaj*, 172; *sifla*, 232–3; see also ignorant
righteous deed, 64, 211, 253, 259–60, 262–3; superior type of deeds, 15; see also good deed; pious deed
righteousness, 246, 258, 259; rewarded with knowledge, 245–6
Rightly-Guided Caliphs, 204
riyā', see ostentatiousness
Ru'ba b. al-ʿAjjāj, 248
ruler, 33, 58, 107, 124, 192, 270; see also king

Saʿd b. Ibrāhīm, 97
ṣadaqa, see charity
Ṣafwān b. ʿAssāl, 46
Sahl b. Saʿd, 39
Saʿīd b. Jubayr, Abū Muḥammad, 95–6, 171
Saʿīd b. al-Musayyab, 156
saint, xv, 133–4, 234–7, 264, 279; see also the truly faithful
Sanḥabra, 69
Satan (*Shayṭān*), 61–2, 100, 103, 139–40; disobedience, 109; the ignorant and, 123–4; knowledge and, 100, 139–40, 163, 176; the most evil of creation arose from, 17; obstinacy, 100; prostration before Adam, 16, 100; protecting oneself from,

140, 141 (contemplation, 275–6); satanic pleasure, 199; scholar and, 54–6, 176; whispering, 141, 176; worshipper, 54–6; see also temptation
Sayyid b. Ibrāhīm b. Ṣādiq ʿImrān, xxvi
scholar/student of knowledge, 17; ʿAlī b. Abī Ṭālib, xix, xxiv, 50, 167–220; analogy of the moon, 43, 44, 47, 48, 49; analogy of the stars, 49; bearing witness to God's Oneness, 6–8; Day of Resurrection, 12; as doctor of the heart, 137; entrusted to preserve and defend the Divine message, 234–8; faith of, 9; God protects those who pursue knowledge, 162, 166; Iblīs, 54–6; intercession by, 48; opposition to, 184; Paradise, 43, 44, 55, 59, 260; prayers for, 42, 43, 46–7, 69; Prophet, 64–5, 68–9; punishment, 261; Qur'ān, 10, 13; *rabbānī*, 167, 171–2; reward, 80, 166; the scholar always remains in prayer, 264; scholar who derived no benefit from his knowledge, 147; scholar without knowledge, 82–3; self-interest, 43; sins, xx, 69–70, 163, 164, 260–1, 263–4; willpower, 147; see also the entries below for scholar; knowers; student of knowledge
scholar, death of, 59, 162, 168, 189, 200–202, 241; death of a scholar is a calamity, 44, 48, 53–4; knowledge fades away with scholar's death, 168, 200–201; see also scholar
scholars and angels, 42, 43, 44, 45, 46, 69; angels/scholars similarities, 44–5; lowering their wings in approval of scholars, 43, 44, 45–6; see also scholar
scholars' higher rank, 11–12, 14, 124, 156, 169, 171–2, 220, 234; the best of God's creation, 17, 78, 179, 200; 'callers to His religion', 169, 220; closest level to that of the prophets, 156, 161, 202; command to obey, respect, support and honour the scholars, 50, 191; Divine command to ask the scholars, 9; heirs of the prophets/Prophet, 43–4, 49–50, 57, 157; importance of, 124, 137–8, 168–9; the most knowledgeable, 64, 79–80, 123, 230; superiority over a martyr, 77, 78; superiority over those who wage battle, 57, 154, 155; superiority over a worshipper, xix, 42, 43, 47–8, 49, 54–6, 163, 164; see also scholar
senses, 89, 118–19, 165; see also body; hearing/listening; vision
al-Shāfiʿī, Muḥammad b. Idrīs, 27, 157, 229, 241, 243, 270
shahāda, see testimony
shahīd, see witness
sharīʿa, see Divine Law
shaykh, 243; *qamarā'* shaykh, 243
Shayṭān, see Satan
al-Shiblī, Abū Bakr, 251
Sībawayh, 171
ṣiddīqūn, see the truly faithful
sifla, see riff-raff
sin, xx, 75, 199; Adam, xviii; Divine Law, 261, 262; ignorance and, 98–9, 116–17, 118, 261, 264; *maʿṣiya*, 116; righteous deeds and, 262–3; scholar's sins, xx, 69–70, 163, 164, 260–1, 263–4; the upright and trustworthy, 238; waging battle and forgiveness of sins, 262
sincerity, 60, 61–2, 82, 100, 172, 265
al-Sirafī, Abū Saʿīd, 228

Sirrī, Abū al-Ḥasan, 224
sleep, 212, 216, 232
Sliti, Abdullah, xx–xxi
Solomon, 29, 51–2, 253–4, 255
speech, 32, 47, 58, 128, 138, 221, 270
spirit, 214, 216; body/spirit relationship, 214, 215, 216; greatest punishment for, 215
spiritual life, 20, 21, 89, 179, 189; evilness is due to privation of spiritual life, 20
stations of the travellers (*manāzil al-sā'irīn*), xiv, 224, 273, 280; *Manāzil al-sā'irīn*, xiv–xv
striving (*jihād*) [for God's sake], xxv, xxvi, 57; against disbelievers and hypocrites, 57–8, 151–2; Qur'ān, striving by using the evidence of, 57, 58; seeking knowledge is a form of, 57, 58, 132–3, 165, 182, 185; see also waging battle
student of knowledge, 167, 169, 171, 172, 200; see also scholar/student of knowledge
subjugation of people, 142, 143–4
Successors, 45, 98, 105
successors, see the truly faithful
al-Suddī, Ismāᶜīl b. ᶜAbd al-Raḥmān, 99, 103
Sufism, 94; Ibn al-Qayyim, xiv, xv; *Madārij al-sālikīn*, xiv; *Ṭarīq al-hijratayn*, xiv, xv
Sufyān al-Thawrī, 98–9, 157, 241
Sufyān b. ᶜUyayna, 59, 156, 258, 269
Sulaymān b. ᶜAbd al-Malik, 240
Sunna, ix, xxii, 82, 238, 243; Ibn al-Qayyim, ix, x; importance of reviving it, 67–8; importance of teaching it, xix; knowledge of, xix, 64
suqūṭ al-taklīf, see antinomianism
ta'ammul, see deep reflection
al-Ṭabarī, Muḥammad b. Jarīr, 235
tadabbur, see pondering
tadhakkur, see recollection
tafakkur, see contemplation
al-Ṭaḥāwī, Abū Jaᶜfar, 244–5
Ṭalḥa, 262
al-Ṭāliqānī, ᶜAbd Allāh b. Bishr, 66
Tammām, 214
tazkiya, see purification
teaching, xix; Abraham, 257; excellence of, 24, 27, 37, 39; following the prophets' guidance and methodology, 50; a form of worship, 264; Gabriel, the most distinguished instructor, 175; importance of, 30, 176; importance of conveying the *ḥadīths*, 59–61, 63–4; learning and teaching *fiqh* is better than supplication alone, 70; punishment for not teaching or spreading knowledge, 252; Qur'ān, xix, 65; reward for teaching, 155, 176, 258, 260–1
temptation, xxiv, 110, 123, 168, 199, 211, 261; contemplation, 275; falsehood, 196; heart, 136, 196; see also Satan
testimony (*shahāda*), 251, 252
Thamūd, 86, 87, 100
theology, xiv; al-Ghazālī, Abū Ḥāmid Muḥammad, xxiv, 205–206; Ibn Taymiyya, xv–xvi, 228; speculative theology, xv–xvi, xxiv, 205–206, 207–208, 228–9
timidity, 164, 244; avoiding timidity when pursuing knowledge, 246–8
al-Tirmidhī, Abū ᶜĪsā Muḥammad b. ᶜĪsā, 23, 68, 71, 128
Torah, 25, 28, 29, 120, 255
the truly faithful (*ṣiddīqūn*), xxv–xxvi, 73; the best of God's creation, 17,

73, 78; al-Ghazālī, Abū Ḥāmid Muḥammad, xxvi; see also saint
al-Tustarī, Sahl b. ʿAbd Allāh, 157, 224, 243
Twelver Shiʿi, belief of occultation, 202–203

ʿUbayd Allāh b. ʿAbd Allāh b. ʿUtba, 249
Ubayy b. Kaʿb, Abū Mundhir, 22
ʿujb, see pride
ʿUmar b. ʿAbd al-ʿAzīz, 270
ʿUmar b. Abī Rabīʿa, 242
ʿUmar b. al-Khaṭṭāb, 69–70, 159,162, 163, 239, 262; death of, 201
Umayya b. Abī al-Ṣalt, 104, 109
Umm al-Dardā', 269
understanding, 36, 90, 249, 275; importance of understanding the *ḥadīth*s, 59–61; Qur'ān, 37, 280, 281
the Unseen, 18, 83, 85, 269
the untrustworthy, 168, 194–5
upright (*ḥanīf*), 151, 232, 256, 257; upright and trustworthy, 7, 237, 238
ʿUrwa b. Ruwaym, 116, 141
ʿUrwa b. al-Zubayr, 249
uṣūl al-fiqh, see jurisprudence
ʿUtbā, 242
ʿUthmān b. ʿAffān, 65, 262
ʿUyāḍ b. Ḥimār, 176

viceroy of God (*khalīfat Allāh*), 169, 216–20, 236
vision, 34, 124, 125, 129, 161; blindness of the heart, 138–9; hearing/vision comparison, 125–6, 127; heart/vision relationship, 126–7; ignorant/disbeliever, described as blind, 8–9, 34, 86, 95, 96, 100, 118–19, 138, 140, 173, 212, 275; vision as a blessing, 128–9, 275; see also senses

waging battle [for God's sake], 26, 57, 58, 91; acquiring knowledge/waging battle comparison, 26, 166; forgiveness of sins, 262; *nafīr*, 26; scholar's superiority over those who wage battle, 57, 154, 155; superiority of, 12, 80–1, 159; see also striving
Wahb b. Munabbih, 270
waḥdat al-wujūd, see monism
al-Wāḥidī, Abū al-Ḥasan, 171–2
al-Wāṣiṭī, ʿImād al-Dīn Abū al-ʿAbbās, xi, xiv
wealth, 110, 116, 143, 267–8; death, 189; extrinsic bliss, 130, 131; 'giving charity does not diminish wealth', 177; harm caused by, 183–4, 190, 268; king, 177, 178; only pursue as much as needed for sustainment, 190; pious deeds and, 267; pleasure from wealth, 179, 180, 182, 185; seduced with gathering wealth, 200; superiority of knowledge over wealth, xix, 15, 52–3, 130, 167–8, 175, 177–90, 192–3, 244–5; those who hoard wealth are spiritually dead, 168, 189–90, 193
willpower, xxv, 1, 2; eminence of, 3; knowledge and, 3, 78–9, 142; laziness, 142; as means to attain Paradise, xviii, xx; patience, xviii; perfection and, 144, 147; scholar, 147; weakening of one's willpower, xxiii, xxiv
wisdom (*ḥikma*), xix, 66–7, 246, 274; creation of Adam, 17; definition, 15; God's wisdom, ix, xvi, xxii, xxiii; humanity, wisdom in the creation of, xviii, 16–17; the lost property of the believer, 67; the Prophet, 15–16

the wise/sage, 38, 96, 179–80, 185, 186, 188, 198–9
witness (*shahīd*), 251–2
women, 136, 217, 261; wives of the Prophet, 136–7, 261
this world, xix, 213, 271–2; as a bridge to the Hereafter, 56; a stranger in this world, 215–16; a transient abode, 212, 214, 215
worship (*ʿibāda*), x–xi, 57; Ibn al-Qayyim, x–xi; ignorant worshipper, 200, 233; knowledge and, 81, 83, 92, 156, 158–9, 160, 225, 245–6; knowledge as one of the best forms of worship, 265; learning as a form of, 264; supererogatory worship, 232; superiority of *fiqh* over worship, 153–4, 156–7; superiority of knowledge over supererogatory worship, 154–6, 157–8, 159–60, 161, 165; superiority of knowledge over worship, xix, 42, 43, 47–8, 49, 54–6, 163, 164, 201, 211, 264; teaching as a form of, 264; worship by the worst of humanity, 145; worshipper, 54–6, 134; see also contemplation; prayer

Yaḥyā b. Abī Kathīr, 132, 198
Yaḥyā b. Aktham, 240–1
Yūnus b. Ḥabīb, 178–9

Zachariah, 52
al-Zajjāj, Abū Isḥāq Ibrāhīm, 96, 102, 103
al-Zamakhsharī, Maḥmūd b. ʿUmar, 251
Zayd b. ʿAmr b. Nufayl, 257
Zayd b. Aslam, Abū Usāma, 14